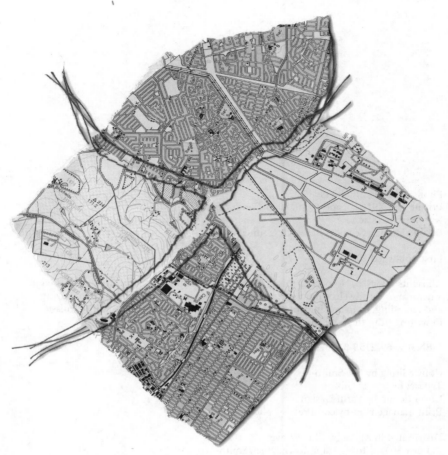

# Democracy and Delivery
## Urban Policy in South Africa

Edited by Udesh Pillay,
Richard Tomlinson &
Jacques du Toit

HSRC
PRESS

Published by HSRC Press
Private Bag X9182, Cape Town, 8000, South Africa
www.hsrcpress.ac.za
© 2006 Human Sciences Research Council

First published 2006

ISBN 0-7969-2156-3

Copy editing by Lee Smith
Typeset by Stacey Gibson
Cover design by Farm Design
Print management by comPress

Distributed in Africa by Blue Weaver
PO Box 30370, Tokai, Cape Town, 7966, South Africa
Tel: +27 (0) 21 701 4477
Fax: +27 (0) 21 701 7302
email: orders@blueweaver.co.za
www.oneworldbooks.com

Distributed in Europe and the United Kingdom by Eurospan Distribution Services (EDS)
3 Henrietta Street, Covent Garden, London, WC2E 8LU, United Kingdom
Tel: +44 (0) 20 7240 0856
Fax: +44 (0) 20 7379 0609
email: orders@edspubs.co.uk
www.eurospanonline.com

Distributed in North America by Independent Publishers Group (IPG)
Order Department, 814 North Franklin Street, Chicago, IL 60610, USA
Call toll-free: (800) 888 4741
All other enquiries: +1 (312) 337 0747
Fax: +1 (312) 337 5985
email: frontdesk@ipgbook.com
www.ipgbook.com

# Contents

**Housing and services delivery programmes**

# List of tables and figures

## Tables

## Figures

# *Preface*

This book is the first publication of an intended series of urban policy research publications of the Urban, Rural and Economic Development Research Programme of the Human Sciences Research Council (HSRC), which is a national programme of policy-relevant urban research.

The book's purpose is to document and assess the policy formulation processes that informed South Africa's foremost urban policies since 1994. It provides an understanding of the origins and goals of the policies; the role of research, advice from international development agencies, and political and economic circumstances and agendas during the policy formulation process; a record of policy implementation; a critical assessment of the policies; and insight into how present polices are being adapted and future policies formulated.

It is anticipated that the book will serve as a record of the first ten years of urban policy formulation processes in democratic South Africa and as a basis for comparative urban and city-based research among scholars worldwide. It is also hoped that the book will inform present and future urban and other policy processes in South Africa and elsewhere. The intended readership of the book includes an informed public, academics and students, policy-makers and government officials.

The conceptualisation of the publication was taken forward with the assistance of a reference group, beginning with a workshop in January 2004. Members of the reference group additionally assisted the editors to review proposals from prospective contributors and, in a number of instances, commented on draft versions of chapters.

At the time of the workshop the members of the reference group and their institutional bases were:

Dr Doreen Atkinson, Chief Research Specialist in the Democracy and Governance Research Programme of the HSRC.

Professor Robert Beauregard, Milano Graduate School of Management and Urban Policy at the New School University, New York.

Andrew Boraine, Chairperson of the South African Cities Network.

Mike de Klerk, Executive Director of the Integrated Rural and Regional Research Programme at the HSRC.

Caroline Kihato, Senior Lecturer in the Department of Town and Regional Planning at the University of the Witwatersrand.

Dr Xolela Mangcu, Director of the Steve Biko Foundation.

Professor Susan Parnell, Department of Geography at the University of Cape Town.

Dr Jennifer Robinson, Senior Lecturer in the Department of Geography at The Open University, United Kingdom.

The composition of the reference group, however, changed over time. One reason was that two members of the reference group chose to submit proposals and withdrew from the reference group in order to avoid a conflict of interest situation. Caroline Kihato and Doreen Atkinson are now contributors to the book.

The determination of the specific urban policies to be investigated in the book started with advertising a call for proposals in the media, and by the use of widely distributed email. The editors sifted through the proposals and selected some for distribution to the reference group. With the recommendations of the reference group in mind, the editors selected a limited number of proposals and the potential contributors were asked to prepare detailed proposal submissions for a second round of assessment. This process led to the identification of the specific policies that would be investigated and the authors that would be commissioned to write these up. In two cases where there were no satisfactory proposals for policy investigation that the editors considered to be essential, the editors solicited pieces from particular individuals.

Each proposal was assessed on the basis of three criteria:
• Relevance of the policy as it pertains to urban development;
• Academic rigour; and
• Different perspectives that could be brought to bear in relation to South Africa's evolving urban environment, and the scholars that could articulate this.

The themes included in the book emerged from the proposals but, in retrospect, are self-evident. First, there are chapters that describe how government set out to restructure and build democratic local governments and to enhance their ability to deliver services and to promote socio-economic development. Second, there are chapters that assess how government has attempted to give effect to 'developmental' local government through integrated development planning and local economic development. Third, there are chapters that describe the policies for the delivery of housing and services.

Two policies that might be said to be 'missing' are also included in the book. One provides an investigation of urban spatial policy and the failure by government to ameliorate the disadvantages associated with the 'apartheid city'. Another concerns the absence of an urbanisation policy that is intended to reverse the consequences of past restrictions on the urbanisation of Africans and to guide the present unintended urbanisation consequences of many government policies.

Unfortunately no proposals were received for urban transport and the recalcitrant authors of a chapter on urban renewal failed to deliver.

A few acknowledgements need to be made. During the later stages of the preparation of the book, the HSRC and the Development Bank of Southern Africa drafted a memorandum of understanding to disseminate the findings of the publication to a select audience of urban practitioners and municipal officials in order to practically impact on the field of urban development. This agreement included funding from the Development Bank of Southern Africa, which is highly appreciated.

During the course of drafting the chapters, some members of the reference group reviewed and commented on draft versions of some chapters. In this respect, we have, in particular, to thank Robert Beauregard, Susan Parnell and Alison Todes for their many contributions.

Adlai Davids from the HSRC Knowledge Systems has also to be thanked for his work on the maps.

Finally, we thank our contributors for what are no doubt important contributions to the field of urban policy, and for their patience and forbearance with many editorial demands. Indeed, one chapter was taken through seven iterations.

Three explanations are required for readers. The first is that the names of many cities and towns referred to in this book changed between 1994 and 2004. A list of old and new names is therefore included on the following page.

The second is that reference to local government changed to municipalities after the 1998 Local Government White Paper. Contributors to the book generally use both references, depending on the timing and context.

The third explanation is intended for foreign readers. South Africans are excessively given to abbreviations: RDP, IDP, DBSA, LED and so on. Whereas South Africans sometimes become so used to the abbreviations that they forget the full name referred to by the abbreviation, a foreigner only becomes operational in South Africa after he or she learns the abbreviations. The editors of the book have removed abbreviations when they occur only a few times, but in other instances please consult the list of abbreviations and acronyms for explanations.

# *List of changes to place names and/or boundaries*

| Old name | New name |
|---|---|
| **Cities** | |
| Bloemfontein | Mangaung Municipality |
| Durban | eThekwini Metropolitan Municipality |
| East London | Buffalo City Municipality |
| East Rand | Ekurhuleni Metropolitan Municipality |
| Pietermaritzburg | Msunduzi Municipality |
| Port Elizabeth | Nelson Mandela Metropolitan Municipality |
| Pretoria | Tshwane Metropolitan Municipality |
| | |
| **Areas** | |
| Vaal and Vaal Triangle | Divided between Emfuleni Municipality and Midvaal Municipality in Gauteng province |
| Witwatersrand | Portions in City of Johannesburg Metropolitan Municipality, Ekurhuleni Metropolitan Municipality and municipalities in Westrand District Municipality |
| | |
| **Secondary cities and towns** | |
| Harrismith | Maluti a Phofung Municipality |
| Kimberley | Sol Plaatje Municipality |
| Kuruman | Ga-Segonyana Municipality |
| Mothibistad | Ga-Segonyana Municipality |
| Nelspruit | Mbombela Municipality |
| Paarl | Drakenstein Municipality |
| Pietersburg | Polokwane Municipality |
| Port Alfred | Ndlambe Municipality |
| Richards Bay | uMhlathuze Municipality |
| | |
| **Former 'homelands'** | |
| Ciskei | Now included within the Eastern Cape province |
| Qwa-Qwa | Now included within the Free State province |
| Transkei | Now included within the Eastern Cape province |
| Gazankulu | Now included within the Limpopo province |

# Abbreviations and acronyms

ANC       African National Congress
CBD       central business district
CSIR      Council for Scientific and Industrial Research
DFA       Development Facilitation Act
DLA       Department of Land Affairs
DoH       Department of Housing
DPLG      Department of Provincial and Local Government
FFC       Financial and Fiscal Commission
GEAR      Growth, Employment and Redistribution programme
GTZ       *Gesellschaft für Technische Zusammenarbeit* (Agency for Technical
          Co-operation)
HSRC      Human Sciences Research Council
IDP       Integrated Development Plan
LED       Local Economic Development
LGNF      Local Government Negotiating Forum
LGTA      Local Government Transition Act
MIIF      Municipal Infrastructure Investment Framework
NGO       Non-governmental organisation
NHF       National Housing Forum
NP        National Party
NSDP      National Spatial Development Perspective
RDP       Reconstruction and Development Programme
SACN      South African Cities Network
SALGA     South African Local Government Association
Sanco     South African National Civic Organisation
UDF       Urban Development Framework
UDS       Urban Development Strategy
UN        United Nations

# 1 Introduction

Udesh Pillay, Richard Tomlinson and Jacques du Toit

A number of books about urban South Africa have been published since the democratic elections in 1994. Their central themes have concerned housing backlogs, policy and delivery, the apartheid city and how the delivery of housing is contributing to urban fragmentation, and governance issues.[1] There have also been a large number of publications on cities, especially on Johannesburg.[2] These books have generally been the product of geographers and planners and one finds in their titles 'fragmentation', 'divided', 'shaping', 'unsustainable' and 'crisis'. 'Post-apartheid', of course, rings most loudly, with a crescendo of journal articles looking at urban South Africa not in terms of its preferred future but in terms of its despised past.

Government has presented issues a bit differently. The conception of the future was defined in the Reconstruction and Development Programme (RDP) by meeting basic human needs, in the 1996 Constitution through giving effect to social rights, and in the 1998 White Paper on Local Government as a 'historic opportunity to transform local government' (RSA 1998: v). It is this sense of opportunity and, indeed, enthusiasm and optimism that underlay the preparation of urban policies in the early years, starting with local government negotiations and in 1992 with the National Housing Forum. The policies were prepared in great haste and driven by political agendas for the future.

The urban policies were at the same time simplistic and complex. They were simplistic in setting targets for delivery whose realisation required ignoring other development criteria; a million houses in five years being the notorious example of a numerical goal overriding the need to build sustainable settlements. They were complex in the transformation of local government and the need to align boundary demarcation, institutional restructuring, financial and fiscal direction and resources, all with a view to building democratic and developmental institutions.

A little has been written about the process of policy formulation and the research and other influences that underlay it, with the focus shifting from housing and urban form to governance and service delivery.[3] There has not been a comprehensive assessment of the urban policies formulated during the first ten years of democracy, the process of formulating the policies and the influences on them.

The process of urban policy formulation covered in this book begins with the 1976 Soweto uprising, pays attention to the intense struggles in the townships during the 1980s, and then proceeds to a close examination of prominent urban policies and policy formulation and implementation during the 1990s and on to 2004. In 2004 South Africa celebrated ten years of democracy.

There have been three components to urban policy in South Africa up to 2004. Policies to which close attention has been paid include those that gave effect to the 'One city, one tax base' slogan that emerged during the township struggles. These policies included re-demarcating municipalities to create integrated and democratic local governments, the comprehensive restructuring of the local government system, and the design of municipal financial systems that support service delivery to the poor. Another set of policies revolves around the creation of 'developmental local governments' and includes integrated development planning and local economic development. A last set of policies refers to the mass delivery of free housing and services within municipalities.

In effect, the national, provincial (in the case of housing) and municipal and sectoral policies included in this book have sought to *enable* local government to undertake delivery, *plan for* delivery and *implement* delivery in consolidating democracy. Thus, government's urban policy has focused on meeting the commitment in the RDP to provide for the basic needs of all South Africans, and building democratic local government institutions and enhancing their ability to promote socio-economic development in urban areas.

A further section of the book is devoted to a chapter on urban spatial policy and another on the absence of an urbanisation policy and present policies that are having unintended consequences for urbanisation. These two chapters provide both a contextual introduction to the book and point to the absence of policies that effectively counter a century of efforts to prevent the urbanisation of the African population.

Most of the urban policies have been debated and evaluated, but there has not been an attempt to document the history of the policy formulation processes in relation to experience with the policies and subsequent revisions to the policies. This book serves this purpose; with the intention also being to evaluate the influence of research, advice from international development agencies and comparative experience, and political and economic pressures during the policy formulation processes. The focus is essentially on the sphere of government where policy is 'passed' (national), and the sphere of government most responsible for implementation (municipal).

## Backdrop

At the time of the 1994 democratic elections, South African cities were characterised by dire housing and services backlogs, inequalities in municipal expenditure, the spatial anomalies associated with the 'apartheid city', profound struggles against apartheid local government structures, high unemployment and many poverty-stricken households.

The African National Congress' (ANC) commitment to addressing these issues can be traced to the 1994 RDP, which committed government to meeting the basic needs of all South Africans. Housing and services such as water and sanitation, land, jobs and others were counted as basic needs. The RDP also included the commitment to the restructuring of local government with a view to meeting these needs. The ANC recognised the key role of local government in delivering services and promoting economic development and called for the re-demarcation of local governments with a view to urban integration and democracy, the creation of a single tax base, and the cross-subsidisation of municipal expenditure. Local governments were to become central to overcoming the backlogs.

However, the ANC confronted a fundamental difficulty. At the time it was unknown how many households suffered from services backlogs; what household incomes were and what services levels they might afford; whether local governments had the capacity to deliver services, as well as knowledge of alternative means of ensuring service delivery such as public–private partnerships; and how the capital and operating costs of the services might be financed. Indeed, there was only inexact data regarding the number of households in urban and rural areas. The same difficulties were not experienced in the case of housing, since the housing backlog had been estimated at the National Housing Forum (1992–1994) in the broadest possible terms, as being 1.5 million units.

It was due to this lack of household and services information, and a lack of clarity regarding options for delivering services, that, in 1995, the first version of the Municipal Infrastructure Investment Framework (MIIF) was prepared (Ministry in the Office of the President and the Department of Housing 1995). All too often based on informed guesstimates, the MIIF provided the 'missing' data and suggested how services might be delivered and financed.

At the same time as the MIIF was prepared, government was putting in place the preconditions for the 'One city, one tax base' policy: re-demarcating and creating integrated local governments in time for the 1995 and 2000 local government elections, with the latter being viewed as the 'final stage' in the creation of 'developmental local government'. Examples of the policies and policy frameworks that emerged over time include integrated development planning, local economic development, free basic services, and municipal services partnerships. Housing policy was an exception to this transformation because, in 1992, negotiations began in the National Housing Forum, and by the time of the 1994 democratic elections what was, in effect, a draft housing White Paper was in place.

Many urban policies have subsequently been revised in the light of experience and, importantly, also as government extended its democratic agenda. Free basic services provide an example. During the 1980s one of the means employed to oppose the Black Local Authority system was a boycott on payment for rent and services. A decade and a half later, after it became clear that the widespread failure to pay for services showed no sign of stopping and also that many households could not afford to pay for services, the ANC and later government adopted the free basic services policy. This represented a break with the earlier principle included in the MIIF that, taking into account the potential for cross-subsidisation, consumers of water and electricity should pay an amount for services consumed.

## The context for urban policy formulation

### Population growth and urbanisation

In the first instance, the context for urban policy is the size of the urban population, its location, how rapidly it is growing, and where it is growing. The South African census defines four types of areas: 'tribal' (former 'homeland'), 'rural formal' or 'commercial farming', 'urban formal' and 'urban informal'.[4]

At the time of the 2001 census, South Africa's population was 44 819 318 with about 57 per cent of the population deemed to be urban and 43 per cent rural. Forty-seven per cent of the urban population lived in formal urban areas and 8 per cent lived in informal urban areas. Thirty-five per cent of the rural population lived in tribal areas and 7 per cent in commercial farming areas. The 3 per cent difference comprises overlapping urban and rural categorisation – institutional housing, hostels, industrial areas and smallholdings – with 2 per cent being found in urban areas and 1 per cent in rural areas.

The location of most of the urban population is depicted in Figure 1.1, which shows the nine largest cities that are members of the South African Cities Network (SACN) and also provincial capitals that are not included in the SACN. The SACN cities are Johannesburg, eThekwini, Cape Town, Tshwane, Ekurhuleni, Nelson Mandela, Buffalo City, Msunduzi and Mangaung. In addition to the cities, Figure 1.1 also reflects population density. Aside from Cape Town, it is apparent that most of the country's population lives in the eastern half of the country.

**Figure 1.1** *Cities comprising the SACN and provincial capitals*

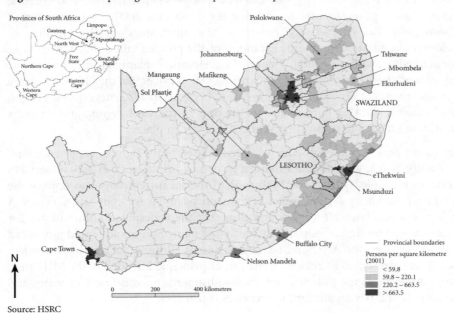

Source: HSRC

Figure 1.2 shows the population size and the number of households living in the cities included in Figure 1.1. Johannesburg and eThekwini have more than three million inhabitants and Cape Town has close to that number. Ekurhuleni and Tshwane follow, with Ekurhuleni having about 2.5 million inhabitants and Tshwane 2 million inhabitants. In practice, the three cities in Gauteng comprise a single conurbation with a population of 7.7 million persons, approximating what the international literature has recently referred to as the emergence of global 'city regions' (Pillay 2004). The last city with metropolitan status, Nelson Mandela, has about a million inhabitants, with Buffalo City, Mangaung and Msunduzi, not classified as metropoles, having much smaller populations. The smaller populations are also true of Polokwane and Mbombela, with a considerable drop to Mafikeng and Sol Plaatje. Sol Plaatje is located in the Northern Cape, which is losing population.

**Figure 1.2** *Population and household numbers of SACN and selected secondary cities, 2001*

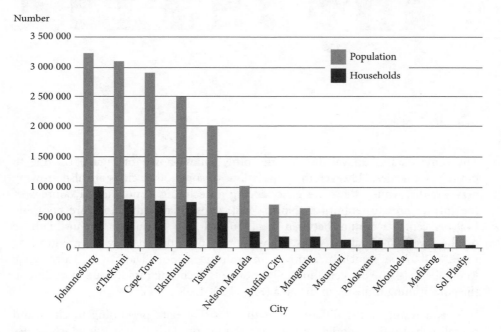

Source: HSRC

In the case of the SACN cities, the most rapid growth is occurring in Gauteng. As can be seen in Figure 1.3, the populations of Johannesburg, Ekurhuleni and Tshwane, at 22.2 per cent, 22.4 per cent and 18.0 per cent between 1996 and 2001 respectively, are growing more rapidly than any other of the SACN cities (SACN 2004: 38). At the same time, cities like Nelson Mandela, Msunduzi, Mangaung and Buffalo City are growing at a rate below that of the nation.

**Figure 1.3** *Population and household growth rates of SACN cities, 1996–2001*

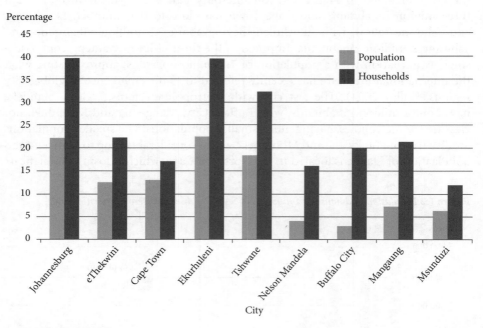

Source: SACN (2004: 38, 81)

The same data is unavailable for the other cities shown in Figure 1.1 due to boundary changes. However, the populations of some other cities are also growing very rapidly, while others are experiencing a declining population. Examples of the former are Rustenburg in North West whose platinum mines are booming (4.9 per cent per annum between the 1996 and 2001 censuses), and uMhlathuze on the KwaZulu-Natal east coast whose port and industrial activities are growing rapidly (8.07 per cent). In contrast, in addition to Sol Plaatje (–0.28 per cent), Mathjabeng (–3.07 per cent) in the Free State is declining rapidly due to decline in the gold-mining industry in the area (SACN 2004: 38).

It is as a result of the different growth rates that data pertaining to cities and overall urbanisation should be read in conjunction with Figure 1.4, which shows population growth between the two census periods, 1996 and 2001. Figure 1.4 points to the population decline in the Northern Cape and also many areas in the former homelands, and also to the fact that in many areas the rural population is growing more rapidly, often considerably more rapidly, than the national average of 2 per cent per annum. Aside from growth in Cape Town, in high value mostly wine farming areas and along the coast north and west of the city, it is apparent that rapid growth is mostly occurring in the eastern and more northern parts of the country.

**Figure 1.4** *Municipal population growth between 1996 and 2001*

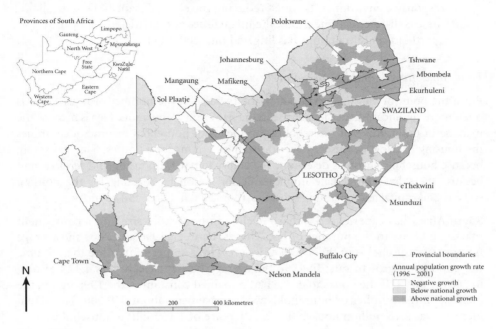

Source: HSRC

It appears that there is also rapid growth in some cities outside Gauteng and also in certain rural areas. The rural-to-rural migration is probably explained by the absence of jobs in the metros and larger urban centres, the availability of social grants that reduce household dependence on cities as possible sources of income, and of subsidised housing and municipal and social services in small towns, predominantly in the commercial farming areas (Bekker & Cross 1999; Cross 2001).

A last observation regarding the location of urban growth is that most of the increase in the cities is occurring on the periphery of cities. This has long been known in the case of the provision since 1994 of subsidised low-income housing projects, which reinforce the disadvantages of poor access to jobs, social services and retail facilities; but this distant location phenomenon is also characteristic of new migrants. This situation is bemoaned by most urban practitioners and by government itself in the Department of Housing's 2004 *Breaking New Ground* policy statement where it is observed that:

> After the 1994 elections, Government committed itself to developing more liveable, equitable and sustainable cities. Key elements of this framework included pursuing a more compact urban form, facilitating higher densities, mixed land use development, and integrating land

use and public transport planning, so as to ensure more diverse and responsive environments whilst reducing travelling distances. Despite all these well-intended measures, the inequalities and inefficiencies of the apartheid space economy, has lingered on. (2004: 11)

### Household growth and housing and services backlogs

From the point of view of urban policy, the increase in the number of households is often more significant than the increase in the size of the population. This is because the increase in the number of households, together with household incomes, determines the housing backlog; because service connections are made to houses, flats and so on; because household incomes determine the ability to pay for housing and services; and because these have immediate implications for national budgeting for the housing subsidy and capital and operating subsidies, municipal finances and so on.

South Africa has experienced a sharp decline in household size and a consequent marked increase in the number of households. Between 1996 and 2001 the average number of households in the SACN cities grew by 27.5 per cent, more than double the population growth rate. In 1996 the average household size was 4.47 persons; in 2001 it was 4. If the household size had remained constant at the 1996 figure, the increase in the number of households would have been about 950 000. The actual increase was 2.13 million households, a difference of 1.18 million households.

**Figure 1.5** *Average household size of SACN and selected secondary cities, 2001*

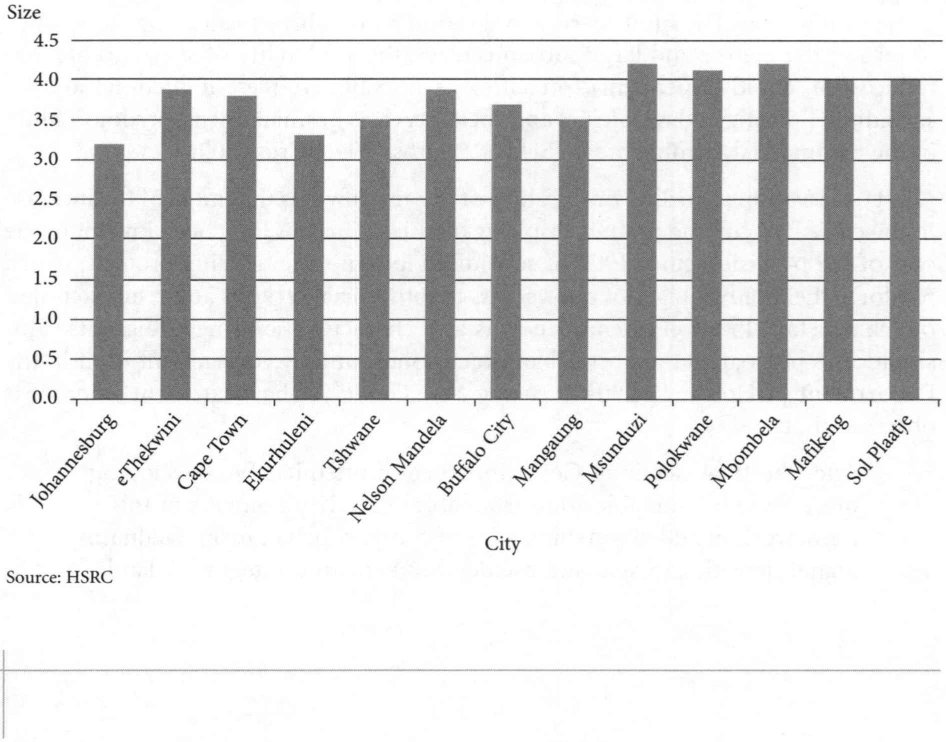

Source: HSRC

Figure 1.3 shows population and household growth rates and Figure 1.5 the differences in household size among the cities. Combining the two is important because rapid population growth coupled with declining household size accentuates the housing and services backlogs in an area. Again it is the cities in Gauteng that stand out. The increase in the number of households in Johannesburg was a remarkable 8.05 per cent per annum, about double the national average. Johannesburg, Ekurhuleni and Tshwane again have the most rapid growth rates. Indeed, with the exception of Buffalo City, the rate of increase in the number of households in the other SACN cities is below the national average. The rate of increase in the number of households in Nelson Mandela and Msunduzi in particular is sharply below the national average.

Possible explanations for the changes in household size include:
- Households that in the apartheid years suffered from massive overcrowding and combined, for example, married children with parents, are unbundling.
- The role of migration may also be a consideration. Cross (2001) suggests that a change in migration patterns is under way. Instead of circular migration, while many householders still talk of returning 'home' to rural areas, in practice what is happening is that families are, de facto, separating into urban and rural households. This view is debated and to some degree supported by Russell (2002). However, Posel (2003) and Cox, Hemson and Todes (2004) disagree with the view that circular migration is giving way to separate urban and rural households.
- The impact of HIV/AIDS on households is unclear. AIDS deaths have picked up rapidly since 2001 but were not as profound between the 1996 and 2001 censuses (Dorrington, Bradshaw, Johnson & Budlender 2004: 24).
- South Africa has a very young population base and the rate at which younger people enter the housing market exceeds the general populations' growth rate, leading to smaller average household sizes.
- In regard to the influx of people from across South Africa's northern borders, people might come in as individuals and not necessarily as families, thus reducing the average household size.
- Reportedly the National Treasury has suggested that the availability of the housing subsidy has caused families to unbundle for the purpose of obtaining the subsidy.

The increase in the number of households among the SACN cities should be read in conjunction with Figure 1.6 which points to the rapid growth of households, in excess of the national average of 4.34 per cent per annum, in many areas of the country aside from the cities. Compared to areas where a population decline is shown (Figure 1.4), there are fewer areas where there is a decline in the number of households. There is at the same time a slower than national average increase in the number of households in many of the former homelands.

**Figure 1.6** *Household growth between 1996 and 2001*

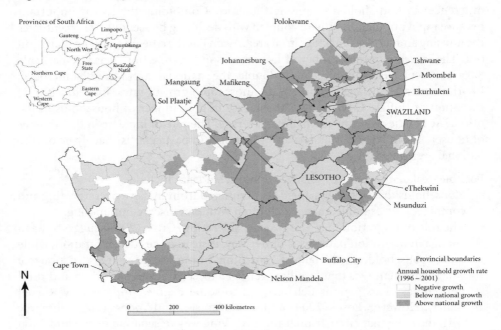

Source: HSRC

The implications of the increase in the number of households are evident in the housing backlog. Despite the delivery of over 1.8 million subsidised housing units completed – or under construction – between 1994 and March 2005, in its 2004 *Breaking New Ground* document the Department of Housing reported that the housing backlog had increased to over 1.84 million units and is growing.

The proportions of households in the SACN cities that lack formal housing or water[5] on the stand or in the house are shown in Figure 1.7. The proportion of households in the cities without formal housing ranges between 20 per cent and 38 per cent, with the three non-metropolitan cities and eThekwini and Ekurhuleni being at the top of the range. With the exception of Ekurhuleni, it is expected that this is partly because their demarcation included former homelands. The proportion of households in the cities without on-site water ranges between 15 per cent and 42 per cent, with eThekwini and the three non-metropolitan cities being at the top of the range. The data is a bit difficult to interpret. On the one hand, it makes sense that the cities whose boundaries include the former homelands will have the largest water backlogs; on the other hand, it is to be expected that formal houses will have on-site water, and this is not always the case, for example in Ekurhuleni. Rather than try to explain the latter differences, one wonders about the data.

**Figure 1.7** *The percentage of households without formal shelter and on-site water in SACN cities, 2001*

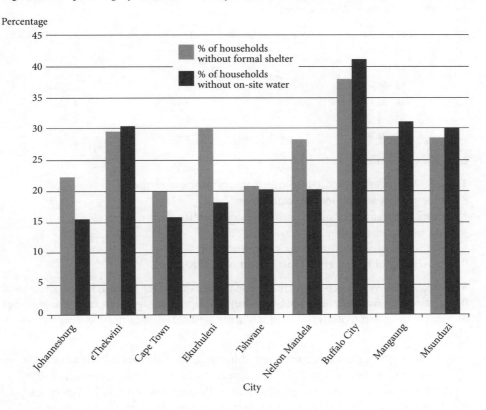

Source: SACN (2004: 27–31, 80)

## POPULATION PROJECTIONS AND THE FUTURE GROWTH OF THE CITIES

One cannot assume that high urban population and household growth rates will continue. South Africa's population is growing increasingly slowly, although the projections that follow do not indicate that HIV/AIDS will lead to negative population growth. Increasingly, urban growth will be propelled less by the natural increase of the urban population and more by internal movement within the country and, perhaps, migration from other countries.

The population projections to 2015, including those for HIV/AIDS, are shown in Table 1.1 and are based on the Actuarial Society of South Africa (ASSA) 2002 model (Dorrington et al. 2004). The projections are for South Africa and none are available for cities and for households. Due to the prevalence of HIV/AIDS, which the Nelson Mandela/Human Sciences Research Council (HSRC) survey reported as 11.4 per cent in 2002, HIV/AIDS is a determining factor of population growth in South Africa.[6]

**Table 1.1** *Projected population, number of HIV positive, AIDS sick and cumulative AIDS deaths for 1990–2015, ASSA 2002 (default scenario)*

| Year | Total population | Annual growth rate % | Total HIV+ | Cumulative AIDS deaths |
|------|------------------|----------------------|------------|------------------------|
| 1990 | 35 538 787 | 1.8 | 38 597 | 326 |
| 1995 | 40 153 091 | 2.7 | 943 590 | 20 662 |
| 2000 | 43 966 756 | 1.4 | 3 731 645 | 318 697 |
| 2005 | 46 156 343 | 0.7 | 5 165 797 | 1 542 169 |
| 2010 | 47 380 126 | 0.5 | 5 408 621 | 3 404 415 |
| 2015 | 48 294 565 | 0.3 | 5 407 945 | 5 358 501 |

Source: Dorrington et al. (2004: 24)

The ASSA projections to 2015 require assumptions regarding:
• information and education campaigns;
• improved treatment of sexually transmitted diseases;
• voluntary counselling and testing;
• mother-to-child transmission prevention; and
• antiretroviral treatment. (Dorrington et al. 2004: 8)

Regarding the overall expected trends for population size, Table 1.1 shows the total population for five year intervals, the annual population growth rate, the number of people infected with HIV and accumulated AIDs deaths. Dorrington et al. observe that:

> The total population continues to increase over the period, although at a decreasing rate. From 2011, the expected annual rate of increase is 0.4%. The number of people infected with HIV peaks in 2013, at just over 5.4 million, after which it starts to decrease slowly. In contrast, the number of people sick with AIDS in the middle of each year continues to rise over the period, reaching nearly 743 000 in 2015. Accumulated AIDS deaths are close to 5.4 million by the same year. By 2004, it is estimated that over 1.2 million people have already died as a result of AIDS, just over 5 million are infected with HIV, and over 500 000 are AIDS sick. (2004: 23)

According to these projections, population growth will slow from 0.7 per cent per annum in 2005 to 0.3 per cent in 2015. At the same time, because HIV infection most affects young adults, beginning at about 20 years old and continuing for another 20 or so years, due to the time lag between infection and death, it is in middle age that most deaths occur. This is when the dying are raising children and caring for the elderly. The death of one or more income-earning household members considerably increases the dependency burden on other household members. This, together with the large number of mostly working-age adults who are AIDS sick and in need of care, points to the burden that will be placed on households and the extended family.

*Household incomes*

So far, the focus has been on the urbanisation of the population, the increase in the number of households, housing and services backlogs, and the location of low-income households within cities. The significance of this material should be interpreted in the light of changing household incomes. This is because household incomes above a certain level enable the household to successfully participate in the private delivery of housing and services, contribute significantly to municipal rates and services, reduce the need for capital and operating subsidies for municipalities, and so on.

In this regard, Table 1.2 provides extraordinary statistics regarding employment and unemployment amongst African and coloured people. Of the urban African and coloured labour force, 38.7 per cent are without employment and 56.5 per cent are without formal employment. Although there has been modest growth in formal sector employment, job creation in this sector has failed to keep pace with the growth in the labour force.

**Table 1.2** *Racial incidence of urban employment and unemployment, 2004*

| | African and coloured | | White | |
| --- | --- | --- | --- | --- |
| | Millions | Percentage | Millions | Percentage |
| Employee, formal sector | 4.3 | 43.5 | 1.4 | 72.5 |
| Employee, informal sector | 1.0 | 10.3 | 0.0 | 0.9 |
| Self-employed, formal sector | 0.1 | 1.3 | 0.3 | 15.6 |
| Self-employed, informal sector | 0.6 | 6.2 | 0.1 | 4.0 |
| Unemployed (broad def.) | 3.9 | 38.7 | 0.1 | 7.0 |
| Total | 9.9 | 100.0 | 1.9 | 100.0 |

Source: Calculated from StatsSA, *Labour Force Survey*, March 2004
Note: The data was provided by Mark Aliber of the HSRC.

The negative implications for household incomes are ameliorated by the availability of social grants. In 1994 government spent R10 billion on social grants and there were 2.6 million beneficiaries. In 2003 the expenditure was R34.8 billion and there were 6.8 million beneficiaries. It is speculated that it is due to these grants that there has been a decline in households with an income of less than R800 per month; conversely, it is speculated that it is due to increasing unemployment that there has been an increase in households with an income of less than R3 500.

## Structure of the book: four sets of urban policies

At the outset it was noted that there are four sets of urban policies: the 'missing' urban spatial form and urbanisation policies; policies that give effect to 'One city, one tax base' prescripts; policies that promote 'developmental local governments';

and policies that promote the mass delivery of housing and services. The structure of this book follows these four sets of policies, plus, of course, provides reflective comment in a concluding chapter.

## Urban and urbanisation

The absence of an urbanisation policy is curious in the light of apartheid policies that historically prevented the urbanisation of the African population. The assumption seems to have been that urbanisation is a natural and inevitable process and that it should be left unattended. As it turns out, Doreen Atkinson and Lochner Marais in Chapter 2 find that a variety of government programmes have had spatial consequences, often unintended and contradictory, and also that the migration from tribal rural to small towns in commercial farming areas could not have been predicted. Urbanisation in South Africa is following an unprecedented course. The Presidency's preparation of the 2003 National Spatial Development Perspective and the 2005 draft Urban Development Framework will provide some guidance in the future, but they occur at a 'higher level' than the complex and diverse array of issues that need to be addressed and should form part of an urbanisation policy.

The absence of effective urban spatial policies is surprising because, since the 1970s, there has been ongoing research into the apartheid city and how urban areas should be restructured. Alison Todes concludes Chapter 3 by referring to these concerns as an 'idea' that captured the enthusiasm of academics and, amongst professionals, planners in particular. It is in the Department of Housing's 2004 *Breaking New Ground* that government has specified its determination to devote resources to acquiring well-located land for low-income housing and to build compact and, a word that now has wide resonance, 'sustainable' cities, human settlements and communities.

## One city, one tax base

The municipal demarcation and local government and municipal restructuring policies follow directly from the set of 'One city, one tax base' policies. They are aimed at creating integrated local governments that are able to deliver services and have the financial capacity to do so.

In Chapter 4 Robert Cameron outlines the hasty process of demarcating local government and ward boundaries for the 1995 elections, and then the 2000 elections. The 1996 Constitution provided for the creation of an independent Municipal Demarcation Board. The criteria for demarcating local government and ward boundaries emerged from the White Paper on Local Government of 1998.

The actual design of local government went through a complex three phases. Mirjam van Donk and Edgar Pieterse in Chapter 5 hold that the first phase started with the struggles of the late 1980s, and came to a close with the municipal elections of 1995/96, when a negotiated transitional system of local government came into effect. The second phase started with the 1996 Constitution, which established local government as an autonomous sphere of government, and then proceeded to the Local Government White Paper and subsequent legislation that further elaborated on what the new local government system would entail. The 2000 municipal elections signified the end of the transitional phase of local government, and the beginning of the new system of local government.

Alan Mabin's Chapter 6 reinforces the salient points made in Chapter 5 through an examination of local government reorganisation around essentially two themes, with the second being the dominant theme. The first has to do with the differences between the 'needs' of the local governments of large cities and local governments of smaller urban centres; and the second, the evolving debates around the purpose of local government. These purposes include service provision, economic development, redistribution, partnership with business, and vehicles for democratic participation. With these purposes not being mutually exclusive, and residing more in relative emphasis, the debate is about the politics of government reorganisation.

None of this would mean a great deal if local governments lacked the finances to provide services and serve as developmental local governments. Philip van Ryneveld contributed to most aspects of the formulation of local government financial policy and provides a detailed record of the changes in Chapter 7. As with Cameron, and Van Donk and Pieterse, he points to the central role of the Local Government White Paper and the municipal finance and service delivery legislation that emerged from the White Paper.

*Developmental local government*

The centrepiece of developmental local government is the Integrated Development Plan (IDP). Philip Harrison (Chapter 8) explains that notions regarding the potential role for such plans emerged from the New Public Management movement and comparative experience in the United States under Clinton, the United Kingdom under Blair, New Zealand and various academic treatises. A substantive conception of developmental local government and IDPs, yet again, emerged out of the Local Government White Paper. IDPs provide a long-term vision for a municipality; detail the priorities of an elected council; link and coordinate sectoral plans and strategies; align financial and human resources with implementation needs; strengthen the focus on environmental sustainability; and provide the basis for annual and medium-term budgeting.

IDPs are intended to give effect to the constitutionally prescribed role of local governments of promoting economic and social development. Local Economic Development (LED) plans are central to this role. LED strategies are integrated into IDPs, and the exploration in the mid-1990s of what they might mean for policy in South Africa was initially based mostly on US experience. Etienne Nel and Lynelle John (Chapter 9) describe the first efforts at the formulation of LED policy that began in the so-called RDP Ministry (the Ministry in the Office of the President), but 'died down' when the ministry was closed. LED was then 'picked up' by the Department of Provincial and Local Government (DPLG) that promoted LED through the creation of a LED Fund, all the while without there being a LED policy as such. It was expected that a LED policy would be finalised in 1995, but it appears that instead a LED Framework will be issued by the DPLG late in 2005.[7]

National policy for tourism is not linked to local efforts to promote tourism. Christian Rogerson, after describing the evolution of national tourism policy in Chapter 10, presents tourism as essentially a vehicle employed by local government and stakeholders to promote the development of the local economy.

## Housing and services delivery programmes

The provision of a free once-off housing subsidy for all qualifying households was negotiated at the National Housing Forum. Over 1.8 million houses and serviced sites have been delivered. A portion of the housing subsidy is used for the installation of services, which means that the housing subsidy has also served as the vehicle for local governments fulfilling their constitutional obligation 'to ensure the provision of services in a sustainable manner'. Housing delivery has repeatedly been used by government to illustrate the extent of its success in meeting the needs of the low-income population. It is ironic that at the time of writing there were riots protesting the slow delivery of housing and services.

Sarah Charlton and Caroline Kihato (Chapter 11) document the key questions addressed during the National Housing Forum and the policy that emerged. They evaluate housing policy and its implementation not through the lens of the time – housing as a basic need and delivery at scale – but through the more ambitious lens that became increasingly prevalent in government discourse, namely, the contribution of the housing benefit to poverty reduction and the creation of sustainable human settlements. They follow how policy was adjusted over the next ten years, with the adjustments essentially being reactions to negative aspects of the policy which become evident through implementation. In 2004 a new, but what government insists is an 'amended' housing policy, was introduced in the form of *Breaking New Ground*, which includes close attention to poverty and sustainability. The authors claim that despite these emphases, the 'amendments' are not clearly related to an analysis of the impact on beneficiaries' lives.

Along with the delivery of housing, government also sought to ensure that all households had access to services. Following the free installation of services infrastructure, with funds drawn from the housing subsidy, the expectation was that households would pay for services consumed. As it turns out, the services payment boycotts that began in opposition to apartheid local government structures in the mid-1980s seem to have been inherited by democratic local governments. Bowing to reality, the free basic services policy was announced at an ANC election rally in 2000. In Chapter 12,

Tim Mosdell explores the motivation and rationale behind this policy shift, identifying and analysing relevant research, policy formulation processes and policy pronouncements. He employs the free basic water policy as an illustration of the origins and subsequent dynamics underpinning the free basic services policy.

An interesting situation has prevailed where a local government system that was premised on the implementation of market principles, for example, user-charges for services, now sets about providing housing and services for free to low-income households.

## Conclusion

In the concluding chapter the editors locate the various policies and policy formulation processes within the changing political and economic context since the 1976 Soweto uprising and describe the major legislation that gave effect to these policies. There follows an assessment of the view of some of the authors that research made a relatively minor contribution to the various policies. Instead, the editors argue that research matters, and have done so through discussing the country's urban policy community and the changing purposes of urban research over time. The editors then turn to government's urban 'policy' initiatives: the National Spatial Development Perspective, the Department of Housing's *Breaking New Ground* housing policy 'amendments', the LED Framework and the draft Urban Development Framework. Government insists that these are not, in fact, urban policies or, anyway, are not new policies. This national urban policy-shy approach is contrasted with the SACN's unabashedly calling for a national urban policy framework, and the SACN and its member cities setting an urban agenda that increasingly influences secondary cities. Responsibility for urban policy appears to be shifting to the cities.

### Notes

1   For example, see Harrison, Huchzermeyer and Mayekiso (2003); Khan and Thring (2003); and Rust and Rubenstein (1996).

2   For example, see Beavon (2004); Tomlinson, Beauregard, Bremner and Mangcu (2003); and Beall, Crankshaw and Parnell (2002).

3   For example, see Bond (2000, 2002) and Tomlinson (2002).

4   These categories are crude. The Development Bank of Southern Africa (2005) points to definitional problems such as when there are large concentrations of people living in rural areas whose existence is better characterised as urban. The Bank also points to extended household survival strategies that include members in urban and rural areas and migration between them. There is considerable potential for debating the conceptual and empirical bases for the urban/rural distinction, but in a sense this is redundant. This introduction serves to situate the reader within the urban policy environment and employs the data commonly used by government and by policy-makers and most academics. It suffices to alert the reader to misgivings regarding the conceptual underpinnings of the data.

5    Water is no doubt the most relevant example of the services backlog, but sanitation backlogs are generally considerably higher.

6    For comparative purposes, the HSRC projects that 4.6 million persons have HIV/AIDS and ASSA 5 million persons.

7    Minister Sydney Mufamadi of the DPLG has the authority to issue a framework document, whereas a policy document has to go to the Cabinet.

## References

Beall J, Crankshaw O & Parnell S (2002) *Uniting a divided city: Governance and social exclusion in Johannesburg.* London: Earthscan Publications.

Beavon K (2004) *Johannesburg: The making and shaping of the city.* Pretoria: University of South Africa Press.

Bekker S & Cross C (1999) Urbanisation factors in land reform, Phase I and II. DBSA, 1998/99. Unpublished report prepared for the Development Bank of Southern Africa.

Bond P (2000) *Cities of gold, township of coal: Essays on South Africa's new urban crisis.* Trenton, N.J.: Africa World Press.

Bond P (2002) *Unsustainable South Africa: Environment, development and social protest.* Pietermaritzburg: University of Natal Press.

Cox K, Hemson D & Todes A (2004) Urbanization in South Africa and the changing character of migrant labour in South Africa, *South African Geographical Journal*, 86(1): 7–16.

Cross C (2001) Why does South Africa need a spatial policy? Population migration, infrastructure and development, *Journal of Contemporary Studies*, 19(1): 111–127.

Department of Housing (2004) *Breaking New Ground: A comprehensive plan for the development of sustainable human settlements.* Pretoria: Department of Housing.

Development Bank of Southern Africa (2005) *Development report 2005 – Overcoming underdevelopment in South Africa's second economy*, chapter 5. Midrand.

Dorrington RE, Bradshaw D, Johnson L & Budlender D (2004) *The demographic impact of HIV/AIDS in South Africa. National indicators for 2004.* Cape Town: Centre for Actuarial Research, South African Medical Research Council and Actuarial Society of South Africa.

Harrison P, Huchzermeyer M & Mayekiso M (eds) (2003) *Confronting fragmentation: Housing and urban development in a democratising society.* Cape Town: UCT Press.

Khan F & Thring P (eds) (2003) *Housing policy and practice in post-apartheid South Africa.* Sandown: Heinemann Publishers.

Ministry in the Office of the President and the Department of Housing (1995) *Municipal Infrastructure Investment Framework.*

Pillay U (2004) Are globally competitive 'city regions' developing in South Africa? Formulaic aspirations or new imaginations, *Urban Forum*, 15(4): 340–364.

Posel D (2003) Have migration patterns in post-apartheid South Africa changed? Conference on African Migration and Urbanisation in Comparative Perspective. Johannesburg. Available at <http://www.pum.princeton.edu/pumconference/papers.html>.

RSA (Republic of South Africa) (1998) *White Paper on Local Government.* Pretoria: Government Printers.

Russell M (2002) Are urban black families nuclear? A comparative study of black and white South African family norms. Centre for Social Science Research Working Paper No. 29, University of Cape Town.

Rust K & Rubenstein S (eds) (1996) *A mandate to build: Developing consensus around a national housing policy in South Africa.* Johannesburg: Ravan.

SACN (South African Cities Network) (2004) *State of the Cities Report.* Johannesburg: SACN.

StatsSA (Statistics South Africa) (2004) *Labour Force Survey.* Pretoria: StatsSA.

Tomlinson R (2002) International best practice, enabling frameworks and the policy process: A South African case study, *International Journal of Urban and Regional Research,* 26(2): 377–388.

Tomlinson R, Beauregard R, Bremner L & Mangcu X (eds) (2003) *Emerging Johannesburg: Perspectives on the post-apartheid city.* New York: Routledge.

# Part 1: Urban and urbanisation

# 2 Urbanisation and the future urban agenda in South Africa

Doreen Atkinson and Lochner Marais

## Introduction

This chapter explores whether there was a coherent national policy after 1994 to address broader urbanisation processes. We will argue that the government approach to urbanisation has been characterised by diverse and unreconciled policy principles; by the unintended consequences of sectoral policies; by contradictory spatial settlement policies; and by a void in thinking about crucial aspects of migration and urbanisation. Until now, government departments have pursued their own developmental priorities, with little concern about the 'where' of development, focusing instead on the 'what' of their sectoral programmes.

This chapter is a review of the most important government policies and strategies that address spatial questions. Briefly, the argument is as follows. Firstly, where policy instruments have, explicitly or implicitly, addressed issues of migration, there have been contradictory and confusing messages about the relationship between rural and urban development. This chapter will first explore the 'Tower of Babel' quality of the prevailing governmental thinking on migration issues.

Secondly, sectoral departments' expenditure decisions have had unintended consequences for urbanisation and migration. We explore the way in which different departments' thinking has remained limited to narrow sectoral concerns, with no appreciation for the impact of their policies and programmes on broader development dynamics. Because of the contradictions in policy, government has been unable to anticipate and prevent the many urban dysfunctions caused by urbanisation, or to exploit some of the potential advantages of rural–urban migration.

Thirdly, where spatial settlement policies have been addressed directly, they have sometimes been in tension with one another. The emerging spatial approaches of the Integrated Sustainable Rural Development Strategy (ISRDS), the Urban Renewal Programme (URP), and the National Spatial Development Perspective (NSDP) will be considered in this context. The NSDP was a major breakthrough; for the first time, there was a strong focus on the 'where' of development.

Fourthly, there are clear signs that these diverse approaches are now starting to converge. Increasingly, the NSDP is becoming the instrument through which the entire government system is starting to focus on 'where' questions.

Finally, in this process, the spatial concept of 'developmental potential' (the 'where' questions) may well serve as an impetus to rethink departments' and municipalities' substantive policy and programme design (the 'what' questions). The stage is now set for numerous hitherto neglected developmental options to come to the fore. The chapter will present some key developmental issues which should be examined by government, with a view to their being incorporated into a more coherent and meaningful policy on urbanisation, migration and spatial allocation of resources.

## Official thinking on urban and rural development, 1994–2002

There has been no clear government position on the desirability of urbanisation, nor have government policies been based on clear spatial assumptions or arguments. The overriding impression is that government seemed to assume that the abolition of influx control would result in the gradual but inevitable, permanent settlement of rural people in towns and cities. No new urbanisation policies would be required, other than to cater for the urban housing needs of rural migrants in the short term (Crankshaw & Parnell 1996). Nevertheless, urbanisation has continued apace. In 1996, South Africa's rural population was 44.9 per cent, and by 2001 – only five years later – this had declined to 42.5 per cent of South Africa's population (StatsSA 2001: 8).[1] The rural population had decreased by 830 000 people.

Several key governmental programmes and strategies make mention of rural or urban development, but an overarching focus on urbanisation or migration dynamics is lacking. At least four government institutions have explicitly raised the issue, albeit in very muted terms. These were the Reconstruction and Development Programme (RDP) Office, which was located in the Presidency, the Department of Housing (DoH), the Department of Social Development, and the Department of Land Affairs (DLA).

The RDP was the first developmental policy document of the new African National Congress (ANC) government, and ten years hence, it exercises a fundamental influence on South Africa's policy thinking. The RDP was concerned about poor spatial planning in the past, which moved the poor away from job opportunities and access to amenities (ANC 1994: Section 2.9.1). 'Almost half the black population was compelled to live in so-called "homelands" where per capita incomes are less than a quarter of the national average…Enforced segregation and industrial decentralisation have located whole communities in areas where their economic viability is threatened' (Section 4.1.2). This has burdened the workforce with enormous travel distances to their places of employment and commercial centres, and thus with excessive costs.

However, the RDP was vague on the issue of urbanisation. Its main concern was that housing and other services should be located 'geologically, environmentally, and with respect to economic opportunities and social amenities' (Section 2.5.11). Throughout the RDP, there is a focus on the needs of all citizens, *regardless of where they may live.*

In order to foster the growth of local economies, broadly representative institutions must be established to address local economic development needs. Their purpose would be to formulate strategies to address job creation and community development (for example, leveraging private sector funds for community development, investment strategies, training, small business and agricultural development, etc.). If necessary, the democratic government must provide some subsidies as a catalyst for job creation programmes controlled by communities and/or workers, and target appropriate job creation and development programmes in the most neglected and impoverished areas of our country. Ultimately, all such projects should sustain themselves. (Section 4.3.6)

Rural development was repeatedly emphasised in the RDP. For example, 'While recognising that rural incomes are far lower, the democratic government must consider rural housing needs in calculating backlogs, and make provision for gradually improving housing in rural areas' (Section 2.5.17). 'Rural areas require more frequent public transport and improved facilities, at an affordable cost' (Section 2.9.2). 'The RDP aims to improve the quality of rural life…It also entails access to affordable services, and the promotion of non-agricultural activities. In the "homelands", where most rural people live, social services and infrastructure remain poorly developed, and this must be remedied' (Section 4.3.8). The RDP framework asserted that substantial transfers of funds from the central government to the rural areas would be required, targeted to meet the needs of the rural poor. Rural communities need practical access to health, education, support for entrepreneurship (including agriculture), financial services, welfare, policing and the courts (Section 4.3.11).

The RDP warned of the 'excessive growth of the largest urban centres, the skewed distribution of population within rural areas, the role of small and medium-sized towns, and the future of declining towns and regions, and the apartheid dumping grounds' (Section 4.3.4). Clearly, the drafters of the RDP felt that something was very wrong with the spatial structure inherited from the apartheid government.

The RDP also paid attention to urban issues. 'The importance of urban development strategies within the RDP is based on a recognition that the urban areas account for over 80 per cent of the country's gross domestic product and accommodate approximately 60 per cent of South Africa's population. Continuing demographic shifts may increase urbanisation to over 70 per cent of the population by 2000' (Section 4.3.16). 'Even with a strong rural development effort, economic activities will remain concentrated in the cities. Ensuring the quality of life, sustainability and efficiency in the urban areas will thus prove critical for renewing growth and promoting equity. The design of a comprehensive national urban strategy will help serve the cities' rapidly growing populations and address the inequities and structural imbalances caused by the apartheid system. The urban development strategy must also be aimed at fostering the long-term development and sustainability of urban areas while alleviating poverty and encouraging economic expansion' (Section 4.3.17). 'The urban programme…must create a functionally integrated, efficient and equitable urban economy, as well as effective and democratic structures of urban governance and management; enhance the position of women in the cities, and initiate a social environment which contributes to a better quality of life' (Section 4.3.18).

In effect, the RDP did not choose to favour either rural or urban development. It suggested that development initiatives in rural as well as urban areas are important. But it barely flagged, let alone addressed, the issue of urbanisation.

Subsequently, in 1995/96, the RDP Office coordinated two strategies: The Urban Development Strategy (UDS) and the Rural Development Framework (RDF).

The UDS was positive about urban growth. 'Urbanisation should not be viewed as a threat. The opportunities it provides to remake our cities and towns as vehicles capable of moving many of our country's people out of poverty, squalor and environmental degradation must be seized…There is little reason to favour policies which may artificially induce or restrain growth in a particular centre, region or tier' (Office of the President 1995: Section 3). The UDS planning process was subsequently relocated to the Department of Housing, which then published the Strategy as the Urban Development Framework (UDF) in 1997. The UDF argued for more efficient and productive cities and towns, through the growth of local economies. It assumed, rather blithely, that such growth would take place, and did little to point the way to *how* it should be achieved. (The fact that the UDF was located in the DoH may explain its relative lack of focus on the productive or economic aspects of urbanisation.) With the benefit of hindsight, this assumption is extremely problematic, as urban formal sector employment has subsequently failed to create sufficient jobs for new migrants.

At the same time as the drafting of the UDF, the RDF was being compiled by the DLA during 1997. The issues of migration and urbanisation can also be glimpsed in the RDF. It acknowledged the fact that many rural people make a living by migrating to urban areas to find work. Like the UDF, the RDF encouraged synergies between rural and urban areas, to promote economic linkages. Small rural towns should be linked to agricultural activities, providing input and output markets, workshops, financial services, and social services such as schools and clinics which would be of benefit to people in the surrounding area.

Unlike the UDF, however, the RDF was worried about the impacts of migration (DLA 1997: 22):

> Labour migration has long been a cause of family breakdown and disruption. It has led to a host of social problems both in the rural areas and the places of in-migration and employment. However, more

recently, there have been problems of increasing numbers of young people in rural areas, unable to find work anywhere. Without productive employment they face a lifetime of poverty, lack of fulfilment and exposure to increasing levels of crime and violence.

Instead, the RDF focused on promoting rural livelihoods, in part to discourage labour migration and urbanisation.

The publication of the UDF and RDF apparently did little to direct the perspectives of sectoral departmental policies. Various departments continued to introduce their own strategies, with their own views on urbanisation and migration. One department which showed some appreciation for the issues of urbanisation and migration, at least at the level of policy discussion, was the Department of Social Development. In April 1998, it produced a White Paper on Population Policy. The White Paper noted that urbanisation was proceeding apace in South Africa, overwhelmingly to the metropolitan areas. The White Paper predicted that Africans would urbanise rapidly during the first decade of the 21st century, which would mean that urban areas would have to provide infrastructure and services for a growing and younger African population. The White Paper was concerned about this: 'Because cities are already large, natural population increase affects the size of cities by the addition of large absolute numbers of people' (DWP 1998: 50). The document proposed two strategies: (1) Increasing alternative choices to migration from rural to urban areas through the provision of social services, infrastructure and better employment opportunities in the rural areas, and (2) reducing backlogs in urban infrastructure and social services. In general, the White Paper regarded urbanisation as normal but problematic, and felt it should preferably be diluted and delayed. (Curiously, when the Department of Social Development six years later published its proposed Strategy on Population and Development for 2004–2009, the topic of urbanisation was totally eclipsed by the HIV/AIDS issue and, to a lesser extent, by the focus on the rural and urban development nodes.)

Generally, not much attention was paid to the issue of urbanisation until the release of the DLA's Green Paper on Development and Planning during 1999. One of the recommendations of the Green Paper was that each province should develop its own spatial plan. The main reason for such a spatial or regional plan is to '…accomplish a greater convergence among sectors and spheres of government and decision-making about where public investment should take place' (DLA 1999: 48). According to the Green Paper, such a spatial development framework should at least consist of the identification of settlements with unique qualities which require special attention on a provincial scale; settlements with significant growth potential which may be realised through provincial investment; the spatial implication of provincial sectoral policies and the testing of the implications of these against other policies and imperatives. For the first time, the issues of spatial targeting of government resources, and possible settlement strategies, were mooted.

In the interim, some provincial governments showed some interest in the topic of urbanisation. For example, the KwaZulu-Natal Provincial Spatial Growth and Development Framework advocated the promotion of 'local strengths' and the building of linkages between towns and their hinterlands, and the creation of development corridors. It proposed the creation of a hierarchy of centres to coordinate the provision of public services.

At national level, however, these themes remained unexplored. A number of research reports noted the lack of a post-apartheid framework for regional development at the provincial and the national levels and within line departments. For example, Kitchin (1997) found that limited coordination existed with regard to regional and development planning and that some government departments had limited or no frameworks at all for regional planning. By 1999, the DLA's Green Paper noted that governmental thinking on urbanisation showed very little coherence: 'There is no evidence of a shared vision of what planning should be trying to achieve in the "new" South Africa…[There] is little evidence that these documents are actively informing the work of other departments or the national allocation of resources. Indeed, there are inconsistencies…Spatial planning requires a political champion… A lack of an integrative focus in South Africa is commonly held to be a major reason for the ineffectiveness of the Urban and Rural Development Frameworks' (DLA 1999: 24, 39).

The UDF and RDF hinted at the importance of a nuanced developmental approach to rural and urban areas and the linkages between them. But largely because the RDP Office was closed down in the mid-1990s, such insights no longer had an institutional champion, and consequently fell off the political map. In this void, the narrow sectoral priorities of government departments have reigned supreme. By default, government's unclear sentiments on urbanisation left the way clear for sectoral government departments to figure out their own spatial strategies, whether they were in concert with one another or not.

The strongest focus on spatial thinking was at the local level. The Development Facilitation Act (DFA) (No. 67 of 1995) was produced by the DLA. It provided several key principles for spatial planning at settlement level. For example, the social, economic, institutional and physical aspects of development should be integrated, and residential and employment opportunities should be promoted in close proximity to one another. Significantly, in Section 3 the DFA stated that land development in rural and urban areas should be undertaken in support of one another, although concrete suggestions on how this should be achieved were not provided.

At municipal level, there was an increasing focus on integrated planning. In terms of the DFA, Land Development Objectives had to be compiled by municipalities. This had the virtue of encouraging municipalities to consider spatial issues in their planning processes. However, the compilation of Land Development Objectives (promoted by the DLA) was gradually eclipsed by the need to compile Integrated

Development Plans (IDPs). The IDP philosophy was promoted strongly by the Department of Provincial and Local Government (DPLG), which devoted many more resources to this enterprise than the compilation of the Land Development Objectives ever received. Officially, Land Development Objectives were supposed to be included in IDPs, but many municipalities dispensed with spatial thinking altogether, and concentrated primarily on issues of infrastructure, poverty and job creation.

Because of their planning activities, municipalities are potentially very strategically placed to influence spatial trends, which may well promote or discourage urbanisation. This potential was not always achieved, at least partly because many municipalities had little experience of issues related to rural areas or rural–urban linkages. But even where municipalities managed to address these issues, they cannot deal with the macro issues of urbanisation and migration. The 'where' of development has to be guided by national level, but until 2002 the resounding silence from national level continued.

## Unintended consequences: the spatial impacts of sectoral departments' spending policies

Despite the lack of clear urbanisation and spatial direction from government, numerous government programmes have indirect spatial consequences. This is a very common phenomenon: 'Indeed, it is often those policies with goals other than migration and urbanisation that have a more powerful (albeit unintended) influence on population redistribution' (Goldschneider 1980: 65). In the words of Peter Morrison, 'Since the most powerful influences often arise from implicit or "hidden" policies (i.e. those without explicit demographic intent), policy makers must focus on the inadvertent demographic effects that result from such policies, and on how these policies might be orchestrated to promote population distribution goals' (1980: 9). Very often, these policies may emanate from different departments, and the interactions between these policies have to be examined. Government policies are important, if indirect, determinants of population distribution. Among these are such diverse policies as incentives to industry, taxation of farm crops, import substitution, family planning, free higher education, and road building. All affect migration and urban growth, even if only contingently. Furthermore, different policies may well have contradictory (and unintended, unanticipated and unexamined) impacts on migration.

Policies and programmes to achieve other goals, including rapid industrial expansion and export promotion, often have a far stronger impact on the geographic allocation of public resources and private investment than do dispersal inducements (Nelson 1980). Furthermore, policies intended to promote rural development may often have precisely the effect of encouraging migration away from rural areas, because of stronger rural–urban economic and transport links (Whitney 1980).

In South Africa, there has also been weak spatial guidance to government departments. Harrison and Todes (2001: 67) refer to:

> …the weak position of integrative spatial planning in relation to sectoral planning and interests; the lack of an effective institutional framework for intersectoral co-ordination; the role of power and factional politics in shaping the 'rationality' of planning frameworks; the ways in which spatial frameworks often expose the varying objectives, interests and sometimes contradictory policy aims of government; and the difficulties in producing meaningful spatial frameworks where spheres of government are overlapping, and roles and responsibilities are open to contestation.

This lack of forceful implementation of the UDF and the RDF has meant that spatial policies have been driven primarily by sectoral concerns. Crankshaw and Parnell (1996) and Bernstein and McCarthy (Centre for Development and Enterprise 1998) rightfully argued that government was already intervening regionally, purely by virtue of the fact that its allocations of bus subsidies, low-income housing subsidies and money for the development of infrastructure are made in favour of certain areas. The result has been a mix of departmental spatial priorities.

In fact, at least seven tendencies have informed different departments' spatial decisions.

First, some departments *allocate resources regardless of where people live.* Sectors such as housing, infrastructure and the allocation of social grants use an 'entitlement' approach towards the allocation of expenditure. People are entitled to these benefits if their income falls below a certain level. This approach runs counter to the assumption of inevitable urbanisation, since it offers incentives for rural people to stay where they are. This is also the case with regards to social grants and infrastructure grants, such as the Consolidated Municipal Infrastructure Programme and the Community-based Expanded Public Works Programme, which have been included in the Municipal Infrastructure Grant, and the Community Water and Sanitation Programme. Once again, these programmes have, implicitly, encouraged people to remain where they are because of 'sunk capital' in those areas. Many rural households receive monthly pensions or other social grants, which enable them to continue to live in areas characterised by widespread unemployment or underemployment.

Second, some departments *have adopted rules which affect spatial allocations, as an unintended consequence.* For example, land economics linked to housing standards have played a critical role in the regional allocation of housing subsidies in the Free State (Marais & Krige 2000; Marais 2003). The construction of housing units of 40 m$^2$ was dependent on a planned and in some instances a serviced stand. The result was that in areas of lower land prices, and with available planned stands, it was much easier to deliver housing. Land prices and the prices of serviced stands in cities are considerably higher than in the middle-order and small towns, which made it difficult to deliver housing in the cities.

In the same category is the DLA, whose Extension of Security of Tenure Act of 1997 has been blamed for the decline in farming employment, and the rapid urbanisation of unemployed farm workers. Tougher labour regulations (in terms of the Basic Conditions of Employment Act of 1997) may have been responsible for a decline in formal employment, and a movement of unemployed people to areas where the informal sector can offer an income, or where a rural base still offers some kind of agricultural livelihood.

Third, some departments *have attempted to streamline their expenditures according to specific spatial criteria*. Departments such as Health made tough choices about the location of services and created a 'step-up' system of health facilities. The consolidation of upper-level facilities (such as hospitals) in specific localities has been associated with the closure of some facilities in other areas. The selection of certain 'pilot sites' for the distribution of HIV/AIDS antiretroviral medication may also encourage people to move to these towns. This may well have had positive or negative economic spin-offs in those localities, possibly resulting in people moving towards or away from those areas. The DLA's decision to focus land reform subsidies on commercial agricultural farms, rather than on peri-urban areas, also has spin-off consequences (as well as potential lost opportunities). In the housing sector, the national department decentralised the allocation of housing subsidies down to the provincial level. The provincial governments can make their own allocations to rural or urban areas. In some provinces, such as the Free State, this has resulted in an urban bias in housing allocations, while other provinces, such as Limpopo, have a much more assertive rural focus.

Fourth, *some programmes are demand-driven, and depend on local project applications, either by municipalities or by communities themselves*. One example was the Local Economic Development Fund, administered by the DPLG. Similar programmes are the Municipal Infrastructure Grant, and the Department of Social Development's Poverty Programme. These programmes depend on local initiative, whether on the part of municipalities, community-based organisations, or individuals, and as such do not discriminate between rural and urban areas. Such programmes – particularly where they were successful – may have made some difference to some households' decisions to migrate or stay.

Fifth, there are *large spatial corridors and zones*. The large spatial programmes, such as the Spatial Development Initiatives (SDIs) or Export Processing Zones, have led to large fiscal allocations to selected regions. Significantly, some provinces, such as the Free State, do not have any SDIs or government-sponsored development corridors at all, which creates disincentives for young people with economic potential to stay in those provinces or areas. Not only are the SDI areas sometimes poorly selected, but the principle of SDIs tends to sit uneasily with the political commitment to prioritise rural development (Harrison & Todes 2001).

Sixth, the *location of administrative offices of government institutions* (with or without actual devolution of decision-making powers) creates major spatial impacts.

In South Africa, impressionistic evidence suggests that provincial departments' location of their regional offices, and municipalities' locational choices for their headquarters, after the amalgamation of municipalities in 2000, are already causing migration pressures towards some localities.

A final issue is the impact of *bureaucratic procedures*. For example, many departments are characterised by an underspending of their budgets. The result is that, as the end of the financial year approaches, money is spent rapidly on available projects, regardless of location. Another bureaucratic feature is that departments which employ non-governmental service providers (such as the Department of Water Affairs, which uses Mvula Trust as a service provider) have a much greater geographic reach than those departments which depend on in-house staff, and are likely to extend their programmes deeper into rural areas.

The result of this diversity of initiatives is that some of these programmes encourage urbanisation, at least to some urban localities. As such, they are not urbanisation policies in any strict sense, nor are they spatial settlement programmes, but they have unforeseen consequences for both urbanisation and settlement hierarchies. Conflicting governmental policies often exist side by side, influencing migration haphazardly (Morrison 1980). There are also cases where sectoral programmes are undermined by migration trends which are simply too powerful to resist. There is the sad tale of subsidised houses in the Free State Goldfields, which were built and the title deeds duly transferred into the names of the beneficiaries, only to discover that the beneficiaries had moved away and could not be traced. There is a great need for more research on the impacts of sectoral policies on local economic dynamics and urbanisation trends.

This is not to argue that contradictory impacts on migration are necessarily a bad thing, because it may well be helpful to balance different stimuli in the economy. But of course, it could lead to local distress, because some services are provided without complementary governmental functions being performed. Whatever the case, it is clear that, for the first ten years of democracy, South Africa has had no coherent approach to urbanisation, or even an exploration of the various spatial dimensions of poverty and livelihoods.

Sectoral policy-makers urgently need an understanding of the multiplier effects (whether in strictly economic terms or more broadly social terms) of the various *types of expenditure*, which may well differ *in different kinds of localities*. Take, for example, the difference between spending on infrastructure or housing, on the one hand, and health, on the other. Whereas infrastructure and houses create lasting physical assets, and possibly create economically productive skills, health is largely a 'consumption' expenditure. It is likely that the relatively large expenditure on infrastructure and housing in small towns may have significant multiplier effects, and thereby encourage people to stay there. Expenditure on skills training (Department of Labour) may encourage people to migrate to areas of greater economic advantage.

In this regard it is hard to disagree with the statement of the Centre for Development and Enterprise (1998: 26) that: 'At the very least, what seems to be required is an open and informed debate about alternative approaches to the "*where*" of development.' This was an insightful comment, but as we shall show, understanding the 'where' is not a simple matter.

## Towards new ways of delivering services

In the past few years, government has made renewed attempts towards finding alternative ways of promoting government service delivery. The ISRDS and the URP find their origin in the Presidency, and the political impetus which President Mbeki gave to the issues of rural and urban poverty. There are some important similarities between them. Both are aimed at addressing the vexed question of intersectoral and interdepartmental coordination, as well as effective intergovernmental cooperation. Both strategies share a goal of encouraging local innovation and creativity, particularly in dealing with poverty. Both also aim at enabling bottom-up approaches to problem solving (although it is in practice not always clear whether the 'bottom' refers to local government, to communities, or to local individuals). And significantly, they are both underpinned by a 'nodal approach', and the conflation of economic and welfarist concerns – possibly to the detriment of both. Together they culminated, by 2004, in the creation of 13 rural nodes and 8 urban nodes.

The ISRDS was born from a deep concern within the ANC government about rural poverty. This problem received top-level attention, from 1999 onwards, when President Mbeki raised the issue with growing concern. From 1995, the issue of rural development had been central in the ANC's thinking. A small group of directors-general (including the departments of Agriculture, Land Affairs, and Minerals and Energy, and supported by Eskom) began working on an appropriate definition of rural development, which ultimately included the following elements: mining, agriculture, conservation (all three items focused on the natural resource base), as well as business, infrastructure and local government. As such, the ISRDS is the product of significant political support and investment by the government (Everatt n.d.).

The ISRDS did not have a clear standpoint on urbanisation. But an underlying assumption was that it would not stop urbanisation, but would delay the process so that it would be more manageable (Everatt n.d.). As such, the ISRDS assumed that people in rural localities would identify and voice their own needs, which would presumably enable government to target expenditures appropriately – thus making life in the rural areas more viable and attractive.

A significant assumption (which was apparently never questioned) was the nodal approach. This idea of 'nodes' can probably be traced back to the concept of 'pilots', which was introduced soon after 1994 in policies such as land reform, where 'pilots' referred to sites of experimentation for new approaches to service delivery. The ISRDS envisaged that the nodes would experiment with new ways of government coordination and bottom-up delivery. Subsequently, these lessons would be rolled out to additional areas (Office of the President 1999).

In 2001, the ISRDS – now called the Integrated Sustainable Rural Development Programme (ISRDP) – was implemented. Nine nodes in eight provinces were identified. It should be emphasised that the ISRDP was not intended to be a spatial approach to development; although it selected spatial localities, it was for the purposes of experimentation with new styles of service delivery, mainly focusing on intersectoral and inter-sphere coordination.

The criteria for selection of the ISRDP's nodes were never made explicit. Issues of economic potential and poverty were apparently equally important in the identification of localities as nodes. Since reliable economic data on the nodes were usually not available, the nodes tended to be selected on the basis of high poverty, low infrastructure and limited capacity (Everatt n.d.).

Despite the lack of economic potential in the nodes, a great deal of government resources has been directed to them. Such high levels of expenditure in the nodes raise important questions. In many nodes, the interminable difficulties of bureaucratic alignment of departmental delivery have not been overcome. Also, the high expenditure in the nodes makes it unlikely that the ISRDP can be replicated elsewhere in the country. It is not clear what lessons could usefully be learned from the nodes.

The unlikely prospects of the nodes being replicated elsewhere may mean that the nodes will remain as the 'select few'. In effect, the nodes may well begin to function – by default – as a new spatial dispersal policy, despite the official intention that the nodes are simply experimenting with new forms of service delivery.

This raises far-reaching questions of what impact the nodes are likely to have on their own hinterlands, as well as on migration to larger centres. The nodes are almost sure to increase migration out of the surrounding rural areas and small towns. Depending on the type of economic activity in the nodes, they may simultaneously trigger economic development of the rural hinterland, particularly if there are strong rural–urban linkages (such as the use of agricultural raw materials in local industry, or the creation of local markets for agricultural products). These are the unintended consequences of the nodal policy of the ISRDP. Whereas the 'nodes' were originally selected with the main purpose of testing new ways of delivering government services in a coordinated way (the 'how' of development), the nodal policy is increasingly functioning – by default – as a spatial dispersal programme.

In sum, by 2002 government had produced an urban strategy (the UDF), a rural strategy (the RDF), numerous departmental strategies, and then yet another urban strategy (the URP) and rural strategy (the ISRDP). None of these dealt explicitly with urbanisation issues, although all of them had implicit spatial consequences. In the meantime, sectoral departments hastened to spend their budgets according to their own spatial criteria. In the midst of this Tower of Babel, the nodal approach of the ISRDP and the URP had become, by around 2003, the beacon of fiscal political correctness in departments' budgeting practices. Government departments are expected to spend a significant proportion of their budgets in the nodes, and most have been happy to oblige, although in some areas (such as the Free State) there is a growing concern amongst officials that the pre-eminence of the nodes is causing other, equally poor, areas to be neglected.

## The 'where' of development: the importance and limitations of the national spatial development perspective

Even before the promulgation of the URP and the ISRDP, the Presidency had become concerned about migration, urbanisation and the spatial aspects of development – in sum, about the 'where' of development. The NSDP was the first real spatial policy to emanate from the ANC government. Like the Green Paper on Planning in 1999, the NSDP noted that spatial allocation of resources in South Africa is currently taking place on an incoherent basis (Office of the President 2003). Current budget constraints mean that some form of rationing in the allocation of funds to infrastructure and development programmes does take place, and spatial choices are either explicitly or implicitly made by sectoral departments. There are no common spatial criteria in use for determining public spending patterns. Funding usually goes to those communities that attract the greatest amount of attention.

The NSDP's main argument is that areas with 'potential' or comparative advantage should be pinpointed, and thereafter receive priority in the allocation of resources – in particular, in the allocation of infrastructure funding ('hard investments'). Government spending on fixed investment, beyond the obligation to provide basic services to all citizens, should therefore be focused on localities of economic growth and/or economic potential in order to attract private sector investment, stimulate sustainable economic activities and/or create long-term employment opportunities.

According to the NSDP, 'development potential' is based on the following criteria (Office of the President 2003: 18):
- Natural resource potential: agricultural potential, environmental sensitivity and the availability of water;
- Human resource potential: levels of skills and human density;
- Infrastructure resource potential: existing and proposed road and rail infrastructure and the main electricity grid;
- Human need: spread of poverty and the size of the poverty gap;
- Existing economic activity.

The NSDP softens its spatial strategy somewhat by suggesting that investment in people ('soft investments') should continue to be made throughout the country, to enable people to acquire the skills to migrate to areas with developmental potential. In localities with low development potential, government spending should focus on providing social transfers, human resource development and labour market intelligence. This will enable people to migrate, if they so choose, to localities that are more likely to provide sustainable employment or other economic opportunities.

Furthermore, in order to overcome the spatial distortions of apartheid, future settlement and economic development opportunities should be channelled into activity corridors and nodes that are adjacent to, or link, the main growth centres. Infrastructure investment and development spending should primarily support localities that will become major growth nodes in South Africa and the Southern African Development Community region so as to create regional gateways to the global economy.

The NSDP made two major contributions, although neither has been sufficiently appreciated. The first contribution was that it actually made an argument for a certain kind of developmental approach, in contrast to the largely rhetorical and vacuous policy statements which had gone before. It is an argument that can and probably should be challenged, and which would benefit from much more critical engagement, but its significance is that it actually begins to confront tough fiscal choices. The NSDP should be the starting point of vigorous public debate about how government can get the maximum 'bang for its buck'. The second contribution was that, between 2000 and 2002, it caused several important studies of migration, urbanisation and spatial developments to be conducted.

The danger is that the NSDP, as published in 2003, may be taken at face value, and that government departments may adopt it naively as their ordained spatial template. Spatial issues – the 'where' of development – are notoriously complex, because they often cannot be clearly separated out from social, economic, demographic, and political factors. The danger exists that the NSDP, if implemented in an unreflective way, may have several unintended consequences.

Firstly, unless the NSDP is implemented on the basis of very careful research, it opens the way to introducing officials' own unexamined biases into the policy. Determining 'development potential' is notoriously difficult, and requires detailed and sophisticated study. It may result in preference being given to urban areas, because economic activity, trade and marketing typically manifest themselves in urban areas, even when those activities are, directly or indirectly, based on rural production.

Secondly, it is generally areas with local professional skills that can lobby for investment in their areas and the identification of urban areas as 'areas with potential' may be promoted by local lobbying. Typically, rural areas have less skills and resources to lobby for their own interests. They may well have explicit or latent comparative advantages, but lack the political ability to articulate this. In such cases, external support would be needed to assist local residents to identify and develop their local economic potential. The current support provided to municipal integrated planning processes has not been nearly sufficient to engage government at this level of lobbying.

Thirdly, it is important to distinguish between actual and latent potential. In some areas, residents have already identified certain local strengths, and have developed these strengths into actual economic activities. But there may be other areas which have latent potential, possibly based on unusual niche markets. In such areas, government could play a crucial role in facilitating or 'animating' the actualisation of this potential. As argued by Hardoy and Satterthwaite, government programmes '…should be based on the understanding that each centre will have its own unique mix of resources, development potential, skills, constraints, and links with its environs and with the wider regional and national economies' (1986: 399). This, in turn, suggests that planning should be as decentralised as possible, so that localities can identify their own needs and potentials.

Furthermore, the NSDP's argument begs the question: 'Potential for what?' The NSDP opens the way for much more debate and research about local potential. Some areas may have potential to become world-class tourist or industrial sites, whereas other areas may have the potential simply to provide a livelihood for local residents – and in a context of widespread unemployment and poverty, this may be good enough to alleviate poverty. Low-key but sustainable use of natural resources (such as smallholder agriculture or informal trade) may be the only possible economic opportunity for millions of people in South Africa. There is a danger that only the more conventional economic strengths are recognised, and unusual economic niches are left to wither. Furthermore, localities may have economic strengths which do not take the form of ostensible economic comparative advantages. Factors such as social cohesion, stable land tenure systems, leadership, and concentrated purchasing power may bestow advantages on unexpected localities. It is possible that areas without ostensible economic strengths may outperform localities that, on the face of it, are blessed with more resources. Given the unpredictability of economic fortunes, it may be safer to spread investment to a wide diversity of places, rather than to favour a smaller number of areas with apparently high potential.

The drafters of the NSDP also assumed that the areas of 'high potential', which will receive these migrants, will be able to withstand the additional strain on public resources, in the form of rapid expansion, poorly designed informal settlements, infrastructure requirements, pollution, and crime.

Interestingly, the NSDP currently functions in some tension with the URP and the ISRDP. In the latter two strategies, the nodes have been selected with primarily welfarist (poverty and need) criteria in mind. This clearly cuts across the NSDP's focus on 'development potential'. This difference in focus is not surprising, since the primary purpose of the URP and the ISRDP was not a spatial strategy, but a new way of organising government institutions to deliver services. In fact, areas with high levels of poverty were specifically targeted. But current realities suggest that the URP and the ISRDP nodes currently have more actual impact *as spatial strategies*, than the NSDP. The sheer scale of expenditure in the nodes is likely to attract more migrants away from nearby areas.

But despite these weaknesses in the NSDP – as it is currently drafted – it makes a specific conceptual contribution which lays the groundwork for a next round of government thinking about development priorities, as the next section shows. Even though the NSDP is primarily about the 'where' of development, it also brushes up against the question of the 'what' of development. Its distinction between infrastructural ('hard') and human ('soft') expenditure deserves to be taken further in policy debates.

## Beyond spatial questions: the alignment process

As mentioned earlier, one of the key strengths of the NSDP is that it focused on the question of economic potential. This took the debate beyond the existing focus on poverty and needs (although these issues also figure in the NSDP). During 2004, the NSDP was given more impetus by a process of provincial and district-level consultations. During this process, key questions were asked: In what way does the NSDP frame the parameters of government actions? How should developmental potential be defined? On what is potential based, and what is required to unlock or sustain it? How should the imperatives of economic developmental potential be traded off against the need to meet poverty alleviation targets? What are the nature and causes of poverty in different localities? And most significantly, how should different agencies of government, at national, provincial and municipal level, interact to achieve agreement on the 'what' and the 'where' of development? (Office of the President 2004) For the first time, explicit 'how', 'what' and 'where' questions are being raised in conjunction with one another – this greatly improves the prospects of meaningful developmental initiatives in different localities throughout the country.

This involves a new use of spatial thinking. Spatial decisions will not be done according to formal and predetermined criteria; rather, the quest is to 'utilise space as a common backdrop against which investment and spending decisions can be considered and made' (Office of the President 2004: 8). National spatial guidelines are intended to facilitate dialogue and exchange of information, to promote understanding of the impacts of policies, to promote the compatibility of policies, and to make connections between various policies and actions more transparent. In this process, municipal IDPs and Provincial Growth and Development Strategies will take on a much more strategic role.

This creates enormous scope for local negotiations about the 'what' of expenditure, the actual economic and livelihoods impacts of specific government interventions, and the most effective balance between hard and soft programmes, *tailored to local circumstances*. Areas with apparent low potential may well – given well-selected hard infrastructure and supportive human development initiatives – perform much better than they have done thus far. Posing questions about spatial location will encourage more creative and penetrating thinking at all levels, about appropriate developmental initiatives. To some extent, this may mean that the fascination with large infrastructural projects may give way to a more nuanced consideration of hitherto poorly designed human development programmes, including skills training, business mentoring, start-up credit, marketing, agricultural extension, transport systems, and rental accommodation for residences and businesses. It opens the way for more careful questions about the different *types* of infrastructure spending and human resources spending, and what their diverse developmental impacts and multipliers might be.

## Urbanisation trends: glimpses and questions

There has been insufficient research regarding urbanisation patterns in the ten years after 1994 and there are currently more questions than answers. A few key texts have opened up key arenas for further enquiry.

Some important findings are that there is a great deal of in-migration into dense settlements, but that these settlements may be rural, peri-urban, or urban (Cross, Harwin, Schwabe, Morris & Kekana n.d.; Cox, Hemson & Todes 2004); that migrant labour is continuing, and that female migrant labour appears to be increasing (Posel & Casale 2002); that many rural families attempt to get urban cash-based livelihoods while many urban families attempt to keep their rural assets; that joblessness is so prevalent that employment prospects are ceasing to become a factor in the motivation of migrants (Schlemmer & Lovell 2000).

Once we have a better idea of how migrants can most effectively be accommodated at their destinations, so that they can achieve their maximum economic potential as soon as possible, a new set of questions should be posed. Given these insights, the paucity of government information about different types of migration becomes a real constraint in the design of policy. We simply do not know enough about the push and pull factors which characterise urbanisation. We also do not know how many people are moving to different kinds of destinations, from where, for what reasons, and what skills they have.

The conceptual apparatus of the NSDP, and the process of intragovernmental debate and alignment, offer the scope to find much more closely tailored developmental solutions for different localities. Various social, economic and demographic dynamics have recently come to light, which will be the basis on which such debates can be conducted. For example, it appears that government expenditure may also create incentives to stay in rural areas, due to the better infrastructure, services and facilities in homeland areas, even where economies are weak or limited (Todes 1999). This also applies to recent government policies, such as the allocation of housing subsidies (Crankshaw & Parnell 1996). The availability of social grants may have major impacts on where people choose to live – especially near pension payout points!

A second dynamic which should influence NSDP debates is that the nature of settlements is changing. Most in-migration is now taking place in rural, peri-urban and metropolitan fringe dense settlements, despite the paucity of formal jobs. These settlements are often poorly integrated in the mainstream of urban life. Such in-migrants are drawn from nearby tribal areas, particularly in KwaZulu-Natal and the Ciskei and Transkei (Todes 1999). This is not surprising. For many migrants – particularly the poor – kin and friends are the main source of information, and the majority of migrants choose to move to places where they already have relatives or friends (Nelson 1980). In the context of South Africa, where so many migrants are poor, this suggests that traditional cultural ties between rural and urban areas continue to exist. It may therefore be the case that kinship ties are a more important determinant of migration than the likelihood of getting a job. This pattern suggests that towns and cities with peri-urban settlement opportunities may be more attractive than cities which do not offer such options. Even within metropolitan areas, the fringes of large metro areas now experience much higher levels of in-migration than the metropolitan core areas (Cross et al. n.d.). This may mean that rural migrants may now be *less* able to access formal urban facilities and livelihoods than previous generations. Is South Africa becoming a society of dense quasi-urban, quasi-rural settlements, with the advantages of neither rural nor urban life?

A third factor is that urbanising farm workers are becoming a prominent category of migrants. Farm workers tend to move to the nearest town, rather than further afield, and have emerged as an important part of housing demand in small towns (Todes 1999; Cox, Hemson & Todes 2004). Compared to migrants from tribal areas, farm workers have very different profiles of skills, experiences, family networks and assets, with quite different prospects for assimilation into urban or peri-urban areas.

Fourthly, many towns have experienced economic decline, but simultaneously continue to experience population growth (Todes 1999). This appears to be a widespread phenomenon in underdeveloped societies. Unemployment does not appear to lead to out-migration (Fay & Opal 2000). Households which lost their employment often do not move out, but by relying on multiple income sources, have preferred to keep their investments in housing in those areas. However, easy generalisations should be avoided. People's responses to unemployment may differ dramatically: in declining mining towns, for example, unemployed miners (who have a more narrow suite of skills) are more likely to leave the towns, whereas other unemployed people are more likely to stay and try different survival skills. This may be due to the characteristics of the towns themselves, or it may be due to the characteristics of the particular individuals, since mineworkers may have closer residual links with rural areas, and therefore a greater likelihood of moving away, than do other types of residents. Such observations need much more empirical investigation.

A fifth consideration is that there is a growing trend towards reverse urbanisation, i.e. people leaving large cities and moving to small towns and rural areas. Factors such as the contraction of employment in the cities, the prevalence of urban crime and violence, the high infrastructure costs, and the value of land and housing in other localities, and the continuation of social relationships with rural communities, may function either as disincentives to migrate to the cities, or as incentives to return to more rural areas (Todes 1999). 'The tendency to characterise migration flows as only rural to urban obscures the reality; indeed, migration flows are as variable as the changing form and spatial distribution, over time, of economic opportunities' (Hardoy & Satterthwaite 1986: 406). For some people, rural areas retain their attraction, possibly due to relatively high levels of communal land access and government expenditure in the deep rural areas. Certain special population categories, such as unemployed mineworkers and HIV/AIDS sufferers, appear to be turning to rural networks for their survival and care.

A new range of secondary cities, large towns and small towns are becoming attractive destinations for migrants. For example, between 1996 and 1998, Johannesburg attracted 22.6 per cent of migrants, but Cape Town only 4.3 per cent; Rustenburg attracted 4.1 per cent of migrants, but Nelspruit only 0.7 per cent (Cox, Hemson & Todes 2004: 9). This may be explained by the fact that metropolitan areas have reached some kind of saturation point, where negative factors (such as unemployment and high costs of living) now outweigh positive opportunities. But different cities and towns appear to have different kinds of attractions. This needs to be investigated empirically in each case, before appropriate plans can be drafted.

## Beyond 'rural' and 'urban': bringing rural–urban linkages into urbanisation policy

A key consideration is the need to transcend the misleading dichotomy of 'rural' and 'urban' areas, and to focus on rural–urban linkages. Many rural households (however 'rural' is defined) have strong links with urban family members. These links include multiple homesteads, commuting, circular migrancy, remittances, shared family responsibilities for rearing children in both rural and urban contexts, the sale of agricultural products in towns and the purchase of urban commodities for consumption in the rural areas. In the South African context, the question of rural–urban linkages is complicated by the particularly South African distinction between commercial farming areas and tribal or traditional areas (the erstwhile 'homelands'). Both these are officially defined as 'rural', even though their spatial, demographic and economic characteristics differ fundamentally. Commercial farming areas typically have far fewer linkages with nearby towns than the much more densely populated smallholder agriculture which characterises the homeland areas.

The international literature has, increasingly, emphasised the linkages between rural and urban areas. For example, Fay & Opal (2000: 26) make the suggestive point that 'the distinctions between urban/rural…may be misplaced in developing countries, especially in Africa'. In South Africa, labour migrancy has continued, despite expectations that the abolition of influx control would gradually cause migrant labour to be phased out (see Posel & Casale 2002). Hardoy and Satterthwaite (1986) argued for more support for small and intermediate urban centres, at least partly because of their important role in providing rural services and promoting rural agro-industries.

The question of rural–urban linkages has repeatedly surfaced in government policy documents, such as the RDF, the UDS and the UDF. The RDF observed that, 'Small rural towns should be a focus for development, providing input and output markets, mechanical and other workshops, financial services, and social services such as schools and clinics which will be of benefit to people in the surrounding area. For historical reasons, these functions and links to the rural hinterland often do not exist or are poorly developed' (DLA 1997: 22). The UDS also questioned the traditional dichotomy between urban and rural areas. It noted that many denser settlements are simultaneously urban and rural. Commuter townships are often on the outer edges of traditional cities, and circulatory migration blurs the distinction between urban and rural dwellers. Urban development should be based on integrated urban and rural development strategies. 'Healthy cities demand healthy country-sides, and vice versa' (Office of the President 1995: 15). The UDF also hinted in this direction: 'There is also a real sense in our cities and towns that everyone's lives are interconnected… There is also recognition that the various urban and rural interest groups can and must work together to remake the cities and towns' (DoH 1997: Section 1.3.4). This perspective was eventually carried through, in 2004, to the NSDP, which asserted that the categories 'urban' and 'rural' as used in South Africa have little meaning, due to high levels of transfers, social interactions, and definitional problems (Office of the President 2004).

There are strong arguments for promoting rural–urban linkages as a way of fostering both urban and rural development (Whitney 1980), and to help migrants secure a foothold in the informal sector. The complex relationships between rural and urban areas are very important, and require explicit recognition in formulating development policy. In this regard, KwaZulu-Natal's provincial White Paper on Integrated Rural Development, published in June 1998, provided a much more nuanced vision of the relationship between rural and urban areas than that of national government. There is a risk of very poor peri-urban communities remaining marginalised on the fringes of cities. In such contexts, essentially 'rural' development programmes should be implemented, by means of measures such as protected communal water sources, alternative sources of fuel, and subsistence and semi-commercial agricultural production. These should be linked, where possible, to urban development strategies, such as tourism, which could create a demand for crafts and fresh produce.

Taking the same logic a step further, the Western Cape government has drafted a policy for the establishment of agricultural holdings on the urban fringes (Western Cape Provincial Government 2000). The policy argues that agricultural holdings should be spatially integrated with other urban fringe land uses. Clearly, this policy envisages strong rural–urban linkages, in contrast with the rather artificial separation of rural and urban policies emanating from national government.

Government departments have not yet taken on board some key international thinking about rural–urban linkages, the important role of agriculture in promoting urban economic development, the advantages of small towns and dispersed urbanisation, and the agricultural potential of cities and peri-urban areas, particularly in the promotion of sustainable livelihoods for the poor. In the same vein, there is a growing interest amongst policy-makers worldwide about the prospects of urban agriculture. In South Africa, only a few municipalities have made any provision for urban agriculture (Tshwane and Cape Town, for example). Some of the possibilities would be to identify local resources and assets, such as land holdings, agricultural skills, community networks, and municipal commonage, which can yield better developmental returns. New spatial localities should be identified, where such assets can be utilised more fully (for example, on peri-urban smallholdings). There are huge unexplored possibilities. In this vein, Chris Rogerson (2001) argues for a framework for rural small, medium and microenterprise promotion; Austin and Visser (2002) advocate urban agriculture; and Stilwell (1997) propounds a much more robust Farmer Support Programme, linked to urban development. As Francie Lund and Andre du Toit (2004) suggested, there are many 'rich connections' between the formal and informal economies in promoting mutually beneficial relationships between poverty and wealth. What is missing, at this stage, is the spatial dimension.

There is a real need to return to the original insights in the UDF and RDF, that urban and rural development should be seen as linked and integrated. As yet, the promotion of rural–urban linkages has not been foregrounded in government policies. This is, arguably, because functions have been allocated to different departments. Whereas the policies of the DoH and the Department of Trade and Industry have focused primarily on urban areas and small towns, the land reform and agricultural policies of the departments of Land Affairs and Agriculture have been directed mainly at rural areas. There has been no political champion for integrated rural–urban development.

## Future research and policy choices

If one were to take the government's own overriding goals – development and poverty alleviation – as the lodestar, what spatial issues should come onto the agenda? Should migration be regarded as a positive or a negative factor? Internationally, there is no consensus on this issue. One view emphasises the positive aspects: 'It is essential to the health of the entire national economy that migration continue and even increase, in the interests of efficient allocation of human and other natural resources' (McNamara 1961: 154). Another view regards urbanisation as a loss of rural community values and agricultural livelihoods, and therefore something to be resisted. Both these views are underpinned by normative and emotive thinking (which is not unusual in social science or policy), but without exploring the real potentials and problems from a spatial point of view, no sensible resolution will be possible.

In the context of South Africa, we need to ask: Has urban migration been good for migrants in South Africa? Does it improve people's livelihoods and life chances? Has urbanisation been good for South African cities? Has it created more multipliers? Or has it compounded urban social problems? Do the new migrants add to economic vibrancy, or are they primarily a drain on social resources?

Changing migration flows and patterns of population settlement have become matters of interest to most of the nations in the world. This concern translates into a series of broad empirical as well as policy questions that must be addressed at least partly through research, but significantly also as part of policy debates (Morrison 1980).

At the empirical level, we need to know, firstly, how many of what types of people are migrating to what destinations, and what form is this movement taking? Secondly, where would current patterns and types of movement lead if they were to continue? Are they likely to continue, intensify, or change in the future? Thirdly, are the effects of these patterns beneficial or adverse, and for whom? Fourthly, should the observed patterns of urbanisation be encouraged, discouraged, or simply allowed to run their course, and to what ends? Finally, how can a national government channel migration within its borders to advance conscious developmental purposes?

In the case of the South African government's policies, it is remarkable how little attention has been paid to these empirical questions. There has been almost no sponsored research in this regard. (Several of these issues have been raised in studies conducted on behalf of departments – notably for the Premier's Office during the compilation of the NSDP – but deserve to be given much more prominence in policy debates.)

We need to ask how South African urbanisation trends compare with those of other developed and less developed countries. There are fundamental differences between urbanisation patterns in industrialised countries and in the less developed countries. In advanced countries (or advanced parts of less developed countries), cities are associated with a culture of 'urbanism', which includes phenomena such as institutional differentiation, specialisation, economic growth, expansion of socio-economic opportunities, and changing family patterns and values (Goldschneider 1980). In contrast, cities in less developed countries experience widespread problems, such as high unemployment, extensive poverty, and the continuation of rural or traditional social networks (a type of 'urbanism without urbanity'). To what extent does South Africa reflect this experience? To what extent do recent migrants in the cities become absorbed effectively into the mainstream of urban economies?

In this context, it should be noted that the nature of poverty, marginalisation and underdevelopment in South African cities is strongly influenced by the pre-1994 legacy. For example, looking back to the pre-1990 influx control policy, the distinction between Section (10)(1)(a) black residents (those who had permanent residential rights in the cities before 1990) and other black residents (whose residential rights were very limited, or who moved illegally) has probably reinforced the class nature of South African cities today (Parnell 2004). The legacy of 'insiders', who could build an asset base, and 'outsiders', who had to fight their way into the city from the informal (and often illegal) shack settlements on the fringes, still remains today. How, then, should this class cleavage be mitigated in the cities? What measures can be put into place to bring the new arrivals more effectively into the mainstream urban economy? And if this is too daunting in practice, what measures can be taken to ensure people's survival in the cities?

Secondly, we need to understand the types of migration that are prevalent. These include commuters, seasonal migrants, sporadic short-term migrants, target migrants (who aim to achieve a specific goal before returning to their place of origin), cyclic migrants, working life migrants, and permanent migrants (Nelson 1980). Different types of migration have very different impacts on people's commitment to rural or urban areas, on their pattern of asset accumulation and livelihoods, and on their social networks. Short-term migrants are not concerned with the long-term opportunities offered by large centres. They tend to be concerned with getting a job quickly; they have less concern with urban amenities; and they tend to be more concerned about travel costs.

This has significant policy implications. If a government wishes to redirect migration (for example, in terms of a spatial dispersal policy), short-term migrants may respond more readily than long-term or permanent movers to incentives offered by employment decentralisation programmes (Nelson 1980).

Thirdly, we need to ask what triggers promote migration to urban areas, and how individuals and households evaluate their options. Who will migrate, to where? It is well known that migrants tend to be opportunity seekers, often younger and with better levels of education than non-migrants (Whitney 1980). A great deal of evidence suggests that migrants' preferences are varied and changing, and they produce complex and often unanticipated responses to altered employment opportunities (Nelson 1980). How do we understand people's propensity to migrate? What push and pull factors encourage people to leave rural areas? What determines their choice of destination? Do people leave because of overcrowding of rural areas, and the lack of access to land and resources? Or do they leave because of their inability to utilise the assets that they do have? Or because they have lost the assets they used to own? Or because they have skills which could be more profitably utilised in urban areas? It is often assumed that most rural out-migration is driven by poverty, that people leave because they are desperate, and that improved rural opportunities and living standards would reduce the exodus. Yet it has been shown that out-migration is often higher from more affluent rural areas than from poor and remote areas. In fact, improved rural economic circumstances often seem to trigger greater out-migration (Nelson 1980).

The complexity of push and pull factors is evident in the migration rates of farm workers away from commercial agriculture towards the towns and cities. Is this rapid out-migration from commercial agriculture due to pull factors (the attractions of the towns and cities) or push factors (mechanisation of agriculture, or pre-emptive evictions to avoid land tenure claims)? Do people leave to seek a better life, or because they are evicted from the farms? Will the migration of farm workers to the towns and cities continue? At what point will the agricultural sector adapt its wage strategies and training policies to entice workers to remain?

These questions will require a great deal of nuanced and focused research in a diversity of communities, but some suggestions can be offered at this stage. Migrants' choices and experiences may be much more complex and varied than we might expect. For example, a survey conducted in the Free State and Northern Cape (Atkinson 2003) found that the reasons for some farm workers preferring to live on farms are factors such as free food, including meat, fruit, and vegetables; free water, electricity and housing; agreeable working hours; less overcrowding than in towns; lower living costs; they like living close to work; they like living with their families in a rural environment; their children are safe when parents are at work; and some farm workers can keep livestock. In contrast, the reasons that other farm workers choose to live in town are that farms are too far from town, and it is difficult to access services such as clinics; they cannot own a house on the farm; workers have no security when they get old and have to retire; on the farm, they are separated from their families; on some farms, workers have to pay for water, housing and/or electricity; the roads are bad and getting to town is difficult; it is difficult to get accommodation for schoolchildren in town; there is a 'better atmosphere' in town; on the farm, 'one has to be too careful not to alienate the farmer' (Atkinson 2003); and there are better services and facilities (eg. housing, sanitation) in town.

This wide variety of responses suggests that social groups cannot be treated as homogenous categories. Different options will appeal to different people, and different categories of people have different propensities to migrate. This will require more detailed locality studies. As Pieter Kok noted, 'A persistent gap in theories to explain migration is the relative lack of behavioural studies which provide a dynamic vs. a static comparison of migration move–stay decision alternatives' (2003: 19).

Furthermore, different types of migration (such as permanent migration and circular migration) depend on different calculations of benefit, and in turn create different developmental spin-offs.

Ideally, government policy should enable and facilitate choices which suit people's life circumstances. This, in turn, would require effective options for rural and urban transport, health, education, income-generating activities, and land ownership.

Even more importantly, a great deal more needs to be known about people's *post hoc* experiences of migration. What are the expectations of potential and actual migrants? Are these expectations fulfilled, or do many fail, and with what consequences? Does migration improve the quality of life, either in the areas of origin or in the point of destination?

Once we understand migrants' experiences, we can begin to propose ways of assisting them to deal with the stress of uprooting from places they know well, to move to difficult and challenging new environments. Such measures would enable migration and urbanisation to be used as a force for progress and development, instead of simply being regarded as a symptom of economic and social distress and policy failure. There is an urgent need for national and provincial governments to assist municipalities to analyse and predict urbanisation trends in their areas, and to work out appropriate responses. The recent round of NSDP-oriented consultations provides a starting point for assisting municipalities to explore these questions, and a 'common platform' to ensure that the various players have sufficient understanding of developmental questions (Office of the President 2004).

Only once we have a much better idea of real developmental and demographic dynamics, will we be able to determine the most effective type of urban hierarchy, creating mutually beneficial linkages between metropoles, smaller cities, small towns, peri-urban areas, and agricultural areas.

## Conclusion

Since 1994, the issue of urbanisation and migration has not been foregrounded as a policy debate in its own right. This is perhaps due to the RDP's basic orientation of avoiding tough choices. This chapter showed how different government strategies have been based on different assumptions about rural and urban development; how sectoral programmes have had unintended spatial consequences; how programmes aimed at improving service delivery have become implicit spatial programmes; and how a spatial policy aimed at promoting areas with developmental potential may, in fact, do the opposite.

The all-pervasive confusion regarding spatial strategies, urbanisation and migration in South Africa is primarily due to the fact that the government's primary goal is to promote development and, more especially, to mitigate poverty. Spatial considerations – and especially tough spatial choices – have always been, at best, secondary, and at worst, simply avoided.

Since 1994, the government's policy principles have not done justice to the full complexity of spatial choices and population movements. There are distinct advantages and disadvantages to living in both rural areas and urban areas. It is becoming increasingly obvious that the main problem confronting South Africa is poverty and the creation of livelihoods, and this raises important spatial questions. Until now, the sectoral approach to poverty and livelihoods has had little success in exploring the interactions between these phenomena, either in an urban or a rural context, or between rural and urban contexts.

There is an overriding impression of a void in policy thinking on urbanisation. Spatial questions have only recently been posed, with the result that government activities have, thus far, remained locked into narrow sectoral concerns. There are good grounds to suggest that government's developmental focus could be immeasurably strengthened by carefully examining spatial trends, and searching for developmental options that build creatively on current and future migration patterns. There is room for some intersectoral and interdepartmental enquiry regarding the type of development emerging in urban, rural and peri-urban areas, including the potential resources, multipliers, livelihoods and assets that these represent.

## Note

1    The figures for 1996 reflect the amended definition of 'rural'. Until 1996, 'urban' areas were defined as 'areas with local authorities', regardless of their spatial features. Since 2001, the definition has been based on spatial form and land use. Consequently, smallholdings, mining towns and residential peri-urban areas were henceforth classified as 'urban'. In traditional areas, villages were still regarded as rural, but the bigger towns were reclassified as 'urban'.

## References

ANC (African National Congress) (1994) *The RDP: Reconstruction and Development Programme.* Johannesburg: Umanyano Publications.

Atkinson D (2003) Life on the farm. Unpublished report. Pretoria: Human Sciences Research Council (HSRC).

Austin A & Visser A (2002) Study report: Urban agriculture in South Africa. CSIR report no. BOU/1243. Pretoria: CSIR.

Centre for Development and Enterprise (1998) South Africa's 'discarded people': Survival, adaption and current policy challenges. Available at <http://www.cde.org.za>.

Cox KR, Hemson D & Todes A (2004) Urbanisation in South Africa and the changing character of migrant labour, *South African Geographical Journal*, 86(1).

Crankshaw O & Parnell S (1996) Housing provision and the need for an urbanisation policy in the new South Africa, *Urban Forum*, 7(2): 232–237.

Cross C, Harwin SJ, Schwabe C, Morris N & Kekana A (n.d.) Rural and urban densification in South Africa: A preliminary review of policy implications for migration and infrastructure. Unpublished document, for Office of the President. Available at <http://www.idp.org.za/NSDP/NSDP>.

DLA (Department of Land Affairs) (1997) *Rural development framework: Thriving rural areas.* Pretoria: DLA.

DLA (1999) *Green Paper on Spatial Development and Planning.* Pretoria: DLA.

DoH (Department of Housing) (1997) *Urban Development Framework.* Pretoria: DoH.

DWP (Department for Welfare and Population Development) (1998) *White Paper on Population Policy.* Government Gazette no. 19230. Pretoria: DWP.

Everatt D (n.d.) Self-critical governance: The evolution of the Integrated Sustainable Rural Development Strategy. Unpublished paper. Available at <http://www.sarpn.org.za/documents/d0000640/P649-isrdsdavid.pdf>.

Fay M & Opal C (2000) *Urbanisation without growth: A not-so-uncommon phenomenon.* Washington DC: World Bank.

Goldschneider C (1980) Modernisation, migration and urbanisation. In P Morrison, *Population movements: Their forms and functions in urbanisation and development.* Belgium: Ordina.

Hardoy J & Satterthwaite D (1986) *Small and intermediate urban centres.* Sevenoaks, Kent: Hodder and Stoughton.

Harrison P & Todes A (2001) The use of spatial frameworks in regional development in South Africa, *Regional Studies*, 35(1).

Kitchin F (1997) Scan of development planning and mapping of government services in South Africa. Unpublished report compiled by the Centre for Development and Enterprise (CDE). Johannesburg: CDE.

Kok P, O'Donovan M, Bouare O & Van Zyl J (2003) *Post-apartheid patterns of internal migration.* Cape Town: HSRC Press.

Lund F & Du Toit A (2004) Livelihoods, (un)employment and social safety nets: Reflections from recent studies in KwaZulu-Natal. Available at <http://www.sarpn.org.za/documents>.

Marais L (2003) Good intentions with negative consequences: The case of housing size in the Free State Province of South Africa, *Africa Insight*, 33(2/3): 54–60.

Marais L & Krige S (2000) Who received what where in the Free State, 1994–1998: An assessment of post-apartheid housing policy and delivery, *Development Southern Africa*, 17(4): 603–619.

McNamara RL (1961) Impact of rural migration on the city. In *Labour mobility and population in agriculture.* Iowa State University: Iowa State University Press.

Morrison P (1980) *Population movements: Their forms and functions in urbanisation and development.* Belgium, Liege: IUSSP.

Nelson J (1980) Population redistribution policies and migrants' choices. In P Morrison, *Population movements: Their forms and functions in urbanisation and development.* Belgium, Liege: IUSSP.

Office of the President (1995) *Urban Development Strategy of the Government of National Unity.* Available at <http://www.anc.org.za/rdp/urbanrdp.html>.

Office of the President (1999) *Integrated Sustainable Rural Development Strategy.* Pretoria. Available at <http://www.idt.org.za>.

Office of the President (2003) *National Spatial Development Perspective* (NSDP). Policy Co-ordination and Advisory Services. Available at <http://www.idp.org.za/NSDP/NSDP>.

Office of the President (2004) Harmonising and aligning: The National Spatial Development Perspective, Provincial Growth and Development Strategies and municipal integrated development plans. Available from the Office of the President.

Parnell S (2004) Constructing a developmental nation – the challenge of including the poor in the post apartheid city. Paper presented at the conference Overcoming Underdevelopment in South Africa's Second Economy. Organised by the Development Bank of Southern Africa. Pretoria, 28–29 October.

Posel D & Casale D (2002) What has been happening to internal labour migration in South Africa, 1993–1999? Paper presented at the Development Policy Research Unit conference on Labour Markets and Poverty in South Africa.

Rogerson C (2001) Towards a framework for rural SMME development in South Africa. In MM Khosa (ed.), *Empowerment through economic transformation.* Cape Town: HSRC Press.

Schlemmer L & Lovell T (2000) Millions of people with nowhere to go: The estimated distribution of the South African population: 1995–2025. Unpublished draft document. Available at <http://www.idp.org.za/NSDP/NSDP>.

StatsSA (Statistics South Africa) (2001) Investigation into appropriate definitions of urban and rural areas for South Africa: Discussion Document. Report no. 03-02-20. Pretoria: StatsSA.

Stilwell T (1997) The farmer support programme revisited: Partnership in the economic survival strategies of the poor. DBSA, Discussion Paper no. 3.

Todes A (1999) Paper for the project on spatial guidelines for infrastructure investment and development. Coordinated by CIU, Office of the Deputy President. Unpublished paper.

Western Cape Provincial Government (2000) Policy for the establishment of agricultural holdings in the urban fringe. Provincial Gazette, no. 6676.

Whitney VH (1980) Planning for migration and urbanisation: Some issues and options for policymakers and planners. In PA Morrison, *Population movements: Their forms and functions in urbanization and development.* Liege, Belgium: IUSSP.

# 3 *Urban spatial policy*

Alison Todes

## Introduction

The notion of urban spatial restructuring, and the idea of 'compacting' and 'integrating' the city spatially, has been an important part of South African post-apartheid urban policy. It emerged early on in policy development, in the 1994 Reconstruction and Development Programme (RDP), and was core to the principles of the 1995 Development Facilitation Act (DFA). It was later embodied in the 1997 Urban Development Framework (UDF) and in several White Papers and other policy statements. The language of urban restructuring and the use of tools such as spatial frameworks to give effect to these ends have become quite standard in local government planning processes.

Policy was built on academic critiques of the apartheid city, campaigns by civic activists for reintegrating the city, and alternative spatial visions produced by planners, activists and academics. Until the mid-1990s, urban spatial policy seemed to be an important arena in which a new government could effect change in the interests of the previously marginalised. From the late 1990s, however, doubts were cast on the project of urban restructuring. With some exceptions, cities continued to develop along socially divided lines, but class began to replace race as a significant socio-spatial divide. Both the feasibility and the desirability of notions of compaction were questioned in the light of rising unemployment, and trends towards a polycentric city. Nevertheless, growing concerns about urban sustainability, housing quality and a divided society have kept notions of urban restructuring (perhaps in more diverse forms) alive, and even seem to be underpinning a resurgence in interest in recent years.

This chapter traces the rise, decline, and seeming resurgence of urban spatial policy. Drawing on existing literature, interviews with key respondents, and documentary evidence, it explores the various influences on policy, and its trajectory. The roles of changing economic conditions and of shifting policy positions within government (Watson 2002; Bond 2003) have been important, but institutional issues have also been critical (Pieterse 2006). The influence of local and international urban planning discourses is clearly evident (Tomlinson 2002). Although the notion of urban restructuring seemed to address black people's disadvantages within the apartheid city, urban spatial policy has largely been driven by technocrats and, in this context, research and argument have been perhaps more important than in other spheres. But the lack of a strong constituency for urban spatial policy has also meant that policy has remained relatively marginal and ineffective, and it remains to be seen whether the current resurgence in interest will be sustained.

## The origins and development of urban spatial policy

Although apartheid-style urban divides are not unique to South Africa (see eg. Abu-Lughod 1980), and several studies have shown the local origins of urban segregation (McCarthy 1991), the violence of state policy after 1948 meant that considerable academic work was devoted to critiques of the apartheid city (see for example collections by Lemon 1991; Smith 1992). Research in particular on Group Areas removals (eg. Western 1981; Hart & Pirie 1984) showed the way it fragmented communities, marginalised their economic activities and undermined their participation in the economy. It located people in areas with poor access to urban services and facilities, raised their transport costs, and sharply increased levels of crime. Research of this sort accorded with popular resistance to forced removals. Later research (eg. Cook 1987) demonstrated the disadvantages faced by the poor on the periphery, especially women, who were forced to travel long distances to work, while also being responsible for housework and childcare.

By the early 1990s, there was little questioning of the argument that the apartheid city was both destructive and economically inefficient. Turok (1994a: 243) began his seminal article on urban planning under apartheid by arguing:

> There can be little dispute about the damaging legacy of urban planning under apartheid in South Africa. Planning was an instrument of crude social engineering, causing great hardship and imposing an unnecessary burden on the economy. The imposition of racial segregation dislocated communities and entrenched inequality in the built environment, marginalising much of the population. The state's hostility to black urbanisation deprived the townships of essential services, housing and economic opportunities.

While research exposed the effects of urban apartheid, a small group of University of Cape Town (UCT) planning academics was key in developing alternative proposals for restructuring the city. Both their arguments and the style of planning proposed proved to be highly influential in shaping urban spatial policy. Influenced by the urbanist critique of modern town planning by writers such as Christopher Alexander, Lewis Mumford, Jane Jacobs, Louis Krier and David Crane, they criticised South African planning not only for its apartheid basis, but also for its application of inappropriate modernist planning (Watson 2002). In common with these writers, they pointed to the qualities of older areas developed on an organic basis over time, and used these to develop a set of normative planning and design principles.

They argued that instead of controlling land use through zoning and other schemes, planning should be minimalist, intervening more often through designing structuring systems, such as grids of interlocking main routes, to which individuals would respond. Such systems could be reinforced by a 'capital web' of public services located at points of high access. Public transport would move along these routes, reinforced by economic activities along the route and higher density residential development close to main routes. In contrast to the emphasis on reducing densities in modern town planning, they argued for compaction and an increase in density to enable higher thresholds for services, facilities, economic activities (especially informal sector) and public transport. A more compact city would also avoid the environmental degradation associated with urban sprawl,[1] and measures such as the use of an urban edge,[2] densification in existing areas, and 'infill' on pieces of well-located land were suggested. Instead of the highly segregated land uses associated with modernist planning, they argued for a mixed-use approach, and for more integrated[3] development.

Through the late 1970s to the early 1990s, this position was developed through a series of papers assessing Cape Town, linking urban spatial organisation to poverty, and making the case for urban compaction and integration (eg. Dewar, Watson, Bassios & Dewar 1990; Dewar & Uytenbogaardt 1991). Research on the international literature on the costs of sprawl and its application in Cape Town – although more equivocal than expected – also served to reinforce the position (Behrens & Watson 1992). Transport research at the Council for Scientific and Industrial Research (CSIR) (Naude 1988) provided further support for integrating cities through urban corridors.

The UCT group was highly influential. The main proponent of the compaction–integration idea, Dave Dewar, was both highly prolific and a passionate speaker who presented his ideas in many forums. As Watson (2002: 35) points out, the ideas formed a central focus of UCT planning education, and successive generations of students went out into practice with a 'vision of a well-performing city'. Variations of these ideas were taken up in several planning schools and by many planners across the country.

The 1980s was a period in which apartheid rule was increasingly challenged and a progressive planning movement keen to contribute to social change emerged. Several built environment non-governmental organisations (NGOs) were established, for example Planact, Development Action Group, and the Built Environment Support Group, comprising professionals and urbanists linking to oppositional civic organisations. Planners linked to these movements interpreted the UCT ideas as a platform for redressing urban apartheid. The critique of the apartheid city seemed to accord with popular experience, and variations of these ideas were presented at the early post-apartheid overseas conferences from the late 1980s, and were taken into struggles around the democratic city.

Although never the main thrust of the business-oriented Urban Foundation, the need to 'reintegrate African townships and core cities' (Bernstein 1991: 327) was accepted and promoted in this quarter as well. A major research initiative exploring and affirming compaction–integration ideas undertaken for the Urban Foundation by progressive planning academics in the late 1980s formed the basis for this position, although the direct influence of the UCT group should not be neglected. Variations of the UCT ideas were accepted more broadly by business, for example in Durban's Tongaat-Hullett Planning Forum of 1989/90.

In 1990, the state conceded that apartheid was no longer tenable, and in the following years several local negotiating forums were established to respond to local crises arising from the fragmentation of local government and the collapse of black local authorities (Turok 1994b). Some forums went much further to consider development needs and to negotiate the future organisation of the city. The forums brought together a wide range of groupings, including civics, political organisations, unions and business, amongst others. Progressive planners and urbanists, built environment NGOs, and the Urban Foundation were present in several forums, including the Central Witwatersrand Metropolitan Chamber – the earliest of these initiatives, and the most influential in terms of later government thinking (Turok 1994b). Urban restructuring was taken up in several forums, for example in Cape Town, Durban and the Central Witwatersrand, all of which produced metropolitan spatial frameworks which were strongly influenced by the UCT ideas. These ideas seemed to address the need to reintegrate the divided city spatially, an issue of considerable concern in some forums, particularly the Chamber.

A significant criticism of the UCT school, and the planning approaches adopted in many of the metropolitan spatial frameworks of the time, was that they were far too physically based and design oriented, and that they did not engage with the economic and social forces shaping the city, or with the role of private property interests as the 'city builders' (Turok 1994b; Tomlinson 2002; Watson 2002). For instance, Turok (1994b: 364) comments that the Central Wits Interim Strategic Framework 'is couched in rather broad terms…it could be used by…developers to justify investment almost anywhere…except in the remote fringes…it may be too simple to assume that improved physical accessibility will lead to social and economic integration, with benefits all-round and no adverse side-effects'. Nevertheless, these broad frameworks became the standard approach thereafter.

Although frameworks were seen as broadly based, considerable research went into mechanisms to facilitate access to land by the poor, particularly in well-located areas. Public land was a particular focus. Research was conducted by the Urban Foundation, progressive NGOs (eg. Wolfson 1991), academics (Tomlinson 1990), by the CSIR linking land to transport corridors (Price 1991), and by the Land and Services Group of the National Housing Forum established in 1992 (Abrahams & Rantete 1996). Considerable work on land availability was also undertaken in the Central Witwatersrand Metropolitan Chamber, and in some cities. Although several municipalities have recently begun to undertake land audits for this purpose, exploration of the 'urban land question' disappeared from national agendas for close to a decade until the 2004 Plan for Sustainable Human Settlements.

Support for the importance of urban restructuring was initially given by a series of World Bank Missions from 1991 to 1993. In the earlier documents, analysis largely accorded with local critiques of the apartheid city form, but added a stronger comparative perspective and a harder analysis of densities, vacant land and land values in South African cities. The economic efficiency of urban restructuring was stressed. A report on the Central Witwatersrand (World Bank 1991) found that densities around the centre were abnormally low, with a peak at 22 to 45 kilometres from the city centre, compared to most city centres internationally where they peak within 5 kilometres. This affected the welfare of the population and resulted in severe inefficiencies in terms of urban services and economic activities. It meant high transport costs, and made it difficult for the unemployed to look for work, particularly in the city centre where more diverse work types were available. The report cited a study demonstrating that peripherally located people have poorer access to employment than those who are centrally located. It argued that a strategy to densify around the city centre was realistic in terms of bulk infrastructure and land costs, and could make a significant difference to efficiency within five years. The CBD-centric view in this document is interesting and may in part account for common misperceptions that urban compaction arguments are essentially about densifying around city central business districts (CBDs). Yet arguments made by Dewar and the UCT group have long focused on a broader process of restructuring around main routes and centres within the fabric of the built-up environment, and are consistent with calls for a polycentric but more compact city.

The Annex to a later World Bank report (Lee 1993), while reiterating the point that South African cities were highly sprawled compared to cities internationally,[4] moved sharply away from the CBD-centric view. It pointed to the emergence of a polycentric city in Central Witwatersrand, and to the growing number of enterprises in townships. Commenting on Soweto, Lee argued that 'there is a wide misconception about Soweto as a poor, sleepy bedroom town' (1993: 14) … 'there are tens of thousands of energetic and innovative self-employed entrepreneurs engaged in various kinds of "informal" activities…A number of transport nodes have been attracting rapidly expanding business activities…a strong indication of developing as CBD type business centres' (1993: 11).

Land values were as high in Soweto as in Sandton, and given the size of these townships they had the potential to grow into economically viable urban centres with some assistance. A strategy of densification in these areas and along routes to the CBD should be followed, rather than any initiatives to undertake 'infill' on large tracts of vacant land between townships and city centres. Lee's (1993) view, however, only proved influential later on.

Notions of urban restructuring were taken up at national level in the National Housing Forum, established as a negotiating forum in 1992 to address the housing crisis (Rust & Rubenstein 1996). The need to address the apartheid geography was taken up in two main task teams: Working Group 5 and, to a lesser extent, in Working Group 1, the Land and Services task group. Research by Working Group 5 culminated in a status report entitled *Restructuring the Built Environment*, undertaken by prominent progressive urbanists and planners (Hindson, Mabin & Watson 1993). It analysed the inherited structure of South African cities and discussed ways to transform it. While analyses and policy proposals were more grounded in the dynamics occurring in cities than the somewhat abstract ideas of the UCT school, the broad ideas were similar. In 1994, a paper assessing the trends and dynamics in the property market, and their implications for urban restructuring, was commissioned. However, it was curtailed early on in the transition from the National Housing Forum to a set of Joint Technical Committees under the new Department of Housing (DoH). While policy areas perceived to be of immediate importance continued under this structure, Working Group 5 was shut down (Rust & Rubenstein 1996).

Questions of urban restructuring were, however, dealt with to some extent within Working Group 1 which, *inter alia*, examined access to land for the poor, land-use policy, and called for a National Land Use Planning Act to redress the spatial inequalities and distortions associated with apartheid planning. The Urban Foundation was strongly represented in Working Group 1, as well as in the Forum in general. It argued for flexible mechanisms to promote land development, and the use of 'performance criteria' to guide planning (Watson 2002). This idea was later included in the 1994 Development Facilitation Bill (Abrahams & Rantete 1996), but modified to Land Development Objectives following parliamentary debate (Mabin 2002). According to Abrahams and Rantete (1996), the principles of the final 1995 DFA, which were intended to guide all development, were based on the National Housing Forum/Joint Technical Committee Land and Services work, including 'promoting efficient and integrated land development through, *inter alia*, promoting social, economic, institutional and physical aspects, the co-location of residence and employment opportunities, optimising resources like bulk infrastructure, discouraging urban sprawl, correcting distorted patterns, and encouraging sustainable development' (1996: 241).

By the early 1990s, ideas of urban restructuring, compaction and integration had become a dominant discourse (Watson 2002; Pieterse 2006). The 1994 RDP called for the 'need to break down the apartheid geography through land reform, more compact cities, decent public transport' (RSA 1994: 83), and by promoting 'densification and unification of the urban fabric' (1994: 86), redressing imbalances, and promoting housing close to work, and 'access to employment and urban resources' (1994). It is not surprising then that these ideas were evident in the 1994 Housing White Paper, and in the principles of the 1995 DFA.[5] In the 1990s, the discourse was strengthened by international visits and connections to places such as Curitiba, where a linear pattern of development seemingly similar to that proposed by the UCT school held sway (but see Watson 2002), and Toronto, where ideas of 'reurbanising the city' and moving away from modernist suburban sprawl were influential.

In 1994, the establishment of an Office for Reconstruction and Development along the lines of a Malaysian-style development planning ministry seemed to put planning (Harrison 2001) at the centre of the task of reconstruction. Spatial planning ideas consistent with the UCT group were introduced into several pieces of legislation (Pieterse 2006). At this stage, urban spatial policy seemed set for implementation, and a parallel process of preparing urban and rural strategies was put in place. Their location in the RDP Office – at this stage a powerful political player – reflected the intention that they would provide cross-cutting policy statements, affecting a variety of policy areas. But instead of strong implementation, the period that followed saw the marginalisation (Parnell & Pieterse 2002; Watson 2002) of urban spatial policy at both national and local level.

## The decline of urban spatial policy

Although the early post-apartheid period allowed for innovation, there were severe constraints on policy. It was difficult to effect change within the bureaucracy at all levels, since innovative integrative policies, and those which required more radical changes, were resisted (Pieterse 2004). Problems were exacerbated by a weak and fragmented local government system. In addition, government had to demonstrate to the world that it was stable. Thus more radical ideas, such as putting low-cost housing next to wealthy white areas, were not in order. High levels of control were exerted to prevent land invasions outside of townships (Tomlinson 2003), without which the shape of the city might have looked very different. As Mabin (1998: 13) put it, the emphasis was on 'making cities safe for capital'. The later shift from the RDP to the Growth, Employment and Redistribution (GEAR) policy in 1996 was associated with a new emphasis on urban competitiveness at local level (Watson 2003), reinforcing relatively *laissez faire* policies with regard to major market-led urban developments (eg. Todes 2000, 2002; Bond 2003). Thus the 1995 Urban Development Strategy (UDS), the first major statement of the urban policy, broadly embraced the idea of urban integration but did not address land markets or suggest mechanisms to acquire land towards the ends of urban integration (Bond, Bremner, Geldenhuys, Mayekiso, Miller & Swilling 1996).

Pieterse's (2006) doctoral thesis on the UDS (1995), which later was transformed into the UDF (1997), provides a fascinating insight into these and other dynamics underpinning the policy. The UDS was formulated by consultants linked to the Development Bank of Southern Africa under the supervision of Chippy Olver in the RDP Office. They reported to an Urban Development Task Team, an interdepartmental committee of senior officials, and to the Forum for Effective Planning and Development, an intergovernmental organisation intended to rationalise and coordinate planning between spheres of government (Pieterse 2006).

The research process included extensive consultations with stakeholders and academics. While the UDS broadly endorsed the compaction–integration model, it moved away from it to some extent. One of the consultants was a recent graduate of the University of California's planning school and drew on international literature on the emerging polycentric city, which was critical of the assumptions of urban compaction proponents. Thus the draft UDS (October 1995) refers to the 'end of the monocentric city', and argues that planners can only harness development, not completely change it. Reference is made to the polycentric nature of Johannesburg and other metropolitan areas. According to Pieterse (2006), the World Bank report on the importance of continued development around townships (Lee 1993) was critical in shifting the discourse away from a more radical spatial restructuring agenda. This position was strengthened by a concern within the Urban Development Task Team, and particularly the Development Bank of Southern Africa, the Department of Finance and Chippy Olver, to establish financially sustainable and effective local government, capable of service delivery. An unwillingness to challenge vested property interests, or to undermine the rate base and economic growth more generally, went along with this approach. Pieterse (2006) comments that these positions were strengthened by engagement with the private sector over the urban economy and economic development. Thus the ideal of urban integration began to recede, although much of the language of compaction remained.

Concerns to establish viable and effective local government underpinned a shift away from a focus on space to governance (Parnell & Pieterse 2002; Watson 2002; Pieterse 2006). While the 1998 Local Government White Paper affirmed the principles of urban restructuring, greater attention was given to Integrated Development Plans (IDPs) as ways of giving effect to developmental local government. Watson (2002) argues that the essentially managerialist approach to IDPs, and the emphasis on the budget as a form of integration rather than on spatial plans, effectively marginalised spatial issues. Added to this, the first rounds of IDPs, undertaken prior to the amalgamation of local government, were often done poorly by old-school physical planners, who treated the IDPs as outdated structure plans without developmental dimensions (Harrison 2001). Thus guides developed to support IDPs are at pains to stress that they are about municipal management, although they do contain a spatial framework.

The closure of the RDP Office in April 1996 further undermined urban spatial policy – and urban policy more generally – as responsibilities were divided between various departments, without any strong centre. Planning and spatial policy were divided between the departments of Land Affairs, Housing, and what later became the Department of Provincial and Local Government.[6] In all cases, urban spatial policy was a minor focus in these departments, a situation that remains today.

With the closure of the RDP Office, the draft UDS was delegated to the DoH. Pieterse (2006) shows how it was marginalised in this context. The UDS became the responsibility of the official previously in charge of the Rural Development Strategy. It was redrafted by a group of Canadian consultants and a Tanzanian academic linked to the University of Toronto,[7] who had previously been appointed by Olver. This group reported in July 1996 and, after a long delay, it was redrafted again by a junior official to bring it into line with the United Nations (UN) Habitat Agenda. Now recast as the UDF, it was published in April 1997 (Pieterse 2006). The department's focus on delivery and the succession of a new and inexperienced Minister of Housing meant that it was not given priority. Without a political champion, and located within a relatively weak department politically, the policy was effectively ignored (Pieterse 2006).

The closure of the RDP Office meant that it was difficult to impose a cross-cutting logic on individual departments (Pieterse 2006). By 1997, the delivery departments were in full force. Thus, in contrast to the UDS which stated a position, the Framework instead drew together existing urban policy programmes, and suggested future overall directions. While the language of urban restructuring remained, no measures were put in place to further these aims or to give effect to implementation (Pieterse 2006). Both Pieterse's (2003) interviews with some key actors in the field, and the DoH's own investigation of the use of the UDF in 2000, suggested that it was largely ignored.[8]

Although the UDF was a DoH policy, the emphasis on housing delivery and the structuring of the housing subsidy directly undermined the urban integration policy (Dewar 2000; Royston 2003; Todes, Pillay & Krone 2003). The housing policy was based on negotiations around the National Housing Forum policies, and while the Forum's Land and Services group called for the development of specific mechanisms to facilitate access to well-located land, the collapse of funding for housing into an individualised housing subsidy meant that these elements disappeared. The capital subsidy programme and the limited funds available per unit led to the production of single detached houses on plots, resulting in a search for cheap land, most often on the periphery. The focus at this time on delivery meant that complicated projects in central areas involving objections by neighbours, land claims and the like were not favoured, and tended to be confined to a few projects, such as Cato Manor, a Special Integrated Presidential Project (Todes 2000). While the DoH initially saw the housing subsidy system as a way of giving the poor a basis for developing their own housing – a policy of 'width', rather than 'depth' – the new Housing minister came from a more state interventionist grouping within the African National Congress, and wanted to ensure the development of more substantial housing. Her insistence on a minimum size for the top structure and a limitation placed on the amount that could be spent on land – also a reaction to concerns about the poor quality of housing which was being produced in housing projects – exacerbated the tendency to locate housing projects on the periphery (Todes et al. 2003).

The question of urban land policy has remained in abeyance. Royston (2003) argues that urban land responsibilities sit uneasily between the departments of Housing and Land Affairs. Thus neither department has actively championed urban land identification, assembly or release, which has also undermined urban restructuring. At the same time, few local governments have been proactive in identifying land for low-cost housing development, particularly in well-located areas (Royston 2003; Todes et al. 2003).

Royston (2003) suggests that the absence of a legal framework for land development and land-use management has also been an impediment to urban restructuring. The DFA was intended as an interim measure, to be replaced by a national planning Act of some sort. This work was part of the task of the Development and Planning Commission, which saw its work as 'the establishment of an efficient, integrated and equitable land planning and development system in South Africa' (DPC 1999: 1). Mabin (2002) argues that the Commission was not seen as a very important body by government, which granted it a budget of only R2 million. Nevertheless, it drew on some prominent urbanists and planners, including those associated with urban compaction ideas, notably Dave Dewar. Established in 1997 under the auspices of the Department of Land Affairs (DLA), the Commission produced the Green Paper on Development and Planning in 1999. Based on comments on the Green Paper, the DLA published the White Paper on Spatial Planning and Land Use Management in 2001, and put out the first version of the Land Use Management Bill for comment at around the same time. It has remained in abeyance since the main actors driving the White Paper left the DLA. Some provinces have put in place their own Acts, but in many provinces the legal situation with regard to land-use management is the same as it was in 1994 (Mabin 2002).

The key tasks of the Development and Planning Commission included a clarification of the principles of the DFA and an assessment of their impact. Several explanatory and 'plain language' documents were produced. The impact of the DFA principles was assessed through a limited set of interviews and reviews of plans[9] (Oakenfull 1998). Despite the limitations of the research, the findings are interesting. They suggest that the DFA principles were largely seen as applicable only to RDP projects and applications taken through DFA tribunals, rather than applying to land-use decisions or planning more generally. Further, Oakenfull (1998) found that the principles were so generally stated that they were seen as difficult to apply, and were not understood by administrators and decision-makers. Principles related to urban restructuring were better understood than others, but were sometimes used inappropriately, contrary to overall intentions. The skill required to use them appropriately was often lacking. There was still a tendency to look for definitive prescriptions, harking back to past planning practices, rather than to seeing the principles as a set of normative values. These problems were exacerbated by a lack of capacity in local government, which was also stressed by a broadening mandate and by processes of institutional reorganisation.

In response to concerns that land-use management remains unreformed in many instances (DPC 1999) and does not link to land-use management (Berrisford 2000), the White Paper on Spatial Planning and Land Use called for spatial frameworks to give effect to DFA principles, and to link to land-use management. Similar provisions were made in regulations for the Municipal Systems Act in 2001, which spelled out the requirements for the spatial framework component of the IDP. Ironically, the limitations of the spatial frameworks were in part a reflection of precisely the flexible indicative style of planning favoured by the UCT school and the Green Paper on Planning. It is unclear what the effect of these measures has been – it is perhaps too early to judge. Nevertheless, research on spatial frameworks conducted for the DLA in 2003 indicated that spatial frameworks were not getting sufficient support – in terms of time, energy, and financial resources – within local authorities to be effective, reflecting the marginalisation of spatial planning.

By the late 1990s, a growing academic literature was beginning to debate the urban compaction idea. Its plausibility was questioned in light of trends towards sprawl (Mabin 1995, 1999; Tomlinson 1997). Research on property market trends suggested that office decentralisation was proceeding apace, and in ways which were contradicting ideas of urban integration (Rogerson 1997; Todes 2000; Turok 2000; Watson 2002; Goga 2003). Instead of a reduction of apartheid divides, old patterns of racial segregation were being maintained, or new socio-spatial divides were emerging, often along class lines. It was clear that the ideals of urban integration were not being realised.

The decline of urban spatial policy begs the question of what interests were served by the policy,[10] and why it was allowed to dissipate. Reflecting on the negotiating forums of the early 1990s, both Turok (1994b) and Watson (2002) comment that civics and unions had limited capacity to engage in the details of the development of metropolitan spatial frameworks, and left this work to 'technical experts'. Thus planning became isolated from communities, despite attempts to maintain these links. Bond (2003) points to a more general demobilisation of civic organisations since 1994, and civic structures that have emerged since then have not focused on these issues. The absence of a political constituency to support more difficult and expensive urban restructuring initiatives was evident in Todes' (2000) study of Durban, where the pressure was for improvement in conditions and extension of housing opportunities 'where people are'. Questions can be raised about whether there is popular support for urban restructuring. The disadvantages of the apartheid city for black people were certainly well established by research and by political movements of the late 1980s and early 1990s. The importance of access to employment is raised in studies on the inner city (eg. Fadane 1993), and in resistance to removal from areas with sources of local income and employment (Charlton 2000). Responses to the Green Paper on Planning and Development include a letter of support by the Congress of South African Trade Unions on urban restructuring and the need to move away from an apartheid geography. Other research, however, suggests that growing unemployment has meant that proximity to areas of employment is less significant for the poor than previously assumed

(Biermann 2003), and that low-density development on the periphery supports the livelihood strategies of some households (Cross, Luckin, Mzimela & Clark 1996; Schoonraad 2000). Thus urban restructuring might have little appeal for parts of the urban population. Yet the urban poor have had limited choice about their location in cities, nor have there been obvious ways in which their 'voices' could be expressed.

At an institutional level, the department with the strongest interest in notions of urban restructuring is the Department of Transport,[11] for which the idea has a strong economic logic, potentially offering a way of reducing transport subsidies, increasing public transport efficiency, reducing car dependence, and improving travel times. The relationship between land use and transport emerged as a key factor in research undertaken for its analysis of the transport problem in the 1997 Moving South Africa Strategy. The Strategy argues for a particular version of compaction, that is the 'Corridor City', with densification around corridors rather than a CBD-centric compaction model, or policies of infill and densification more generally. It is claimed that the additional cost of purchasing well-located land can be recovered in 7 to 20 years through transport savings (including subsidies). These ideas were given effect in the National Land Transport Transition Act of 2000, which calls for transport planning to guide land-use and development planning, and for the integration of transport plans into IDPs.

Although this legislation seems to support the notion of urban restructuring, there are difficulties in implementing these concepts in practice. Wilkinson (2001) argues that the form of planning adopted in IDPs does not lend itself to transport planning, and most IDPs have not incorporated these elements. More fundamentally, a set of pilot corridor projects initiated in several cities from the mid-1990s has highlighted the constraints on the corridor approach, and suggests that they are difficult to achieve (Del Mistro 2002).[12]

The limits of a corridor approach were highlighted in the Fundamental Restructuring of Durban's Public Transport System, a national flagship project undertaken in 1999 by the Department of Transport in partnership with the provincial transport department and the Durban metro. The aim of the pilot project was to restructure Durban's public transport system (taxi, bus and rail) and gain insights around the implementation of national policy. The project modelled transport usage, using existing user data and projected changes, and suggested that a much more limited set of corridors would be possible than that assumed by the Spatial Framework (Todes 2002). Further, although considerable savings from transport restructuring would be possible through the development of a rail-based corridor, it was dependent on significant pre-investment to make the integrated system work effectively (Aucamp 2001). There were questions as to whether the system could work, as it was dependent on good intermodal integration and on an ability to shift transport usage away from modes preferred by users. It might threaten the interests of taxis, leading to conflict, and could be undermined by crime and by contrary spatial trends over the long term (Aucamp 2001).

The question of whether spatial planning can bring about the changes necessary to support corridors, or urban restructuring more generally, has been raised by both transport planners (Cameron 1997) and critical academics. A 1998 workshop organised by two NGOs, the Isandla Institute and Planact, and the Graduate School of Public and Development Management of the University of the Witwatersrand, raised fundamental issues about notions of urban compaction. Robinson (1998) and Simone (1998) argued that urban compaction–integration ideas as embodied in policy documents and plans did not come to terms with the complexity of social and economic dynamics in cities, and moreover made the questionable assumption that 'the apartheid city can be remade through a coherent set of policy instruments' (Simone 1998: 1).

By late 1990s, the plausibility and desirability of compaction were increasingly debated. Debates were reflected in the CSIR's *State of Human Settlements Report* (1999) produced for the Department of Housing, which reviewed human settlement policy and its impact. Drawing on existing literature, it noted the absence of a coordinated programme to promote well-located high-density settlements, and pointed to research demonstrating that the peripheral location of new (greenfields) development had 'unintentionally accentuated economic disadvantage, social exclusions, institutional isolation, and a lack of employment opportunities' (Friedrich Ebert Stifting and National Housing Forum Trust Study[13] in CSIR 1999: 60). It nevertheless noted the way households had come to survive in peripheral areas, and argued for an acceptance of existing settlement patterns. Drawing in part on this work, South Africa's report on the implementation of the Habitat Agenda (DoH 2001) conceded that the reality of South African cities had fallen short of the UDF, with trends towards sprawl and the location of the poor on the periphery. These were seen largely as a result of dynamics linked to land and property. Its summary of the debate demonstrates the way policy thinking had shifted: while notions of compaction were not abandoned, they were modified in the light of urban realities:

> The current debate is then on the feasibility of achieving the envisioned compact city in a market economy, where most land is in private ownership and settlement development is often largely a private sector activity. There is an emerging trend to emphasise integration and not compaction,[14] using compact city principles where practical but also accepting the reality of sprawl in a market driven urban land market, and to concentrate on mitigating its negative impacts by, for instance, upgrading informal and low-income settlements to improve quality of life. The main realisation is that there is not a single development imperative suitable for all circumstances. (DoH 2001: 7)

Thus by the beginning of the millennium, the limits of policy had been recognised, and a more modified policy approach had begun to develop. This was reflected both in the 'more realistic' approach adopted in the CSIR report, in the transport studies, and in some locally generated metropolitan spatial frameworks which had begun to adopt more modest approaches to urban restructuring (eg. see Todes 2002 on the case of eThekwini).

## The resurgence of urban spatial policy?

Towards the end of 2004, ideas of integrating and compacting the city seemed to be resurgent, although in a more muted form than in 1994. In 2000, responsibility for the UDF shifted from the DoH to the Department of Provincial and Local Government following criticism that the former had done little to promote the policy. Spurred by the National Spatial Development Perspective (NSDP),[15] which pointed to the important role of cities in development, an initial document in 2002 argued for a stronger urban policy, particularly to address urbanisation and urban poverty, and to promote an integrated approach. The distorted spatial organisation of the city was seen as an issue to be addressed in this context, a theme that has remained in drafts of policy since then. At the time of writing, a document entitled *Towards an Urban Policy/Strategy* had been tabled to Cabinet, and had been referred to an Urban Task Force in the Office of the President for further consideration (Patel 2004). This document recognised the failings of past urban spatial policy, and argued for a pragmatic approach focused on creating polycentric cities 'through the development of a dense, well connected network of nodes' (2004: 29), drawing in both specialised and day-to-day activity. This approach, however, goes along with an emphasis on many elements of compaction–integration: densification, land-use mix, transit and development corridors, and urban edges. Nevertheless, a cautious approach exploring plausible options and designing appropriate policy instruments was adopted.

In 2004, the DoH produced a new policy document, *Breaking New Ground: A Comprehensive Plan for the Development of Sustainable Human Settlements*, which included an emphasis on urban restructuring and integration. It went well beyond its previous and rather limited focus on medium-density social housing as a means of increasing densities. The new policy was accepted by Cabinet in September 2004. Cast within a broader vision of sustainable human settlements and efficient cities, the Plan proposed to explore measures to give effect to intentions to integrate the city. These included several policy areas, which had seemingly fallen off government's agenda for ten years:

- A densification policy (also referred to in *Towards an Urban Policy/Strategy*), possibly using planning policies, property tax, and land mechanisms;
- Residential permits, requiring developers to set aside 20 per cent of units for low-cost affordable housing (not necessarily on site);

- Fiscal incentives to encourage densification and discourage sprawl;
- Strategies to access well-located land owned by the state and parastatals, or even the private sector;
- Special funding for well-located land for housing.

Given the marginalisation and decline of the urban restructuring agenda within government, it is useful to question why this emphasis seems to have re-emerged. Within the DoH the resurgence of urban integration as a theme can be seen as a reflection of broader shifts in government policy. Interviews and documents highlight the importance of the Ten Year Review and President Mbeki's 2004 State of the Nation address, both of which stress the need to respond to poverty and to the challenges of a dual economy. Both make some mention of urban restructuring. The Ten Year Review refers to the need to overcome spatial disjunctures between home and work, to increase residential densities, and to create more compact designs. Similarly, President Mbeki's speech in the context of housing includes 'addressing the broader question of spatial settlement patterns and implications of this in our efforts to build a non-racial society' (Mbeki 2004).

Changes, however, also reflect a shift within the DoH from a focus on delivery to a greater emphasis on the quality of housing and the creation of sustainable human settlements. The influence of the UN Habitat Agenda and its Local Agenda 21 programme needs to be noted here. While the UDF never set up reporting structures, government was required to report on the Habitat Agenda in terms of its agreements with the UN. This created a channel for the influence of sustainability ideas, but also meant that a level of ongoing reflection on policy occurred. Thus both the strengths and deficiencies of South Africa's settlement policies have been subject to international scrutiny and debate in terms of international discourses. Urban compaction ideas were debated in a session of the 2000 conference on Sustainable Urban Development, organised by the departments of Housing and of Environment and Tourism. Research commissioned by the DoH on sustainable settlements and housing found that the spatial structure of South African cities, and the predominant form of low-cost housing, was unsustainable (Du Plessis 2002; Irurah & Boshoff 2003). The World Summit on Sustainable Development in 2002 highlighted these concerns.

In 2002, the DoH embarked on a process of consultation and research to assess past policy and to identify future directions. Some 14 workshops with national, provincial and local stakeholders were held, and a survey of housing beneficiaries was undertaken (SMM 2003). The need to create better quality housing environments and well-located developments, and to address 'dysfunctional human settlements' emerged as an issue in this context. Studies of beneficiaries (Zack & Charlton 2003), based on 28 focus groups, found that they were better off than before but experienced a range of problems, including poor location and increased costs. Few beneficiaries had been able to choose their location. They were poorly located relative to work, and projects had limited ability to sustain income generation, thus their economic activities were largely survivalist. Poor access to facilities, amenities, and work opportunities was raised repeatedly. A clear distinction between better and poorly located settlements emerged. The cost and availability of transport was also a concern for most groups, preventing their participation in the urban system.

Similar points were made in the Urban Sector Network's (2003) evaluation of the housing subsidy scheme for the Public Services Commission. Based on an assessment of 40 projects, and beneficiary surveys, problems associated with persistent patterns of location on the periphery were raised. Beneficiaries were forced to choose between owning houses and renting in areas closer to work. Examples of people living in cars to be close to work were noted (Charlton, Silverman & Berrisford 2003). These beneficiary surveys were reportedly influential in the shift to a greater emphasis on urban restructuring. The overall review of the policy (Charlton et al. 2003) found that while the delivery of basic services, security and tenure had fostered pride and dignity, the quality of houses, neighbourhoods and locations remained a problem. It recommended a broader conceptualisation of well-located land, and a wider range of mechanisms to support integrated development.

The housing research also drew on literature debating urban integration, including a collection of papers brought together by University of Witwatersrand academics (Harrison, Huchzmeyer & Mayekiso 2003), which was workshopped with several sets of stakeholders. While authors pointed to problems with the somewhat simplistic social and economic ideas contained in the earlier versions of urban integration and compaction, the general thrust was not so much to discard these ideas, but to argue for a more nuanced, socially informed and contextual approach to urban restructuring.

The findings of the Urban Sector Network and the housing research stand somewhat in contrast to a major study by the CSIR, initiated in 2002. The study was commissioned by the Johannesburg Development Agency in response to concerns that Johannesburg's adoption of compaction policies, and the establishment of an urban edge, limited investment in some important settlements which were defined as poorly located. The research compared Alexandra and Diepsloot on a range of social indicators based on a sample survey of the two settlements. Research was extended by an analysis of six low-income settlements in Durban with variable locational characteristics. It found that patterns of decentralisation within the city had brought what were assumed to be marginal settlements into reasonable accessibility limits. Further, since levels of unemployment were low, access to formal work opportunities was less important than informal opportunities, including access to domestic work. Low-income households had diverse locational needs and meanings of 'good' location varied (Biermann 2003). Households adjusted their transport patterns to spend between 15 per cent and 16 per cent of income on transport, no matter which city or locality they were found in. The CSIR research is important as it seems to challenge the basis of arguments for urban integration. Some of its findings are not consistent with transport studies, which stress locational disadvantages (eg. Behrens & Wilkinson 2003). Arguments about adaptation to the spatial and economic environment by localising work needs have to be set against qualitative studies by Zack and Charlton (2003) and the Urban Sector Network (2003), which argue that the poor are trapped in peripheral locations. The CSIR study, however, is important in developing a much more nuanced approach to understanding accessibility and actual patterns of the use of space in contemporary South African cities.

Debates over the urban integration concept continue in other forums as well. For instance, in his opening address at the launch of a new volume on the city (Khan 2004), which contained critical debate on the idea of urban restructuring, Elroy Africa, Deputy Director-General in the Department of Provincial and Local Government, called for new and creative ways of thinking about the city, beyond the sterile and rather physically oriented debates of the past. Pieterse (2004) argues for a much greater engagement with politics, moving beyond the consensual approach inherent in notions of urban integration. Ideas about what urban integration would entail and require seem to be broadening, and there is a growing engagement with actual patterns of urban spatial change. For instance, systematic studies of changing urban spatial patterns have been undertaken by the City of Cape Town (CCC 2003a) and in 2004 by the DLA, for an assessment of the impact of policies on settlement patterns.

The growing importance of a sustainability agenda, and links made between urban restructuring and sustainability, seem to be raising the profile of urban integration ideas more generally. At a City Energy Strategies Conference, organised by the influential South African Cities Network and Sustainable Energy Africa in 2003, the inefficiency of sprawling cities in terms of transport and energy usage was highlighted in several papers. For instance, Cape Town's *State of Energy Report* noted that some 54 per cent of Cape Town's energy usage is on transport (CCC 2003b). The social, environmental, and energy costs associated with the sprawling, fragmented South African city were raised in a keynote speech. The Network's 2004 *State of the Cities Report* (SACN 2004) drew on UCT academic Gasson's (2003) work on the ecological footprint of South African cities, and made strong links between patterns of sprawl, energy usage and environmental problems.[16]

Although there appears to be a new interest in urban integration, it is not clear how far it is likely to go. Some local authorities, such as Johannesburg and eThekwini, have put in place urban edges and are encouraging urban compaction. In the case of eThekwini, studies have highlighted the infrastructural costs of development beyond the edge, and are affirming a commitment to compaction. The DoH's new policy also appears to have encouraged an exploration of ways to increase population in the central areas.

It remains to be seen what support the new policies will develop at national level. The DoH's policies require a significant increase in funding, which may not be forthcoming. Further, the emphasis on addressing informal settlements is much more central to the plan, and of greater political importance. In some of the thinking, densification and addressing informal settlements are linked together, for example in the Cape Town N2 corridor project, where it is envisaged that medium-density social housing could, *inter alia*, replace informal settlements (Sisulu 2004). Following research by Syn-Consult et al. (2003) for the DoH, a wider range of housing typologies is included in medium-density social housing. However, there are still concerns that it is inappropriate for people currently living in informal settlements, and that maintenance costs will put this type of housing beyond the reach of the poor. Nor is it clear that the political will exists to challenge patterns of spatial inequality in more substantial ways than in the past (see Charlton and Kihato in this book for a more extensive discussion).

## Conclusion

This chapter has shown how the ideas of urban restructuring, compaction and integration became a dominant policy discourse, which was incorporated into policy statements and legislation with regard to urban land development, planning, housing, transport and local government. Nevertheless, it was marginalised in the post-apartheid era. While modified forms of the urban restructuring idea – now accepting a more diverse range of settlements and housing needs, and a polycentric city – appear to be resurgent, it is not clear how much commitment there is to change. One weakness of urban spatial policy was that it was founded on a planning approach which did not address the economic drivers of spatial form, or take into account the way politics shapes cities, or the diversity of social needs for space. Too little was done to investigate how the ambitious aims of urban restructuring could be realised or to explore the types of instruments which would be required to do so. Current policy at least promises to research mechanisms for change after a decade in which urban land questions were largely forgotten. However, the weakness of urban spatial policy was not purely the consequence of the limits of ideas. Rather, the constraints of a newly emerging democracy, and a later shift from RDP to GEAR, underpinned an unwillingness to challenge patterns of urban spatial inequality. The absence of a vocal and organised constituency in the post-apartheid era, and the lack of political or even bureaucratic champions have also been crucial. Current concerns by government to address poverty and social division, and to respond to at least survey-based evidence of popular perceptions of the dysfunctionality of the apartheid city, may lead to some form of redress. It is not clear, however, whether government and local governments are willing to take on property interests and other social forces perpetuating at least class divides in cities. Current skirmishes around gated communities and spatial exclusion may be indicative of emerging battles around the right to the city. The lack of a strong institutional base for urban spatial policy also remains, and it will be interesting to see whether current moves towards some form of built environment cluster will lead to change.

It is ironic that a new interest in urban restructuring is emerging at a time when the project of urban integration is being challenged by research. There are notable contradictions between some pieces of research, but this work highlights the need for a close reading of urban spatial and social dynamics within cities, and the importance of moving beyond a reliance on unpeopled spatial concepts. Urban spatial policy is one of the few areas of urban policy where research has shaped policy, and the development of closer ties in this regard could be important in designing policies that more closely respond to social realities and development challenges.

## Acknowledgements

I would like to thank the interviewees for their ideas, but particularly Gemey Abrahams, who also spent considerable time in the interview and in searching for relevant documents. Edgar Pieterse was extremely generous in allowing me to read and cite from his draft PhD thesis. Dirk Osborne put together material on transport.

## Notes

1   Lateral spread of urban development, generally at relatively low densities, which may encroach on agricultural or environmentally important areas. Sprawl is associated with suburban development, but also with townhouse complexes, peripherally located housing projects, and increasing densities on land held under traditional tenure on the edge of cities.

2   An urban edge creates limits to formal urban development on the urban periphery, particularly where such development is likely to lead to demands for infrastructural development. It does not, however, exclude small-scale agriculture and the like.

3   'Integrated development' has several meanings: spatial integration (where diverse but mutually supportive land uses coexist or are in reasonable proximity, potentially reducing distances between home and work, and enabling easy access to various services and facilities); a mix of housing types; and a much greater mixing of income (and race) groups than is generally the case in areas developed by modernist planning; and administrative integration, where the social, economic, environmental and institutional dimensions are brought together and the various institutions work in a mutually supportive way. Different dimensions are emphasised by various authors. Some lay greater emphasis on social and racial integration than spatial integration. In the South African context, integrated development also means moving away from the apartheid form of the city.

4   Lee notes that Greater Cape Town's land area with 3 million people was more than double the size of Mexico City with 25 million people.

5   Although aspects of the DFA were influenced by a Canadian-funded local government and planning think tank established in 1991, which drew together a network of progressive organisations, activists and academics (Watson 2002), the influence of the Urban Foundation ideas and of discourse seems to be more important with regard to spatial

principles. The focus of the think tank was more towards governance questions, and while the appropriate form of planning was debated, little attention was given to its content.

6   Arguably the Department of Environment and Tourism should be added to this list since its environment impact assessment processes overlap with planning processes. However, urban spatial policy has never been an explicit focus.

7   After a three-week consultation around the country.

8   According to documents in DoH (2000), a short questionnaire was sent to several government departments, institutes, parastatals, academics and some local and provincial governments. In addition, some informal consultation occurred. The questionnaire enquired whether they were aware of the Urban Development Framework, whether it informs government programmes and tasks, and its shortcomings and areas needing improvement. The response to both the questionnaires and the recorded workshops was, however, extremely poor. Of the 12 who responded to the questionnaire, only 8 had seen it before. These respondents felt that it was important, but that it didn't influence their daily tasks.

9   Interviews were conducted with planners and a few members of local and provincial government. Some Land Development Objectives and Spatial Development Frameworks were assessed.

10  The absence of a constituency for these policies was stressed by Alan Mabin and Mark Oranje in interviews, and earlier on by Jeff McCarthy in the case of Durban.

11  This point was suggested by Mark Oranje.

12  Marrian's (2001) review of corridors for the Department of Transport suggests that they are contingent on a number of mutually supporting factors, including: a critical mass of existing and future economic activity; integrated and enforceable land-use management aimed at providing thresholds for supporting corridors; integrated public transport systems and strong demand for movement between nodes; favourable public image and ongoing political commitment; a cooperative attitude across role-players and a culture of public transport use; and an integrated metropolitan planning process.

13  The CSIR notes that this was a qualitative study based on personal interviews in four settlements in Gauteng, including an upgraded informal settlement and two core housing settlements.

14  See endnote 3 for a definition of integration. Compaction refers to increasing densities within a given boundary, rather than continuing to spread beyond it.

15  Published officially in 2003, but largely completed by 2000. The NSDP did not specifically address the spatial organisation of cities, but its arguments on the need to move beyond apartheid spatial organisation are sometimes seen as supporting urban spatial restructuring (eg. see SACN 2004).

16  Biermann's (2003) study, however, challenges the assumptions that peripheral location of the poor leads to high energy use since the limited extent of travel and high occupancy in taxis mean that the energy impacts of low-income households are relatively low. These patterns need to be seen within the context of high unemployment. Significant economic growth could put paid to arguments around energy usage.

## References

Abrahams G & Rantete J (1996) The delivery of land and services for housing. In K Rust & S Rubenstein (eds), *A mandate to build: Developing consensus around a national housing policy in South Africa.* Johannesburg: Ravan.

Abu-Lughod J (1980*) Rabat: Urban apartheid in Morocco.* New Jersey: Princeton University Press.

Aucamp A (2001) The fundamental restructuring of Durban's public transport network: Interim results. Unpublished paper. Durban: Durban Unicity, Traffic and Transportation Department.

Behrens R & Watson V (1992) Spread city! Evaluation of the costs of urban growth in metropolitan Cape Town. Urban Problems Research Unit Working Paper 46. Cape Town: University of Cape Town.

Behrens R & Wilkinson P (2003) Housing and urban passenger transport policy and planning in South African cities: A problematic relationship? In P Harrison, M Huchzermeyer & M Mayekiso (eds), *Confronting fragmentation: Housing and urban development in a democratising society.* Cape Town: UCT Press.

Bernstein A (1991) The challenge of the cities. In M Swilling, R Humphries & K Shubane (eds), *Apartheid city in transition.* Cape Town: Oxford University Press.

Berrisford S (2000) IDP/Land-use management linkage. Unpublished paper. Pretoria: GTZ and Department of Provincial and Local Government.

Biermann S (2003) Investigation into the energy consumption implications of alternative locations for low income housing development in South African urban areas. Unpublished paper. Pretoria: Housing Finance Resource Programme.

Bond P (2003) The degeneration of urban policy after apartheid. In P Harrison, M Huchzermeyer & M Mayekiso (eds), *Confronting fragmentation: Housing and urban development in a democratising society.* Cape Town: UCT Press.

Bond P, Bremner L, Geldenhuys O, Mayekiso M, Miller D & Swilling M (1996) Response to government's draft Urban Strategy document II, *Urban Forum,* 7(1): 101–120.

Cameron J (1997) Spatial development plans and corridors. Paper presented to SA Transport Conference, Pretoria.

CCC (Cape Town City Council) (2003a) *Metropolitan spatial development framework review. Phase 1: Spatial analysis, trends and implications.* Cape Town: CCC.

CCC (2003b) *State of energy report for Cape Town.* Cape Town: CCC.

Charlton S (2000) Infill and integration in the post apartheid city: Two low-income housing projects in Durban. Paper presented to the Johannesburg Conference on Urban Futures, 10–14 July.

Charlton S, Silverman S & Berrisford S (2003) Taking stock. Review of the Department of Housing's programmes, policies and practices (1994–2003). Unpublished paper. Pretoria: Department of Housing.

Cook G (1987) Time budgets of working women in disadvantaged society, *Bluestocking,* 37: 33–35.

Cross C, Luckin L, Mzimela T & Clark C (1996) On the edge: Poverty, livelihoods and natural resources in rural KwaZulu-Natal. In M Lipton, F Ellis & M Lipton (eds), *Land, labour and livelihoods in rural South Africa.* Durban: Indicator Press.

CSIR (Council for Scientific and Industrial Research) (1999) *State of human settlements report: South Africa 1994–1998*. Pretoria: Department of Housing.

Del Mistro R (2002) Improving the probability of corridor development. Paper presented to SA Transport Conference, Pretoria, 15–19 July.

Dewar D (2000) The relevance of the compact city approach: The management of growth in South African cities. In M Jencks & R Burgess (eds), *Compact cities. Sustainable urban forms for developing countries*. London: Spon Press.

Dewar D & Uytenbogaardt R (1991) *South African cities: A manifesto for change*. Cape Town: University of Cape Town.

Dewar D, Watson V, Bassios A & Dewar N (1990) The structure and form of metropolitan Cape Town: Its origins, influences and performance. Urban Problems Research Unit Working Paper 42. Cape Town: University of Cape Town.

DoH (Department of Housing) (2000) *Settlement policy revision: Urban Development Framework*, Vol. 1. SP/10/3/3/11.

DoH (2001) South African Country Report to the Special Session of the United Nations General Assembly for the Review of the Implementation of the Habitat Agenda. Pretoria: DoH.

DPC (Development and Planning Commission) (1999) *Green Paper on Development and Planning*. Pretoria: Department of Land Affairs.

Du Plessis C (2002) Sustainability analysis of human settlements in South Africa. Unpublished report. Pretoria: DoH.

Fadane N (1993) An examination of gendered housing needs of informal sector operators in Warwick Triangle. Unpublished Master of Town and Regional Planning dissertation. Durban: University of Natal.

Gasson B (2003) The ecological footprint of Cape Town in relation to energy consumption. Paper presented to the Cape Town Conference on City Energy Strategies, 19–21 November.

Goga S (2003) Property investors and decentralization: A case of false competition? In R Tomlinson, R Beauregard, L Bremner & X Mangcu (eds), *Emerging Johannesburg: Perspectives on the post-apartheid city*. New York: Routledge.

Harrison P (2001) The genealogy of South Africa's Integrated Development Plan, *Third World Planning Review*, 23(2): 175–192.

Harrison P, Huchzermeyer M & Mayekiso M (eds) (2003) *Confronting fragmentation: Housing and urban development in a democratising society*. Cape Town: UCT Press.

Hart D & Pirie G (1984) The sight and soul of Sophiatown, *Geographical Review*, 74(1): 38–47.

Hindson D, Mabin A & Watson V (1993) Restructuring the built environment. Report to Working Group 5. Unpublished paper. Johannesburg: National Housing Forum.

Irurah D & Boshoff B (2003) An interpretation of sustainable development and urban sustainability in low-cost housing and settlements in South Africa. In P Harrison, M Huchzermeyer & M Mayekiso (eds), *Confronting fragmentation: Housing and urban development in a democratising society*. Cape Town: UCT Press.

Khan F (ed.) (2004) The city and its future? The eternal question, *Development Update*, 5(1): 81–104.

Lee K (1993) South Africa. Urban economic mission. World Bank. February 12, 1993. Aide Memoire. Annex 1. Unpublished paper. Washington: World Bank.

Lemon A (ed.) (1991) *Homes apart: South Africa's segregated cities.* Cape Town: David Philip.

Mabin A (1995) On the problems and prospects of overcoming segregation and fragmentation in South African cities in the postmodern era. In S Watson & K Gibson (eds), *Postmodern cities and spaces.* Oxford: Blackwell.

Mabin A (1998) Commentary on 'Vusani Amadolobha – Urban regeneration and integration plan for city, town and township centres'. In *Cities in transition.* Proceedings of the Urban Development Symposium. Johannesburg: Planact, Isandla Institute, Wits School of Public and Development Management.

Mabin A (1999) Dynamics of urban spatial growth (particularly 'sub-urbanisation') and their implications for spatial guidelines. Unpublished paper. Pretoria: President's Office.

Mabin A (2002) Local government in the emerging national planning context. In S Parnell, E Pieterse, M Swilling & D Wooldridge (eds), *Democratising local government: The South African experiment.* Cape Town: UCT Press.

Marrian B (2001) Towards a general theory of corridor development in South Africa. Paper presented to SA Transport Conference, Pretoria, 16–20 July.

Mbeki T (2004) State of the Nation. Address to the Joint Sitting of the Houses of Parliament, Cape Town, 21 May. Available at <http://www.gov.za>. Downloaded on 27 September 2004.

McCarthy J (1991) Class, race and urban locational relationships. In M Swilling, R Humphries & K Shubane (eds), *Apartheid city in transition.* Cape Town: Oxford University Press.

Naude A (1988) Urban activity corridors: Suggestions for a strategy to contain urban sprawl and promote public transport. Unpublished paper. Pretoria: CSIR.

Oakenfull L (1998) *The Chapter 1 principles: Practical experiences.* Development and Planning Commission Document 67/98. Pretoria: Development and Planning Commission.

Parnell S & Pieterse E (2002) Developmental local government. In S Parnell, E Pieterse, M Swilling & D Wooldridge (eds), *Democratising local government: The South African experiment.* Cape Town: UCT Press.

Patel Y (2004) National perspective on city development strategies and the Urban Strategy. Paper presented to the Durban Cities Alliance Conference, 1–3 November.

Pieterse E (2003) Unravelling the different meanings of urban integration: The Urban Development Framework of the South African government. In P Harrison, M Huchzermeyer & M Mayekiso (eds), *Confronting fragmentation: Housing and urban development in a democratising society.* Cape Town: UCT Press.

Pieterse E (2004) Recasting urban integration and fragmentation in post-apartheid South Africa. In F Khan (ed.), The city and its future? The eternal question, *Development Update,* 5(1): 81–104.

Pieterse E (2006) Re-building amongst ruins: The pursuit of urban integration in South Africa (1994–2001). PhD thesis. London: London School of Economic and Political Science.

Price F (1991) A review of instruments of land development policy. Cuta Land Use-Transport Technical Committee Task 9. Unpublished paper. Pretoria: CSIR.

Robinson J (1998) Planning the post-apartheid city. Comments on the Metropolitan Spatial

Development Framework – Cape Town. In *Cities in transition*. Proceedings of the Urban Development Symposium. Johannesburg: Planact, Isandla Institute, Wits School of Public and Development Management.

Rogerson J (1997) The central Witwatersrand. Post-elections investment outlook for the built environment, *Urban Forum*, 8(1): 93–108.

Royston L (2003) On the outskirts: Access to well-located land and integration in post-apartheid human settlement development. In F Khan & P Thring (eds), *Housing policy and practice in South Africa*. Cape Town: UCT Press.

RSA (Republic of South Africa) (1994) *White Paper on Reconstruction and Development*. Cape Town: Government Gazette.

Rust K & Rubenstein S (eds) (1996) *A mandate to build: Developing consensus around a national housing policy in South Africa*. Johannesburg: Ravan.

SACN (South African Cities Network) (2004) *State of the Cities Report*. Johannesburg: SACN.

Schoonraad M (2000) Cultural and institutional obstacles to compact cities in South Africa. In M Jencks & R Burgess (eds), *Compact cities: Sustainable urban forms for developing countries*. London: Spon Press.

Simone A (1998) Discussion paper on the Urban Development Framework. In *Cities in transition*. Proceedings of the Urban Development Symposium. Johannesburg: Planact, Isandla Institute, Wits School of Public and Development Management.

Sisulu L (2004) Cities without slums. Presentation to the Durban Conference of the Cities Alliance, 1–3 November.

Smith D (ed.) (1992) *The apartheid city and beyond: Urbanization and social change in South Africa*. London: Routledge.

SMM (Sigodi Marah Martin) (2003) Report on the consultative process on national housing policy and strategy: Towards second generation housing programme of the government. Unpublished paper. Pretoria: DoH.

Syn-Consult, Poulsen L, Silverman M, Wilson A, Ashira, CUBES, Ronald Schloss and Associates, Viruly Consulting (2003) Research report for the development of a medium density housing programme for the national Department of Housing. Unpublished paper. Pretoria: DoH.

Todes A (2000) Reintegrating the apartheid city? Urban policy and urban restructuring in Durban. In S Watson & G Bridges (eds), *A companion to the city*. London: Blackwell.

Todes A (2002) Spatial change and Durban's spatial framework. In A Bouillon, B Freund, D Hindson & B Lootvoet (eds), *Governance, urban dynamics and economic development: A comparative analysis of the metropolitan areas of Durban, Abidjan and Marseilles*. Durban: Plumbline Publishing.

Todes A, Pillay C & Krone A (2003) Urban restructuring and land availability. In F Khan & P Thring (eds), *Housing policy and practice in South Africa*. Cape Town: UCT Press.

Tomlinson R (1990) *Urbanization in post-apartheid South Africa*. London: Unwin Hyman.

Tomlinson R (1997) Urban sprawl problem hard nut to crack, *Business Day* 29.09.1997.

Tomlinson R (2002) International best practice, enabling frameworks and the policy process: A South African case study, *International Journal of Urban and Regional Research*, 26(2): 377–388.

Tomlinson R (2003) HIV/Aids and urban disintegration in Johannesburg. In P Harrison, M Huchzermeyer & M Mayekiso (eds), *Confronting fragmentation: Housing and urban development in a democratising society.* Cape Town: UCT Press.

Turok I (1994a) Urban planning in the transition from apartheid. Part 1: The legacy of social control, *Town Planning Review,* 65(3): 243–259.

Turok I (1994b) Urban planning in the transition from apartheid. Part 2: Towards reconstruction, *Town Planning Review,* 65(34): 355–374.

Turok I (2000) Persistent polarisation post-Apartheid? Progress towards urban integration in Cape Town. Urban Change and Policy Research Group Discussion Paper 1. Glasgow: University of Glasgow.

Urban Sector Network (2003) Evaluation of the national housing subsidy scheme. Unpublished paper. Pretoria: Public Services Commission.

Watson V (2002) *Change and continuity in spatial planning: Metropolitan planning in Cape Town.* London: Routledge.

Western J (1981) *Outcast Cape Town.* London: George Allen and Unwin.

Wilkinson P (2001) Integrated planning at the local level? The problematic intersection of integrated development planning and integrated transport planning in contemporary South Africa. Paper presented to the Planning Africa Conference, 18–20 September.

Wolfson T (1991) Access to urban land. In M Swilling, R Humphries & K Shubane (eds), *Apartheid city in transition.* Cape Town: Oxford University Press.

World Bank (1991) South Africa. Urban sector reconnaissance. World Bank Mission, 6 December 1991. Aide Memoire. Unpublished paper. Washington: World Bank.

Zack T & Charlton S (2003) Better off, but … Beneficiaries' perceptions of the government's housing subsidy scheme. Unpublished paper. Pretoria: DoH.

## Interviews and discussions

Abrahams G, Urban Planning Consultant, 13 July 2004.

Berrisford S, Planning Law and Policy Consultant, 21 June 2004 (telephonic).

Cobbett B, Cities Alliance, 1 November 2004.

Davies G, Development Bank of Southern Africa, 21 July 2004 (telephonic).

Heymans C, Development Consultant, 17 September 2004 (telephonic).

Lewis S, Department of Finance, 14 July 2004.

Mabin A, Professor, Graduate School of Public and Development Management, University of the Witwatersrand, 13 July 2004.

Magni P, Department of Housing, 14 July 2004.

McCarthy J, Urban Development Consultant, 28 September 2004.

Napier M, CSIR, 21 September 2004 (telephonic).

Oranje M, Professor, Department of Town and Regional Planning, University of Pretoria, and Van Huyssteen E, CSIR, 14 July 2004.

Silverman M, Consultant, 8 September 2004 (telephonic).

Swartz M, Department of Land Affairs, 2 September 2004 (telephonic).

Tomlinson R, Visiting Professor, Wits Business School, 13 July 2004.

# Part 2: One city, one tax base

# 4 Local government boundary reorganisation

Robert Cameron

## Introduction

During the course of the rent and services boycotts in the 1980s, 'One city, one tax base' became a national rallying cry in the townships. Municipal demarcation gave effect to this cry.

The demarcation of local government boundaries will always be a contested issue. This is because boundaries redistribute political power, with some organisations standing to gain power and others standing to lose power. Boundaries also influence communities' access to local government services. Incorporation with richer jurisdictions can lead to a better standard of services while inclusion in poorer jurisdictions often leads to a lower quality of services. This inequality is generally more pronounced when there is fragmented local government (Magnusson 1981; Keating 1995). In South Africa spatial fragmentation was exacerbated by racially based local government, which led to massive disparities in levels of service provision. Thus it was that local government boundary demarcation became a key instrument in the transformation of apartheid urban systems.

This chapter describes the process of demarcation. Its defining features were the pre-interim, interim and final phases of local government transformation and the dates associated with these phases; the rush to prepare for and to demarcate local government and ward boundaries in time for the 1995 and 2000 local government elections; the criteria used for this purpose; and the effects the rush had on the demarcation process.

The chapter begins with a description of the pre-interim phase and the demarcation process that preceded the 1995 elections, with the elections introducing the interim phase of local government transition. The chapter then continues with an in-depth look at the final phase, which concluded with the 2000 local government elections. The interim phase required the determination of the types of municipalities, demarcation legislation, the appointment in 1999 of a Municipal Demarcation Board (MDB), the demarcation of municipal boundaries and the delimitation of wards. It is the two dates – the appointment of a Demarcation Board in 1999 and municipal elections in 2000 – that explain the rush involved in the demarcation process and many aspects of the process. The chapter then proceeds with a description of a few demarcation issues that are being addressed in the final phase. The chapter concludes with an evaluation of the influences on the demarcation process and, due to the contested nature of the process, the questions that were raised about the independence of the MDB.

Finally, the author was a member of the first MDB in South Africa (February 1999–January 2004). This chapter is an attempt to reflect upon that experience. The chapter also draws on information gleaned from a number of local government research projects over the past few years.

## The pre-interim phase

### Preparing for the 1995 elections

Emerging out of the struggles in the 1980s and agreements reached in 1990 and thereabouts were numerous local negotiating forums, with the most prominent being Johannesburg's Central Witwatersrand Metropolitan Chamber (Tomlinson 1999). It soon became apparent that these local forums were, on their own, unable to substantively change fundamental aspects of the apartheid urban system. Thus, in 1992/93 those negotiating the interim Constitution realised that a national framework was needed to guide the local transition via the local forums.

The Local Government Negotiating Forum (LGNF) was created in 1993 comprising 60 members, 30 of which were nominated by representatives of statutory organisations and 30 by non-statutory organisations. The statutory delegation consisted of representatives of central, provincial and local government. The non-statutory side was represented by the South African National Civic Organisation, although its delegation included a number of key African National Congress (ANC) figures. The recommendations of the LGNF were mostly included in the 1993 interim Constitution and the Local Government Transition Act (LGTA) of 1993 (Cloete 1995; Robinson 1995; Cameron 1999a). The LGNF was the midwife of local government democratisation.

Three phases of local government transformation were prescribed by the LGTA. They were:
- The *pre-interim phase,* which was intended to cover the period from after the country's first democratic national and provincial elections in April 1994 until the first democratic local government elections, which took place in 1995/96.
- The *interim phase* began with the first local government elections and ended with the implementation of the final constitutional model at local government.
- The *final phase,* which began with the final constitutional model in 1997, although some of the constitutional provisions only took effect after the 2000 local government elections. (Cloete 1995; Cameron 1999a)

The local government election in 1995 was the culmination of the pre-interim phase and the 2000 elections were the culmination of the interim phase.

The 1995 elections were based on three different categories of local government that were provided for in the 1993 interim Constitution, namely, metropolitan, urban and rural.

The electoral system for local government first involved amalgamating apartheid local government structures, that is, the demarcation of the outer boundaries. Since the local government system for the 1995 and the 2000 elections was based on a combination of ward and proportional representation (PR), preparation for the elections also required the delimitation of ward boundaries. These two tasks and also the need to draw up voters' rolls led to the decision to hold local government elections in November 1995, some 17 months after the national and provincial elections (Botha 1993).

The electoral system for the 1995/96 elections involved 40 per cent of the councillors being elected by PR, while the remaining 60 per cent were elected on a ward basis. The 60 per cent ward representation was further divided:
- Half of these councillors (50 per cent) represented traditional white local authority areas, including coloured and Indian areas (Category A wards).
- The other half (50 per cent) represented areas outside the jurisdiction of white local authorities, which were in mostly black local authority areas (Category B wards). (Cameron 1999a: 95–96)

What was generally agreed upon by the major parties was that local government, because of its grassroots-based nature, needed at least some form of constituency-based system to coexist along with the PR system used at national and provincial level in the country. However, there was some tough bargaining about the nature of the ward system. This ward formula was one of the compromises reached between the National Party (NP) government and the ANC in bilateral negotiations. The NP originally wanted power-sharing arrangements based on property ownership and the financial loading of wards. While the ANC was not opposed to minority over-representation in principle, it was against financial criteria being used in this regard. The formula was a power-sharing agreement reached to over-represent white people on a non-financial basis, particularly in the erstwhile Transvaal and Orange Free State where, in some areas, they formed only 5–10 per cent of the local electorate (Cloete 1995; Cameron 1999a: 95–96).

It also needs to be stressed that the emphasis was on protecting minorities, not racial groups. Thus, the provision ended up over-representing white people in many city councils in most provinces. However, in the Western Cape, where black people are in the minority, they were the beneficiaries of this clause and, accordingly, were over-represented in local councils.

### Demarcation process for the 1995 elections

The negotiated basis of the LGTA led to provinces assuming major responsibilities for local government transformation. The LGTA made provision for the establishment of a Local Government Demarcation Board in each of the nine provinces. These Boards had advisory powers only and could advise the administrator, in practice the provincial Minister of Local Government, regarding the boundaries and wards of local government jurisdictions. The ministers of local governments had to consult provincial committees, which were set up in each province to supervise and implement the transformation of local government. These generally consisted of representatives of both statutory and non-statutory organisations and meant that there had to be multiparty support for boundary decisions. If provincial committees could not reach consensus, deadlocked boundaries were sent to the special electoral court. Provincial ministers and provincial committees appointed the Board members on the basis of technical expertise (Cameron 1999a).

All Demarcation Boards were established in the first half of 1994 with the exception of KwaZulu-Natal, where the Board became operational in September 1994 (Elections Task Team 1996). In metropolitan areas a two-tier system was created consisting of Transitional Metropolitan Councils (TMCs) and Transitional Metropolitan Substructures (subsequently Metropolitan Local Councils). In urban areas stand-alone Transitional Local Councils (TLCs) were created. District councils, along with a menu of options for primary local government, were created in rural areas.

These provincial Boards had to consider certain statutory criteria when demarcating boundaries (see Annexure 1). Their major political objective was to combine apartheid boundaries into single municipalities. Apartheid boundaries were broken down, but because of the decentralised nature of demarcation, this tended to be uneven, particularly in some smaller towns and rural areas. In total, 843 municipalities were created in the country.

One of the problems of the demarcation for the 1995 elections was unevenness in the reports of the provincial Boards. Some provincial Boards were technically very competent while the reports of some of the other Boards were not of a particularly high standard. Some of the problems of non-viability of certain municipalities were due to poorly designed boundaries (Cameron 1999b).

Attempted gerrymandering of local boundaries was a major problem. Some provincial ministers of local government attempted to demarcate local government boundaries which would have advantaged their respective parties' electoral chances rather than support provincial demarcation boards' proposals for more rational boundaries that would, at least theoretically, have facilitated service delivery and promoted development. A study of the demarcation process in the interim phase in the three major cities in South Africa, namely Johannesburg, Cape Town and Durban, showed that the respective provincial ministers of local government attempted to gerrymander metropolitan boundaries in each city. The three provinces were in fact controlled by three different political parties, namely the ANC, the NP and the Inkatha Freedom Party (IFP) respectively. Boundary disputes had in fact led to boundary deadlocks being sent to the special electoral court, which led to the delay of local government elections in KwaZulu-Natal and the Western Cape (Cameron 1999a; Mabin 1999; Pillay 1999).

## The final phase

### Types of municipalities

Preparations for the 2000 elections and the beginning of the final phase required identifying types of municipalities. The types of municipalities were determined in the final Constitution that was certified by the Constitutional Court in December 1996 and took partial effect in January 1997. Section 155(1) of the final Constitution made provision for Category A, B and C municipalities (RSA 1996). The definitions are:
a) Category A: A municipality that has exclusive municipal executive and legislative authority in its area.
b) Category B: A municipality that shares municipal executive and legislative authority in its area with a Category C municipality within whose area it falls.
c) Category C: A municipality that has municipal executive and legislative authority in an area that includes more than one municipality.

The attempt to introduce flexible structures had been influenced by the experience of the interim Constitution, which had made provision for fixed categories of metropolitan, urban and rural local governments. This had led to numerous demarcation disputes around differences between metropolitan and stand-alone urban areas, such as the dispute between the Cape Metropolitan Council and the fringe areas of Paarl, Stellenbosch and Somerset West in the Western Cape. There were also demarcation disputes between stand-alone towns and their surrounding rural areas (Cameron 1999a; Mabin 1999; Pillay 1999).

The drafters of the Constitution accordingly came up with this A/B/C formulation that provided greater flexibility to the demarcation of local government structures.

### Metropolitan

Prior to 1994 no form of metropolitan government existed in the country. In 1994 a two-tier system of metropolitan government was established. The ANC had long preferred single-tier authorities as a way of redistributing resources and services. It was of the view that strong lower-tier authorities were preventing metropolitan government from enforcing metropolitan-wide development and redistribution (Wooldridge 2002). Given that the final constitutional phase was shorn of power-sharing clauses, it was able to push the megacity option through.

The White Paper on Local Government stated that metropolitan government created a basis for equitable and just metropolitan governance; provided strategic land-use planning; and is able to develop a city-wide framework for economic and social development which can enhance the economic competitiveness and well-being of cities.

The ANC argued that a single-tier body was best suited to implement these goals. It was felt that a two-tier system led to fragmented metropolitan governance.

Legislation was accordingly passed replacing the two-tier system with single-tier Category A municipalities (Cameron 2000; Wooldridge 2002).

## DISTRICT AND LOCAL MUNICIPALITIES

The White Paper argued that even boundaries created in the interim phase had divided settlements irrationally and that there was a need to create municipal institutions that recognised the linkages between urban and rural settlements. It suggested that almost all towns are linked functionally to rural areas, relying on their hinterlands for productive economic activity and providing centres for the delivery of social services (Ministry of Provincial Affairs and Constitutional Development 1998). In particular, concern was raised that the service needs of farm workers and those forcibly removed to bantustans (pseudo homelands for black people) during apartheid were not catered for under the existing system of rural local government. Rural local government structures that were set up in the interim phase were largely political shells without any formal administration, with district councils providing most of the functions on an agency basis.

The Local Government Municipal Structures Act of 1998 (RSA 1998a) embodied the spirit of the White Paper recommendations and made provision for more hierarchical two-tier local government systems in non-metropolitan areas. Following on from the Constitution, district councils were now called district municipalities and became the upper-tier (Category C) authority. One fundamental change has been in functions, with district municipalities assuming many responsibilities. In the past, districts had no jurisdiction in large urban towns. Now, district municipalities have assumed upper-tier responsibilities of some primary local government functions such as planning and environmental health.

At the lower-tier level, there were Category B structures. Provision was made for only one form of B local government structure, namely local municipalities. The Structures Act did not distinguish between urban and rural local government. This legislation both strengthened the role of districts and proposed one integrated form of non-metropolitan local government (Cameron 2001; Pycroft 2002). This had important implications for demarcation, which will be discussed later in the chapter.

Table 4.1  *Types and numbers of municipalities*

| Category A | 6 | |
|---|---|---|
| Category B | 232 | (of which 8 were cross-boundary local municipalities) |
| Category C | 46 | (of which 7 were cross-boundary district municipalities) |
| Total | 284 | |

Source: MDB (2000a)

The final demarcation of boundaries agreed to by the MDB is shown in Table 4.1. Whereas the 1994 demarcation exercise led to the creation of 843 local government structures, the later demarcation exercise consolidated these to 284 municipalities, a few of which crossed provincial borders.

## The development of demarcation legislation

### THE GREEN PAPER ON LOCAL GOVERNMENT

What type of research informed the demarcation policy? This author was approached to be the technical consultant on demarcation for the Green Paper on Local Government. A major part of the brief was to look at international models of demarcation. The gist of the report was included in the Green Paper on Local Government (Ministry of Provincial Affairs and Constitutional Development 1997). The Green Paper listed some of the most prominent international approaches to demarcation:

- Functional approaches which derived boundaries from the optimal area for which particular areas should be delivered, for example water catchment areas. This approach aims to minimise externalities and spillovers that occur in the provision of particular services. The problem is that different functions, for example water, electricity, and health, have different optimal areas and some prioritisation is required.
- Socio-geographic (socio-economic) approaches analyse spatial behaviour in order to understand social, economic and cultural linkages between and within local areas. An advantage of this approach is that abutting fringe areas are not excluded from the town/city whose infrastructure or services contribute to such development. The problem is that it is difficult to ascertain the 'cut-off' point between socio-economically dependent areas.
- Economies of scale approaches are about the need to ensure that there are high enough thresholds (population and/or territory) for municipal services. It is held that local government efficiency will be improved by enlarging their jurisdictions.
- Institutional approaches focus on administrative and financial viability and the need to ensure that each municipality has a viable tax base.

Although the White Paper on Local Government did not specifically indicate any approach, it was clearly influenced by the socio-geographic model.

### THE WHITE PAPER ON LOCAL GOVERNMENT

This theme of demarcation approaches was taken up in the White Paper on Local Government wherein it is argued that there was a need to create municipal institutions that recognised the linkages between urban and rural settlements. The White Paper had shown a clear preference for the socio-geographic demarcation approach mentioned in the previous section and it is worth discussing some of the research that went into the White Paper process that underpinned this model.

The socio-geographic approach attempts to correlate local government boundaries with their respective interdependent socio-economic areas (Cameron 1999a). This is due to the belief that when government areas no longer correspond to spatial behaviour, such as economic and social linkages of communities, then this often leads to the reform of local government systems (Smith 1985).

The socio-geographic approach attempts to map the areas of influence of urban areas by analysing economic and social activity, showing the socio-economically interdependent areas for which cities provide services and financial facilities. This requires a great deal of knowledge, not only about the spatial distribution of settlements, but also about the spatial patterns of socio-economic activity. This requires systematic research into behavioural relationships between spatially-defined groups; economic transactions; employment catchment areas, most notably commuter patterns; spending patterns; cultural linkages and recreational habits (Smith 1985, 1993).

Another important component of the White Paper research was Bennett's typology of bounded municipalities (1989). Bennett's approach is a useful way of operationalising this socio-geographic approach. Firstly, he introduces the concept of 'truly-bounded'. Here, there is direct correlation between socio-economic activity spaces and administrative structures. More commonly, administrative structures are 'under-bounded': the activity space crosses over many local government boundaries with resultant 'spillover' problems – when the administrative size of municipalities is less than the range of socio-economic activities of many of its citizens. 'Over-bounding' occurs where the activity space is only a small part of an administrative division (also see Meligrana 2004); when the administrative size of muncipalities exceeds the range of socio-economic activities of many of its citizens. Local government reforms in countries such as Britain, Sweden and Eastern Europe have been influenced by the 'truly-bounded' concept. The less developed the social and economic life of the community, the easier it is to identify the 'natural' boundaries of communities (Smith 1993).

There are problems in achieving 'truly-bounded' administrative spaces. For example, there is no consensus about the level of aggregation of preferences and activity spaces that is required. Another problem is the frequency of journeys and activities – some are frequent, while others are infrequent. There are also different types of activities, such as commuting, recreation and shopping. The functional concept therefore tends to increase administrative size beyond the range of normal activities of the majority of people. As a result, 'over-bounding' is a frequent outcome of reforms based on activity spaces (Bennett 1989; Sharpe 1995; Cameron 1999a).

## THE LOCAL GOVERNMENT MUNICIPAL DEMARCATION ACT

The Local Government Municipal Demarcation Act of 1998 (RSA 1998b) was lifted out of the White Paper on Local Government process and 'fast-tracked' because of the constitutional requirement that all local government boundaries had to be demarcated before the December 2000 elections. This Act was the major policy instrument for demarcation and was arguably the most important transformative piece of local government legislation. This was because it was the major policy instrument for dismantling segregated local government.

## The Municipal Demarcation Board

The 1996 Constitution required that municipal boundaries should be demarcated by an independent Board and this principle of independence was embodied in the Demarcation Act. The appointment of a single national Board involved a change from nine provincial Boards. This was supported by this author in his Green Paper submission (Cameron 1997). It was argued that it would ensure uniform application of policy and better coordination, allow the concentration of limited expertise in demarcation, and be less costly than the previous system of nine provincial Boards. It was also felt that removing demarcation from provincial control would prevent future gerrymandering. This decision was also supported by the ANC for political reasons, which felt that a national Board could promote transformation more strongly.

The appointment procedure conformed to the independence requirements. Advertisements were put in newspapers calling for applicants with relevant local government experience. Public interviews were held with shortlisted candidates by a selection panel headed by the Deputy President of the Constitutional Court, Justice Pius Langa. The President, Nelson Mandela, made 11 appointments from the 14 names given to him. There was one representative from each province along with a chairperson and a vice-chairperson (Cameron 1999b). All the appointees were part-time except for the chairperson, Dr Mike Sutcliffe, who was a full-time member.

Unlike the provincial Boards, the MDB was the final decision-making body when it came to the demarcation of boundaries. The system of advisory provincial Boards making recommendations, provincial ministers of local government deciding in conjunction with provincial committees and deadlocks then being sent to special electoral courts, had turned out to be cumbersome and contributed to the delay of the 1995/96 local government elections. The decision-making process was now crisper. Provision was made for an appeal mechanism enabling stakeholders who are aggrieved by the determination of boundaries to appeal against the decision. Appeals also had to be considered by the MDB.

It is rare in international terms for politicians to grant decision-making powers of this sort to an independent structure, so the MDB was novel in many aspects and unprecedented in Africa where there is a weak tradition of local government (Cameron 1999b; Olowu 2003).

In January 1998 the then Department of Constitutional Development (subsequently Provincial and Local Government) created the Demarcation Steering Committee to undertake the basic, technical work for demarcation (MDB 2004). This was a low-key body that prepared the way for the MDB, which was formally established on 1 February 1999.

## The determination of outer boundaries

A paper by the chairperson, Dr Sutcliffe (1999), at the MDB's inaugural meeting indicated some of the inconsistencies of demarcation in the interim phase:

- Local governments were largely defined according to subjective needs and preferences, rather than on the basis of any national norms and standards. For example, in certain provinces there were some TLCs with fewer than 100 registered voters, whereas in the same provinces, some urban communities with over 15 000 voters had no primary local government. In the case of district councils, they ranged from some 1 984 voters to over 1.5 million voters in size.
- There were major disparities in council sizes. In the cases of TLCs, the average number of registered voters per councillor ranged from 10 to 7 192 voters.
- Approximately one-third of all TLCs and rural councils were quite small and had fewer than 2 000 voters.

Furthermore, problems emerged around situations where communities were split by provincial boundaries.

Sections 24 and 25 of the Demarcation Act also laid down the criteria that the Board had to take into account (RSA 1998b). These criteria are shown in Annexure 2. Section 24 deals with demarcation objectives and Section 25 lists the factors that have to be taken into account when determining municipal boundaries. Synthesising Section 24, it states that when a Board determines a municipal boundary its objective must be to establish an area that would enable the municipality for that area to fulfil its constitutional obligations, provide effective local governance and integrated development, and have a tax base as inclusive as possible of users of municipal services in the municipality.

These demarcation objectives are largely lifted from Section 152 of the Constitution, which lays down the objectives of local government. There is a strong emphasis on the need to promote socio-economic rights, which is an important element that the Board needs to take into account when demarcating boundaries.

Section 25 lists the factors that have to be taken into account when determining municipal boundaries. Synthesising Section 25, the factors concern, *inter alia*, the interdependence of people, communities and economics; the need for cohesive, integrated and unfragmented areas, including metropolitan areas; financial viability; and the administrative capacity of the municipality to perform municipal functions efficiently and effectively.

There was no weighting of the criteria and the MDB had discretion on how to interpret them. There was, however, a strong focus on interdependence of people, communities and economics, including employment, commuting, spending, commercial and industrial linkages, and amenities. The issue of bounded municipalities featured prominently in the MDB's deliberations.

## Metropolitan government boundaries

The task of the MDB was initially to determine the boundaries of metropolitan authorities, taking into account the definition of a Category A municipality (which was a definition of a metropolitan area) in the Municipal Structures Act. Section 2 of the Act stated that areas that must have single Category A municipalities are those that can reasonably be regarded as:
(a) A conurbation featuring:
  (i)   areas of high population density;
  (ii)  an intensive movement of people, goods, and services;
  (iii) extensive development; and
  (iv)  multiple business districts and industrial areas;
(b) A centre of economic activity with a complex and diverse economy;
(c) A single area for which integrated development is desirable; and
(d) Having strong interdependent social and economic linkages between its constituent units.

It was originally the responsibility of the Minister of Provincial Affairs and Constitutional Development to determine whether an area should be an A category metropolitan authority. The then opposition-controlled Western Cape and KwaZulu-Natal argued that the Structures Act encroached unconstitutionally on the powers of local government and of provinces and took the matter to the Constitutional Court, the final arbitrator of intergovernmental relations. The major objection of these two provinces was the imposition of unitary-tier structures in metropolitan areas. The court ruled that the application of criteria for metropolitan areas formed part of the boundary determination, which through the Constitution is vested in the Demarcation Board. This meant that the declaration of metropolitan areas by the minister was invalid. This judgement was aptly captured in a local government publication: *Provinces vs Structures Act Demarcation Board walks off with the spoils* (Constitutional Court 1999; Local Government Bulletin 1999; Cameron 2000).

The Act was accordingly amended and the MDB was given the powers to determine whether an area must have a Category A municipality and thereafter to determine boundaries.

The research process coordinated by the MDB involved an evaluation of the existing TMCs and TLCs. Three research reports were compiled by its Urban Conurbations working group with the support of a consultant. These research findings indicated that some non-metropolitan TLCs such as Port Elizabeth showed greater metropolitan characteristics than some existing metropolitan governments such as Khayalami and Lekoa/Vaal. Based on this the MDB developed a strategic framework for assessing the criteria (MDB 1999a, 1999b). The MDB's research was originally based on the need to advise the Minister of Provincial and Local Government on the advantages and disadvantages of declaring possible nodal points as metropolitan areas. After the Constitutional Court hearing the determination of metropolitan areas became the responsibility of the MDB. The MDB accordingly used the same set of data but abandoned the notion of nodal points and set about determining boundaries directly.

The MDB created six metropolitan authorities in the country. It confirmed that Greater Johannesburg, Cape Metro, Greater Durban and Greater Pretoria met all the criteria for metropolitan areas, although there were boundary changes to all of these local governments. The MDB found that neither the Khayalami nor the Lekoa/Vaal metros met the requirement for a metro. In the case of Khayalami, the MDB argued that the area was not 'truly-bounded' in that there was not a consistent correlation between activity spaces and administrative structures. In particular, it felt that there were stronger linkages with Johannesburg. In the case of Lekoa/Vaal, the MDB concluded that it was too small and that its level of economic activity was comparable to that of large TLCs (MDB 1999b, 1999c).

The MDB did, however, create two new metros. The East Rand metro was created to the east of Johannesburg and consisted of a number of previously independent municipalities. While it had no single traditional core, it was felt that in many aspects, including size, density and social and economic activity, the area conformed to the requirements of a metro. The MDB also established a new metro in the Port-Elizabeth–Uitenhage–Despatch industrial complex in the Eastern Cape. It was felt that there was sufficient economic interdependence between these areas to warrant including them in a single metro and that the creation of such an entity would facilitate growth in the region (MDB 1999b).

The MDB felt that the best means of determining the interdependence of people, communities and economies was through commuting patterns. This was an attempt to create truly-bounded municipalities. This was because commuting is probably the best single measure of the relationship between human settlements on the one hand, and employment, spending and amenity usage patterns on the other. The MDB was of the view that a metropolitan or local council should encompass at least 50 per cent of all people who live, work and shop within that area (MDB 1999b).

The MDB's statistics for metropolitan governments indicated that they encompass areas in which people, communities and the economy are interdependent. For example, in Cape Town, 95 per cent of people who work in the area also reside in the metropolitan area of jurisdiction. In Durban the figure was 86 per cent, in East Rand 87 per cent, 84 per cent in Pretoria and 64 per cent in Johannesburg (MDB 2000b). Johannesburg's figures were perhaps low, but what the MDB found was that there was spillover between the three metros in Gauteng (East Rand, Pretoria and Johannesburg), particularly between Johannesburg and East Rand where it was difficult to determine a precise boundary. As the South African Cities Network *State of the Cities Report* (2004: 24) states, these three cities – along with two abutting local municipalities – constitute a virtually continuous urban extent of some 8.6 million people. This option of a single urban region was never considered. It would have meant creating a municipality that would be almost as big as the province, which was an unrealistic option. There were also concerns about whether such a municipality would have the capacity to service such a large population.

## DISTRICT MUNICIPALITIES' BOUNDARIES

The MDB, through its district working group and with the support of consultants, undertook research for district boundaries (C municipalities). It released a general framework for nodal points for district boundaries simultaneously with metropolitan boundaries. This report argued that while there were well-defined guidelines for defining metropolitan boundaries in legislation, the criteria for district boundaries were less prescriptive. Districts were also more diverse than metropolitan areas which made it more difficult to develop a national framework. The MDB (1999a) suggested four principles which should underpin the determination of nodal points for districts:

- There should be functional linkages showing a coherent social and economic base around which the district would coalesce. This would include looking at spending patterns, sectors of economic activity and migration.
- The districts should not be too large: in settled areas a radius of 50–100 kilometres was utilised.
- While the population of districts should not be too large, for economies of scale it was felt districts should have a base population of at least 100 000 persons.
- Wherever possible, there should be some coherence to the economic and social base of districts.

The MDB also tried to create bounded municipalities for districts although it was not always easy to do so.

## LOCAL MUNICIPALITIES

When it came to the demarcation of local (B) municipalities, the MDB decided on the following principles, based on Sections 24 and 25 of the Demarcation Act. The full text is shown in Annexure 3. The principles were geographical continuity and coherence, capacity development, resource sharing, manageable size, and functionality. These principles attempted to redress the effects of apartheid-era displacement and made provision for future growth.

However, in practice there were two main components to the MDB's approach to demarcating local boundaries. Firstly, based on international and local experience, commuting and to a lesser extent shopping from other cities and fringe areas gave an indication where people belong in terms of boundary demarcation. Secondly, the application of the Group Areas Act and 'homelands' development strategies resulted in an attenuated settlement pattern in and around urban areas, most notably the relocation of poor communities to the fringes of the urban areas. Commuting patterns were a good indicator of the spatial dislocations caused by apartheid. Although the MDB did say that these factors have to be balanced by other criteria such as administrative capacity and financial viability, these latter factors played a minor role in demarcation (MDB 1999b). It can be seen that the MDB was strongly influenced by the socio-geographic approach with its emphasis on economic linkages.

The MDB accordingly came up with integrated urban–rural municipalities as a way of redressing rural poverty. This was seen as a way of redressing apartheid social patterns by including poor black people from rural areas and ex-bantustans in towns and in so doing implementing a key goal of the White Paper.

CROSS-BOUNDARY MUNICIPALITIES

The Constitution was amended to make provision for an Act of Parliament, the Cross-Boundary Municipalities Act of 2000 (RSA 2000a), authorising the establishment of cross-boundary municipalities, which was duly legislated for. The reason for this was that the hastily drawn provincial boundaries that were put in place in 1994 had in some cases divided settlements.

After conducting its research, the MDB noted that there were a number of areas in the country where socio-economically interdependent areas, including different parts of the same town, straddled provincial boundaries. It made recommendations to provincial and national governments on possible cross-border municipalities such as Kuruman–Mothibistad, Umzimkulu–Mount Currie, Bushbuckridge–Kruger National Park, and East Rand Metropolitan Area–Mpumalanga (MDB 1999b: 11–13). Principled agreement was eventually reached between provinces for the proposed cross-boundary areas with the exception of KwaZulu-Natal, where the then majority party, the IFP, indicated that it was opposed to the linking of Umzimkulu with Mount Currie in the Eastern Cape and this proposal was shelved.

However, while there was principled agreement amongst provinces for most of the cross-boundary municipalities recommendations, getting consensus around operational issues – such as which province would administer and financially support such cross-areas – has proved difficult. They have generally been recognised to be a failure and were abolished in late 2005. All cross-boundary municipalities were consolidated into single provinces.

## The delimitation of wards

The electoral system for the final phase of local government was based on an integrated PR and ward representation formula. Metropolitan councils and local municipalities with wards consisted of 50 per cent ward councillors and 50 per cent PR councillors (on party lists nominated by political parties or groupings of civics/independents). District municipalities consisted of 40 per cent PR councillors elected directly by all voters in the district areas and 60 per cent of councillors elected indirectly by local municipalities in that district municipality. These councillors had to be elected from party lists to proportionately represent parties in the district municipality.

In the final phase of local government the delimitation of local government wards was initially the responsibility of the Independent Electoral Commission (IEC). The IEC, using a Geographic Information System (GIS), divided the country into 86 000 enumerator areas, each containing between 120 and 150 households. These areas were combined into 14 484 districts, purportedly determined by limits on the walking distance from a polling station (Lodge 1999: 28–29). However, the IEC voting districts were technical constructs and in many cases did not conform to local perceptions of community.

The Municipal Demarcation Act removed the responsibility for the demarcation of wards from the IEC and gave it to the newly created MDB. The policy-makers felt that the specialist Demarcation Board would best carry out the delimitation of wards.

A comparison of the average number of registered voters and the average number of seats in the interim-phase municipalities by the MDB revealed that there were substantial provincial differences. For example, rural councils in the Northern Cape had on average less than 2 000 voters while rural councils in the Northern Province (now Limpopo) had on average 4 000 voters. Gauteng had very large TLCs (average close to 90 000) while the Western Cape (average 5 331) and Northern Cape (average 4 745) had very small TLCs.

There were similar variations between provinces in the number of councillors per registered voters. A comparison of the average number of registered voters per councillor between provinces reveals some interesting statistics:
- In the Eastern Cape, Western Cape, KwaZulu-Natal and the Northern Cape, over 50 per cent of the councils had less than 500 voters per councillor.
- In the Free State and North West, over 50 per cent of the councils had between 500 and 1 000 voters per councillor.
- In Gauteng and Mpumalanga, over 50 per cent of the councils had between 1 000 and 2 000 voters per councillor. In the Northern Province, over 50 per cent of the councils had over 2 000 voters per councillor. (MDB 2000c)

## THE LEGAL PROCESS

In terms of the Municipal Structures Act, the Minister of Provincial and Local Government published a formula for the number of councillors for municipal councils. The formula had to be based on the number of voters registered on that municipality's segment of the national common voters' roll.

The provincial ministers of local government could decide on a deviation from the formula and increase or decrease the number of councillors due to reasons such as distance, responsiveness and accountability of councillors, and affordability. A deviation could not exceed 3 of the number decided if 30 or fewer councillors had been determined for the municipality in terms of the formula. A council of fewer than 7 could not be decreased. If more than 30 councillors had been determined for the municipality in terms of the formula, the deviation could be 10 per cent of this number.

The MDB then delimited each municipality with seven or more councillors into wards, taking into account the criteria listed in the next section. Finally, the MDB published its delimitation of wards. It had to allow 14 days for considering objections (MDB 2000d, 2001).

## DELIMITATION CRITERIA

The MDB had to consider certain criteria, a number of which were logistical. The criteria are shown in Annexure 4. The two most important criteria were, firstly, that the number of registered voters in each ward could not vary by more than 15 per cent of the norm. The norm was determined by dividing the total number of registered voters by the number of wards to ensure that each ward had approximately the same number of voters. Secondly, fragmentation of communities had to be avoided as far as possible (MDB 2000d).

## THE MINISTER'S FORMULA

The important electoral timetable issue was that the MDB could not commence with the delimitation of wards until the minister had determined the councillor formula (Ministry for Provincial and Local Government 2000). The ministry released its draft policy framework in February 2000. It stated that there were 11 883 councillors in South Africa. There were, however, no existing norms in terms of the number of voters per councillor. It suggested that there were two options for rationalising the number of councillors. It could either choose a specific proportion by which the overall number should be reduced or it could come up with an approach that allows national norms, but allows for variations depending on settlement patterns. The draft policy framework showed a preference for the second approach. It came up with three options for the determination of councillors in metropolitan areas, namely, 'maximum', 'middle-range' and 'minimum' models. It provided a similar formula for local municipalities. For district municipalities, it proposed a range of options, depending on the number of voters. It did recommend that because district municipalities are primarily indirectly elected structures, they should not be too large (Ministry for Provincial and Local Government 2000).

The minister's final formula was released in April 2000 (RSA 2000b). The formula was a technical document and will not be repeated here. It can be said that the minister went for a middle-range option, which meant that the cut in councillors was not as drastic as the reduction in municipalities. Provincial and Local Government Minister Sydney Mufamadi said that 'we do not want to have a vast number of people that feel underrepresented' (*Business Day* 08.02.2000).

In most cases, provincial ministers of local government, under political pressure from existing councillors competing for reduced seats, increased the number of councillors by the maximum allowable. In total there was a 27 per cent reduction in councillors from 11 368 to 8 951. This can be compared to the 197 per cent reduction in outer boundaries, from 843 municipalities to 284.

Table 4.2 *Councillor breakdown*

| Province | Ward 1996 | Proportional representation 1996 | Total 1996 | Total 2000 | Wards 2000 | Cross-boundary municipalities included* |
|---|---|---|---|---|---|---|
| Eastern Cape | 789 | 1 146 | 1 935 | 1 449 | 602 | |
| Free State | 844 | 464 | 1 308 | 732 | 291 | |
| Gauteng | 559 | 484 | 1 043 | 983 | 446 | Cross-Boundary Local Council (CBLC)2, CBLC8, East Rand, Pretoria |
| Mpumalanga | 598 | 504 | 1 102 | 912 | 393 | Cross-Boundary District Council (CBDC)4, CBDC6 |
| Northern Cape | 466 | 345 | 811 | 388 | 162 | CBDC1, CBDC7 |
| Northern Province | 364 | 195 | 559 | 1 102 | 448 | CBLC3, CBLC5 |
| North West | 380 | 375 | 755 | 828 | 337 | |
| Western Cape | 959 | 695 | 1 654 | 781 | 330 | |
| KwaZulu-Natal | 993 | 1 208 | 2 201 | 1 776 | 742 | |
| Totals | 5 952 | 5 416 | 11 368 | 8 951 | 3 751 | |

Source: MDB (2001: 17)
* CBDC and CBLC refer to the names of the councils.

## THE WARD DELIMITATION EXERCISE

The wards were delimited at breakneck speed. Firstly, there were delays to the electoral timetable. Secondly, the wards were not created from a clean slate. The census enumerator areas were used by the IEC, at great expense, as the basis of voting districts, which in turn were the building blocks of wards. If these enumerator areas were discarded, the IEC would have to re-register voters at the cost of R200–R400 million. This was because voters had to register at voting stations within voting districts. If voting districts were split, voters had to re-register. The MDB accordingly took a policy decision to avoid splitting voting districts as far as possible.

However, this turned out to be difficult to implement in practice. As noted, one of the ward requirements was that wards could not vary by more than 15 per cent of the norm. In some cases, this requirement could only be met by splitting voting districts. Furthermore, in non-metropolitan local government, it was particularly difficult to implement this ward formula. As pointed out, non-metropolitan local government consisted of both urban and rural local government. Conforming to this 15 per cent requirement in some municipalities entailed combining far-flung rural communities with portions of urban towns.

The casualty in this process was the ward criterion 'as far as possible to avoid the fragmentation of communities'. The MDB did not debate the controversial sociological issue of what a community is, mainly because of time constraints. It did not really matter because the constraints of the voting districts and the 15 per cent norm were major impediments against unifying communities. In addition, some of the IEC's enumerator areas had already split communities. This led to many complaints that the Board was in fact splitting communities (*Cape Argus* 01.05.2000; *Constantiaberg Bulletin* 27.04.2000; *False Bay Echo* 04.05.2000; *Southern Suburbs Tatler* 04.05.2000).

Because the electoral system was ultimately determined proportionately, it was not possible to gerrymander wards. Nevertheless, political parties disputed the ward delimitation process. When quizzed on this issue, one party organiser acknowledged that in terms of political power ward delimitation did not matter, but added: 'Control of a ward is far more preferable to a proportional representation seat. It gives you a constituency and linkages to local communities.'

The Board was accused of gerrymandering in favour of the ANC (*Business Day* 18.04.2000; *The Star* 02.05.2000; Lodge 2002), but in reality, given the constraints mentioned earlier, it was more a case of trying to put a giant jigsaw puzzle together. It was not nor could it be a rational process. There was no reference to international models of ward redistricting. The IEC's enumerator areas and the 15 per cent deviation formula meant that it was really a case of finding out what works. In some cases, it was only possible to stay within the 15 per cent limitation by splitting enumerator areas. In addition, the MDB had to delimit wards at undue haste in order to conform to the electoral timetable. This led to complaints from communities that the process was being bulldozed through (*Cape Argus* 16.03.2000; *Constantiaberg Bulletin* 20.04.2000).

Finally, one of the issues to be considered within divided societies is whether to delimit ward boundaries on racial grounds or to create integrated multi-ethnic wards

(Allen 1990). The Board did try to create integrated wards where possible as a way of breaking down apartheid settlement patterns. However, this was limited because, as pointed out, in-between the enumerator areas and the 15 per cent deviation, there was not much room to manoeuvre.

### THE NEW DEMARCATION BOARD

The second MDB commenced office on 1 February 2004. It is examining whether there should be an increase in the number of metropolitan municipalities. The MDB is unlikely to create any new metropolitan governments before the next local government elections. The issue of the failure of cross-boundary municipalities has been mentioned. Gauteng is trying to shed its rural areas to neighbouring provinces and become a province of metropolitan authorities only. This has run into resistance and may not be implemented in time for the next local government elections.

The major task of the new Board has been to delimit wards for the next elections. This is because the number of registered voters has increased, which in a number of cases has led to the 15 per cent norm being exceeded. This has led to an increase of wards in many municipalities and, because of the knock-on effect, has necessitated the complete redelimitation of wards.

## Evaluation of the demarcation process

The evaluation of the demarcation process refers to the Board's policy, the influence of public participation on demarcation policy, resistance to change, and the independence of the Board.

### Evaluation of the Board's policy

Due to time constraints arising from the electoral timetable, the MDB did not debate appropriate theoretical approaches to demarcation that could guide the process. Nevertheless, the MDB was influenced implicitly by some of these approaches, most notably the socio-geographic approach with its emphasis on creating 'truly-bounded' municipalities where boundaries correspond with socio-economic activity spaces (Cameron 2004).

The MDB primarily used commuting as a means of dealing with the illogical spatial apartheid distortions in an attempt to create 'truly-bounded' boundaries. While this approach was largely uncontroversial in metropolitan areas, it has turned out to be one of the central issues in post-2000 non-metropolitan local government. When it came to the actual determination of the local municipalities, the time pressure more than anything else led to inconsistencies in the way the research was used and ultimately how boundaries were demarcated. There was simply not the time to carefully consider alternative demarcation options.

For Category B municipalities, the Board also used minimum area sizes of $3\,500\ \text{km}^2$ as a guideline. Underpinning this decision was the contestable economies-of-scale argument, which posits that efficiency will be enhanced by enlarging local government areas. Most literature suggests that there is not a positive relationship between size and performance (Smith 1985, 1993; Keating 1995; Cameron 1999a).

The major criticism is that many of the MDB's boundaries are 'over-bounded'. Given the symbiotic relationship between urban and rural areas exacerbated by apartheid settlement patterns, there were perhaps good reasons why the MDB went for this integrated urban–rural policy option. One must also remember that the adoption of the socio-geographic approach was an attempt to embody a goal of the White Paper. At one level, many of these boundaries appear to conform to the socio-economic interdependent areas. The problem, in terms of service delivery, is that the greater the degree of interdependence, the larger a municipality will become. It was pointed out that this socio-geographic approach to demarcation tends to increase administrative size beyond the range of normal activities of the majority of people.

This in some cases has arguably led to 'over-bounded' boundaries in that communities with little in common were amalgamated. Not only were peri-urban and black dormitory towns included, but in some cases deep rural areas with few linkages with urban areas were included. This not only signalled a retreat from the more logical settlement pattern approach, but has also led some local municipalities to complain that their areas of jurisdiction were too big to service properly. Many local managers said that their municipalities were stretched financially and administratively in delivering services to the vast rural areas that were now part of urban municipalities. Research by Atkinson (2003) and Cameron (2003) suggests that some of these B municipalities, such as Mbombela (Nelspruit) and Umlathuze (Richards Bay), are too big to service their rural hinterlands.

This issue had reared its head during the demarcation process. The Department of Finance had opposed the MDB's preliminary proposals. A memorandum by the Director-General of Finance argued that the MDB's proposed boundaries would weaken the fiscal position of non-metropolitan cities and towns structurally and, as a consequence, constrain rather than enhance their ability to raise capital and develop infrastructure (water, power, etc.), which is their key responsibility. Already before demarcation, the long-term debt market had largely dried up (Department of Finance 2000). The concern was that the resultant diminished creditworthiness would mean that the only source of capital available in some municipalities would be government transfers.

The department undertook an analysis of three existing towns in which it was shown that non-metropolitan towns (B municipalities) generally would face a marked structural decline in their fiscal position as a result of the inclusion of considerably disadvantaged poor rural areas into their jurisdictions. The MDB was asked to revisit its demarcation of non-metropolitan towns and cities (Department of Finance 2000).

What is seemingly becoming urban myth is that the MDB did not respond to the department's criticism and more generally ignored the question of financial viability. This mistake is repeated by Van Donk and Pieterse (see their chapter in this book), who use interviews from secondary sources and do not draw on publicly available primary MDB documentation.[1] In fact there was a substantial rebuttal by the MDB, which disputed the methodology used by the department. It argued that the department's report gave no indication of what power and functions were being analysed against available income; ignored the fact that the smaller the boundaries, the greater would be the spatial inequalities and the greater the correlation to the old apartheid order; and incorrectly presumed that boundary demarcation is a primary determinant of financial viability and creditworthiness. The MDB accused the department of boundary determinism because of the latter's inference that boundaries are the prime determinant of creditworthiness and financial viability. It did not change its boundary proposals significantly (MDB 2000d).

The MDB also responded to the department by emphasising that it had never stated that all its municipalities would be financially viable. Its own research showed that 102 new municipalities – mostly B categories in the former independent and self-governing territories – are weak and have limited financial resources. Given spatial inequalities arising from apartheid underdevelopment, the task of making all municipalities viable was simply impossible. This was exacerbated by lack of finality on national financial policy for local government. The MDB made a number of recommendations for extra sources of revenue, including a surcharge on personal income tax and a substantial increase in the equitable share (MDB 2000c). This was not accepted by national government, which had adopted the financially restrictive Growth, Employment and Redistribution strategy as its macroeconomic framework.

What this meant is that many local governments were established without the extra sources of revenue recommended by the MDB.

### The influence of public participation on demarcation policy

Due to the tight electoral timetable, the MDB had to demarcate boundaries in an extremely short time period. There was no systematic analysis of theoretical boundary approaches along the lines of the Redcliffe Maude Commission in England in 1969 or even the Western Cape Provincial Demarcation Board in 1994/95 (Cameron 1999a).

Due to this time frame, the MDB held a couple of hastily arranged internal workshops in which it worked out its general approach to demarcation. It later developed more specific frameworks for Category A, B and C municipalities. There was a reasonable period for the development of metropolitan and district frameworks, but extremely limited time to demarcate local municipalities and delimit wards. Arguably, this limited time period contibuted to the inconsistencies in the way that B municipalities were demarcated.

Meetings were held with a number of stakeholders where the process of the demarcation research for the demarcation of boundaries was outlined and draft and final boundaries were presented. Important stakeholders consulted included the National Parliamentary Portfolio Committee on Provincial and Local Government, the minister and officials of the Department of Provincial and Local Government, provincial ministers of local government, the South African Local Government Association and its provincial affiliates, Houses of Traditional Leaders, national departments, political parties in the legislatures, key private-sector agencies and key non-governmental organisations (MDB 2000b). In addition, although it was not a statutory requirement, the MDB held a number of public meetings for its Category B hearings.

The MDB invited comment on the determination of all its boundaries. There were 787 Category A and C submissions and 816 Category B submissions. Sixty-five per cent of the Board's A and C submissions were from the three wealthier provinces – Western Cape, KwaZulu-Natal and Gauteng – and public contribution tailed off for the poorer provinces. For B submissions, most of the contributions (67.6 per cent) came from the Western Cape, Eastern Cape and KwaZulu-Natal. There was a similar pattern of contribution, although there was more public input, from the Eastern Cape, a large if poor province (Gauteng only had a few B municipalities). Input came from a variety of organisations including political parties, ratepayers' organisations, civic organisations, business chambers and traditional leaders. After the MDB's provisional boundaries were published, provision was made for public objections. In total there were 750 objections received (MDB 2001: 10, 12, 15).

One problem with this participation process was the limited time given to comment on these proposals. There were also complaints that the MDB failed to listen to community concerns. The demarcation process was certainly not well understood amongst the public. Part of the problem was that many of these stakeholders did not convey information gleaned at these workshops to their constituencies. The lack of knowledge on the ground about the demarcation process can partially be attributed to communication problems within some of the above-mentioned organisations.

However, there was perhaps a more fundamental issue. Public participation is a cornerstone of the final Constitution and is integral to the principle of developmental local government. Yet public participation operated a bit differently at the level of demarcation. The demarcation frameworks were based on the criteria listed in Sections 24 and 25 of the Act, which were planning, economic, geographical and other functional considerations. Good demarcation suggests that boundary choices cannot be reduced to the will of the community only, particularly when they fly against the more objective demarcation criteria (Cameron 1999a). A number of submissions were dismissed because they failed to conform to the Board's framework.

On the positive side, the MDB made extensive use of its website to enable the public to get access to information on demarcation activities and maps of boundaries. This site received over one million visitors between October 1999 and February 2000 (MDB 2004: 53). One major factor which helped facilitate the Board's demarcation was the GIS, which captured spatial data from a variety of sources, including census data from Statistics South Africa, Project Viability and municipalities.

(The MDB in fact won a 'Special Achievement in GIS award' at the Environment Systems Research Initiative annual conference in San Diego, California, in July 2002. It was selected to receive this award from over 100 000 websites worldwide [MDB 2004: 51].)

The role of consultants also had to be considered. Because of the tight time frame the MDB had to begin demarcating before they had offices or staff. This meant they had to rely extensively on consultants. While the MDB's primary consultants were of a high quality, some of those who did fieldwork were of a poor quality. A number of demarcation investigations were carried out by consultants with mixed results. Many consultants ignored these demarcation criteria and simply looked at community consensus as a basis for their reports. Also, consultants had to draft justification reports for each demarcated municipality. The quality of some of these reports was so poor that the Board decided not to make any of them public (MDB 1999e). This led to complaints from the public that the MDB was not transparent in making decisions (Cameron 2004). This probably contributed to some decisions being made around B boundaries that were not properly grounded in research.

*Resistance to change*

Local government boundary reform is often met with heavy resistance. There are strong vested interests at stake in boundary reorganisation. Such reforms affect the interests of politicians, bureaucrats and residents (Leemans 1970; Keating 1995; Leach & Stoker 1997). Metropolitan governments have been particularly contested given the scale of such entities (Barlow 1991). It has already been pointed out that the metropolitan boundaries were disputed in the 1994/95 demarcation exercise (Cameron 1999a). The 1999/2000 demarcation process was also heavily contested. For example, in Durban, the question of traditional areas was a hotly contested issue, as it had been during the 1995/96 elections. Pillay (1999) has shown how traditional leaders' concern about losing functions and powers to local government had stalled the finalisation of the metropolitan boundary in 1995/96. This was still a pressing issue during the 1999/2000 demarcation. The Greater Durban urban landscape consisted of intertwined urban and informal areas. The MDB argued that many of the people who live in informal settlements located in tribal areas do not enjoy the benefit of representation and servicing by the municipalities in which they work and shop. The general poverty in such traditional areas was in fact exacerbated by their exclusion from the Durban metro area. The MDB included some traditional areas into the Durban metro as part of the 1999/2000 demarcation exercise (these were in fact largely the disputed areas of 1995/96 which were excluded from the metro). Around 5 per cent additional population was added to the metro (MDB 1999e).

### Independence of the Board

How independent was the MDB? There was one representative from each province except for KwaZulu-Natal and Northern Province (subsequently Limpopo), which each had two. However, Board members were not mandated representatives. It has already been pointed out that they were appointed on the basis of expertise. Some provincial ministers did think that the role of Board members was to implement their proposals. The overwhelming view in the MDB was, however, that it was a national body there to transform apartheid boundaries and it was not politically accountable to provincial ministers (MDB 2004).

Another contentious issue was the role of the chairperson, Mike Sutcliffe. Sutcliffe was a high-powered ANC politician before he was appointed to the Board (he was previously a member of the KwaZulu-Natal executive legislature). The criticism of opposition parties, most notably the Democratic Alliance and the IFP, was that the MDB, through Sutcliffe, was a Trojan Horse for ANC policy.

In reality Sutcliffe focused on the big picture and allowed Board members a great deal of operational autonomy to determine the boundaries of their respective provinces. While the question of metropolitan areas was probably approved by high-level ANC political structures before being finally approved by the MDB, there was less interest in non-metropolitan boundaries, including secondary cities. For example, outside of the Cape Metropolitan Area I had a great deal of discretion to determine boundaries within the context of the MDB's framework. It is also worth mentioning that the Board never voted. All decisions were reached by consensus (MDB 2004).

### Conclusion

It is apparent that the demarcation exercise has given full effect to 'One city, one tax base'. It is also apparent that this was a complicated and demanding exercise and, ultimately, a rushed exercise in order to meet the 2000 election dates.

It can be concluded that there was a reasonable amount of demarcation research that went into the White Paper and the Municipal Demarcation Act. However, once the MDB began operating, due to the electoral time frame the research became more of the 'quick and dirty' variety. Some systematic research went into the framework for metropolitan and district municipalities but the framework for local municipalities and wards was rushed.

It could be argued that the end result of all of this was that the MDB's research was, particularly for local municipalities, not as systematic or thorough as it could have been. However, it was recognised in government circles that the MDB, due to its rigid adherence to electoral deadlines, was probably responsible more than any other organisation for keeping the December 2000 elections on track.

Certainly, the jury is out on whether the MDB made a major mistake when demarcating local municipalities' (B) boundaries. Perhaps the MDB's most defining contribution to urban policy was in fact to deny the existence of something specifically urban and create integrated urban–rural municipalities. This has led some urban observers to argue that the MDB has created 'over-bounded' municipalities where urban core areas are struggling both administratively and financially to serve their rural hinterlands. However, one must avoid boundary determinism whereby there is a temptation to blame boundaries for all of local government's ills. Cameron (2003) argues that there is evidence suggesting that the biggest problem facing municipalities is the poor quality of political leadership, which is far more important than boundaries. One could also argue that the MDB's recommendations were a holistic package and that the failure of the government to accept the proposals for substantive financial relief for poorer local governments was a contributory factor to some of the problems that some local municipalities now face.

The MDB made many enemies. There were complaints about lack of public participation in policy and there was strong resistance to some of its proposals. However, this was often due to the nature of demarcation. Demarcation or delimitation boards are generally not popular anywhere in the world. Many stakeholders could not understand that the MDB was not simply there to rubber-stamp organisations' proposals, particularly when they did not conform to the Board's framework. The limited time frame also made it difficult for thorough public participation.

In conclusion it can be argued that the MDB, although controversial, made an incontrovertible contribution to dismantling the apartheid landscape in South Africa.

### Note

1    Van Donk and Pieterse respond to the criticism in their chapter in this book (see endnote 46 in Chapter 5).

## Annexure 1: Demarcation process for the 1995 elections

The nine Provincial Demarcation Boards had to take the following criteria into account:

1. Topographical and physical characteristics of the area concerned.
2. Population distribution within the area concerned.
3. Existing demarcation of areas pertaining to local government affairs and services, including existing areas of local government bodies and areas existing before 1971 as areas of such local government bodies (if any), as well as areas of regional services councils and joint service boards.
4. Existing and potential land usage, town and transport planning, including industrial, business, commercial and residential usage and planning.
5. Economy, functionality, efficiency and financial viability with regard to the administration and rendering of services within the area concerned.
6. Development potential in relation to the availability of sufficient land for a reasonably foreseeable period to meet the spatial needs of the existing and potential residents of the proposed area for their residential, business, recreational and amenity use.
7. Interdependence of and community of interest between residents in respect of residency, work, commuting and recreation.
8. The integrated urban economy as dictated by commercial, industrial and residential linkages.

(Schedule 6 of the LGTA)

## Annexure 2: The determination of outer boundaries

Section 24 of the Municipal Demarcation Act deals with demarcation objectives which are to establish an area that would:

(a) Enable the municipality for that area to fulfil its constitutional obligations, including:
    (i) the provision of democratic and accountable government for the local communities;
    (ii) the provision of services to the communities in an equitable and sustainable manner;
    (iii) the provision of social and economic development; and
    (iv) the provision of a safe and healthy environment.
(b) Enable effective local governance;
(c) Enable integrated development; and
(d) Have a tax base as inclusive as possible of users of municipal services in the municipality.

Section 25 of the Municipal Demarcation Act lists the factors (criteria) that have to be taken into account when determining municipal boundaries:

(a) The interdependence of people, communities and economics as indicated by:
    (i) existing and expected patterns of human settlement and migration;
    (ii) employment;
    (iii) commuting and dominant transport movements;
    (iv) spending;
    (v) the use of amenities, recreational facilities and infrastructure; and
    (vi) commercial and industrial linkages.
(b) The need for cohesive, integrated and unfragmented areas, including metropolitan areas;
(c) The financial viability and administrative capacity of the municipality to perform municipal functions efficiently and effectively;
(d) The need to share and redistribute financial and administrative resources;
(e) Provincial and municipal boundaries;
(f) Areas of traditional rural communities;
(g) Existing and proposed functional boundaries, including magisterial districts, health, transport, police and census enumerator boundaries;
(h) Existing and expected land use, social, economic and transport planning;
(i) The need for coordinated municipal, provincial and national programmes and services, including the needs for the administration of justice and health care;
(j) Topographical, environmental and physical characteristics of the area;
(k) The administrative consequences of its boundary demarcation on:
    (i) municipal creditworthiness;
    (ii) existing municipalities, their council members and staff; and
    (iii) any other relevant matter.
(l) The need to rationalise the total number of municipalities within different categories and of different types to achieve the objectives of effective and sustainable service delivery, financial viability and macroeconomic stability.

## Annexure 3: Local municipalities

The Demarcation Board decided on the following principles, based on Sections 24 and 25 of the Demarcation Act for local municipalities:

*Geographical continuity and coherence:* Because municipal government is so closely tied to local identity and accessibility to local representatives, rationalisation should generally follow 'nearest neighbour' principles, that is, there should be geographically coherent, consolidated Category B municipalities.

*Capacity development:* There should be a critical mass of municipal capacity (staff, assets, finances), especially where there were under-resourced municipalities.

*Resource sharing:* Wherever possible, existing municipalities should be combined with the view to realising fiscally sustainable units, with weaker areas being paired with stronger areas to achieve a sharing of existing or potential sources.

*Manageable size*: A statistically derived indicator of 3 500 km² and 80 000 persons was suggested as the possible norm for Category B municipalities. However, deviations from the norm were inevitable given the uneven geographical distribution of population and economic activity throughout the country. The Board's empirical research suggested that populations of less than 20 000 are generally undesirable for Category B municipalities given the objectives of realising economies of scale in municipalities.

*Functionality*: Amalgamation of places with commuting, shopping and social links was another important consideration. This linked rural areas and ex-bantustan areas with urban towns. (MDB 1999d)

## Annexure 4: Delimitation criteria

Schedule 1 (4) of the Municipal Structures Act states that:

The Demarcation Board after consulting the Electoral Commission must delimit a municipality into wards, each having approximately the same number of voters, taking into account the following criteria:

(a) The number of registered voters in each ward may not vary by more than 15 per cent of the norm, where the norm is determined by dividing the total number of registered voters on the municipality's segment of the national common voters' roll by the number of wards in the municipality.

(b) The need to avoid as far as possible the fragmentation of communities.

(c) The object of a ward committee, which is to enhance participatory democracy in local government.

(d) The availability and location of a suitable place or places for voting and counting if appropriate, taking into consideration:
  (i) communication and accessibility;
  (ii) density of population;
  (iii) topography and physical characteristics; and
  (iv) the number of voters that are entitled to vote within the required time frame.

(e) The safety and security of voters and election material.

(f) Identifiable ward boundaries.

## References

Allen HJ (1990) *Cultivating the grassroots: Why local government matters.* The Hague: International Union of Local Authorities.

Atkinson D (2003) *A passion to govern: Third generation issues facing local government in South Africa.* Johannesburg: Centre for Development Enterprise.

Barlow IM (1991) *Metropolitan government.* London: Routledge.

Bennett R (ed.) (1989) *Territory and administration in Europe.* London: Pinter.

Botha T (1993) Address given at the Second Annual Conference of Freloga. Randburg.

Cameron RG (1997) A Framework for Local Government Boundary Demarcation. Research study for the Local Government Green Paper process. Unpublished paper. Cape Town.

Cameron RG (1999a) *Democratisation of South African local government: A tale of three cities.* Pretoria: Van Schaik.

Cameron RG (1999b) *An overview of the Local Government Municipal Demarcation Act 27 of 1998.* Johannesburg: The Electoral Institute of South Africa.

Cameron RG (2000) Megacities in South Africa: A solution for the new millennium? *Public Administration and Development,* 20(2): 155–165.

Cameron RG (2001) The upliftment of South African local government, *Local Government Studies,* 27(3): 97–118.

Cameron RG (2003) Decentralisation to non-metropolitan local government in South Africa. Paper presented at International Association of Schools and Institutes Conference, Miami, 14–18 September.

Cameron RG (2004) Local government reorganisation in South Africa. In J Meligrana (ed.), *Redrawing local government boundaries: An international study of politics, procedure and decisions.* Vancouver: UBC Press.

Cloete F (1995) *Local government transformation in South Africa.* Pretoria: Van Schaik.

Constitutional Court of South Africa (1999) *In the matter between The Executive Council of the Province of the Western Cape and The Minister for Provincial Affairs and Constitutional Development of the Republic of South Africa, The Municipal Demarcation Board.* Johannesburg.

Department of Finance (2000) *Municipal Demarcation Board proposals.* Pretoria: Department of Finance.

Elections Task Team (1996) *Local Government Elections in South Africa 1995/1996.* Johannesburg.

Keating M (1995) Size, efficiency and democracy: Consolidation, fragmentation and public choice. In D Judge, G Stokes & H Wolman (eds.), *Theories of urban politics.* London: Sage.

Leach S & Stoker G (1997) Understanding the Local Government Review: A retrospective analysis, *Public Administration,* 75(1).

Leemans AF (1970) *Changing patterns of Local Government.* Netherlands: International Union of Local Authorities.

Local Government Bulletin (1999) *Provinces vs Structures Act Demarcation Board walks off with the spoils,* 1(4). Available on http://www.sn.apc.org/users/clc/localgovt/bulletin.htm

Lodge T (1999) *Consolidating democracy: South Africa's second popular election.* Johannesburg: Electoral Institute of South Africa/Witwatersrand University Press.

Lodge T (2002) *Politics in South Africa from Mandela to Mbeki.* Cape Town: David Philip/Oxford: James Currey.

Mabin A (1999) From hard top to soft serve: Demarcation of metropolitan government in Johannesburg for the 1995 elections. In RG Cameron, *Democratisation of South African local government:. A tale of three cities.* Pretoria: Van Schaik.

Magnusson W (1981) Metropolitan reform in the capitalist city, *Canadian Journal of Political Science,* xiv(3): 587–585.

MDB (Municipal Demarcation Board) (1999a) *Nodal points for metropolitan and district council areas in South Africa.* Pretoria, 26 June.

MDB (1999b) *The determination of metropolitan and district council boundaries.* Pretoria, 4 October.

MDB (1999c) *Assessment of large urban centres.* Pretoria.

MDB (1999d) *The Board's approach to the determination of Category B municipalities.* Pretoria.

MDB (1999e) *Justification reports.* Pretoria.

MDB (2000a) *Final number of municipal boundaries published.* Pretoria.

MDB (2000b) *Statistics.* Pretoria.

MDB (2000c) *The delimitation of wards.* Discussion document. Pretoria.

MDB (2000d) *Memorandum: Municipal Demarcation Board response to Department of Finance.* Pretoria, 21 February.

MDB (2001) *Annual Report 2000/01.* Pretoria.

MDB (2004) *Shaping South Africa. Reflections on the first term of the Municipal Demarcation Board, South Africa 1999–2004.* Pretoria.

Meligrana J (ed.) (2004) *Redrawing local government boundaries: An international study of politics, procedure and decisions.* Vancouver: UBC Press.

Ministry for Provincial and Local Government (2000) *Policy Framework for Full-Time Councillors and Formulae for Number of Councillors.* Pretoria: Ministry for Provincial and Local Government.

Ministry of Provincial Affairs and Constitutional Development (1997) *Green Paper on Local Government.* Pretoria: Government Printer.

Ministry of Provincial Affairs and Constitutional Development (1998) *White Paper on Local Government.* Pretoria: Government Printer.

Olowu D (2003) Local institutional and political structures and processes: Recent experience in Africa, *Public Administration and Development,* 23: 41–52.

Pillay U (1999) Demarcating South Africa's metro areas: A cautionary lesson from the Durban Metropolitan Area. In RG Cameron, *Democratisation of South African local government: A tale of three cities.* Pretoria: Van Schaik.

Pycroft C (2002) Addressing rural poverty: Restructuring rural local government. In S Parnell, E Pieterse, M Swilling & D Wooldridge (eds), *Democratising local government: The South African experiment.* Cape Town: UCT Press.

Robinson J (1995) Transforming spaces: Spatiality and re-mapping the apartheid city. Paper presented at the Centre for African Studies Seminar, University of Cape Town.

RSA (Republic of South Africa) (1996) *The Constitution of the Republic of South Africa. Act no. 108 of 1996.* Cape Town: Government Printers.

RSA (1998a) *Local Government: Municipal Structures Act, no. 117 of 1998.* Cape Town: Government Printers.

RSA (1998b) *Local Government: Municipal Demarcation Act, no. 27 of 1998.* Cape Town: Government Printers.

RSA (2000a) *Cross Boundary Municipalities Act, no. 29 of 2000.* Cape Town: Government Printers.

RSA (2000b) *Local Government: Municipal Structures Act, no. 117 of 1998: Formulae for determination of the number of councillors of municipal councils.* Government Gazette Vol. 418. Pretoria: Government Printers.

Sharpe LJ (ed.) (1995) The future of metropolitan government. In LJ Sharpe (ed.), *The government of world cities: The future of the metro model.* Chichester: John Wiley & Sons.

Smith BC (1985) *Decentralisation: The territorial dimension of the state.* London: George Allen and Unwin.

Smith BC (1993) *Choices in the design of decentralisation.* London: Commonwealth Secretariat.

South African Cities Network (2004) *State of the Cities Report.* Johannesburg: SACN.

Sutcliffe M (1999) Opening Remarks at Inaugural Demarcation Board Meeting. Cape Town.

Tomlinson R (1999) Ten years in the making: A history of metropolitan government in Johannesburg, *Urban Forum,* 10(1): 1–40.

Wooldridge D (2002) Introducing metropolitan government. In S Parnell, E Pieterse, M Swilling & D Wooldridge (eds), *Democratising local government: The South African experiment.* Cape Town: UCT Press.

# 5 Reflections on the design of a post-apartheid system of (urban) local government

Mirjam van Donk and Edgar Pieterse

## Introduction

The purpose of this chapter is to identify the key driving forces that have brought about the current system of urban local government in South Africa. Whereas our particular interest is to review what contribution research has played in the policy process, we are acutely aware of the difficulty in ascertaining its impact with some certainty. During the final days of apartheid and the first years of democracy in South Africa, ideological considerations and political dynamics – much of it obscure even to well-informed outsiders – tended to shape policy in more significant ways than rigorous assessments or empirical studies. Because many of these (party-) political dynamics and processes have not been documented or analysed, it is difficult to ascribe particular policy inclusions (or exclusions) to research.

The present situation can only be understood in the light of events since the 1980s, when the apartheid system of local government became the focal point of community resistance. In this chapter, we distinguish between three phases since the late 1980s until 2004, summarising the key ideas and processes that have influenced local government policy during these various phases.[1] Because much of this is 'unwritten history',[2] the information is drawn from interviews with key informants.

The first phase starts with the late 1980s, when throughout the country mass action compelled local-level negotiations, which eventually resulted in national-level negotiations on local government in the early 1990s, and appointed councils in 1993. The first phase comes to a close with the municipal elections of 1995/96,[3] when a negotiated transitional system of local government came into effect. The second phase starts with the Constitution of 1996, which established local government as an autonomous sphere of government. The White Paper on Local Government and subsequent legislation further elaborated on what the new local government system would entail. The 2000 municipal elections signified the end of the transitional phase of local government and the beginning of the new system of local government. Finally, attention will be given to three critical policy issues that have come to signify some key challenges and conceptual weaknesses associated with urban local government in the post-2000 period: powers and functions, municipal viability, and operationalising the Integrated Development Plan (IDP).

These three policy issues are illustrative of the challenges facing key role-players in the local government sphere to ensure a stable and effective system of urban local government in the near future. We therefore give cursory attention in this regard to the roles and contributions of the Department of Provincial and Local Government (DPLG), the South African Local Government Association (SALGA) and the South African Cities Network. Before concluding this chapter, we briefly return to the relationship between research and policy processes.

## Key phases in local government policy

### 1980s to mid-1990s: community mobilisation, negotiations and transitional arrangements

During apartheid, local government structures in South Africa were designed to reproduce the urban system in accordance with the policy objectives of the state (Swilling 1991). Until influx control was abolished in 1986, the state projected an image of urban areas as white areas, where black labourers would stay temporarily – in racially segregated areas – for the duration of their employment. It was therefore only in areas designated as 'white' that fully fledged municipalities (white local authorities) were set up. Management committees – called 'local advisory committees' in Natal – were set up in coloured and Indian group areas, yet these only had advisory powers and limited delegated powers from the white local authorities these areas fell under. Although the official policy allowed for management committees and local advisory committees to become independent local government structures, with the exception of four Indian local advisory committees no other management committee or local advisory committee has ever evolved into an independent local authority (Cameron 1991). Black local authorities, introduced in 1982, were responsible for service provision in African townships, yet from the outset these structures had virtually no tax base and limited powers and capacity to execute their functions.

From the early 1980s, local conditions, and specifically the lack of urban services, in black townships became a rallying point for mass mobilisation across the country. On occasion, and increasingly over time, the focus of mass action shifted to the system of urban local government, particularly as awareness grew that black South Africans were cross-subsidising white standards of living. Not only did black residents spend most of their income in shops in white group areas, all economic activity – even if located in black townships – was considered part of the white tax base. The black local authorities lacked the revenue, capacity and legitimacy to provide services to African townships. With rents and service charges providing the only source of revenue for black local authorities, many councils saw no alternative but to raise rents and service charges. At the same time, residents were faced with deteriorating services whilst the economy was slipping into decline. Civic organisations,[4] many of which had been formed in protest against the establishment of black local authorities, mobilised local communities against local conditions in general and rents and service charges in particular (Shubane 1991). Across the country, widespread protest erupted against rents and service hikes in townships. One of the first and most visible of these was the Vaal uprising of September 1984, which left over 30 people dead, including four councillors (Seekings 1991).

Community mass action took on a variety of forms, from rent boycotts and consumer boycotts to attacks on those associated with the apartheid system, for example black councillors. The Vaal rent boycott, following the 1984 Vaal uprising, was a long-term and large-scale campaign. By mid-1986, about 50 townships were participating in rent boycotts nationwide (Swilling, Cobbett & Hunter 1991: 188). Following intensified repression by the apartheid state during the period 1986–1989, many residents in smaller towns started to pay rent and service charges, but by the middle of 1990 rent boycotts had spread again from a small number of townships to 49 in the former Transvaal province alone (Swilling et al. 1991: 188).

In the Eastern Cape, consumer boycotts were more prevalent (Atkinson 1991). Civic associations in Port Alfred, East London and Port Elizabeth sought support from white local authorities to re-supply local services, given that black local authorities were ineffective, and to provide protection against harassment by the security police. Although the white local authorities were receptive, such an arrangement went against the grain of apartheid policy and by mid-1986 local negotiations came to an end (Atkinson 1991).

Recognising the ability of mass action to undermine the apartheid urban system, the apartheid government initially thought it could hold on to power and maintain the apartheid urban system through the provision of urban services to black communities, yet without conceding the right to political citizenship of the black majority. In pursuing the 'winning-hearts-and-minds' strategy, the government of the day underestimated the extent to which black residents saw their material and political concerns as interconnected (Swilling 1991). More importantly, civil resistance had become a widespread and accepted form of political expression. The psychic stranglehold of the apartheid machinery was effectively broken through the mass campaigns in the townships across most urban areas in South Africa. New political identities had taken hold.

Rent boycotts clearly exacerbated the financial crisis faced by black local authorities and forced local negotiations to resolve the crisis. By early 1990, around the time of the unbanning of political movements and the release of Nelson Mandela, there were hundreds of local-level negotiations across the country, resulting in the establishment of local negotiating forums (Swilling & Boya 1995). Initially, these forums were little more than crisis management structures, attempting to resolve the rent boycotts and address the community grievances underpinning mass action targeted at local government. Many future councillors, (local) government officials, community leaders and Members of Parliament (MPs) cut their teeth in these local forums. An invaluable role was played by non-governmental organisations (NGOs) like Planact and other affiliates of the Urban Sector Network, which provided policy advice (often based on pioneering and thorough empirical research)[5] and training to civic associations in these processes. The impact of community mass action on the local government system, particularly its financial viability, was also recognised by then Minister of Provincial Affairs Hernus Kriel when he launched a report on possible options for local government in May 1990 (Swilling et al. 1991). Whilst premised on the report of the Thornhill Committee, whose recommendations generally sought to reinscribe white domination through more subtle means, by highlighting the possibility of bringing about a non-racial municipality with a common tax base through the process of local-level negotiation, Kriel's report gave civics (and the urban policy organisations supporting them) a significant boost.

The most well known and one of the longest running rent boycotts, the Soweto rent boycott, eventually led to the establishment of one of the most prominent local negotiating forums, the Central Witwatersrand Metropolitan Chamber, which proved very influential in the local government transition process. There were similar processes in other cities and towns as well, but none of these achieved the degree of influence of the Johannesburg/Central Witwatersrand process.[6] We therefore restrict our discussion here to this process.

## The Soweto rent boycott

The Soweto rent boycott started in June 1986 and was based on five demands: a write-off of arrears; the transfer of houses to residents; an upgrade of services and the provision of affordable services; a single tax base across the city of Johannesburg; and the establishment of a non-racial and democratic municipality. A critical contribution of the Soweto People's Delegation (the negotiating team formed to negotiate an end to the boycott) was a 1989 study, which demonstrated how the apartheid local government finance system was based on a redistribution of local resources from African townships to white group areas (Swilling et al. 1991).[7] This gave rise to the slogan 'One city, one tax base', which became a national rallying cry.

For four years, 80 per cent of formal rent-paying households in Soweto withheld rent and service payments. By 1990, this situation had clearly become untenable and negotiations were entered into to end the boycott. In September of that year, negotiations culminated in the Soweto Accord, which had been ratified by Cabinet and included writing off R500 million in arrears. The remaining demands of the boycott were referred to a new negotiating forum, the Central Witwatersrand Metropolitan Chamber. Although the Soweto Accord became a model for local-level negotiations in other areas in the Transvaal, in practice it proved difficult to reproduce the process and outcomes elsewhere (Swilling et al. 1991).

## THE CENTRAL WITWATERSRAND METROPOLITAN CHAMBER

The Central Witwatersrand Metropolitan Chamber can be seen as a laboratory for ideas on a new, non-racial system of urban local government. Set up in April 1991 as a negotiating forum between the 10 main local government bodies in the then Central Witwatersrand and 5 civic associations representing African and coloured communities, by the time of its disbandment 3 years later the Chamber had 53 members and 32 official observer bodies (Swilling & Boya 1995). The Metropolitan Chamber went through a thorough process of negotiating a new system of urban governance and planning. For this purpose, six working groups were set up with task teams that were responsible for the formulation of policy proposals.[8]

It has been suggested by Mark Swilling that the Metropolitan Chamber represents 'the biggest urban research project' to date in South Africa.[9] Extensive research was conducted on issues such as:
*   How to integrate tax bases across the Central Witwatersrand;
*   The existing electrification infrastructure and its management in the Central Witwatersrand, how to integrate this (racially disparate) infrastructure and how to provide it as a local government function (as opposed to privatisation);
*   The existing water and sewerage system in the Central Witwatersrand and the implications for where housing for the poor could be located;
*   The extent of state-owned housing and appropriate mechanisms for the transfer of state-owned housing to families (as opposed to individual ownership).[10]

This empirical and action-oriented research has had a direct and significant impact on policy coordination and analysis pertaining to metropolitan government in the Central Witwatersrand specifically and – through the national negotiations on local government – the system of urban local government more generally.

One of the hallmarks of the Metropolitan Chamber was that its working groups represented a wide range of stakeholders across the political and institutional spectrum, including civics and organisations providing advisory and policy support to civics (eg. Planact), municipal officials from different sectors, organised business and professional associations. A key strength of the Metropolitan Chamber, which in the end turned out to be its major weakness, was that it was a consensus-based structure. For this reason, it was unable to resolve a number of critical issues relating to the densification of white suburbs and redistribution through the tax basis. In the end, it needed decision-making and statutory powers to deal with resistance from entrenched (white) interests and to implement the recommendations of its working groups.[11]

## FROM LOCAL TO NATIONAL NEGOTIATIONS: THE LGNF AND LGTA

The Central Witwatersrand Metropolitan Chamber was not the only local negotiating forum that reached this point. Across the country, there was growing recognition that the issues debated in local negotiating forums transcended local boundaries.

It was increasingly obvious that a common national solution to the problems associated with local government was required. At the same time, the system of local government – particularly the demand for a single tax base – was among the most strongly resisted issues during national negotiation processes. With the police and military, it was one of three outstanding crunch issues that Codesa (Convention for a Democratic South Africa, 1991–1992) was unable to resolve.[12]

In 1993, the national Local Government Negotiating Forum (LGNF) was set up, consisting of national government, organised associations of local governments, political parties, trade unions and the South African National Civic Organisation (Sanco). One of the most urgent issues facing the LGNF was to deal with the financial crisis of local government and non-payment of rent and service charges. This resulted in the Agreement on Finance and Services, which facilitated writing off arrears to black local authorities.

Within a year, the LGNF negotiated a national framework to guide the transition towards a new local government system, the Local Government Transition Act (LGTA) of 1993 (Act 209 of 1993). This framework and its implications became entrenched in the interim Constitution of 1993 as Chapter 10, meaning that local government became an autonomous sphere of authority. Throughout the negotiations, the non-statutory delegation was acutely aware of the need to overcome white resistance and not to give white conservative forces a pretext to take up arms.[13] In contrast to national government, where the National Party was the governing party, a significant proportion of white local authorities outside the metropolitan areas were controlled by the Conservative Party. Against this background, the LGTA reflected a number of significant compromises which bedevilled the local government transition, including the delimitation of wards in a manner that skewed representation in favour of entrenched interests and the requirement that municipal budgets had to be approved by a two-thirds majority (RSA 1998).

The LGTA envisaged a three-phased transition period for local government: a pre-interim, interim and final phase. During the pre-interim phase, local negotiating forums became statutory structures and were tasked with the appointment of temporary councils which would govern until municipal elections. This involved defining municipal boundaries, appointing councillors and establishing a financial system. Between 1993 and 1996, by the time municipal elections had been held across the country, 843 new local authorities were established in accordance with the LGTA. Because the LGTA endorsed locally negotiated solutions, the result was a variety of forms of local government across the country.

The pre-interim phase came to a close with the municipal elections of 1995/96, which allowed for transitional local government structures to be established. With the exception of metropolitan areas, single-tier local government structures (Transitional Local Councils) were set up in larger cities and smaller towns. In six metropolitan areas, a two-tier system was set up, allowing for a Transitional

Metropolitan Council and Metropolitan Sub-Structures. The fact that both tiers of local government in metropolitan areas were given original powers (meaning that each structure could authorise budgets and was an independent employer body) and had overlapping mandates severely complicated intra-municipal relations, financial management and human resource management.[14] One particularly problematic consequence of the two-tier system was poor financial control, with the substructures having little incentive to control expenditure (SACN 2004), which in no small measure contributed to the financial crises in most metropolitan areas by the second half of the 1990s.

During the interim phase (1996–2000), the LGTA envisaged that the new local government system would be finalised in legislation. During this period, local government operated on the basis of transitional arrangements derived from the LGTA and from local processes of negotiation. The municipal elections of 2000 heralded the final phase, when the new local government system would be fully operationalised. Both phases are further discussed later.

One of the criticisms levelled against the LGTA is that it reflected an urban bias. This is not surprising, as it drew heavily from the experiences and policy proposals of the Central Witwatersrand Metropolitan Chamber. In fact, there was a significant amount of overlap in terms of the people involved in both processes (Swilling & Boya 1995). In particular, members of Planact played quite central roles in both the Central Witwatersrand Metropolitan Chamber negotiations and in the LGNF.[15] Another reason for the urban bias in local government policy is perhaps a historical one: during the apartheid years, systems of traditional leadership tended to provide services to the African majority living in homeland areas, whereas national departments or provincial administrations provided public services to areas largely under the control of white commercial farmers. It was only in 1987 that Regional Services Councils were set up as a limited form of local government for African rural communities (Pycroft 2002).

### 1996–2000: designing a new local government system

The Constitution of 1996 established local government as an autonomous sphere of government and gave it a new development mandate. The White Paper on Local Government of 1998 and subsequent legislation (see Box 1) further expanded on this mandate of 'developmental local government' and on the political, administrative and institutional systems to fulfil it.

---

**Box 1: Key legislation affecting local government in South Africa**

Among the key Acts that have been passed to give effect to the constitutional directives on local government and the policy framework reflected in the White Paper on Local Government are:

– Local Government: Municipal Demarcation Act, 1998 (Act 27 of 1998), which provided for the establishment of the Municipal Demarcation Board, tasked with the determination of municipal boundaries in a manner that would facilitate integrated development, effective service delivery and participatory local democracy.

– Local Government: Municipal Structures Act, 1998 (Act 117 of 1998, with three subsequent amendments in 2000, 2002 and 2003), which allowed for the establishment of different types and categories of municipalities in different areas (i.e. single-tier municipalities for metropolitan areas and two-tier municipalities outside metropolitan areas), defined two options for executive systems in metropolitan areas (mayoral executive system or collective executive system), and allowed for the establishment of ward committees to facilitate community participation in council matters.

– Municipal Electoral Act, 2000 (Act 27 of 2000), which regulated all aspects of the municipal elections, including the requirements on parties and ward candidates to contest the elections, voter education and election observers, voting and counting.

– Local Government: Municipal Systems Act, 2000 (Act 32 of 2000, with an amendment in 2003), which established a framework for the operation of municipalities, with guidelines for development planning and service provision (including a partnership-based approach), staffing matters and performance management systems.

– Local Government: Municipal Finance Management Act, 2003 (Act 56 of 2003), which created a framework for municipalities to borrow money and determined the conditions for short-term and long-term borrowing.

– Local Government: Municipal Property Rates Act, 2004 (Act 6 of 2004), which established a uniform property rating system across South Africa.

In his Foreword to the White Paper, the then Minister for Provincial Affairs and Constitutional Development, Mohammed Valli Moosa, asserts that the policy framework was the outcome of an 'intensive 18-month period of consultation and research' (RSA 1998: no page number) since the Green Paper on Local Government was released in October 1997. In fact, most of the research had been commissioned prior to the Green Paper, although not all of it found its way into the discussion document.[16]

The White Paper Working Committee commissioned research related to four themes (political and institutional systems, developmental local government, municipal finance and 'reality check').[17] Under these four themes, a host of research papers was prepared on topics ranging from financial systems, service delivery mechanisms, globalisation and integrated development planning, to metropolitan local government, rural local government, and gender. It was envisaged that the research papers would be collated into the Green Paper, but undisclosed political dynamics thwarted this intention.[18] Around this time, the ministry – anxious to deliver a policy framework by 1998 to allow sufficient time for the final system of local government to be finalised by 2000 – became more closely involved in the process and pushed for a more strategic and coherent approach to the Green Paper. Instead of the research findings culminating in a comprehensive policy framework for local government, the minister and the White Paper Political Committee opted for a more practical approach whereby each section in the Green Paper had to answer a number of specific questions.

The extent to which the research findings and proposed policy options were eventually reflected in the White Paper was contingent on a number of factors. Firstly, all the different pieces of information, potentially conflicting views and recommendations had to somehow be reconciled in the editing process.[19] It is in this process that an editorial team held significant discretionary power to determine what needed to be reflected in the policy framework. This is not to say that there were no checks and balances in place to overcome whatever policy preferences, blind spots or conceptual flaws the editorial team may have had. The White Paper Working Committee and particularly the White Paper Political Committee played an important role in ensuring that the outcome reflected a politically acceptable policy framework. In addition, parliamentary public hearings created an opportunity to comment on the White Paper to ensure that subsequent legislation would benefit from as many ideas, perspectives and experiences as possible.[20]

Secondly, rather than the editing process, a much more significant factor in diminishing the possible impact of research on policy relates to politics, more specifically (perceived) political pressures and party-political dynamics, and ideology. At the time, when the democratic system was not yet fully consolidated and the majority of policy-makers lacked prior experience in parliamentary policy processes, policy critiques and recommendations were generally interpreted and appraised through an ideological lens, rather than on the merits of the proposals.[21]

For example, the re-demarcation of municipal boundaries was in large part driven by an ideological perspective that redistribution is best facilitated by linking municipalities with a tax base and significant institutional capacity to those that lack a proper tax base and adequate human resources. Yet, this assumption was never tested through empirical assessments or statistical modelling to inform various policy options.[22] If anything, this ideological perspective found fertile ground in the fact that those considered to be on opposite sides of the political spectrum opposed it.[23]

In a similar vein, it has been suggested that the concept of ward committees was introduced to pre-empt the criticism of liberal forces that single-tier metropolitan government would be undemocratic and too far removed from the populace. Yet, this insertion into the policy framework was not informed by any considered assessment of whether the ward committee system would be an effective mechanism to facilitate inclusive local governance in the context of a hybrid electoral system.[24]

In addition to research and politics, a third factor shaping the policy framework on local government is the fact that it had to reflect a balance of negotiations between stakeholders representing a wide divergence of interests. National and provincial governments, municipal unions, organised local government, organised business and civil society groups all sought to influence the local government system, often with varying – if not conflicting – outcomes in mind.[25]

During this period, a significant number of municipalities, including those in metropolitan areas, experienced a severe financial crisis. This crisis was in large part brought on by increased spending (to meet more service delivery needs) combined with unstable revenue streams (largely due to inability to pay) in a dysfunctional, poorly capacitated and inefficient institutional context (Parnell 2004a; SACN 2004). Partly as a result of this, the system of two-tier metropolitan government was scrapped in favour of a single-tier system in the new policy framework. Yet, outside metropolitan areas a two-tier system was introduced, which means that secondary cities and large towns (at least in theory) have to engage with district councils as well.[26] This became particularly confusing, complicated and financially onerous in the first two years after the 2000 municipal elections, as the following section on powers and functions illustrates.

Generally, the bigger cities were quite vocal in the policy formulation phase.[27] For one, some national departments like National Treasury and DPLG, conscious of their size and economic role, felt that their perspectives warranted special attention. Secondly, whenever the realities facing secondary cities and smaller urban areas came up, the tendency was to highlight the urban–rural link and relate their concerns to the ideological perspective that they had a role to play in regional redistribution.[28]

In recent years, with the consolidation of the local government system, it has become increasingly clear that the fairly uniform model of local government presented in the White Paper is problematic. Seen in historical context, it is understandable that policy-makers at the time opted for a common and rather prescriptive framework for local government in an attempt to overcome a deeply fragmented system of local government.[29] At the time it was already suggested that this uniform portrayal failed to appreciate the diverse challenges and possibilities facing urban areas of variable sizes, ranging from small towns to large cities (Bernstein 1998). Clearly, the political atmosphere was not receptive to considering a more diversified and flexible system of local government.[30]

It is important to recognise that the ideological perspectives of (political) decision-makers at the time were heavily influenced by a veritable maelstrom in shifting development discourses (Parnell & Pieterse 1999). Neo-liberal policy precepts remained profoundly influential after becoming hegemonic internationally during the 1980s, but were increasingly softened by the recognition that the state had a vital role to play in guiding and facilitating development processes (eg. World Bank 1997). The detrimental environmental and poverty effects of crude neo-liberal policies were also widely recognised (Edwards 1999). At the same time, policy emphasis on greater civil society participation in development processes and democratisation had become accepted across the ideological spectrum, reflected in vibrant debates on the importance of local democracy, identity politics, decentralisation, social capital and sustainable livelihoods (Parnell & Pieterse 1999). The unresolved tension that existed between neo-liberal economic prescripts and social/human development perspectives was mediated by the rise of Third Way social democracy, à la Anthony Giddens and Tony Blair (Giddens 2000). At the core of this policy perspective was a renewed role for the state whereby concerns with greater state efficiency and effectiveness were combined with a focus on equity and individual responsibility (Rose 1999).

In South Africa these strands were clearly in evidence, which was unsurprising since policy networks supporting the new state drew heavily on development and public sector reform debates in the United Nations system (especially the United Nations Development Programme), the World Bank and think tanks of New Labour in the UK (Khan 2004).[31] As a consequence of these often contradictory policy streams, South African urban policies were characterised by a form of schizophrenia: being torn by neo-liberal financial and institutional precepts, on the one hand, and social development and environmental redistributive precepts on the other (Pieterse 2004). What is significant though is that formal policy documents such as White Papers would never acknowledge even the potential for contradiction and conflict between the government's neo-liberal macroeconomic programme, the Growth, Employment and Redistribution programme (commonly referred to as GEAR),[32] and the social democratic agenda in the Reconstruction and Development Programme (RDP).[33] It is therefore not surprising, with the benefit of hindsight, to observe that the developmental local government approach consolidated in the White Paper treated local government in a fairly homogeneous and singular manner.

Finally, the one surprising issue that was not considered at all by policy-makers involved in shaping the new local government system was the challenge of HIV/AIDS. This gap existed despite the profound implications of the epidemic for the viability of local development processes and services (Van Donk 2003).

*Post-2000: trials and tribulations of operationalising the local government system*

With the municipal elections of December 2000, the period of designing a post-apartheid system of local government came to a close. Attention then shifted to the effective operationalisation of the new system. After almost a decade of perpetual flux and uncertainty, the relative stability brought about by the 2000 municipal elections is most welcome. Yet, it is obvious that significant challenges remain and that unresolved policy dilemmas beleaguer the current phase. By way of illustration, this section will elaborate on three key policy issues that have vexed the post-2000 period, namely powers and functions, financial viability and how to operationalise the IDP.

## POWERS AND FUNCTIONS

The Constitution provides for the division of powers and functions between national, provincial and local government. Box 2 summarises the areas of competency that fall under local government. The powers and functions dilemma has two dimensions, which tend to affect different types of municipalities differently. On the one hand, there are problems with 'unfunded mandates', when municipalities perform functions that are supposed to be done (and/or funded) by other spheres of government. This intergovernmental dimension mainly affects larger urban municipalities, including metropolitan councils. On the other hand, there is intra-municipal confusion about powers and functions where two-tier local government structures exist, i.e. between district councils and local municipalities. In this instance, metropolitan areas and the larger 20 well-functioning cities are not affected, but smaller urban municipalities are. In both instances, the confusion stems in large part from legal and constitutional ambiguity and omission.

---

### Box 2: Powers and functions of local government

Municipal powers and functions are derived from the 1996 Constitution which states that: *A municipality has executive authority in respect of, and has the right to administer (a) the local government matters listed in Part B of Schedule 4 and Part B of Schedule 5* (Constitution, Section 156(1)). The relevant local government matters are listed as follows:

| SCHEDULE 4, PART B | SCHEDULE 5, PART B |
|---|---|
| – Air pollution | – Beaches and amusement facilities |
| – Building regulations | – Billboards/advertisements in public places |
| – Childcare facilities | – Cemeteries, funeral parlours and crematoria |
| – Electricity and gas reticulation | – Cleansing |
| – Fire-fighting services | – Control of public nuisances |
| – Local tourism | – Control of undertakings that sell liquor to the public |
| – Municipal airports | |
| – Municipal planning | – Facilities for the accommodation, care and burial of animals |
| – Municipal health services | |
| – Municipal public transport | – Fencing and fences |
| – Municipal public works (limited to functions assigned under the Constitution and law) | – Licensing of dogs |
| | – Licensing and control of the selling of food to the public |
| – Pontoons, ferries, jetties, piers and harbours (excl. national/international aspects) | – Local amenities |
| – Stormwater management systems | – Local sport facilities |

---

| SCHEDULE 4, PART B | SCHEDULE 5, PART B |
|---|---|
| – Trading regulations<br>– Water and sanitation services (potable [drinkable] water supply systems, domestic waste water and sewage disposal systems) | – Markets<br>– Municipal abattoirs<br>– Municipal parks and recreation<br>– Municipal roads<br>– Noise pollution<br>– Pounds<br>– Public places<br>– Refuse removal, refuse dumps and solid waste disposal<br>– Street trading<br>– Street lighting<br>– Traffic and parking |

In addition, municipalities have potential powers and functions that may be devolved or delegated to them from provincial and national government. These national and provincial powers and functions are listed in Part A of Schedules 4 and 5 of the Constitution. The Constitution makes provision for the delegation of powers and functions to local government by agreement, provided municipalities have the necessary capacity and are considered the most effective site from which these powers may be exercised.

Source: RSA (1998); DPLG (2001: 2–3)

The *intergovernmental* issue related to powers and functions arises from Schedules 4 and 5 in the Constitution, which define the powers and functions of each sphere of government. Yet, in practice, considerable confusion exists regarding the precise meaning and delineation of each function (Palmer 2004). The Municipal Systems Act of 2000 attempted to address the issue of 'unfunded mandates', where municipalities found themselves executing and funding certain functions without having access to prerequisite resources from other spheres of government. The Act allows for the allocation of powers and functions to local government through assignment (the transfer of authority) and delegation (the transfer of provider responsibility). Although the Act outlines clear mechanisms for assignments from national or provincial government, no such mechanisms are elaborated on with respect to delegations. Given that provinces tend to favour delegations over assignment, often without clear contractual agreement and financial arrangements, the misalignment between functions and finance (or 'unfunded mandates') continues to exist (Palmer 2004). This was confirmed by the Ministerial Advisory Committee on Local Government Transformation,[34] which found that '…the "underfunded" and "unfunded" mandates delegated to local authorities is [sic] creating huge financial strain for municipalities attempting to address the backlogs for service provision in their constituencies' (Ministerial Advisory Committee 2001: 20). On a more positive note, a recent Human Sciences Research Council study in the Free State suggests that intergovernmental relations are improving, although some caveats in terms of resource constraints, resource flows and unfunded mandates remain (Zingel 2004).

Problems with *intra-municipal* functional assignments are not a post-2000 phenomenon, having pervaded debates about metropolitan government until the two-tier system was replaced by the one-tier system in metropolitan areas (Savage n.d.). The origin of recent intra-municipal problems with powers and functions lies in the Municipal Structures Amendment Act of 2000 (Ministerial Advisory Committee 2001; Palmer 2004). Just two months prior to the municipal elections of 2000, one of the amendments to the Municipal Structures Act of 1998 transferred the most significant powers and functions vested in local municipalities (electricity, water, sanitation, health) to district municipalities, without prior consultation or public debate.[35] The Municipal Structures Amendment Act made provision for the minister to authorise local municipalities to fulfil these functions. The minister in turn immediately gave temporary authorisations for the status quo to be maintained until further notice. Because the authorisations were of a temporary nature, significant uncertainty arose, which impacted negatively on financial planning, the willingness of local municipalities to allocate resources to these services and staff morale.[36] It took until October 2002 for the minister to make final proclamations (taking effect from December 2002), with all municipal health functions assigned to district level and water and sanitation split between local and district councils (Savage n.d.).[37]

It has been argued that the timing of the amendment, when most local government stakeholders were focused on the impending municipal elections of December 2000, meant that it could slip through unnoticed, without much contestation.[38] Officially, the argument given by those supporting the amendment (the Municipal Demarcation Board, in particular its chairperson Dr Mike Sutcliffe, and the DPLG) was that redistribution was best facilitated at district level. Yet, this assumption was not tested and, in fact, became strongly contested, particularly when related to issues of capacity and financial viability.[39] The Ministerial Advisory Committee on Local Government Transformation came to the following strongly worded conclusion:

> It is apparent from the bulk of evidence presented to the MAC [Ministerial Advisory Committee] that the conferral of substantial powers on district municipalities does not, in fact, invest them with real capacity. The non-alignment of services with revenue may retard the real transformation that the Act seeks to achieve and is a serious structural problem, which the amended version of section 84 fails to adequately address. This, in turn, could lead to arrested, rather than accelerated, transformation. There is no evidence of any considered investigation into the direct and indirect repercussions of transferring the most significant powers and functions of local municipalities to district municipalities. In addition, the Amendment Act may raise real questions of constitutionality. (Ministerial Advisory Committee 2001: 8)

In fact, it referred to the fact that the two-tier local government system proved unsuccessful at metropolitan (Johannesburg) level between 1995 and 2000, which is seen to have contributed to the liquidity crisis faced by the city in 1996/97 (see also Parnell 2004a). Not surprisingly, its main recommendation was to nullify this particular provision in the Municipal Structures Amendment Act. Since December 2002, there has been greater clarity on the intra-municipal assignment of powers and functions, but the main challenge is to ensure concomitant alignment of capacity and of fiscal and expenditure powers, particularly at district level (Harrison 2003). The deeper policy question about how developmental local government is best achieved in terms of powers and functions remains unexplored in the public sphere.

## Financial viability

The Ministerial Advisory Committee has defined financial viability as 'the ability of a local authority to fulfil constitutional and legislative responsibilities' (Ministerial Advisory Committee 2001: 18). Municipal resources to fulfil these responsibilities come from two key avenues: the equitable share and local revenue. It has been noted that in many municipalities the equitable share is very low and even continues to decrease (Ministerial Advisory Committee 2001).[40] According to the Medium Term Budget Policy Statement 2004, the equitable share going to municipalities is just over 4.5 per cent (National Treasury 2004: 55).[41]

A municipality's ability to generate local revenue hinges on the level of wealth (and, conversely, the scale of poverty) within its municipal boundaries and on economic activity. Where high levels of poverty exist, cost recovery is unlikely for municipal service provision. Where economic activity is low (often in direct correlation to high levels of poverty) or declining, municipalities are unable to generate revenue from economic activity (Fast, quoted in Ministerial Advisory Committee 2001). This has important implications for urban local government, where poverty and unemployment have increased in recent years (Parnell 2004b; SACN 2004). The *State of the Cities Report* notes that between 1996 and 2001 the 21 largest urban centres in South Africa experienced rapid urbanisation (SACN 2004: 37), yet this dynamic context (and the associated rise in urban poverty and inequality) is insufficiently taken into account in the intergovernmental grant system.[42]

Financial considerations have been primary throughout different stages of local government transition, albeit in different shapes and with different emphases over time. In the absence of a uniform accounting and financial management system (which has only been established recently), it was impossible to get a clear picture of the exact nature and scope of the financial and fiscal situation in local government. Consequently, key policy decisions have been made without an in-depth understanding of the factors influencing the financial viability of municipalities.[43]

During the re-demarcation of municipal boundaries prior to the 2000 municipal elections, the issue of financial viability was a particularly contested one. The Municipal Demarcation Board asserted, without prior investigation or proper assessment, that the rationalisation of local municipalities from 843 to 284 was in large part necessitated by the need for financial viability.[44] In response, National Treasury argued that the proposed boundaries would structurally weaken the fiscal position of many non-metropolitan municipalities and, as a result, constrain their ability to raise capital and develop infrastructure in line with their core mandate.[45] Yet, according to interviewees, its intervention had little impact and its memorandum to the Municipal Demarcation Board was not responded to.[46]

As mentioned earlier, financial viability is closely linked to powers and functions. On the one hand, national and provincial governments tend to assign and delegate functions to municipalities without ensuring that appropriate financial arrangements are in place. In large part, this is brought on by the fiscal squeeze experienced by provincial and national governments (Olver 1998). On the other hand, the assignment of core revenue-generating powers and functions from local to district councils undermines the financial viability and capacity of non-metropolitan local government whilst adding to the complexity of the intergovernmental fiscal system (Ministerial Advisory Committee 2001; Savage n.d.).

In addition to the shift in municipal powers and functions, employment costs, the constitutional imperative to ensure access to basic services (i.e. through subsidised service provision), rising bulk supply costs and the costs associated with the process of amalgamation create financial pressures on municipalities (submission of National Treasury to the MAC, quoted in Ministerial Advisory Committee 2001). With respect to employment costs, overstaffing at middle and senior levels and inherited service conditions (which make it extremely costly to retrench or reassign staff) create a serious financial drain on the budgets of many urban municipalities (SACN 2004).

## Integrated Development Plan

Since 1996, the IDP is the centrepiece of planning. It is supposed to provide strategic guidance to municipalities whilst linking sectoral plans and processes (Harrison 2001). The chapter by Harrison in this volume deals in much greater depth with the IDP. Our purpose here is to highlight the fact that although the IDP is considered a critical instrument of post-apartheid local government, in practice it is beset with many challenges and problems. The first round of IDPs (between 1996 and 2002) revealed many shortcomings in the formulation and implementation of these plans (Harrison 2001; Ministerial Advisory Committee 2001). The Ministerial Advisory Committee (2001) found that many interim IDPs merely reflected shopping lists, rather than a strategic and long-term vision of the development of a municipal area. Furthermore, many IDPs tended to overemphasise infrastructure development at the expense of social and economic development. To be fair, these IDPs were developed in a rather difficult and volatile context, when newly established municipalities lacked experience in planning, had limited capacity and resources and were faced with multiple demands from national and provincial government (Harrison 2001).

IDPs developed in the post-2000 period provide the basis for a fairer assessment, although the second round of IDPs clearly shows that it continues to be a learning process, in terms of its preparation, operationalisation and implementation (Harrison 2003). Drawing on an assessment of IDPs within six districts, Harrison (2003) identified 16 key areas of concern, ranging from the lack of real strategic planning and analysis to weak linkages between the IDP and budgets and inadequate intergovernmental alignment, amongst others.

Other assessments have also suggested that the lack of financial analysis into the viability of planned interventions and weak links between the IDP and municipal budgets continue to be a hallmark of many IDPs (Ministerial Advisory Committee 2001; Carter 2004; Palmer 2004). A study into IDPs funded by the German agency for development cooperation GTZ (*Gesellschaft für Technische Zusammenarbeit*) found that municipalities tend to see IDPs and budget processes as separate, even though the Municipal Finance Management Act requires that the budget be aligned with the priorities reflected in the IDP (Carter 2004).

Specific questions have been raised about the role and usefulness of IDPs for planning in metropolitan areas. The South African Cities Network (SACN), currently representing the nine main urban centres in the country, promotes the adoption of city-wide development strategies which are longer term than the IDP and, unlike the IDP, are not restricted to municipal boundaries (SACN 2004).[47] A similar observation about the limitations of IDPs as an instrument for planning in metropolitan areas is made by Harrison (2003). He argues that these areas need to have scope for more experimentation and creativity than the IDP framework allows.

## *Challenging key role-players*

The three critical policy issues outlined earlier are illustrative of the challenges facing key role-players in the local government sphere to ensure a stable system of urban local government. Based on experiences to date, questions remain about the capability of role-players like DPLG, SALGA[48] and, perhaps to a lesser extent, the recently formed SACN to be proactive in this regard.

As a conceptual starting point, role-players have to recognise and articulate the variety of interests that characterise local government. Clearly, the developmental realities and challenges faced by metropolitan areas, secondary cities, large and small towns or rural districts vary fundamentally, which has implications for the system of local government. Yet, both DPLG and SALGA (and its provincial affiliates) are seen to reflect a rather standardised approach to local government, in which the needs and constraints of smaller municipalities tend to take precedence.[49] Given that the policy and legislative framework promotes a significant level of conformity and uniformity, it is perhaps not surprising that SALGA and DPLG follow this approach and tend to prioritise those aspects of the local government system that are not functioning well – which tend to be rural and district councils. Furthermore, in light of the capacity constraints that have characterised SALGA since its inception, it is questionable whether it will be able to execute its mandate (i.e. to represent local government in its multiplicity of interests) effectively (Ministerial Advisory Committee 2001).

Perhaps another reason why SALGA and DPLG tend to concentrate on the interests of smaller municipalities and district councils is that specific urban areas, particularly the metropolitan areas, have tended to be quite vocal and influential throughout the local government transformation process.[50] In contrast to rural and district councils, urban municipalities also had access to knowledge-based networks such as the Local Government Learning Network (commonly referred to as Logon).[51] Logon attempted to pioneer a new approach to policy research and development by linking senior municipal managers to policy researchers in NGOs and academia. The working assumption was that the everyday experiences of practitioners was a richer terrain for policy learning than anything coming out of independent analysis.

Logon served as a critical precursor to the SACN, which was formally launched in October 2002 by South Africa's nine main urban centres as a knowledge-sharing network.[52] Although initially intended to facilitate knowledge sharing between its members, it is estimated that perhaps as much as 70 per cent of its work has been related to information sharing between cities and other spheres of government, particularly national government.[53] A key rationale for its existence is the realisation that the role and impact of cities exceed municipal boundaries – and thus the traditional remit of urban local government (SACN 2004). During its relatively short lifespan to date, the SACN has already brought about a significant policy shift to urban development across a number of national departments by highlighting the role (and 'burden', in terms of the concentration of poverty in urban areas) of cities in national development.[54] According to the chairperson of the SACN, Andrew Boraine, its flagship publication, *State of the Cities Report*, has made a significant contribution to this shift in thinking.

SACN consciously does not position itself as an interest group of urban (or specifically metropolitan) local government (which it considers part of SALGA's mandate), or even of cities – although arguably a grey area exists between sharing information with national government simply to enhance knowledge or to somehow encourage action, based on that knowledge. Perhaps the most useful avenue for SACN to help refine the system of urban local government is to influence SALGA in a manner that allows SALGA to appreciate and take up the specific interests of urban and metropolitan local government.

A discussion on the key role-players in the local government sphere is incomplete without some reference to the role of donors. It is important to recognise that a significant proportion of research (evaluations, assessments, materials development, international reviews, etc.) informing the work and positions of key role-players like DPLG, SALGA and SACN remains funded by anchor donors that have given significant support throughout the local government transition process.[55] In the past, particularly during the initial phases of the design of the new local government system, some donors tended to make extensive use of non-South African consultants, who often promoted predetermined policy options without due consideration or understanding of the South African context (Tomlinson 2002). In more recent years, however, the dominant trend among donors has been to use local consultants for implementation assessments, policy review and more detailed policy design. This trend is encouraging for ensuring better understanding of and responses to the challenges of urban local government in South Africa.

## The question of research revisited

A decade after formal political freedom it is probably time for the relationship between research and policy processes to 'normalise' around three distinct categories of research: academic, policy and (participatory) action-oriented. These loose categories have clearly been entangled and sometimes blurred during the past decade and a half. As a consequence, one could argue that forms of participatory action research gave rise to the first generation of NGOs in the late 1980s that became so central in formulating the first round of policy thinking on urban democracy and development. In the early days of policy renewal, most of the research was of a highly activist nature to reinforce the social mobilisations of new urban social movements. However, with the advent of democracy in the early 1990s, the mode of policy research shifted into a different gear, because there was a focus on proposing alternatives to the apartheid norm. Up to that point, most research was of course focused on critiquing the lies and policy positions of the apartheid state and local authorities. The shift from activist support to more formal policy development also signalled the beginning of a break between NGOs and grassroots movements.

With the advent of the pre-interim phase in 1993, most of the research on local government issues was in a propositional policy development mode, with a heavy emphasis on designing the primary elements of the new dispensation. At this moment, more academics stepped into the arena, often on commission of former NGO policy researchers who were now senior managers in the state. This process produced very little independent critical academic research in the mid- to late-1990s. In fact, one is hard-pressed to identify any original and compelling theory-building work on local government/governance during this period. Most interventions were of an overly descriptive or prescriptive nature. This has left current (policy) debates on the history and future of the emergent South African local government system impoverished. One can only hope that the next ten years will be marked by a more balanced and productive period wherein academic, policy and action research will find its rightful place and flourish. As this chapter demonstrates, there certainly is not a shortage of vital issues that demand further theorisation and policy sophistication.

## Conclusion

Since the late 1980s, a variety of forces and processes have helped bring about the current local government system in South Africa. At various moments and with varying degrees, social mobilisation, advocacy based on empirical studies, intense negotiations, financial pressures and incentives, donor interests, ideology and (perceived) political imperatives have proven particularly influential in shaping the system of urban local government. In the midst of these forces, it is difficult to unravel the exact contribution of research in decision-making on local government policy. Undoubtedly, action research by organisations like Planact played an important role in motivating and sustaining mass action against the apartheid system of urban local government. Subsequently, the negotiation phase of the early 1990s provided an unprecedented opportunity for innovative ideas and policy options on integrating the apartheid city to surface. This is evident in the negotiations at the Central Witwatersrand Metropolitan Chamber, which were underpinned by a highly sophisticated and elaborate urban research project, ultimately informing the LGNF and the LGTA. However, even then – and more obviously so during the policy formulation period in the latter half of the 1990s – research was not an objective and 'clean' process unaffected by political pressures and imperatives. Undoubtedly, the political context of most of the past decade has been such that policy options tended to be filtered through particular ideological lenses and, vice versa, that ideology largely predetermined policy outcomes. With many factors and dynamics influencing political decision-making unrecorded or unanalysed, it remains difficult to ascertain the contribution and impact of research on the system of urban local government with certainty.

### Acknowledgements

We would like to thank the interview respondents for their time and for sharing their insights and Richard Tomlinson for his editorial feedback. We also appreciate the feedback received from Alan Mabin and Robert Cameron on earlier versions of the chapter.

## Notes

1   The system of urban local government in South Africa has never been static. Throughout previous decades, urban local government underwent continuous changes and amendments to maximise its efficiency in fulfilling its key purpose. Of course, the object of local government has changed fundamentally since South Africa's transition to democracy. Consequently, its powers, functions, actions and structure have been altered significantly in recent years. At the heart of apartheid urban policy was the intent to curb African urbanisation, residentially segregate classified racial groups and eliminate urban unemployment through a combination of influx control, 'urban labour preference' and legislation pronouncing residential segregation (i.e. the Group Areas Act of 1950) (Mabin 1991; Posel 1991). However, even in the decades before apartheid became the official government policy, residential segregation and restricted residential rights to the employed was a reality administered by municipalities (Davenport 1991). In contrast, the current local government system has been designed to overcome and rectify the apartheid legacy of discrimination, underdevelopment, segregation and exclusion.

2   As noted by Robert Cameron in response to an earlier draft of this chapter, a substantial amount of literature on local government restructuring exists. The question is, however, to what extent existing documentation and recorded events adequately capture the intricacies of (party-)political decision-making and horse-trading involved in policy processes. Our view is that much of it has happened below the surface and has not been adequately documented or analysed. In the same vein, there are also the structural/cultural features of dominant political cultures which shape decisions and outcomes. Very little of this is properly documented, let alone analysed or theorised.

3   In most parts of the country, local government elections were held in 1995 in accordance with the Local Government Transition Act of 1993. In parts of the Western Cape and in KwaZulu-Natal, the elections were postponed until 1996.

4   Civic organisations are residents' associations in black communities that were part of the mass democratic movement in the late 1980s and early 1990s. Civics were initially formed to deal with local issues and, more specifically, to campaign for an improvement in the conditions in townships. Because local issues were so intertwined with national politics, their role transcended community boundaries. In 1992, civic associations established a national federation, called Sanco.

5   Swilling interview.

6   See, amongst others, Watson (2002) on the process in Cape Town and Maharaj (2002) on Durban.

7   The study included an empirical assessment of the proportion of money spent by black consumers in white shops in central Witwatersrand. The researchers involved made use of the fact that tills had two buttons: one for white consumers and one for black consumers. Empirical research was also conducted into the property rates system in the Johannesburg area, which found that property rates in the township of Soweto were higher than those in the formerly white area of Houghton (Swilling interview).

8   The six working groups were: Constitutional Development, Institutional Development, Physical Development, Social Development, Economic Development and Financial Development.

9   Interview with Mark Swilling. As a member of Planact at the time, he was closely involved in various research projects to inform the negotiations about an appropriate metropolitan system of local government in Johannesburg.

10  Interview with Mark Swilling. Planact was integrally involved in these research processes.

11  In 1993, the Metropolitan Chamber was restructured into the Greater Johannesburg Negotiating Forum in accordance with the Local Government Transition Act of 1993. In terms of the Act, the Greater Johannesburg Negotiating Forum was tasked with negotiating the appointment of a transitional council to govern the city until the local government elections of 1995 (Tomlinson 2005).

12  Interview with Andrew Boraine, who was seconded to the LGNF by Planact as adviser to the non-statutory component.

13  Interview with Andrew Boraine. It is important to bear in mind that the parallel negotiations in Codesa attracted more political attention from liberation movements. The local government negotiations were regarded as secondary, which made it easier for the right wing to wring concessions.

14  The LGTA did not decide on the allocation of powers and functions between the metropolitan council and metropolitan local councils, but allowed for local negotiations on this matter (RSA 1998; Wooldridge 2002).

15  Andrew Boraine, who worked for Planact at the time, was involved in the Central Witwatersrand Metropolitan Chamber and was subsequently seconded by Planact to the LGNF as adviser to the non-statutory component. Subsequently, members of Planact took on central roles in national and local government positions, where they continued to influence policy on local government. Similarly, between 1993 and the municipal elections of 1995/96 the organisation Inlogov (Institute for Local Government) in Cape Town played a key role in terms of training, policy development and capacity building of the non-statutory side related to the implementation of the LGTA. Its staff members at the time included Thozamile Botha (who became Deputy Director-General for Local Government in the Department for Constitutional Development, later renamed the Department for Provincial and Local Government), Andrew Boraine (who succeeded Thozamile Botha as Deputy Director-General for Local Government and subsequently became City Manager of Cape Town) and Dr Crispian (Chippy) Olver (who worked for the RDP Office on local government matters and also eventually became Deputy Director-General for Local Government in the DPLG).

16  Some additional research was commissioned in the period between the Green Paper and the White Paper, but this tended to be of a more politicised nature. For example, prior to the Green Paper a thorough study on systems of metropolitan government comparing experiences in 20 countries had been conducted. After the Green Paper, a second study on metropolitan government was conducted by Mike Sutcliffe, reflecting the position of South Africa's main urban centres rather than policy options. Dr Sutcliffe subsequently became Chairperson of the Municipal Demarcation Board, before taking up his current position as City Manager of eThekwini (Durban).

17  Responsibility for the four research themes was located in different institutions. The Graduate School of Public and Development Management at the University of the Witwatersrand was responsible for political and institutional systems, the Centre for Policy Studies for

developmental local government, whilst municipal finance fell under Treasury. The cluster 'reality check', which included research papers on gender, environment and demarcation, was coordinated by the Urban Sector Network/Foundation for Contemporary Research.

18  Interview with Dominique Wooldridge. At a workshop with the White Paper Political Committee, the people driving the process of producing the Green Paper were sidelined.

19  Whereas the Green Paper reflected options (for example, for metropolitan government or the role of traditional leaders in local governance), the White Paper presented the final policy on particular issues. Yet, although the Green Paper signalled alternatives, by that time certain policy positions had already been taken (Wooldridge interview).

20  Interview with MP Yunus Carrim, who became the Chairperson of the Portfolio Committee on Provincial and Local Government on 1 March 1998, weeks before the White Paper on Local Government was released. He argued that it was unprecedented at the time to have public hearings on a White Paper, which was a Cabinet approved policy framework rather than a discussion document.

21  This point was conceded by Lechesa Tsenoli, who was a member of the White Paper Political Committee between 1996 and 1998 and a member of the Portfolio Committee on Provincial and Local Government between 1994 and 1999 (Tsenoli interview).

22  This point was made almost unanimously by interview respondents.

23  Tsenoli interview.

24  Gotz interview.

25  Interview with MP Yunus Carrim, who was Chairperson of the Portfolio Committee on Provincial and Local Government from 1 March 1998 until the end of the second democratic Parliament in 2004.

26  Some remote rural areas with very low population densities (referred to as District Management Areas) are governed by district municipalities only.

27  This is not to imply that cities spoke in one voice on these matters.

28  Tsenoli interview.

29  This point was also made by MP Lechesa Tsenoli.

30  One of the background papers for the White Paper (on 'human settlement trends') implicitly argued for more differentiated policy and structures, but that merited only a mention in the White Paper and the symmetrical system was adopted. As Alan Mabin, the author of the background paper observes, 'The research was ignored no doubt for good political reasons' (personal communication).

31  Since the early 1990s there were numerous study missions to various countries in both the north and the south to look at comparative local government models. Specialised training courses were also organised to forge shared policy understandings of relevant international models. These interventions brought together politicians (from all sides of the ideological divide), community activists, NGO researchers and sometimes academics. These observations were confirmed by MP Lechesa Tsenoli.

32  GEAR was adopted in 1996 as the government's macroeconomic policy and is premised on the notion that improved economic performance is essential to sustain social development.

However, the neo-liberal instruments adopted to pursue the policy agenda of GEAR have served to undermine this broader policy intent.

33 The RDP was released a few months before the first democratic elections in 1994 and served as the election manifesto for the African National Congress-led alliance. It sets out a robust development agenda and includes clear targets for realising socio-economic rights of previously disadvantaged social groups. In November 1994 the RDP supposedly became official government policy when the White Paper on Reconstruction and Development was passed. In reality the policy framework reflected a significant departure from the original RDP, particularly in terms of economic policy (Pieterse & Van Donk 2002). In 1996, the RDP Office was suddenly closed and GEAR replaced the RDP as the overarching policy framework.

34 The Ministerial Advisory Committee on Local Government Transformation was appointed by the Minister for Provincial and Local Government in March 2001. Its brief included an assessment of the financial viability and capacity of municipalities, which included a review of the impact of the Municipal Structures Amendment Act (2000). The Committee produced its interim report in November 2001. Its final report was never made public. When some of its findings were reported in *Business Day* in July 2002, a stinging rebuke from the Minister for Provincial and Local Government, Sydney Mufamadi, followed (see <http://www.dplg.gov.za/speeches/draft8jul02.htm>).

35 Interview with Mark Pickering. This point is confirmed in the interim report of the Ministerial Advisory Committee, which found that contrary to constitutional provisions, the Financial and Fiscal Commission (FFC) and organised local government had not been consulted on the amendment (Ministerial Advisory Committee 2001). However, according to MP Yunus Carrim, in deciding on the amendment the Portfolio Committee took into account that there was a convergence on this issue between the Municipal Demarcation Board, DPLG and SALGA (Carrim interview).

36 Interview with Mark Pickering, Palmer Development Group, 15 December 2004, who observed that resignations in the affected sectors were not uncommon as relevant staff were insecure about their job prospects and many did not want to be reassigned to district councils. Both points (lack of financial planning and impact on staff morale) are confirmed by DPLG in its submission to the Ministerial Advisory Committee (see Ministerial Advisory Committee 2001). See also Carter (2004).

37 Because proposals to restructure the electricity distribution industry were in an advanced state, the minister proclaimed that the status quo would be retained until this process would be completed (Savage n.d.).

38 Pickering interview.

39 See the submissions of the FFC, National Treasury, the Banking Council, Free State Local Government Association and various other stakeholders to the Ministerial Advisory Committee on Local Government Transformation (Ministerial Advisory Committee 2001).

40 The Institute for Democracy in South Africa's Budget Watch is a useful source of information and analysis on budgetary matters, including the equitable share and municipal finance (see <http://www.idasa.org.za>).

41  For the financial years 2004/05, 2005/06 and 2006/07, the equitable share stands at 4.6 per cent, only to increase marginally to 4.7 per cent in 2007/08.

42  Interview with Paul Whelan. MP Lechesa Tsenoli also identified the system of intergovernmental relations, with particular reference to fiscal relations, as an area of weakness that has remained under-explored in the White Paper process.

43  Whelan interview.

44  Gotz interview. Of the 284 municipalities, there are 6 metropolitan municipalities, 231 local municipalities and 47 district municipalities.

45  See Memorandum on the Fiscal and Financial Implications of Proposed Municipal Boundary Demarcations from the Director-General: Department of Finance to the Municipal Demarcation Board, 16 February 2000.

46  Gotz interview. Cameron in this volume takes issue with this perspective, referring to it as 'urban myth'. Yet this perspective has also been articulated by the Banking Council in its submission to the Ministerial Advisory Committee (2001). Clearly, the extent to which the Municipal Demarcation Board took questions of financial viability into account in deciding on municipal boundaries is contested. Perhaps the Board has not sufficiently and/or publicly clarified its position at the time, allowing the 'urban myth' to live on.

47  Not surprisingly, this point was made quite strongly by Andrew Boraine, who is the Chairperson of the SACN (Boraine interview).

48  The Constitution makes provision for an Act of Parliament to recognise national and provincial associations representing municipalities. SALGA and its provincial affiliates have been recognised by law (the Organised Local Government Act, Act 52 of 1997) as bodies representing the interests of municipalities. The Act further allows for representation of SALGA at the National Council of Provinces and the FFC.

49  Interview with Andrew Boraine. A similar observation regarding SALGA is made in the interim report of the Ministerial Advisory Committee (2001), without the explicit reference to urban municipalities.

50  Tsenoli and Wooldridge interviews.

51  Logon was set up in the latter part of the 1990s to facilitate exchange of knowledge and experiences between urban municipalities.

52  The nine cities include the six metropolitan areas (Cape Town, Ekurhuleni/East Rand, Johannesburg, eThekwini/Durban, Nelson Mandela/Port Elizabeth, Tshwane/Pretoria) and three local municipalities (Buffalo City/East London, Mangaung/Bloemfontein and Msunduzi/Pietermaritzburg).

53  Boraine interview.

54  Interestingly, one of the departments considered least susceptible to this insight is DPLG (Boraine interview).

55  A list reflecting donor support to local government (via DPLG) between 1999 and 2003 gives insight into what donors considered to be critical aspects of the emerging local government system. Apart from more general capacity-building support, three topics stand out for getting significant support from a number of donors: 1. the IDP (funding is made available for IDP assessments, technical support, the development of a guide pack and

training by the UK Department for International Development [DFID] and Netherlands Donor Aid); 2. the development of a performance management system (including United States Agency for International Development [USAID] funds for an international review, funds from the Norwegian aid agency NORAD for a manual and implementation guide, and DFID funds for piloting and finalisation of the system); and 3. financial and fiscal aspects of local government (including work on financial reform, credit control and national guidelines for tariffs, all funded by USAID) (Source: Undated document, titled 'Current Status of Donors within DPLG'). Although GTZ is not mentioned in the document, it is well known that GTZ plays a major role in IDP-related policy issues.

## References

Atkinson D (1991) One-city initiatives. In M Swilling, R Humphries & K Shubane (eds), *Apartheid city in transition*. Cape Town: Oxford University Press.

Bernstein A (1998) Response to the White Paper by the Centre for Development and Enterprise, *Development Southern Africa*, 15(2): 297–306.

Cameron R (1991) Managing the coloured and Indian areas. In M Swilling, R Humphries & K Shubane (eds), *Apartheid city in transition*. Cape Town: Oxford University Press.

Carter J (2004) Integrating planning and budgeting at local level. Produced and published July 2004. Available at <http://www.idasa.org.za>.

Davenport D (1991) Historical background of the apartheid city to 1948. In M Swilling, R Humphries & K Shubane (eds), *Apartheid city in transition*. Cape Town: Oxford University Press.

DPLG (Department for Provincial and Local Government) (2001) *Review of powers and functions. Report for consultation*. Pretoria: DPLG.

Edwards M (1999) *Future positive: International co-operation in the 21st century*. London: Earthscan.

Giddens A (2000) *The third way and its critics*. London: Polity.

Harrison P (2001) The genealogy of South Africa's Integrated Development Plan, *Third World Planning Review*, 23(2): 175–193.

Harrison P (2003) *Towards integrated inter-governmental planning in South Africa: The IDP as a building block*. A report for the Department of Provincial and Local Government and the Municipal Demarcations Board. January 2003.

Khan F (2004) The city and its future? The eternal question, *Development Update*, 5(1): 5–51.

Mabin A (1991) The dynamics of urbanization since 1960. In M Swilling, R Humphries & K Shubane (eds), *Apartheid city in transition*. Cape Town: Oxford University Press.

Maharaj B (2002) Segregation, desegregation and de-racialisation: Racial politics and the city of Durban. In B Freund & V Padayachee (eds), *(D)Urban vortex: A South African city in transition*. Pietermaritzburg: University of Natal Press.

Ministerial Advisory Committee on Local Government Transformation (2001) Interim report on the challenges facing local government. Report submitted to the Minister of Provincial and Local Government, 22 November 2001.

National Treasury (2004) *Medium term budget policy statement 2004*. Pretoria: National Treasury. Available at <http://www.treasury.gov.za>.

Olver C (1998) Metropolitan Government for the 21st Century: Anticipated changes need maximum flexibility, *Development Southern Africa*, 15(2): 289–291.

Palmer I (2004) Local government powers and functions. Idasa Occasional Papers. Cape Town: Idasa.

Parnell S (2004a) Building developmental local government to fight poverty: Institutional change in the city of Johannesburg, *International Development Planning Review (IDPR)*, 26(4): 355–377.

Parnell S (2004b) Constructing a developmental nation – the challenge of including the poor in the post-apartheid city. Paper presented at the conference Overcoming Underdevelopment in South Africa's Second Economy. Organised by the Development Bank of Southern Africa. Pretoria, 28–29 October.

Parnell S & Pieterse E (1999) Developmental local government: The second wave of post-apartheid urban reconstruction, *Africanus*, 29(2): 68–85.

Pieterse E (2004) Untangling 'integration' in urban development policy, *Urban Forum*, 15(1): 1–35.

Pieterse E & Van Donk M (2002) Incomplete ruptures: The political economy of realising socio-economic rights in South Africa, *Law, Democracy & Development*, 6(2): 193–229.

Posel D (1991) Curbing African urbanization in the 1950s and 1960s. In M Swilling, R Humphries & K Shubane (eds), *Apartheid city in transition*. Cape Town: Oxford University Press.

Pycroft C (2002) Addressing rural poverty: Restructuring rural local government. In S Parnell, E Pieterse, M Swilling & D Wooldridge (eds), *Democratising local government: The South African experiment*. Cape Town: UCT Press.

Rose N (1999) *Powers of freedom: Reframing political thought*. Cambridge: Cambridge University Press.

RSA (Republic of South Africa) (1998) *White Paper on local government*. Pretoria: Government Printers.

SACN (South African Cities Network) (2004) *State of the Cities Report*. Available at <http://www.sacities.net>.

Savage D (n.d.) Uncertainty over powers and functions set to continue. Available at <http://www.idasa.org.za>.

Seekings J (1991) Township resistance in the 1980s. In M Swilling, R Humphries & K Shubane (eds), *Apartheid city in transition*. Cape Town: Oxford University Press.

Shubane K (1991) Black local authorities: A contraption of control. In M Swilling, R Humphries & K Shubane (eds), *Apartheid city in transition*. Cape Town: Oxford University Press.

Swilling M (1991) Introduction. In M Swilling, R Humphries & K Shubane (eds), *Apartheid city in transition*. Cape Town: Oxford University Press.

Swilling M & Boya L (1995) Local governance in transition. In P Fitzgerald, A McLennan & B Munslow (eds), *Managing sustainable development in South Africa*. Cape Town: Oxford University Press.

Swilling M, Cobbett W & Hunter R (1991) Finance, electricity costs, and the rent boycott. In M Swilling, R Humphries & K Shubane (eds), *Apartheid city in transition*. Cape Town: Oxford University Press.

Tomlinson R (2002) International best practice, enabling frameworks and the policy process: A South African case study, *International Journal of Urban and Regional Research*, 26(2): 377–388.

Tomlinson R (2005) Reinterpreting the meaning of decentralization in Johannesburg. In K Segbers, S Raiser & K Volkmann (eds), *Public problems – Private solutions? Globalizing cities in the South*. Aldershot: Ashgate.

Van Donk M (2003) Planning for a 'positive' future: HIV/AIDS as an integral component of urban development in South Africa, *Urban Forum*, 14(1): 3–25.

Watson V (2002) *Change and continuity in spatial planning. Metropolitan planning in Cape Town under political transition*. London: Routledge.

Wooldridge D (2002) Introducing metropolitan government in South Africa. In S Parnell, E Pieterse, M Swilling & D Wooldridge (eds), *Democratising local government: The South African experiment*. Cape Town: UCT Press.

World Bank (1997) *World development report 1997: The state in a changing world*. New York: Oxford University Press.

Zingel J (2004) Position paper: A case study analysis of the implications of the concept of the developmental state for skills development in the Free State province. Report prepared for DPSA. Bloemfontein: Human Sciences Research Council.

## Interviews

Boraine A, Chairperson of the South African Cities Network, 9 December 2004.

Carrim Y (MP), former Chairperson of the Portfolio Committee on Provincial and Local Government in the National Assembly (1998–2004), 10 January 2005.

Gotz G, Independent Researcher and Consultant, 14 December 2004.

Pickering M, Palmer Development Group, 15 December 2004.

Swilling M, formerly with Planact, 19 January 2005.

Tsenoli L (MP), former MEC for Local Government in the Free State (1999–2004) and member of the Portfolio Committee on Provincial and Local Government in the National Assembly (1994–1999), 7 January 2005.

Whelan P, formerly Researcher with IDASA Budget Watch, 6 January 2005.

Wooldridge D, who headed up of one of the research clusters for the Green Paper on Local Government and was the editor of the Green Paper and the White Paper, 25 January 2005.

# 6 Local government in South Africa's larger cities

Alan Mabin

## Local government in metropolises

> Great strides have been made with regard to urban development over
> the last decade. Racially divided, fragmented and unrepresentative local
> government structures have, in varying degrees, been transformed
> into integrated and representative municipalities, and the focus on
> traditional municipal service delivery has been partially transformed
> into a developmental local government approach where municipalities
> acknowledge their responsibility to contribute towards economic growth
> and job creation. Yet the challenges facing South African cities seem to
> be greater than ever. (Smit 2004: 76)

As Smit implies, the shift from apartheid local government to 'one city' municipalities
has been a very special experience. Politicians and senior officials in the major cities
generally feel that the transition has left institutions, ways of doing and ways of
thinking profoundly altered (Mbanga interview).[1] In this context, the formation
of policy on large city government has raised new challenges at each step in the
transformation process. South Africa has a long history of attempts to grapple with
cities and a deep collective inclination to think that local government at substantial
scale can do something to solve crises, manage growth, reconstruct or remake
the city (Mabin 1995). Yet local government in larger cities is always contestable,
debatable. This chapter is concerned with changing understandings of the purpose,
role and possibilities of such government.

The chapter concentrates on the larger cities within the context of wider changes in
local government in the country. The literature generally distinguishes 'metropolises'
in their complexity, cultures and representations from smaller places (see Mbembe
& Nuttall 2004). The South African Cities Network's (SACN) existence as a body
including just nine of the largest urban centres in the country reflects a similar
distinction. Harrison (2003) illustrates a need to consider larger cities and their
government separately when he outlines limitations of the standard integrated
development planning instrument in larger cities, and argues that they need scope
for more creativity and experimentation. Mirjam van Donk and Edgar Pieterse
make a similar point in their chapter in this book when they write that 'with the
consolidation of the local government system, it has become increasingly clear
that the fairly uniform model of local government presented in the White Paper is

problematic'. They contend that new ways of dealing with a real set of differences may be needed. Whilst this chapter does not intend to take up that argument, it does seek to provide an eclectic history of thinking (and in some cases, its relationship to research) around large city government in South Africa, and to outline some of the issues which problems in the model adopted may raise.

Much of the debate around city government seems to concentrate on structural issues. Yet, '[T]he dictates of a country's constitution and the nature of its economic system and governing coalition are poor predictors of what local authorities actually do' (Tomlinson 1994: 90), and similarly there is a tenuous relationship between structures and actions (not to mention effects) of local government. 'Theory-building work on local government/governance' (Van Donk & Pieterse in this book) can hardly be confined to debating structures or powers and functions of local government. Rather, it must surely explore perceptions, ideas and thinking about the place of local government in the country, within a wider global context. As stated some time ago by the Foundation for Contemporary Research (1998: 1), '[M]etropolitan government has many meanings...political victory...threat...means of redistribution...attack on lifestyle...city-wide democracy...'. There is certainly space to explore the changing meanings of city government.

This chapter accepts that larger cities have their own individual characters but are also distinct (however loosely defined) from the other kinds of human settlements in the country (see SACN 2004: 22–24). On this basis, the chapter investigates how approaches to, and understanding of, local government in the larger cities have shifted. The chapter is based on some available literature, select documents and interviews with more than a dozen people who have a long-standing involvement from rather diverse perspectives in the development of policy for local government in the cities.[2] Interviewees were selected on the basis of identifying individuals who could claim: (1) involvement in local government change since 'early' struggle days in the 1980s; (2) involvement in local negotiations in the early 1990s; (3) involvement in the (national) Local Government Negotiating Forum (LGNF) and later in the White Paper policy process around issues of metropolitan government; (4) and some who were later arrivals during the period of transition, or select external observers. The selection of interviewees was necessarily eclectic and thus the chapter does not claim any degree of closure on the questions which it raises. The issues raised by respondents are so diverse and point in such a variety of directions that the interviews proved most rewarding; but they also showed just how uncertain the present and future meanings attached to city government actually are.

## Elements of change in larger city local government

This section will indicate the major changes which have occurred in larger city local government since democracy arrived in 1994. Some of the larger urban concentrations (including Johannesburg, Pretoria, Cape Town and Durban) gained 'transitional metropolitan' status under the Local Government Transition Act (LGTA) of 1993, granted by provincial demarcation boards and governments in 1994/95. The legislation required that such 'metros' have two 'levels' of local government – both 'metropolitan' and 'local' or 'substructure' components. Together with the crucial inclusion of former black and white areas under a 'one city' government, several of these metros also included most of the previously autonomous suburban areas surrounding older cities, a remarkable development by comparison with many other parts of the world such as the United States and Australia. In most cases these metros could be described as 'soft top' rather than 'hard top'.[3] However, not all the larger cities followed this route, places such as Port Elizabeth, Bloemfontein and East London instead having single councils, and in several cases not really bringing together all of the elements of a single urban region – exemplified by Port Elizabeth and Uitenhage maintaining separate municipalities. (For a more detailed description see Cameron 1999.)

These 'transitional' arrangements gave way after the 2000 local government elections to something quite different. Some transitional metro[4] councils disappeared (Vaal/Lekoa, Khayalami). Six of the largest urban areas (Johannesburg, Cape Town, eThekwini/ Durban, Tshwane/Pretoria, Ekurhuleni/the East Rand, Nelson Mandela/Port Elizabeth) were recognised by the new national Demarcation Board as 'metropolitan' in terms of the Municipal Structures Act of 1998. These new metros have single level or 'unicity' local government bodies. Beyond them, several of the larger cities find themselves the bases of municipalities which include large rural areas (Mangaung/Bloemfontein, Buffalo City/East London, Msunduzi/Pietermaritzburg – these three being the non-metro members of the SACN – and several others such as Mbombela/Nelspruit, Polokwane/Pietersburg, Sol Plaatje/Kimberley) (SACN 2004).

But this crude structural account does not address the ways in which actors have understood these varied local government arrangements and their purposes, and the chapter is more concerned with those issues than the organisational detail of each particular city government.

## Issues in city government

Much of the debate in South Africa has ostensibly revolved around the *structures* of bigger city local government. For example, throughout the period of negotiation (1989–1994) and local government transition (1995–2000) an absolutely central issue persisted: the question of adopting a single or dual-level approach to 'metro' government. Indeed, in the issue of 'regions' or 'subcouncils' within the metros, the question is still present if dormant in most places.

A symbol of this area of debate is the sometimes controversial contradiction between the 'local', and the scale of 'metro' government. Can a single big city government (a unicity) be 'locally' responsive? The same issue exists in many parts of the world.

Is local government something which allows citizens to deepen the meaning of *democracy* precisely through being smaller-scale, indeed local, unlike other elements of government? It is this issue which leads authors such as Boudreau (2003) and Brodie (2000) to ask: What is local democracy? The latter remarks, 'Despite the growing importance of the local...the literature is frequently unclear about what, in fact, is meant by the term. Is it an opposition to the national and global, a community, a discursive field, a level of government, the city?' (Brodie 2000: 117).

Local government in cities is therefore a terrain on which issues concerning meanings of democracy can be played out. Discussions of these questions, as Boudreau (2003) shows, also raise issues of the role of local government by comparison with other actors – civil society, business, individuals as well as other spheres of government, and indeed actors on a global scale. The meaning of local government *in relation to such other actors* is contested. As one peruses the literature related to these issues, it becomes clear that many aspects of local government are changing rapidly in large cities in other parts of the world. This observation may most readily be supported from Europe, where a rapidly growing body of research and literature is demonstrating the depth of the impact of shifting local socio-economic conditions as well as of stronger non-local, subnational government (the French regions, or Catalonia) and the significance of relationships between local government and the almost supranational European Union. The literature also reveals the painfulness of shifting decades-deep ideas about the place of local government in relation to citizens, their collective organisations and their businesses (Le Galès 2002). It is equally apparent that similar issues are emerging around the city-regions of Asia (Bishop, Phillips & Yeo 2003). In South Africa a rich vein of discussion of similar questions is found in the work of Maliq Simone and of Graeme Gotz on the dilemmas of city governance in relation to the poor (eg. Simone 2002; Gotz & Simone 2003), although these enquiries are far from exhausting the broader subject. South African cities are a particular theatre of contest over local government, with special features which arise from the legacy of apartheid, but they face change and restructuring which is common throughout the world.

## Paths to city government: histories, context and contest

Many accounts have been and will be written of the paths to present large city government in South Africa, particularly in the major cities (Cameron 1999; Tomlinson 1999; Pieterse 2002; Wooldridge 2002). During the struggle years of the 1980s, none of the largest cities had anything approaching a metropolitan government. Only the introduction of metropolitan transport boards and Regional Services Councils in the eighties introduced real practices of large city government (Olivier interview).

As the struggle rooted in the townships and based on mass mobilisation plus boycotts of payments to black local authorities developed, the overwhelming demand was for 'one city' government (see Van Donk & Pieterse's chapter in this book). But what such a form would mean in the larger cities remained far from clear. The non-governmental organisations which advised the civic participants in local negotiating fora which developed from 1989, tended to think of local governments of the future essentially as 'deliverers of public services to the poor' (Sutcliffe interview). Their research, including that of Planact (see the Van Donk & Pieterse chapter in this book), demonstrated the unified nature of urban areas, but did not explore the nature of city government actions and their effects. Research emphasised the disjuncture between spaces of opportunity and where the poor actually lived, supporting a sense of a role for local government in changing those patterns without much consideration of how that would be accomplished. While a general view of city government was derived from these perspectives, rooted in the social movements and their demands, the daily work of local governments even as service providers was little appreciated – 'there was not much on fire engines, even water' (Sutcliffe interview). 'Detailed research on various aspects of local government and urban planning was being conducted within the progressive academic networks *in order to support these broad political demands with technical analysis*' (emphasis added) (Robinson 1996: 215). A lack of substantial research engagement with the trajectories of the cities and a disproportionate influence of particular formal voices meant that the scope of urban issues remained narrowly defined – and it was only as negotiations became national in 1993 that this realisation haltingly emerged (Sutcliffe and Boraine interviews).

## From local struggle to the LGTA

The LGNF's emergence was spurred by the fact that the national constitutional negotiations had not addressed local government (Boraine interview). The Forum began with a consultative conference early in March 1993 (Robinson 1996). On the oppositional or 'non-statutory' side of the Forum, 'no one had a national perspective on local government' (Boraine interview). The beginnings of a national perspective were contributed through research shaped by a Local Government Policy Research project, which evolved into the Institute for Local Governance in 1992. However, the contributions made were somewhat partial, again not analysing the complexity of large city government operations either in South Africa or elsewhere in any depth.

Thus in the LGNF, 'The starting point was housing, services, the demands of the civics, and the framing of those demands came largely from Planact and the other service organisations' (Boraine interview). Local government meant something which could solve the problem. With some exceptions, discussions did not single out the larger cities as a particular focus of attention. 'The apartheid regime tried initially to argue for differentiation of larger cities. It was not recognised that it was possible to have an equitable system with differentiation and thus the non-statutory side was opposed and argued against' (Boraine interview). The constituencies arguing for more attention to be paid to the larger cities included key people from the mostly Democratic Party (or allied) management committees of the existing big city councils – Peter Mansfield from Durban, Ian Davidson from Johannesburg, and Clive Keegan from Cape Town. They presented themselves as a 'Major Urban Areas Association' and their arguments for paying specific attention to the larger cities were supported by research conducted through the Urban Foundation on 'big cities'. But those constituencies were opposed by both the National Party (NP), which still found such forces too liberal, and the African National Congress (ANC), which tended to avoid a big city agenda in the context of its own rural–urban political make-up, and which did not identify with a politics of 'seizing the heartland of the economy' (Boraine interview). In this context the Urban Foundation's research 'undermined further the possibility of thinking through the question' despite its quality. Thus there was 'a consensus between old and new power to close down the big city stuff' (Boraine interview).

Many conservative elements flowed from the deal struck in the LGNF, mostly in the shape of the LGTA. A key compromise reflected in the LGTA was the composition of councils, with former white council areas having 50 per cent of the ward seats in the interim councils to be elected (and actually elected in 1995 in most of the country, and 1996 in Cape Town and KwaZulu-Natal).[5] Presumably the reason why the non-statutory forces agreed to this compromise was the threat to delay the national democratisation process issued by the government side (Robinson 1996). Certainly a consequence was that the balance of forces in the transitional councils elected from 1995 under the LGTA retarded reconceptualisation of big city local government. Well-organised and experienced sections of minority political parties predominated in several local councils within the metros established under the Act. For the dominant national political party the struggle to accomplish a 'full' democratisation of local government continued. That struggle played itself out in all of the structures under the LGTA, such as the provincial demarcation boards which drew boundaries for elections. For example, in Gauteng the demarcation board was chaired by a government-nominated NP local politician-cum-official, who most certainly played a highly conservative role in the process of arriving at structures of government for Pretoria, Johannesburg and the other cities of Gauteng (Mabin 1999).

Metropolitan government as defined in Schedule 2 to the LGTA was something intended to achieve 'metropolitan coordination', without distinguishing clearly between local and metropolitan roles (Tomlinson 1999: 9). The poorly developed idea of large city government which this represented was a notion of a body which would cement – or perhaps paper – over many cracks. While the ANC and associated forces clung to a notion of city government which would mean delivery of services to those who did not have them, and overcoming the discrimination which the apartheid city represented, they did not develop a new vision of city government adapted to the turbulent global times to which the cities were increasingly exposed. The LGNF, then, lent a conservative meaning to city government for the next period, during which a larger policy process began to shift interpretations attached to city government by different actors.

*From transitional local government to unicities*

It was suggested as the local government transition began in earnest that the 'inertia of transition coupled with the dynamism of the local environment and struggles around "bread and butter" issues…created a setting conducive to development planning' (Tomlinson 1994: 92), and indeed many expected that stakeholder discussion would shape coalitions and agendas for city development. But the largest political organisation carried a belief that it would be able to make local government *the* actor in development planning, and that view attached a dominant meaning to city government, including attempts to bend city government to such transformation. Despite the energetic engagement of a wide range of parties in earlier negotiations in the larger cities over the reshaping of local government, the pre-interim appointed authorities of 1993–1995 and the newly elected councils of 1995/96 onwards simply did not continue that engagement. The result was the exclusion of parties crucial to investment, response to regulation, use of infrastructure and capacity for capacity building. Consequently, given the nature of the society, its urban economies and the shifting global engagement of the country, development when it did seem to occur had in most cases relatively little to do with the efforts of city governments. Burgeoning suburbs symbolised the problem (Mabin 2005). The realisation of the problem underlay some of the debates which continued in the policy process towards the White Paper on Local Government in 1997 and 1998.

While a key theme within that process was one of further development of the idea of city government as central actor in development, there were important shifts in the expectations of local government. The culmination of the White Paper policy process encouraged others to write, perhaps exaggeratedly:

> In an obvious break with the past, the post-apartheid state has radically transformed and extended the role of local government. Now the municipality becomes the primary development champion, the major conduit for poverty alleviation, the guarantor of social and economic rights, the enabler of economic growth, the principal agent of spatial or physical planning and the watchdog of environmental justice. (Parnell & Pieterse 2002: 82–3)

In the shift from driver to champion lies a considerable move from what might be characterised as an older social democratic idea of the role of the local state – captured in the image of 'big public housing estates done properly' (Sutcliffe interview). What are the components of this shift, and why did it occur? To answer these questions requires a review of the White Paper process from the specific perspective of larger city government.

According to Dominique Wooldridge, whose role at the time involved refracting debate, the process was informed by 'the need to deal with the legacy of urban apartheid and address urgent "inherited" problems, while simultaneously establishing a viable mid- to long-term framework within which metropolitan government can be restructured' (2002: 127). However, it took several years to merge these prerogatives.

From a national perspective, delay in the necessary process of reorganising local government was presumably because of the three years taken (1994–1997) to negotiate a new Constitution in the National Assembly, although some important turns in the approach to local government took place as those negotiations proceeded. For example, the 1993 Constitution (on which the 1994 elections were based, subsequently revised) had given provinces substantial powers over local government, at the very least of oversight. Despite the forces interested in the maintenance and even expansion of provincial power, the tendency within the ANC for greater autonomy for municipalities won the day in the constitution-making process, resulting in 'getting local government away from the provinces' in the 1996 Constitution (Wooldridge interview). By extension, metropolitan government thus began to take on a more substantial meaning than before – though within limits. 'Constitutionalising local government as an equal sphere came from the strength of local contributions to struggle' (Boraine interview) – setting up a tension which has thus far been managed largely through the centralised deployment of personnel by the ruling party.

The White Paper process was driven by a Political Committee, as well as by the relevant national department's local government section. Particular individuals were very important to the shaping of ideas about city government in the period. The Political Committee set out many of the initial terms of discussion, including the removal of some of the 'highly critical left' influences from contributing directly to the process of discussion (Wooldridge interview). It also set the process on a path towards significant change in the form of large city government. The first major step on the road to a new conception was expressed in the Green Paper on Local Government (Ministry of Provincial Affairs and Constitutional Development 1997). This document set out policy direction for discussion, arguing implicitly for single city governments for the larger cities rather than multiple municipalities or two-level forms of metropolitan rule. For example, the Green Paper argued in several places that 'both the single city and integrating two tier types of metropolitan government' could accomplish identified goals, but always noted the weaker ability of the latter to do so (see 1997: 47–48). The existing arrangements were termed 'ambiguous and inadequate' and a strong argument advanced for change. The research which informed this view, however, was largely in the form of a survey of literature on large city government in other parts of the world (Wooldridge 2002: 129; Wooldridge interview) rather than a detailed exploration of what was happening in South African cities. It was not until the White Paper process was complete that a modicum of research on the conditions of existing metro governments and the views of prominent actors within them was conducted.

The Green Paper claimed that metropolitan government could 'create a basis for equitable and socially just metropolitan governance, help to minimise spillovers and externalities, promote rational and integrated planning and coordinated public investment, (and) enhance the economic competitiveness and well-being of the city' (1997: 39). In other words, the Green Paper advanced an argument for a partly economic development role, but in particular for a redistributive role for large city government. Whilst the economic role was relatively new and certainly more developed than that emerging from the LGNF, the redistributive idea continued the primary expectation of large city government developed by anti-apartheid forces from the 1980s. The White Paper, completed in 1998 (DPLG 1998), extended the same lines of thinking. There was an absence of thinking about a social development role; even guidelines for administrative structures able to carry out the intended tasks were absent from the White Paper, left to the department to develop in great haste ahead of the 2000 local government elections in the shape of a Municipal Structures Bill (Wooldridge interview), or indeed left to local governments themselves to sort out in a process still incomplete at the time of writing (Davidson, Mdunyelwa and Swaminathan interviews). The idea that city government could achieve a new city through redirecting, redistributing and redeploying remained strong, but perhaps in tension with the growing sense of city government as 'champion' of a development process rather than its sole or even major driver.

On the structural side, the White Paper's city government proposals were welcomed by many, but strongly criticised by some, particularly with respect to 'strong views [which] emerged with respect to the so-called mega-city proposals' (Sutcliffe 1998: Chapter 1). Not only was there considerable noise from circles opposed to the ANC in Durban, Pretoria and Johannesburg, but in some places – especially Cape Town – significant sections of the ANC itself 'resisted full consolidation' (Boraine interview). Because of the different political situations prevailing in different cities, 'there was a lot of parochialism' in the process (Boraine interview). As much as any other motive, the strong push for single metro councils without 'substructures' required further justification for several constituencies. Thus, following the adoption of the White Paper in 1998, further research on 'metropolitan government systems' was commissioned by the department. This research aimed explicitly to 'fine-tune aspects of the administrative, financial, political and legal frameworks suggested by the White Paper' (Sutcliffe 1998: Preface). Research was rapidly undertaken on four cities (Cape Town, Durban, Johannesburg, Pretoria) by three consultants, leading to strong conclusions on a single administrative system, single valuation roll and single budget for each of the metropolitan areas (Sutcliffe 1998: esp. Section 8.8). The conclusion to the overall report was very much in favour of a single metropolitan system or 'unicity' approach.

The research chapters in the report are also suggestive of a shift towards understanding the larger cities as single entities which, although having internally varied needs, would best be served by so-called unicity governments. Perhaps most significantly, the report closed with calls for more research to inform the other spheres of government, with a view to supporting the development of metropolitan government in the service of 'the engine rooms of economic growth' (Sutcliffe 1998: Section 8.8). The emphases in the idea of city government had certainly shifted in directions rejected at the time of the LGNF five years earlier, and these lines of development have remained strong ever since.

Whilst most public attention probably focused on the 'unicity' question as the White Paper policy process moved towards implementation, a further debate concerned what the White Paper termed 'municipal service partnerships'. To some extent this debate represented 'a huge but narrow debate on privatisation...only around traditional municipal services' (Boraine interview). It reflected the growing awareness of limitations of capacity in municipalities, and also the international debate on partnerships. That awareness was driven, through precisely the period in which the White Paper was in preparation, by events in the actually existing metros, particularly Johannesburg.

## Impact of fiscal crisis

Even prior to the emergence of major problems in metro administration, however, the extent to which the options open to city government were actually limited had increasingly impressed itself, sometimes painfully, on those who came into power in the nineties (Olivier and Swaminathan interviews). However, it was only when metropolitan government began to run into very significant problems that the approach began to be questioned rather more seriously. It was perhaps these events which encouraged a shift from thinking of city governments as *the* major actors, to thinking of them as *contributors* to shaping the environment within which development would happen. 'It took time for new actors to appreciate that cities are not equal to municipalities' (Boraine interview).

A prominent actor in Johannesburg noted that transitional local government's initial inclination was 'to respond with: it's going to be like that, it's going to be great, etc., and it fails to recognise that there's a lot of other things happening, that people have to survive and that they're going to create ways of surviving, and how do you incorporate that into your own processes' (Graeme Reid, CEO of Johannesburg Development Agency, quoted in Lipietz 2004: 10). A tension developed in the new city governments trying to realise the vision of the integrated, democratic, functioning, equitable city, expressed in the new understanding that much of the time city government could only hope to 'reach some kind of control in an inordinately confused, fluid and chaotic environment' (Lipietz 2004: 11). The material side of these ambiguities revealed itself in the increasing fiscal difficulties of several municipalities.

By 1997 the ANC-ruled state in South Africa had already committed itself to a development path in which fiscal discipline became the key to economic growth (and in a more hopeful scenario, employment growth). Of course, it took time for this commitment to be realised in different parts of the broad governmental apparatus. For example, some departments of state were still budgeting mostly for equity and redistribution a few years later, until the discipline of the medium-term expenditure framework and other instruments wielded by the Treasury began to bite. In local government the same fiscal discipline took longer to develop. Symbolic of the distance between local government practice and that of other spheres, was the relatively high remuneration of many municipal officials. It took major shocks in the system for larger city government to shift powerfully towards new understandings of the business of city government.

The most prominent of these shocks was the fiscal crisis of Johannesburg. 'Inefficiency, overspending and bad budgetary planning plunged Johannesburg into bankruptcy by 1997' (*Financial Mail* 11.02.2005: 19). The consequences of the fiscal crisis included a collapse in the capital budget of the city, falling from around R1.25 billion in 1997 to less than half that figure for the next four years, and reaching as low as R250 million in 2000 – not much over a tenth of the current estimates of required capital expenditure for maintenance and new infrastructure (*Financial Mail* 11.02.2005: 19). The Johannesburg saga, most prominently written up in Beall, Crankshaw and Parnell (2002), is the story of a city administration which conceptualised itself as the primary actor in the city, attempted to pursue a highly redistributive path, underestimated the political problems of doing so, and overestimated its own capacities. Fiscal crisis was the result.

The Johannesburg case informed national thinking about the future of metropolitan government to a very substantial extent. Wooldridge (2002; interview) suggested that the media attention given to the Johannesburg case was significant; sensitivity to the interests affronted by Johannesburg fiscal policy may have been at least as important. Interviewees concur that the Johannesburg case had a profound impact on policy discussions (Boraine, Sutcliffe, Ralikontsane and Wooldridge interviews).

The resolution of the fiscal crisis in Johannesburg is associated with the adoption of a strategy to reorganise the structure of the city's operations, including the 'corporatisation' of many entities (electricity, roads, water, garbage collection, zoo), the sale of a few units (minor airport, gas), and the pursuit of a far more prominent strategy to seek investment and economic growth rather than an overt redistributive agenda. The consequence of the Johannesburg saga has been wide rethinking, clearly present in each of the larger city governments, to the effect that, 'Now the view is if you get local economic development right, stability will follow, resources will flow, and service delivery can take place' (Mdunyelwa interview).[6] That this linkage is optimistic is indicated by much of the international literature, for many city administrations have pursued fiscal austerity and 'active engagement in transforming the city into a potent productive node in the global economy' (Lipietz 2004: 2), but they have frequently done so at the expense of other understandings of local government (see Brenner & Theodore 2002).

Nonetheless, the White Paper continued the 'language of township resistance [as]…the hopeful language of urban reconstruction' (Robinson 1996: 219), as it had been established in the earlier negotiation period but to some extent frustrated by the long five-year interim period of local government. The effect in some of the cities was to put off the day of reckoning which the Johannesburg experience indicated loomed over each one's future. The notion of city government as central development actor continued, awaiting modulation only as problems deepened.

## Prospects of alternative views and approaches

Just as those who entered city government from 1995 onwards found that their understandings of those institutions had to alter, so the process of realising the White Paper's policies led to new understandings of city government. For example, as the Municipal Demarcation Board worked feverishly to define much more than the boundaries of cities in time for the 2000 local government elections, both it and the Treasury commissioned more substantial fiscal research than had occurred in the policy drafting process. Amongst other results, that allowed actors to appreciate that capacity in the large cities to understand their integrated urban systems was weak. It led some to a view that sustainability of city government *itself* required 'much more than a focus on service delivery' (Sutcliffe interview).

The contradiction between the concept of city government as responsible for 'delivery' of the sophisticated version of basic needs, and the capacities of the city governments actually to do so, is the structural cause of the financial crisis which confronts each of the cities from time to time. 'Not even in Sweden can city government live up to this vision' (Olivier interview). The difficulty of the contradiction is manifest in the near impossibility of a ward councillor campaigning on anything other than better service delivery. Yet the evidence suggests that in many cases city government is actually 'bad on the basics' (Wooldridge interview).

Along the route to present city government, alternative visions have certainly been noted but seldom seriously entertained. For example, the White Paper (DPLG 1998) notes that municipalities could think of their actions in terms of developing the social capital of their communities; but that view was not developed at the time, nor pursued in detail by city governments. What is more, given the lack of serious exploration of such issues through sensitive research, the rather crude notion that such social capital is somehow available to be called up at will is clearly problematic (Harrison 2002). A lack of detailed research means that such local government roles are still in their infancy, although in Johannesburg in particular, the social development work undertaken more recently suggests that they are being explored.

The most evident area of change lies in partnerships – particularly with private business – which have developed in different cities with their own momentum.

## Partnership as key theme in city government

'Partnerships are now the thing' (Nkahle interview).

In a probably apocryphal aside the former city manager of a major city mentioned that during a substantial term of office after apartheid there had never once been a scheduled exchange of views between the city manager and business leaders in the city. Such anecdotes are supported by business people. The lack of engagement between local government and business has often been bemoaned (De Jager and Leissner interviews), even if there are partial exceptions (such as those in Durban – see Freund 2001), which in any event may become more typical. It is equally apparent that more recently, perhaps particularly since 2000, a more or less complete change in municipal–business relationships has occurred, even if weaknesses in the relationship continue in terms of misunderstandings and misinformation (Mdunyelwa interview).

The vastly increased preparedness of city governments to enter into partnerships with business arose from a perhaps belated 'recognition that municipal powers alone cannot transform cities' (Boraine interview). The consequences have been multidimensioned. Materially, where some of the cities have been most successful is where they have identified and assisted things happening already, as in the Cape Town central business district (CBD) and certain other areas, or in the Msunduzi/ Pietermaritzburg CBD (Davidson and Swaminathan interviews). In these cases, it is precisely partnership arrangements which have led to new lines of development.

Yet these forms of progress in turn raise new challenges, as in Msunduzi where the management of a crime prevention strategy is theoretically in the hands of a safety and security forum, but where it appears that the real management and delivery under the partnership is outside civic centre and not really in council hands (Swaminathan interview).

Far from the history of not talking to business, in some cases now the approach looks more like 'involving them every step of the way'. The 'role of the city is no longer to set terms, but to discuss and engage' (Sutcliffe interview). Whilst this may mean a leading role in some cases, in others it is easy to imagine how direction and even control may ultimately pass to business constituencies – not necessarily meaning the current leading or long-term established white-led businesses, but over time also the emerging larger black businesses. Thus there is a challenge, and as 'more transformed business' emerges city governments 'will have to engage differently' (Sutcliffe interview).

What allows municipalities to lead? In the longer run the 'critical issue is economic intelligence not political intelligence' (Sutcliffe interview) – something recognised by the increasing role accorded to economic research activities in most of the major cities. The point here is that partnerships in practice have the potential to unleash very different meanings of city government from those which populate the pages of earlier policy documents, and are already doing so. Lurking around the corner is the difficulty which has confronted politicians in other environments, where a shift from hands-on service delivery to 'community leadership' and 'convenor of partnerships' has sometimes led to detaching local political leaders from their traditional party roots (Cole & John 2001).

## City government autonomy in economic development

Whilst city governments have plunged into partnerships, which have delivered new forms of traditional services (street cleaning, security), it is not at all obvious that the approach has really delivered economic growth and development. The idea that city government is always on the brink of 'getting cracking' is popular, has some substance, is punted even by journals like the *Financial Mail* (the quote is from a cover story on Johannesburg on 11.02.2005), but is not yet believed even by senior officials in many administrations (interviews). In the face of these ambiguities city government easily ends up being about control rather than regeneration (Lipietz 2004). The disappointments of local economic development can be temporarily contained by a rhetoric built on words and phrases like 'gradual', 'promising', 'projects initiated', and 'momentum to be maintained' (see for example Nel & Binns 2003: 181). But it is by no means clear that the way to move beyond these disappointments is through more support (from other spheres) and more human resource capacity. It is at least as likely that reconceptualisation of practical 'developmentalism' is required – and it is clear that many city administrators are engaged in such rethinking.

Some of the more intriguing examples come from cases of shrinking city economies, which at least in some views would be a way to characterise Kimberley, Vereeniging and East London (in Sol Plaatje, Emfuleni and Buffalo City municipalities). In those places, there is some development of the idea that less is more, in other words, 'if the municipality tries to do less it may succeed in focusing its actions and accomplishing something (such as) slowing disinvestment patterns…by finding a few new areas of potential and partnering to pursue their development' (Olivier interview). These shifts perhaps begin to illustrate new lines of thinking on 'issues like influencing the market, getting markets to work in areas of failure' (Boraine interview). There are some signs of wealthier city government moving in these directions. For example, elements of the strategic plan in Johannesburg, *Joburg 2030* (City of Johannesburg 2003), concern identifying roles for city government in building success factors, in this case the top priorities emerging as bringing down crime rates and building skills. In Durban the notion exists that 'success is going to be based on African entrepreneurship' connected to a role for the city government in 'broadening the entrepreneurial base' (Sutcliffe interview).

On a larger scale and perhaps in more dramatic ways, clues to developmental city government come from the shift from state control in China to much greater local autonomy. Jieming Zhu (2004: 424) writes, 'China's local governments have become economic interest groups with their own policy agenda, and thus the local developmental state.' The idea of the local state as highly autonomous is present in some previous local discourses (for example, the idea of 'metro charters' bestowing considerable power in Sutcliffe 1998). South African local government transformation has certainly included 'decentralisation plus consolidation of each local authority' (Boraine interview), and the consequence is the potential for powerfully autonomous city governments. Indeed, some officials note that 'to an extent the strategic path is carved by the city alone and aligned to national policy' (Mdunyelwa interview). But city autonomy remains contentious.

If cities are 'collective actors, aggregations of groups and interests capable under certain circumstances of purposive initiative', the issues which confront the progressive city 'engaged in local struggles for economic wellbeing and cultural autonomy' (Walton 2004: 237) are substantial. Among them is the question of whether the individual city strategic paths will at some point diverge from and even contradict national directions – a question which has seldom been raised (but see Lootvoet & Khan 2002), but is obviously potent in many other countries. The consolidation of large metros has created something 'which suits cities that want to get into global strategy' (Boraine interview) and has perhaps created the potential for them to do so autonomously. As a result, a recent survey of the urban condition asks, 'Can locally based growth coalitions…form significant alliances that may have national political implications?…it is too early to tell…so far the ANC has put in place measures that firmly control any deviant local development but with time and the possible decline of the centralizing post-liberation ethos, this may become a fruitful way of looking at future city development' (Freund 2006: 317).

South Africa is a tissue of contradictory trends. At present these trends suggest a superficial calm, since they appear to balance each other (Lee 2004). At some point, however, if one alignment of forces gains strength over others, one would anticipate a lurch in the direction of the trends which overwhelm 'the surface quiet of 2005' (Lee 2004: 4). The potential for cities to emerge as collective actors in the sense noted by Le Galès (2002) is present. It is also being managed by the SACN, which seeks discussion of these roles and exploration of 'particular city strengths within the urban system' (Mbanga interview), perhaps as an alternative to growing city autonomy.

## Intergovernmental relations

More immediately, another area which demonstrates patches of stability is that of relationships between city governments and the larger scales of government. The weaknesses of larger city government have allowed the provinces a new lease on life with respect to their management (Wooldridge interview). Such creeping hierarchical roles coalesce with other trends towards a heightened role for provinces, including not least the victory of the ANC in all provinces in the 2004 elections, meaning that the ten years of a central emphasis on reducing provincial roles in the interests of reducing opposition power, could at least for the foreseeable future be relaxed.

Some provinces certainly envisage a more activist role. For example, Western Cape Premier Ebrahim Rasool's state of the province address on 18 February 2005 explicitly called for a more interventionist role for the province, and the new taxes which he proposed at least potentially suggested a diminution of municipal developmental roles in favour of provincial action (*Cape Argus* 19.02.2005). At least the relationship between city governments and provincial institutions is openly under negotiation. Behind that lies a degree of blurring in the roles of local politicians *vis-à-vis* provincial politicians (Mdunyelwa and Mbanga interviews).

To separate between the relevant roles is difficult, and sheds a little light on the difficulties of further developing city government. Some point to the fact that city governments tend to have 'more capacity in most areas than provincial governments' (Sutcliffe interview). Yet provinces may have greater capital resources to contribute to city development, as the Gauteng Blue IQ projects demonstrate.[7] Thus 'city development strategies are intergovernmental strategies' (Boraine interview), leading to new thinking on cities within intergovernmental relations, new structures in the relationships (agency, partnering, merged offices in some sectors), awareness of contradictions and the statement of a 'need for tightening IGR [intergovernmental relations]' (Mdunyelwa and Boraine interviews). The most ambitious ideas come from Gauteng, where the new image of joint management of the province between the provincial government and at least the three metro municipalities within it, is the stuff of a new discourse.

## The imagined city government

The Gauteng example indicates that thinking about what the city is, and how its government and governance relates to that reality, are once more subject to debate, investigation and negotiation. What is the city which our city governments imagine? Is it the surface city or the city underneath? (Mbembe & Nuttall 2004). A possible answer is that the problems of city government stem from the limited knowledge, ways of seeing and readings of cities, in turn related to the narrowness of research and the overconfident presentations of knowledge without negotiating their meanings for diverse elements which make up, at least, the city. If city government is meant to create a terrain for the engagement of citizens in spite of their divergences, 'in Johannesburg this formula is still in the making' (Caldeira 2004: 236). The same is true of the rest of the country.

Thierry Paquot, the editor of the excellent French publication *Urbanisme*, a magazine widely read by urban practitioners and intellectuals in the francophone world, cites Georges Perec: 'Ne pas essayer trop vite de trouver une définition de la ville' (Don't try to find a definition of the city too quickly) (Paquot 2003). One could take this as an aphorism for a process of continuously revisiting the understandings of the city shared, and not shared, by different parties to city government and to shaping the city. The question is perhaps not *what* the city is, but *why* it is, as Perec further notes, and he comments that different disciplines do not on their own achieve finality on the question – the struggle to inform action through concept and reconceptualised knowledge is continuous (Perec 1974).

Many aspects of urban change confound a simple and linear view of the tasks of city government. The contradictions of gentrification, for example, present the city with patterns of change not contemplated in the linear model of addressing the legacy of apartheid, an instance where much more research might assist (Visser 2002). Parallel but not identical, is the highly uneven pattern of changes in residential segregation and possibly integration. Some of the former white group area sections of larger cities (Bloemfontein, Fourways [Johannesburg]) are now reaching demographic proportions of a third or a half black, with a major role of local government probably being purely as one public sector employer of the 'new' middle-class populations concerned (Fife & Larsen 2004). Negotiating meanings could prove creatively important in these new circumstances. An illustration can be found in the difficulties city government faces in relation to the highly mobile South African urban population. 'Linkages with the rural are critical to advancing the national city interest' (Nkahle interview), yet city governments have not found means of dealing with the very different perceptions of intervention across marginalised groups of poor urban residents – who almost always have complex linkages with others, other spaces – and whose priorities for development may be very different from those of councillors and officials in municipal positions. Indeed, it is too easy to assume 'false consensus on what the community wants' (Olivier interview). There seems to be a long road to city government which draws together and enables negotiation of collective action.

> There is no more urgent task in our new democracy than to embark on
> the long journey of re-dreaming our urban future firmly grounded in the
> values of social justice, human solidarity and equity. In this endeavour
> we must be careful not to confuse constructive visioning or utopian
> thinking with utopian plans and planning... (Khan 2004: 43)

Execution of this task has not proved simple. Despite widespread requirements of participation and a vast calendar of meetings, ward committees and representative forums, many barriers separate people from influence (transport, language, etc.) and 'a lot of trust has been lost' (Nkahle interview). In a cynical view one would stress how city government remains an institution from which something is expected but people are able to scale down to the situation where some groups have thus accepted city government's participation initiatives 'as a source of supper not of influence' (Nkahle interview).

Of course, city government has functioned as a source of employment and the realisation of the hopes of many for a more secure and comfortable life, especially in the managerial echelons (Mbanga interview). And there has been a degree of movement between city government and business, between appointed and elected status, which suggests that to some extent a relatively unbounded elite has emerged around city government. However, that does not mean that South African city governments have become vehicles of a 'politics of the belly' (Bayart 1993). For example, a degree of separation between those who do official work and those who become contractors to city government does appear to persist. But some participants in city government do appear to think of enrichment through their roles in relation to the broader state apparatus as just what the 'game is about' (see Bayart 1993). And of course most of those employed in city government are in no strong position to shape its actions, except when coalitions between ordinary employees and other constituencies appear to frustrate change (eg. Pieterse 2002).

In short, the processes which have given us existing city governments have not yet fully engaged ways of exploring and negotiating, not only the imagination of the city, but even the imagination of city government itself.

## Conclusion

City government has clearly struggled to become 'a powerful tool that would forever help the poor to realise the dream of a life free of poverty, free of hunger, free of unemployment and free of underdevelopment' (President Thabo Mbeki in *Sunday Times* 20.02.2005: 18). Simple and complex images akin to the values of the eighties have only very partially been achieved. 'Integration shows just a few glimmers – like Summer Greens' (Davidson interview). 'The groups that seem to have used the new structures of democracy the most are from the middle classes,' observes Teresa Caldeira (2004: 236). Presumably this limit is a consequence of the lack of civil society organisations which conceptualise themselves as urban actors engaging at the scale of the city as a whole (Pieterse 2003). What are the moments, in the history recounted here, when different meanings have emerged, when creative ideas about the city and its government have flowered?

Significant breaks have occurred in the understandings of city government in South Africa's larger urban places over the period of struggle, negotiation, transition and transformation. Those intriguing moments seem to have been associated with the pursuit of an open, creative research agenda. At present local government in the larger cities seems reasonably settled on a modest idea of what local government can do, mostly in partnerships and through 'special interventions' (Mdunyelwa 2004: 16–17) rather than broad programmes and city-transformative agendas. These understandings seem to indicate that the cities are not empowered to pursue the 'freedom to operate beyond constraints imposed by any stakeholder' (Mdunyelwa 2004: 17). In this sense one may revisit a perceptive comment made by Udesh Pillay during the development of the project of which this chapter forms a part, a comment for which the chapter provides significant support:

The shaping of understandings of local government in the larger cities has been deeply affected by a relative lack of research, of narrowness of such research as has been undertaken, political framing of research, disjunctures between national and local forces, ideological biases, and different versions of genesis. (Points made by Udesh Pillay at a seminar at HSRC on 29.09.2004)

## Acknowledgements

Many thanks to those who shared time and thoughts in formal interviews, and also to those whose ideas and recollections have implicitly entered the text from less formal discussions.

## Notes

1   A list of interviews is appended at the end of the chapter.

2   Inevitably a major influence on the ideas in the chapter arose in the course of an executive development programme led by the author over many months in 2003/04, from extended discussions with City of Johannesburg participants with whom I chose not to conduct formal interviews. Prominent among them were Blake Mosley-Lefatola, Jakoob Makda, Lawrence Boya, and Pat Lephunya.

3   A phrase introduced by Mark Swilling in the early nineties; in most cases the primary power remained with local/substructure councils, leaving metros 'soft'.

4   The abbreviated term 'metro' is used in the chapter to denote the specific forms of metropolitan government adopted since 1995.

5   An incidental consequence was that where African sections were factually a minority, their representation was overweighted, as in most Western Cape towns and, indeed, in Cape Town itself, with the result that the ANC was able to win control of Cape Town's major local council, though not of the metro council itself.

6   Similar points have been made in my interviews in Mbombela, Msunduzi, Mangaung, eThekwini, etc.

7   Major capital projects initiated and financed by Gauteng provincial government.

## References

Bayart J-F (1993) *The state in Africa: The politics of the belly*. London: Longman.

Beall J, Crankshaw O & Parnell S (2002) *Uniting a divided city: Governance and social exclusion in Johannesburg*. London: Earthscan Publications.

Bishop R, Phillips J & Yeo W (eds) (2003) *Postcolonial urbanism: Southeast Asian cities and global processes*. New York: Routledge.

Boudreau J (2003) Questioning the use of 'local democracy' as a discursive strategy for political mobilization in Los Angeles, Montreal and Toronto, *International Journal of Urban and Regional Research*, 27(4): 793–810.

Brenner N & Theodore N (2002) Cities and the geographies of 'actually existing neoliberalism', *Antipode,* 34(3): 349–379.

Brodie J (2000) Imagining democratic urban citizenship. In EF Isin (ed.), *Democracy, citizenship and the global city.* London: Routledge.

Caldeira T (2004) Review of Beall, Crankshaw & Parnell 2002, *International Journal of Urban and Regional Research,* 28(1): 235–236.

Cameron R (ed.) (1999) *Democratisation of South African local government: A tale of three cities.* Pretoria: Van Schaik.

City of Johannesburg (2003) *Joburg 2030.* Johannesburg: City of Johannesburg.

Cole A & John P (2001) *Local governance in England and France.* London: Routledge.

DPLG (Department of Provincial and Local Government) (1998) *White Paper on local government.* Pretoria: DPLG.

Fife I & Larsen P (2004) Transformation: The new cosmopolis: Johannesburg leads way to racially integrated suburbs, *Financial Mail* 29.10.2004.

Foundation for Contemporary Research (1998) *Metropolitan government 1994–1997: Case studies of Durban, Johannesburg and Cape Town.* Cape Town: FCR.

Freund B (2001) City Hall and the direction of development: The changing role of the local state as a factor in the economic planning and development of Durban. In B Freund & V Padayachee (eds), *[D]Urban vortex: A South African city in transition.* Pietermaritzburg: University of Natal Press.

Freund B (2006) The state of South Africa's cities 2005. In S Buhlungu et al. (eds), *The state of the nation 2005-2006.* Cape Town: HSRC Press.

Gotz G & Simone A (2003) On belonging and becoming in African cities. In R Tomlinson, R Beauregard, L Bremner & X Mangcu (eds), *Emerging Johannesburg: Perspectives on the post-apartheid city.* New York: Routledge.

Harrison K (2002) Social capital and local government. In S Parnell, E Pieterse, M Swilling & D Wooldridge (eds), *Democratising local government: The South African experiment.* Cape Town: UCT Press.

Harrison P (2003) *Towards integrated inter-governmental planning in South Africa: The IDP as a building block.* A report for the Department of Provincial and Local Government and the Municipal Demarcations Board. January 2003.

Khan F (2004) The city and its future? The eternal question, *Development Update,* 5(1): 5–52.

Lee R (2004) Deceptively quiet year. In South Africa in 2005, *Financial Mail* 03.12.2004: 4–5.

Le Galès P (2002) *European cities: Social conflicts and governance.* Oxford: Oxford University Press.

Lipietz B (2004) 'Muddling through': Urban regeneration in Johannesburg's inner city. Paper presented at N-Aerus Annual Conference, Barcelona.

Lootvoet B & Khan S (2002) La decentralisation Sud-Africaine et les métropoles: Les défis de Durban, *Autrepart 21*: 145–160.

Mabin A (1995) Urban crisis, growth management and the history of metropolitan planning in South Africa, *Urban Forum,* 6(1): 67–94.

Mabin A (1999) From hard top to soft serve: Demarcation of metropolitan government in Johannesburg for the 1995 elections. In RG Cameron, *Democratisation of South African local government: A tale of three cities*. Pretoria: Van Schaik.

Mabin A (2005) Suburbanisation, segregation and government of territorial transformations, *Transformation*, 57: 47–63.

Mbembe A & Nuttall S (2004) Writing the world from an African metropolis, *Public Culture*, 16(3): 347–372.

Mdunyelwa L (2004) From urban distress to global city: Cape Town's improved districts, *Development Update*, 5(1): 161–168.

Ministry of Provincial Affairs and Constitutional Development (1997) *Green Paper on local government*. Pretoria: Government Printer.

Nel E & Binns T (2003) Putting developmental local government into practice: The experience of South Africa's towns and cities, *Urban Forum*, 14(2–3): 165–184.

Paquot T (2003) Que savons-nous de la ville et de l'urbain? In J Levy, O Mongin, T Paquot, M Roncayolo & P Cardinali (eds), *De la ville et du citadin*. Marseille: Parenthèses.

Parnell S & Pieterse E (2002) Developmental local government. In S Parnell, E Pieterse, M Swilling & D Wooldridge (eds), *Democratising local government: The South African experiment*. Cape Town: UCT Press.

Perec G (1974) *Espèces d'espace*. Paris: Galilée.

Pieterse E (2002) From divided to integrated city? Critical overview of the emerging governance system in Cape Town, *Urban Forum*, 13(1): 3–37.

Pieterse E (2003) Problematising and recasting vision-driven politics in Cape Town. In C Haferburg & J Ossenbrügge (eds), *Ambiguous restructurings of post-apartheid Cape Town*. Munster: Lit Verlag.

Robinson J (1996) *The power of apartheid: State, power and space in South Africa's cities*. Oxford: Butterworth.

SACN (South African Cities Network) (2004) *State of the Cities Report*. Johannesburg: SACN.

Simone A (2002) Dilemmas of informality for African urban governance. In S Parnell, E Pieterse, M Swilling & D Wooldridge (eds), *Democratising local government: The South African experiment*. Cape Town: UCT Press.

Smit W (2004) The urban development imagination and *realpolitik*, *Development Update*, 5(1): 53–80.

Sutcliffe M (1998) Further research into metropolitan government systems. Report for Department of Provincial and Local Government. Available at <http://www.dplg.gov.za/documents/wpaper/resourswhitepaper/furtherresdoc.htm>.

Tomlinson R (1994) *Urban development planning: Lessons for the economic reconstruction of South Africa's cities*. Johannesburg: Wits University Press.

Tomlinson R (1999) Ten years in the making: The evolution of metropolitan government in Johannesburg, *Urban Forum*, 10(1): 1–40.

Visser G (2002) Gentrification and South African cities, *Cities*, 19(6): 419–423.

Walton J (2004) Review of P Le Galès (2002) European cities, *International Journal of Urban and Regional Research*, 28(1): 236–239.

Wooldridge D (2002) Introducing metropolitan government in South Africa. In S Parnell, E Pieterse, M Swilling & D Wooldridge (eds), *Democratising local government: The South African experiment*. Cape Town: UCT Press.

Zhu Jieming (2004) Local developmental state and order in China's urban development during transition, *International Journal of Urban and Regional Research*, 28(2): 424–447.

### Interviews

Boraine A, Cape Town Partnership/South African Cities Network, 17 February 2005.

Davidson B, City of Cape Town, 10 September 2004.

De Jager M, Johannesburg Chamber of Commerce and Industry, 25 January 2002.*

Leissner G, AngloProps, 11 January 2002.*

Mbanga S, South African Cities Network, 1 March 2005.

Mdunyelwa L, City of Cape Town, 18 February 2005.

Nkahle S, South African Cities Network and former Planact fieldworker, 14 February 2005.

Olivier A, Organisation Development Africa, 8 November 2004.

Ralikontsane K, Mangaung Municipality, 6 August 2004.

Sutcliffe M, City of eThekwini, 23 February 2005.

Swaminathan T, Msunduzi Municipality, 22 February 2005.

Wooldridge D, Johannesburg, 27 January 2005.

* These interviews were conducted by Alan Mabin for a consulting project led by Susan Parnell.

# 7 The development of policy on the financing of municipalities

Philip van Ryneveld

## Introduction

This chapter examines the processes and influences which led to the development of current policies on the financing of municipal government, while noting some of the more significant bodies of research which informed this.

It is through municipalities that many of the most basic needs are provided, such as water, electricity, sanitation, refuse services, roads, and fire and emergency services. The financial resources that municipalities have at their disposal are thus critical to issues of poverty alleviation, redistribution and economic growth.

But there is a further, less obvious, yet equally significant dimension. The manner in which revenue and capital are mobilised for local governent is also critical to the structure and nature of accountability and, therefore, to the design and functioning of municipal institutions and their position within the overall intergovernmental system. In essence, where municipalities are reliant upon other spheres of government for resources, they will inevitably focus much of their attention on these other spheres in order to ensure that resource levels are maintained or expanded. Where they are dependent upon their own residents for such resources their focus will generally shift accordingly.

Underlying much of the policy development in the arena of municipal finance in recent years has been the issue of how to provide acceptable levels of municipal services to poor households at affordable rates which, in turn requires a degree of redistribution. That source of redistribution can be either local, through cross-subsidisation within the municipality, or from grants financed from national taxes, or a combination of the two.

The slogan 'One city, one tax base' which was developed during the struggles of the late 1980s on the Witwatersrand places the emphasis on local redistribution which, while it may suffice under certain circumstances in wealthier areas, has serious limitations in poor regions of the country where the tax base is very weak.

The conventional view internationally is that redistribution is best effected from the national level. This is because strongly redistributive local jurisdictions will tend to attract poor residents, while wealthier residents will be attracted to less redistributive municipalities, thus increasing the need while reducing the scope for redistribution.

The broad thrust of government policy has placed the emphasis on financing redistribution from the national tax base through the equitable share and other grants, although there is significant local-level redistribution in the bigger centres – to a far greater degree than that financed by national grants. Certainly, the concept of redistribution through a local tax base has been a significant presence in policy-making. In some cases this appears to be functioning reasonably effectively, although in others this approach has led to anomalous outcomes such as the manner in which Regional Services Council (RSC) levies raised in larger secondary towns have been used for redistributive purposes in their rural hinterlands.

Ultimately, balances need to be struck so as to achieve redistribution while not overly compromising either local accountability or economic growth. This tension has underlain much of the policy development.

Policy around some of the key mechanisms for financing municipal government is still being developed. Most notably, in the 2005 Budget speech the Minister of Finance announced that the RSC levies were to be 'eliminated' from 1 July 2006, and replaced with other instruments. National Treasury is conducting research into this and a number of other issues as part of the review and further development of a 'local government fiscal framework', and has made some of this material available on its website.[1] On the other hand, important broader themes of the policy are well established.

Indeed, despite the contentious nature of the subject, these broader themes, which are highly significant and relate in particular to the establishment of local government as a properly independent sphere of government, have not been seriously questioned. The focus has rather been on policy development and implementation within the terms of these themes. For example, there have been numerous calls for an increase in the 'equitable share' allocated to local government; but there has been little resistance to the concept of the equitable share. There has been debate around how property tax should be reformed, but little debate around the fundamentals of retaining the property tax as a local revenue source. This suggests that the framework that was established when the Constitution was written was generally robust.

In the first part of this chapter I attempt briefly to articulate this broad framework. This is followed by a section tracing its formulation, originating in anti-apartheid struggle, through developments which followed the Soweto uprising of 1976 to the period of intense negotiations regarding the role and financing of local government at the beginning of the 1990s. I then highlight some of the main policy developments and refinements which have taken place subsequently, and follow this with a section identifying and discussing the most significant current policy issues and debates, some of which are addressed by research being conducted by National Treasury. The chapter concludes with some remarks on the relationship between research and policy-making, and the influence of research organisations and donor agencies.

The focus of the chapter is on the framework whereby revenue is raised for the provision of municipal services, rather than on financial administration. Thus some of the important debates on financial governance which are addressed in the Local Government: Municipal Finance Management Act (No. 56 of 2003), are not discussed.

At the outset I should note that I was personally involved in many of the processes described and analysed here. In this respect this chapter is partially a personal account and perhaps in some cases the benefits of a relatively intimate insight into what occurred are diminished by a lack of objective perspective. Consequently, I have footnoted my involvement.

## Seven key features of the current system of municipal finance

South Africa's post-apartheid system of municipal finance could be characterised by seven key features. These features are now largely unquestioned, but are of considerable importance in seeking to build municipalities as an effective sphere of government, independent, yet able to draw on national resources to address the service delivery needs of poor areas and households. Many of these features are absent in other countries. This section mentions some of the main elements that constitute each of these seven features, some of which have been the subject of debate and revision that will be dealt with in subsequent sections.

### Substantial own revenues

First, local government is substantially financed by means of own revenues. Whereas provincial government is financed almost entirely through grants from national government, municipal government as a whole raises most of its own funds through taxes and service charges. Table 7.1 shows the composition of municipal finance by revenue source.

**Table 7.1** *Budgeted municipal operating revenue (all municipalities), 2003/04*

| Revenue Source | Amount (Rbn) | Proportion |
|---|---|---|
| Regional Service levies | 5.2 | 7.1 |
| Property rates | 14.3 | 19.5 |
| Electricity charges | 21.4 | 29.3 |
| Water charges | 9.6 | 13.2 |
| Sanitation charges | 2.8 | 3.8 |
| Refuse charges | 2.4 | 3.2 |
| Subsidies and grants | 8.3 | 11.3 |
| Other income | 8.9 | 12.1 |
| Total | 73.0 | 100.0 |

Source: RSA (2004)

Currently property rates, constituting 19.5 per cent of operating revenue, are levied in a variety of ways across the country in terms of legislation from the four former provinces. This includes some taxes based on land only, some on both land and improvements, and some on a composite basis weighted to emphasise land value. This is changing with the coming into effect of the new Local Government: Municipal Property Rates Act (No. 6 of 2004), which will shift all municipalities onto a system where the full market value of the property (including land and improvements) is taxed. Property rates are assigned to metropolitan and local councils, but not district councils.

RSC levies, constituting 7.1 per cent of operating revenue, are a tax on business and consist of a small levy on turnover (between 0.10 per cent and 0.20 per cent) and the cost of remuneration (between 0.25 per cent and 0.38 per cent). For historical reasons the rates differ slightly across the country, but have been frozen by the Minister of Finance. As noted, the Minister of Finance indicated in his February 2005 Budget speech the elimination of this tax from 1 July 2006. The accompanying *Budget Review* proposed that the levies 'be replaced with alternative tax instruments or funding arrangements to ensure the continued independence and financial viability of municipalities' (RSA 2005: 94). The Review stated further that 'the alternative tax instruments and/or funding arrangements will be finalised in consultation with all stakeholders by the end of September 2005 in order to enable draft legislation to be tabled before the end of 2005' (RSA 2005: 94). However, it would appear that for the first year at least the tax is to be replaced by a grant from the centre pending agreement on a new tax source.

Although taken as a whole, local government is funded largely by own resources, this disguises substantial differences amongst municipalities. The metropolitan areas and larger cities account for most municipal financing, and are largely self-funded. The six metropolitan areas receive between 3 per cent and 8 per cent of their operating revenue from grants, in contrast to 11.3 per cent for all municipalities (RSA 2004: Appendix B). Many other areas do not have sufficient tax bases to finance basic services adequately.

### Grants from national government

Second, own revenues are supplemented by substantial grants from national government, determined three years in advance, mainly to ensure that poor households receive basic services and service backlogs are addressed. In terms of the Constitution local government (and each province) is 'entitled to an equitable share of revenue raised nationally to enable it to provide basic services and perform the functions allocated to it' (Constitution s227(1)[a]). The Constitution specifies broadly what needs to be taken into account in determining the transfers. A permanent, independent Financial and Fiscal Commission (FFC), created in terms of the Constitution, gives advice on all aspects of intergovernmental fiscal relations.

The division of revenue has been surprisingly uncontentious since 1994, although there have been voices, often articulated within government by the Department of Provincial and Local Government (DPLG), to the effect that the total amount of resources allocated to local government is insufficient.

The objective has been to ensure that transfers are formula driven, based on objective criteria, well publicised, and determined well in advance. There has been ongoing debate around the formula, although no questioning of a formula-driven approach. The Division of Revenue Bill, 2005, introduces a new formula. This is discussed in a later section.

All transfers from national government have to be legislated. Thus, each year a Division of Revenue Act is passed together with the national Budget. This Act explains the basis for the transfers, and sets out grants to each province and municipality for the coming three financial years. The outer years can be adjusted in subsequent budgets, but such adjustments are minimal. Three-year allocations are regarded as highly desirable since they provide scope for forward planning; yet internationally they are surprisingly uncommon.

Transfers to local government are divided into 'equitable share' (unconditional) and conditional grants. The latter include grants for capital purposes such as the Consolidated Municipal Infrastructure Programme that since 2004 has been incorporated into the Municipal Infrastructure Grant. Grants to local government have been increasing significantly in real terms in recent years as indicated in Table 7.2.

**Table 7.2** *Conditional and unconditional transfers from national to local government (R millions)*

| Year | 2000/01 | 2001/02 | 2002/03 | 2003/04 | 2004/05 |
|---|---|---|---|---|---|
| Equitable share | 2 415 | 3 184 | 4 187 | 6 350 | 7 678 |
| Conditional | 3 121 | 3 336 | 4 519 | 6 039 | 6 568 |

Source: RSA (2004)

The Municipal Infrastructure Grants are largely aimed at eliminating infrastructure backlogs in poor residential areas and the equitable share grant at financing the operating costs of the provision of basic services to poor households. They include an amount which is intended to enable low levels of basic services to be provided to poor households free. The housing subsidy, part of which is used to finance service reticulation within the housing development area, is not included in these figures.

*Single channel for the provision of grants*

Third, a single channel for the provision of Municipal Infrastructure Grants is being introduced. Until recently the different sectoral departments at the national sphere have designed allocations and set conditions for municipalities in receipt of various conditional grants aimed at addressing services backlogs in poor areas. In addition, provinces have controlled housing subsidies, which are intended to finance the reticulation of services within any new subsidised housing settlement. This has led to complex and diverse reporting requirements and a tendency to compromise the Integrated Development Plans (IDPs) which municipalities are required to draw up.

For grants other than housing grants, the Municipal Infrastructure Grant is being introduced with a single reporting channel in which the national departments participate. This grant is allocated according to fomulae largely based on infrastructure backlogs, and is intended to give more autonomy to municipalities in terms of how they prioritise the use of resources. At the same time, the conditions place greater emphasis on ensuring that intended outputs are achieved and the investments are done in a financially sustainable manner.

The issue of how housing subsidies should be distributed remains a matter for debate and is discussed later.

## Borrowing to finance capital expenditure

Fourth, while substantial capital grants are provided for addressing infrastructure backlogs, it is envisaged that municipalities borrow to finance capital expenditure.

Since 1994 a very substantial proportion of capital expenditure of municipalities has been financed by capital grants from national government, especially if housing subsidies, which are often implemented by municipalities and thus recorded in their budgets, are included. These resources have, in turn, been raised by a combination of taxes and borrowing by the national government. However, it is envisaged that municipalities finance a substantial part of their capital budgets directly through borrowing, especially amongst larger, wealthier municipalities.

Significant attention has been paid to constructing an appropriate regulatory environment for facilitating borrowing. While borrowing has been somewhat slow in recent years this now appears set to increase, especially after the successful floating of two municipal bonds by Johannesburg.

## Avoidance of national guarantees for local loans

Fifth, redistribution is effected through grants rather than through interfering in the financial system; national government may not guarantee repayment of local borrowing.

In many countries national governments intervene in the financial markets in order to improve the availability of capital resources to municipalities. This generally takes the form of some kind of risk enhancement, where national government carries some of the risk, often through providing repayment guarantees to the lender. This does reduce the direct cost of borrowing, but at the cost of severely confusing accountability. If national government guarantees the loans it must either take steps to ensure there is no default by the local authority, or must be prepared to repay the loan in case of default. The former results in the need for much greater control by national government over local authorities – often very poorly or inappropriately exercised. The latter leads to large, ad hoc, forced transfers, with those making decisions not required to bear responsibility if they fail. Where parastatal lenders enjoy some form of implicit or explicit guarantee, private lenders are generally unable to compete and exit the market.

If municipalities are to be able to borrow from the private financial sector at reasonable rates, lenders need to be assured of being repaid. If this is not to be done by national government guaranteeing repayment of loans, then it can only be done by ensuring that the finances of local governments are sufficiently rigorous that such guarantees are not required.

Since 1994 the use of guarantees has been strictly avoided, with the Constitution itself precluding guarantees other than under carefully controlled conditions. This has re-enforced a strong emphasis on the need for sound financial management, evident most clearly in the Local Government: Municipal Finance Management Act (No. 56 of 2003).

Guarantees are a form of hidden subsidy where the degree of subsidisation is not clearly defined or understood. Taking an approach whereby guarantees are avoided does not amount to excluding redistribution or only financing projects which provide a market return. Instead, borrowing is made feasible through transparent grants, with risks and returns priced in this context.

One key merit of this approach is that municipalities wishing to borrow are required to demonstrate to private lenders well-argued strategies and implementation plans into the medium and long term.

### Widely drawn local boundaries

Sixth, boundaries are widely drawn so that each metropolitan area and large city is governed by a single municipality. Indeed, in some cases the boundaries of local municipalities extend well beyond this.

The key motivation for widely drawn boundaries is that it allows areas which are a single social, functional unit to be governed as such. This is critical in managing complex regions such as metropolitan areas. Uniting rich and poor areas within a single city into a single municipality also enhances the scope and pressure for redistributive spending.

As indicated earlier, in terms of conventional public finance theory redistribution is better effected by national rather than local government. In South Africa the call for 'One city, one tax base' during the anti-apartheid period tended to lead to a strong, if not excessive, emphasis on drawing wide local boundaries in an attempt to create the conditions for redistribution, rather than, perhaps, the need for functional coherence.

### Provinces play a monitoring role

Seventh, municipal finance is governed by national legislation, with provinces playing primarily a monitoring role. In many three-tier systems local government is a responsibility of the second, usually provincial tier. South Africa's three-sphere system gives responsibility for determining the local legislative framework to the national sphere. The result is the introduction of new systems which are common across the country. This greatly facilitates the efficiency of governance and transparency.

Furthermore, of critical importance is that grants from the national to the local sphere do not need to pass through the provincial sphere.

## Events and influences leading to the establishment of the broad framework for financing municipal government

While the decade after the end of apartheid saw the introduction of many new features to the system of financing local government, the extent to which the new system was able to build upon key characteristics from the previous period is sometimes underestimated. Professional municipal bureaucracies had been in place in the key cities for more than a century, the property tax was well established, as was the notion of payment of fees for services. There was a history of municipal borrowing and even a history of issuing municipal bonds, although this had largely ceased with the termination of the prescribed asset requirements[2] in the 1980s.

Most important in the development of the new system was the extent to which anti-apartheid struggles from 1976 onwards were focused on or related to municipal issues. Furthermore, the banning of the national anti-apartheid movements led to an emphasis on local civic movements, brought together in the United Democratic Front (UDF) in the 1980s, as part of the vanguard of the anti-apartheid movement.

In constitutional negotiations, the key opponents of the African National Congress (ANC), such as the National Party, the Inkatha Freedom Party and a number of others, placed considerable emphasis on structuring decentralisation – particularly at provincial level – to their advantage. This was where they would most likely be able to build an ethnic power base. They also sought through the Constitution to weaken the centre, which they were unlikely ever to control.

A significant number of those in the ANC who had been in exile tended to have a somewhat centrist approach in their response to the federalist opposition. However, much of the internal membership, which had been closely involved in civic struggles, saw many advantages in building strong local government. At the same time, they were concerned that strong provinces would control and weaken local government. Thus within the ANC a common approach – characterised by some as 'strong-weak-strong'[3] – needed to be forged.

The fact that these issues had to be negotiated both between political parties and within the ANC resulted in far more rigorous attention being paid to issues of decentralisation, including local government matters, than in most national constitutions.

### The 1976 Soweto uprising and policy responses on urban financing

The 1976 Soweto uprising marked the first major resistance directed at the apartheid system of local government in black areas. While these protests were aimed mainly at the education system, amongst the first targets for attack were the state-run beerhalls, which were the main source for financing services in black townships.

The 1976 uprising resulted in a number of new initiatives from business organisations and the state. Most notably, the Urban Foundation was established by more progressive, larger, mainly English-speaking businesses, with strong support from the Anglo American Corporation, the large mining and industrial corporation which dominated South African business. The objective of the Urban Foundation was to influence the policies of the apartheid government in respect of black urban areas. For example, it sought recognition from the government of the permanence of black residents in the cities and pushed for black South Africans to be allowed to own residential property outside the former homeland areas. It argued for the 'upgrading' of living conditions in black areas.

The Urban Foundation was well financed, and conducted significant research. While the apartheid government's actions were driven primarily by political pressures, the ideas promoted through the research and lobbying conducted by the Urban Foundation did have significant influence.[4]

One of the important responses from government was the Black Local Authorities Act (No. 102 of 1982) which provided for the establishment of separate black local authorities, with locally elected councils having significant powers which had previously been exercised by officials answerable to central government. This was associated with a drive to improve urban services in black areas. Significant amongst these initiatives was the electrification of black townships. Remarkably, while South Africa had a large electricity industry, and many power stations were located on the outskirts of black townships, none of these townships had electricity prior to 1980.

### The failure of the post-1976 initiatives and the call for 'One city, one tax base'

The new initiatives failed for a number of reasons. While politically the notion of separate black local authorities was never going to be acceptable to the anti-apartheid movements, the financing arrangements were also unworkable.

On the one hand the revenues from the beerhalls were lost as these were privatised in response to the actions of the youth in 1976, and in line with new policies aimed at establishing a black middle class. On the other hand, the improved services had to be financed alongside the financing of the new local councils themselves. Minimal provision was made for this in the national Budget; it was expected that the revenues be raised locally. Thus the introduction of new, locally elected black councils was associated with very significant increases in service charges payable to the local black administrations which, until then, had been negligible.

There was a widespread popular response of refusing to pay the new charges while rejecting the new black local authorities. It was in the context of protests and marches around these issues that the army was called into the townships of the Vaal Triangle in 1982 to put down protests, and remained present in black urban areas until the end of apartheid.

Belatedly the government responded in 1987 by introducing RSCs, financed by RSC levies. The boundaries of the RSCs were drawn so as to link black and white areas, with indirect representation from each constituent municipality based on revenue contribution. The RSCs were required to spend their revenue largely on overcoming infrastructure backlogs.

As indicated in Table 7.1, the levies have now become a critical element in the financing of municipalities in major urban areas. Johannesburg raised close to R1.5 billion from levies in the 2004/05 financial year.[5] This is further discussed later.

In 1983 the UDF was established and began to articulate a common agenda around a range of urban issues in particular, including municipal finance issues. The obvious response to the failure of the new reforms was to call for the unification of separate black and white local authorities. The slogan 'One city, one tax base' arose in this context in the late 1980s. If cities could be united, it was argued, then the resources from the richer areas could be used to finance improvements in the poorer areas.

During this period a significant network of technical organisations working in association with the civic associations began to emerge. These non-governmental organisations (NGOs), which came to be funded by international donor agencies, began to support, at a technical level, the formulation of strategies and programmes amongst the civic associations. Foremost amongst these organisations was Planact, which was closely involved in places such as Soweto and Alexandra. Others included the Development Action Group[6] in Cape Town, and the Built Environment Support Group in Durban. While initially the work of these organisations was project specific, they began to create a network and a body of ideas which were subsequently to have a significant impact on research and policy-making in the early to mid-1990s.

Through the 1980s, apart from the Urban Foundation, which continued to conduct research into urban policy, the Development Bank of Southern Africa (DBSA) also began to research municipal finance issues. The DBSA had been established in 1984, aimed in particular at the financing of development in the black 'homeland' areas. However, towards the late 1980s the DBSA introduced a strong focus on urban and local issues, including a lending programme. Through people such as the CEO, Dr Simon Brand, the DBSA had important links with key, more progressive figures within the apartheid regime who were seeking new approaches. Thus their research was important in paving the way from the regime's side towards new negotiated approaches to resolving urban conflicts.[7]

Within the Department of Finance a project called KIFVSA (*Komitee vir Inter-goewermentele Fiskale Verhoudinge in Suid-Afrika* [Committee for Inter-governmental Fiscal Relations in South Africa]) was also established during this period. This created a culture of discussion around issues of fiscal decentralisation within the department which contributed subsequently to constitutional negotiations in this area.

By 1989 it was increasingly recognised by government that a new local dispensation was required which would involve the amalgamation of black and white local authorities.

## The Local Government Negotiating Forum

After the unbanning of the ANC in 1990 most attention began to be given to the development of a new Constitution. Nevertheless, considerable momentum had already developed around local-level negotiations aimed at combining black and white areas. In 1991 the government passed the Interim Measures for Local Government Act. This Act provided the scope for ad hoc interventions to set up joint structures that crossed the town/township divide and that would facilitate the delivery of services in areas where black local authorities had collapsed. Although the Act was implemented, resistance groups rejected it, calling for the full abolition of race-based local structures and the creation of metropolitan and local structures that would be able to address urban inequities effectively.

The result was the creation of the national Local Government Negotiating Forum (LGNF), driven by the anti-apartheid civic movement in response and partial opposition to the Interim Measures for Local Government Act, and seeking to create a single framework to give direction and consistency to the myriad of emerging local processes. Fortunately, it gained the cooperation of the apartheid authorities, with the national department responsible for constitutional development eventually providing the secretariat.

The two sides to the negotiations were termed the 'statutory' and 'non-statutory' sides. The 'statutory' side represented the associations of statutory municipal authorities while the 'non-statutory' side represented the local civic associations, trade unions and the ANC and other parties which had previously either boycotted, or been excluded from, the formal local political systems.

The LGNF was organised into three working groups – the legal and constitutional, the finance and services, and the administrative working groups. The main focus of the Forum was to establish a process whereby the previous racially fragmented municipal areas could be combined into single bodies, which was seen as the basis for ending racial division and providing the fiscal resources necessary to improve conditions in the black townships.

Each side had its own technical advisers who helped to formulate positions. On the non-statutory side the technical advisers were drawn largely from the NGOs, noted earlier, which had supported the civics in the 1980s. By now the Local Government Policy Project (known as Logopop) had been established, creating a more formal network of these researchers and technical policy advisers. This network played a key role in policy formulation.

Some municipal councils, such as Cape Town, had conducted research into new municipal policy, but on technical issues the statutory side had a somewhat disparate approach. The key ideas established in these negotiations, such as the definition of functional areas for the purposes of creating interim municipalities, were largely driven by the technical advisers on the non-statutory side.[8] At a political level, however, significant, albeit temporary compromises were required to avoid disruption of the process of change by Conservative Party councils in particular.

### The broader constitutional debate and the key ideas on fiscal decentralisation

Initially the local government negotiations ran somewhat separately from national-level negotiations. However, decentralisation soon became a critical national issue. As indicated, it did so essentially because a collection of ethnically based regional interests saw this as a means to secure some power, while others saw it as a mechanism to weaken a national government which they were unlikely to control. The position of the ANC had been that there should be a Constituent Assembly prior to decisions on issues such as regional government; however, this proved untenable if agreement was to be reached. Thus it somewhat hurriedly sought to develop positions on decentralisation, in the process drawing in a number of the Logopop network.

In early 1993 the ANC Constitutional Committee held a conference to develop a mandated position on provincial[9] government to be taken into negotiations. This was preceded by the compilation of a discussion document used for consultation amongst ANC structures prior to the conference. The document, entitled *ANC Regional Policy*, was compiled under the auspices of the ANC's Constitutional Committee and its Department of Local and Regional Government and Housing, after discussions between drafters and the ANC's Constitutional Committee. Key members of the team involved in the drafting were linked to local civic struggles and the Logopop research project.[10] Thus the debate was influenced by a strong local perspective. Much of the substance of the discussion document became the basis of the ANC negotiating position, and subsequently found its way into the interim and final Constitutions. A number of elements had a particularly important effect on the system that emerged after 1994.

The document accepted that consensus had developed around creating three tiers of government, but emphasised the interdependent nature of the tiers. It also placed the notion of metropolitan governments firmly on the agenda, stating that, 'The ANC views the creation of metropolitan governments in certain parts of the country as essential to the cause of unifying, deracialising and democratising cities, in addition to the more efficient and effective provision of affordable services' (ANC 1992: 7). This was a reflection of the calls for 'One city, one tax base', and the desire to exercise coherent authority across functional urban areas.

The section on finance and resources, which laid out significant elements of the basis for the intergovernmental fiscal system that eventually emerged through the negotiating process, was written against the backdrop of attempts by federalists to argue for the devolution of taxes to the provincial tier. It sought to counter this, while at the same time creating the basis for fiscal decentralisation to the local level. It argued that a new system 'must be appropriate to modern economic conditions, seeking to enhance democratic accountability while ensuring that the public resources of the country are shared fairly amongst the whole population. The starting point should be a strong emphasis upon the need to strengthen local control over the use of public resources. This helps to ensure that usage is efficiently and appropriately tailored to local conditions. The link between paying taxes and receiving public services must be recognised as an important element in the strengthening of democratic accountability, and is most direct at local level' (ANC 1992: 9).

But, it also argued that there were constraints to fiscal decentralisation. It should not compromise the capacity for the authorities to exercise sound management over the economy as a whole nor, in a country of profound regional inequalities, should it compromise the capacity for redistribution. Furthermore, there were significant technical constraints on the devolution of taxes, most of which were difficult to administer at subnational level. The conclusion was that while some taxes could be retained at local level, especially property taxes and possibly some excise duties, such as fuel levies, the bulk of taxes should be collected nationally and, to the extent that expenditure took place at lower levels, should be distributed by fair and transparent means through fiscal transfers. It was perhaps the first document relating to local financing which clearly placed the emphasis for providing for redistribution on the national fiscus, rather than through redrawing local boundaries, stating that more important than the notion of 'One city, one tax base' was the notion of 'One country, one tax base'.

It spelled out the need for transfers to be formula driven, and to comprise both conditional and unconditional tranches. These grants would have to 'take into account the capacity of various lower level governments to raise their own resources so that inequalities amongst regions and localities could be counteracted' (ANC 1992: 11). The document also argued it would be unwise to leave control over the transfers entirely to central government. Instead, the Constitution should contain a set of guidelines to govern transfers while at the same time a 'permanent Advisory Fiscal Commission structured on a non-party-political basis' should be created in which certain powers for 'advising on the structure and mechanism of fiscal decentralisation would be vested' (ANC 1992: 11). Such guidelines should ensure that 'transfers are made in such a way that lower levels of government are able to plan properly; that they are structured so as to enhance efficiency and local accountability and that they are open to clear and effective monitoring. The guidelines must seek to redress inequalities between regions' (ANC 1992: 11).

It was also stated that the Fiscal Commission should have a say in granting powers of taxation to lower levels of government within this overall framework, thereby indicating the need for adaptation to the system of tax devolution over time.

Many of these concepts became embedded in the interim and final Constitutions, and underlie the current system of intergovernmental fiscal relations. Most of the seven key features mentioned at the outset were either explicitly or implicitly contained in the document.

Apart from the arguments on the need for national government to be able to exercise macroeconomic control – which implies a degree of control over sub-central borrowing – the one key policy area not dealt with in the *Regional Policy* document was that of local borrowing. Nevertheless, both the interim and final Constitutions recognised the right of municipalities to borrow, while significantly limiting the extent to which the granting of guarantees by national government in respect of local and provincial borrowing was permissible. This was driven by the experience of lending to the homelands in the late apartheid years. Technically the homelands, consisting of both 'independent states' and 'self-governing territories', had a high degree of independence. Furthermore, the late apartheid regime did not wish to act firmly against potential political allies. The result was a huge increase in borrowing by these territories which they were clearly unable to repay, but which was either implicitly or explicitly guaranteed by the central South African government. Both the ANC and the government negotiators responded to this experience by strongly opposing central government guarantees of subnational debt or entities created by subnational governments.

## Research and policy developments since 1994

### The provision of services and the Municipal Infrastructure Investment Framework

As part of its election campaign and process of preparing to govern, the ANC drew up the Reconstruction and Development Programme, popularly known as the RDP. It was a detailed document setting out a number of targets, including in the area of housing and municipal service provision. With regard to housing it sought to construct 'a million low-cost houses' over five years. With respect to municipal services there was a short-term aim of 'establishing a national water and sanitation programme which aim(ed) to provide all households with a clean, safe supply of 20–30 litres per capita per day within 200 metres, an adequate/safe sanitation facility per site, and a refuse removal system to all urban households' (ANC 1994: 29). Regarding electrification it stated that, 'An accelerated and sustainable electrification programme must provide access to electricity for an additional 2.5 million households by the year 2000, thereby increasing the level of access to electricity to about 72 per cent of all households (double the present number)' (ANC 1994: 33). Most of these targets have now been met and, indeed, exceeded, although this did not happen in the first five years.

In 1995, the Department of Housing together with the RDP Ministry drew up a Municipal Infrastructure Investment Framework (MIIF), which laid out financial mechanisms and an institutional approach for overcoming service delivery backlogs. The MIIF argued for a ten-year, rather than a five-year programme to overcome backlogs, stating that the programme would require a significant capital grant from central government 'in the order of R30–R35 billion' (RSA 1995: ii). The MIIF defined three broad levels of service, and envisaged that an investment programme of between R60 and R70 billion over ten years, funded partly at local level and partly through national grants, would result in a 55:25:20 configuration of urban services nationally between full, intermediate and basic levels (RSA 1995: ii).

Municipalities were to finance capital expenditure through a combination of the redirection of existing local resources together with recurrent and capital grants and loans for capital development.

The MIIF set out a number of key elements of a new financial framework for the provision of service infrastructure. In particular, it emphasised the principle of financing capital expenditure through borrowing, while current expenditure should be financed by current income. Of particular significance was the view taken that redistributive mechanisms should be transparent and addressed through fiscal flows in the context of the emerging system of devolved taxes and grants, rather than by manipulating the financial sector. And capital finance should be accessed by integration into the mainstream private financial system, rather than through special public sector lending institutions; where public sector lending institutions existed they should support this process.

The MIIF was drafted by a team of South African consultants[11] supported by a World Bank team, and thus represented the first time that international experts became involved in the development of elements of municipal finance policy. On the financial side the key contribution of the World Bank team was the emphasis on providing subsidies through grant mechanisms rather than manipulating the financial sector, and was based on the experience of countries such as India where the reverse had happened to the severe detriment of subnational finances. It was a position consistent with the approach to guarantees already agreed to by all parties in the development of the interim Constitution.

For a variety of reasons, many to do with uncertainty in the system, the municipal sector has not raised as much capital from the private financial sector as was envisaged. At the same time, capital grant funding from national government has been larger than expected. Nevertheless, the principles of the MIIF have remained prominent ideals, with redistribution through manipulating the financial system – especially through guarantee mechanisms – largely being avoided, and the use of borrowings to finance current expenditure outlawed in terms of the Municipal Finance Management Act. Currently there are indications that there is a significant increase in the readiness of the private financial sector to lend to local government. As noted, Johannesburg has recently successfully launched two sets of municipal bonds.

The MIIF has been through a number of iterations since it was first published, with responsibility shifting from the Ministry in the Office of the President (RDP Ministry) to the Department of Housing and then to the current DPLG. This has resulted, in particular, in a more sophisticated approach to modelling of the costs and a refinement of certain other elements.

## White Paper on Local Government

It was agreed in the LGNF that the first round of local government elections in terms of the interim Constitution would represent an 'interim phase' of local government during which, after the final Constitution was passed by the Constituent Assembly, there would be a Local Government White Paper process. This would then lead to a new legislative framework for local government consistent with the new national Constitution.

The research for the White Paper on Local Government was initiated in 1996 and the White Paper was eventually published in March 1998. The work on municipal finance was largely done by the National Treasury (then known as the Department of Finance). The White Paper did not break significantly new ground on municipal financing issues but was important in reinforcing many of the approaches developed in constitutional negotiations and subsequently. It did give prominence to issues related to municipal borrowing.

It recognised that problems in municipal finance lay in shortcomings in policy as well as poor implementation, that redistribution and growth needed to be balanced, and that differences across municipalities needed to be accommodated. It argued that changes were needed in four areas, namely, local revenue instruments and policies, national to local transfers, gearing in private investments, and the budgeting, accounting and financial reporting systems.

On local revenue instruments and policies it recognised that local choice over the tax rate was the most significant element in strengthening local accountability. Regarding property taxes specifically, it argued for a simpler system applied nationally and based on the market value of property rather than the variety of systems then in place across the country. Systems varied between those based only on the site value, those based on site and improvements and those that had a composite of the two. The White Paper stated that deciding whether this should remain a local choice was a key decision.

It viewed RSC levies as inefficient taxes but recognised their importance and that they would need to be retained until a suitable alternative, yielding the same net revenue, was introduced. It also suggested that a municipal fuel levy might be introduced.

On user charges it largely repeated the principles for service tariffs that were already contained in the first MIIF, but strengthened them somewhat, arguing that all households other than the indigent should pay the full costs of services consumed, rather than the minimum level of operations and maintenance costs referred to in the MIIF. Municipalities should develop a set of targeted subsidies to ensure all had access to a minimum level of basic services.

It stressed that grants should be transparent, equitable and predictable and recognised the need for changes to be introduced here, including a properly constituted 'equitable share' in line with the Constitution. The formula-based system should 'enable municipalities to provide a basic level of services to low income households in their areas of jurisdiction at affordable cost' (Ministry of Provincial Affairs and Constitutional Development 1998: 120). The funds should not be allocated via the provinces.

The White Paper strongly reinforced the importance of municipal borrowing stating that 'ultimately, a vibrant and innovative primary and secondary market for long and short term municipal debt should emerge' (1998: 122). It stressed 'the importance of achieving financial discipline through decentralised market relationships (between borrower and lender) rather than the direct, centralised control of local government' (1998: 122). It went into some detail on the need to develop approaches that would enhance credit without central guarantees. It did also recognise the need for concessional loan finance and the role that should be played by public sector financial intermediaries, which should support rather than replace market development.

It gave attention to the need to modernise accounting and budgeting practices.

The section concluded by emphasising 'the total commitment of government to building a financially independent and viable system of local government in the long term' (1998: 127).

Between 1998 and 2004 the White Paper led to the passing of key legislation such as the Municipal Structures Act, the Municipal Demarcation Act, the Municipal Systems Act, the Municipal Property Rates Act, and the Municipal Finance Management Act.

*Key institutions conducting policy research since the White Paper*

Since the White Paper various parts of the state administration have done research and taken forward the agenda on municipal finance issues.

### FINANCIAL AND FISCAL COMMISSION

The FFC, created as recommended in the ANC's *Regional Policy* document as a constitutional body, focused mainly on provincial financing in its earlier years, but subsequently began to focus more on local government. It has done thorough research into municipal finance issues, not all of which has been included in its submissions to Parliament. It has done extensive work on the equitable share formula where it has called, *inter alia*, for the introduction of a revenue-raising capacity component to the formula and the inclusion of health and lifeline tariff expenditure within the equitable share. It has also made important contributions in defining basic municipal services, and recommendations on the division of powers and functions between district and local municipalities, the remuneration of councillors, the future of the RSC levies – which it argues should be replaced by another instrument over which local government has control – municipal borrowing, and the financial impact of the reform of the electricity distribution industry.

### DEMARCATION BOARD

The Demarcation Board,[12] established in terms of the Demarcation Act, was required to do research in order to determine the boundaries of new local authorities.

One of the key contributions of the Demarcation Board in terms of research has been to develop sophisticated Geographic Information System databases of municipal information. The research of the Demarcation Board has focused on drawing boundaries in such a manner as to capture functional linkages within a single jurisdiction and provide for municipalities to have as much financial and administrative capacity as possible. This has sometimes tended to lead the Board to take quite controversial approaches with respect to redistribution and the division of powers between Category B and C municipalities. It could be argued that, as an entity with no control over national redistributive processes but able to demarcate boundaries, it has emphasised the notion of redistribution through drawing wide local boundaries.

### DEPARTMENT OF PROVINCIAL AND LOCAL GOVERNMENT

The DPLG has a responsibility for ensuring a sound local government system in South Africa. As such it is one of the key centres for procuring research into municipal finance issues.

Probably the most important municipal finance area in the recent period has been research into the new Property Rates Act, but there have been many others, including the equitable share formula, RSC levies, and indigent policy.

In the early 2000s there was a large research programme conducted under the auspices of the Research Triangle Institute and focused in particular on DPLG. The single most useful paper to emerge from this was one by Bahl and Solomon (2000) on RSC levies. A book was subsequently published on the research, written largely by the international participants, but this has not been widely circulated or used in South Africa and the research appears to have had relatively little direct impact on the actual policy development process.

## NATIONAL TREASURY

While DPLG is responsible for ensuring a sound local government system in South Africa, National Treasury is responsible for a sound fiscal system. Thus it is also deeply involved in municipal finance issues.

Apart from drafting the municipal finance sections of the White Paper, important areas where National Treasury has driven the agenda include the issue of borrowing, where the department took a comprehensive policy on municipal borrowing through Cabinet, the introduction of a consolidated Municipal Infrastructure Grant, and RSC levies.

Currently the National Treasury is conducting a review of the Local Government Fiscal Framework with the intention of making progress in a number of areas, including the reform of RSC levies, regulations on the property tax, borrowing, free basic services and tariff guidelines, consumer debt, and the financial implications of restructuring the electricity distribution industry.

National Treasury's *Inter-governmental Fiscal Reviews*, which it seeks to publish annually, contain a wealth of information on local government. Not only do they qualify as research, but they have also facilitated research by others.

## INSTITUTE FOR A DEMOCRATIC SOUTH AFRICA

While all the bodies mentioned so far are government departments or constitutional bodies, one body doing notable research into municipal finance which falls outside that category is the NGO Institute for a Democratic South Africa.

While it does not have the extensive capacity and budgets of a government department it has produced thorough and useful papers summarising the workings of the municipal finance environment and making proposals around the equitable share in particular (Wheelan 2002, 2004).

## Recent, current and future research issues

While the broad framework and direction of municipal finance policy is in place there are a number of research topics which in recent years have been the subject of important debates, some of which are not yet resolved, and where the outcomes could still affect the long-term development of the municipal fiscal system in profound ways. Some of the more significant ones are noted here.

### Replacement of the RSC levies

Much the most important issue still to be resolved is what replaces the RSC levies. For more than a decade commentators have criticised the RSC levies as poorly designed taxes. The turnover element means that high turnover, low margin activities are taxed proportionately more, while the tax on the wage bill has been criticised for dampening employment demand. However, with the rates so low, the impact has been minimal. Another key criticism has been that administration is poor. Underlying this is the fact that, in enforcing the tax, municipalities do not have the legal right to inspect company books.

On the expenditure side, in those districts which contain a reasonably strong secondary town the revenues tend to be used for redistributive purposes to provide residential services in municipalities at a distance from where the tax is generated. This is not an appropriate use for a local business tax. Such services would be better funded from the centre, especially considering that two-thirds of the districts have insignificant tax bases.

On the other hand, the revenues have become highly significant to the metropolitan authorities in particular. Given that these areas are the drivers of the country's economy and currently, along with the secondary cities, offer the best chance for absorbing the large numbers of unemployed, it would be highly counterproductive to remove this revenue source. The announcement that the tax is to be eliminated raises the question as to what it will be replaced by.

The various options can be divided into one of two alternatives. The revenue could be replaced by a national tax and distributed on a formula basis.[13] If the idea is to support economic growth, this distribution would need to be based on origin. Alternatively it could be replaced by a different local tax. The various role-players concerned with developing the local government system have largely supported the latter approach. The problem lies in the design of the tax, given technical and constitutional constraints. Bahl and Solomon (2000) favoured the abolition of the turnover component and the concomitant increase in the wage component. However, this is unlikely to prove politically acceptable in the face of high unemployment. National Treasury is currently seeking other options.

The replacement of the levies with a grant from the centre creates much greater long-term uncertainty for individual local governments. Grant formulae can easily be changed. Furthermore, there is a tendency for grants over time to tend towards distribution on a population or poverty basis, not on the basis of economic activity. A grant approach runs the risk of seriously undermining the vision that has been adopted regarding borrowing, with lenders increasingly seeking assurance from the centre about the long-term distribution of funds, thus undermining the emphasis on local autonomy and responsibility.

The resolution of this issue is further complicated by the lack of clarity surrounding the role of district municipalities and their relationships with local municipalities.

### Equitable share formula

The initial work on the equitable share formula was done by what was then the Department of Constitutional Development, and subsequently taken up by the Department of Finance. The initial approach was very simple and based the distribution on the number of poor households in a municipality and what it cost, on average, to provide each of them with basic services. The amount actually provided was constrained by what was available from the budget.

There have been widespread calls for the total amount to be increased, and this has been done, as indicated in the first section of this chapter. Over time the grant became complicated by adding 'windows' for the financing of free basic services, and the urban and rural development nodes identified by national government, as well as other adaptations to favour poorer municipalities. Many commentators have argued for the need to introduce the criterion of 'revenue-raising capacity' into the formula to reduce the proportion of the grant flowing to richer municipalities and increase the flow to poorer ones. One of the complications in designing the grant has been the lack of consistent official data available across the country to base it upon.

A new formula was announced in the February 2005 Budget, which was the product of joint work between National Treasury and the DPLG. This simplifies the formula, largely reverting to its original form, but adding a revenue-raising capacity element. It creates a new 'development' component to the grant, but at this stage the parameter for this is set at zero.

### The Municipal Infrastructure Grant and housing subsidies

From 1994 numerous capital grant mechanisms were introduced by the different sectoral departments for addressing service backlogs. Each of these carried different sets of conditions, often leading to inefficiency and placing large compliance costs on municipalities, which were required to adapt their behaviour to meet grant requirements.

The National Treasury thus initiated a process to consolidate these into a single window, now referred to as the Municipal Infrastructure Grant. This approach unsurprisingly resulted in some resistance from the line departments. Nor, because of long-term commitments, could grant programmes be rapidy shifted. However, the Municipal Infrastructure Grant has now been established and was implemented from fiscal year 2004/05. Capital grants are now focused on funding municipalities' own programmes, as devised in their IDPs.

The Housing Act provides for the accreditation of municipalities which should permit the same approach in the distribution of housing grants. Yet, despite the provision being in place, provinces have continued to administer housing subsidies and often to take direct responsibility for delivering housing. This is an issue which will need to be addressed.

### Property rates

The Municipal Property Rates Act was passed in 2004, and implemented from 2 July 2005. Property tax represents the biggest element of local government tax revenue and is central to municipal finance. It is also the tax which generates the greatest amount of emotion in relation to the revenue collected.

After some dispute it was agreed between National Treasury and the DPLG that the latter would take responsibility for the legislation. In the course of a large number of drafts over four years it was agreed that a uniform system based on market value of the whole property would be introduced. This is the most common approach internationally and used currently by a third of the country, and was agreed fairly early in the process.

More contentious issues were those relating to the taxation of public infrastructure and government properties, and the extension of the system to agricultural areas and areas where traditional tenure forms still prevail. Generally, National Treasury sought to limit the taxation of public infrastructure and government properties while DPLG was more in favour. Eventually, however, it was the parliamentary committee which was decisive in including all these areas in the tax net, while providing for a number of mechanisms whereby decisions could be made on the extent of rebates and exclusions locally. The Minister of Finance is also permitted to set limits on the difference between the tax rates imposed on residential and non-residential categories.

Property tax legislation is always highly complex. In most respects the legislation which has eventually emerged could be regarded as sound, although there are some areas which could be improved, and technical issues yet to be tested. The major challenge will be in its practical implementation, especially managing the shifts in incidence which will arise in places such as Johannesburg where there will be a change from taxation based on the site value only to taxation based on the total market value of the property. A poorly managed implementation across a number of larger municipalities could threaten the legitimacy of this critical component of municipal finance. It is of great importance that municipalities embark on detailed research backed by modelling to ensure successful implementation; the shifts in incidence and the options for managing the impact need to be understood at a local level and not merely at a general, national level.

## Indigent policy

The term 'indigent policy' has come to be used to refer to how poor households should be managed in respect of delivery of services, charging for services, and responding in the case of non-payment where consumption has exceeded the amount of services provided free.

This is clearly a highly contentious and politically charged issue, with which most municipalities are struggling. Most municipalities have introduced policies, but many of them have proved difficult or impossible to implement.

A comprehensive report and suggested policy approach was commissioned by the City of Cape Town in 2003. More recently DPLG has commissioned work on developing a national approach.[14]

Apart from establishing appropriate levels of cross-subsidisation, perhaps the area where the biggest difficulty is experienced in devising a policy is around the extent to which it is feasible to adminstratively apply means tests to individual households to assess the level of poverty. The work done in Cape Town argues strongly that automatic mechanisms need to be devised for identifying 'indigent' households, based on location, consumption levels and behaviour in the face of possible sanctions. Dignified mechanisms whereby poorer households can limit their consumption to reasonable set levels and thus receive free services is one of the keys to a successful approach. There cannot be a decisive cut-off point between households which are indigent and those which are not; a much more graduated approach is required.

## Borrowing

Borrowing has already been discussed in previous sections. However, there remain a number of unresolved policy issues. There seems little doubt that for the strongest 25 to 30 municipalities the approach adopted is bearing fruit. There is increasingly a strong interest in lending to these municipalities, and the competition amongst lenders is already driving the terms down to favourable levels. Where members of this group are not able to borrow the causes lie in matters which could and should be addressed locally, rather than in the system. This group accounts for most of the significant urban centres in South Africa.

However, there is not the same readiness to lend to the next 100 or so municipalities other than at significantly higher interest rates. The Infrastructure Finance Corporation (known as INCA), which is a private finance institution, has lent to more than 120 municipalities and experienced very low default, but structurally, this second group of municipalities experiences difficulties in borrowing. This needs to be addressed by intermediaries such as the DBSA together with other mechanisms. Policies need to be developed to enhance the scope and reduce the costs of borrowing by this group without interfering in rigorous assessment of risk or squeezing the private lenders out of markets they could otherwise service.

National Treasury did extensive work on creating the appropriate environment for borrowing, including getting agreement on a small amendment to the Constitution, and writing extensive sections into the Municipal Finance Management Act in order to establish the 'rules of the game'.

Research into borrowing is being conducted by National Treasury and the DBSA on an ongoing basis.

### Financial implications of the restructuring of the electricity distribution industry

The electricity distribution undertakings of the bigger municipalities represent, in each case, their biggest single component. For more than ten years there have been attempts to shift electricity distribution from the municipalities into independent dedicated utilities.

In the late 1990s a large research project was undertaken by PriceWaterhouseCoopers to develop a way ahead on the matter. Unfortunately the issue of the implications for municipalities was not sufficiently addressed.[15] Given that electricity distribution is a municipal function in terms of the Constitution, this was a significant gap, and is currently leading to deadlock in attempting to push the agenda further.

This matter is likely to remain contentious for a number of years with Eskom, National Treasury, DPLG, Electricity Distribution Industry Holdings, the major municipalities and the Department of Mineral and Energy Affairs all involved in the developments.

### Transport

The funding of transport infrastructure and the subsidisation of public transport are two areas that continue to receive insufficient attention within the municipal finance debates. An example of the anomalies which exist is that currently provincial government has a significant influence as to where new low-income housing is located through the housing subsidy mechanism, and national government bears the costs of subsidising the expensive public transport arising from the poor location. Logically, the trade-off should be made by municipal government, which should control both.

In many cities there is scope for building on and significantly upgrading commuter rail services. This will become rapidly more expensive as land use intensifies. There is a need to urgently address how new, effective public transport infrastructure can be financed and managed, and this needs to be integrated into the municipal finance framework.

## Concluding reflections on research and the policy development process

As indicated at the outset, I have been closely involved as a participant in much of the development of municipal finance policy in South Africa, working with civic associations in the 1980s, with the ANC and associated organisations during the Constitution-making period of the early 1990s, as a contributor to government policy-making subsequently, and as an implementer while holding the position of Chief Finance Officer for the City of Cape Town from 1997 till 2001.

In their chapter in this book, Van Donk and Pieterse distinguish broadly between academic, policy and (participatory) action-oriented research. I have largely contributed within what I understand to be their latter two categories, although would argue that policy-making can be both participatory and action-oriented. What follows in this section is a set of personal insights based on my experience of working on South African municipal finance policy.

Van Donk and Pieterse's categories are useful, but the distinction lies largely in the interests driving the work. In what they refer to as 'action-oriented' research a particular interest group is being consciously served; research is aimed at building their case.[16] In policy research the emphasis is on developing practical approaches which promote the key aims of the ruling political representatives while recognising that all interests need to be accommodated to a greater or lesser degree. While the former might be characterised as the art of being constructively vocal, the latter is the art of the possible. In academic research, interests are intended to be largely latent, and not to intrude too heavy-handedly into analysis. In South Africa a number of researchers who have presented themselves as academics have lost credibility in recent years through allowing narrow loyalties to distort not only their analysis but even their facts.

One important distinction between working as an academic and working as a policy-maker or 'action researcher' is the extent to which 'bright ideas' should be owned. It is part of being a good academic to 'own' the ideas you generate. A good policy-maker, especially working as an official, will achieve most by ensuring his or her ideas are owned by others, especially politicians. Consultants straddle an uneasy space in-between! This does influence the nature of the work published, how it is published and how the link is made between research and policy.

The key to successful policy-making in South Africa in the current environment and probably in most countries is not the researcher but the senior government official, working closely with the political representatives on balancing interests with what is possible. This calls in turn for a particular type of researcher, who can understand what the official requires to do his or her job most effectively. The ability of government officials currently to manage the policy-making process is mixed. There are pockets of excellence, but there is a tendency across various government departments towards a lack of experience.

At a more fundamental level, however, it would seem that policy formulation is driven more by material forces than abstract ideas. That is not to say that policies cannot influence how events unfold, yet at the time at which they are devised there are generally only a limited range of responses possible. Good policy will use that space creatively to open up new opportunities for the future. But policies which do not realistically take current circumstances into consideration are likely to fail; compromise is required.

Part of the brief in writing this chapter was to examine and identify how research has influenced policy development. A further underlying theme has been to examine the extent to which a locally shaped agenda was influenced or even redirected by experts and ideas from the multilateral and aid agencies. What, instead, has unfolded has been a story of how the key ideas were shaped by material forces and events, and the responses they elicited.

In essence, a period of intense thought, discussion and negotiation amongst local stakeholders and their 'intellectual' partners, who had become involved in the 1980s with the democratic political organisations, together with the process of negotiating – rather than dictating – a new Constitution, led to a vision for a future system of local government and the financing framework which went with it. Why the *Regional Policy* document (ANC 1992) cited in some detail earlier is significant is that it articulates the key elements of the vision as early as 1992, prior to any significant multilateral agency involvement. Most of what has unfolded since then can be seen to be consistent with that vision.

This chapter has also sought to demonstrate how local experience has driven key technical elements of what was put in place. It was not the World Bank, for example, which stressed that it was bad practice, if South Africa wanted independent local government, to guarantee loans from the centre; it was the experience with homeland governments in the late apartheid period.

That said, the role played by agencies such as the World Bank has been significant. In particular, one of the senior in-country World Bank staff members was highly effective in engaging with key local intellectuals and policy-makers and instrumental in introducing some of the most able and experienced international skills into local debates. This strengthened local insights and perspectives as well as confidence. But the fact that the World Bank has never lent significant amounts to South Africa meant that the relationship tended more towards a partnership than is probably the case in many other contexts.

The original vision appears to be increasingly established and accepted. However, the process of bedding down the detail in terms of that vision is not complete, as the previous section has shown. Serious errors could be made. Nor is it possible to claim that South Africa's local government system is running easily and efficiently; there are many shortcomings, largely arising from the intense institutional change which the sector has experienced over the last decade, and which is not yet complete.

But if these matters are successfully addressed over the coming five years or so, it is not impossible that South Africa's municipal finance system will begin to be viewed as an important contribution to the development of ideas on how best to approach these matters.

## Notes

1   The author of this document is the core consultant in the team of external consultants working with the National Treasury on this project.

2   Until abolition of the prescribed assets requirements, all pension funds had to keep a certain proportion of assets in government stock and other related investments, including municipal stock.

3   A three-tier system characterised by strong national government, weak provincial government and strong local government.

4   While initially most of the work of the Urban Foundation was aimed at lobbying the apartheid regime to accept the permanence of black residents in urban areas, subsequently it contributed significantly to housing policy, including promoting the idea of the individual capital subsidy for the provision of social housing, which remains the central thrust of current policy.

5   This is equivalent to over half of what is expected to be collected in property taxes.

6   The author was employed by the Black Sash (a women's human rights organisation) at the time and worked closely with a number of civic associations. He was a founder member of the Development Action Group.

7   Dr Simon Brand was personally involved in a significant DBSA study into the finances of Soweto.

8   The author was responsible within Logopop for municipal finance and fiscal decentralisation issues and was one of the technical advisers to the non-statutory working group on finances and services.

9   In its discussions the federalists, including government and others, used the term 'states' to describe the second-tier governments they sought. The ANC used the term 'region', indicating it saw this tier as much weaker. Eventually the term 'provinces' was used as a compromise. Many of the documents of the time referred to SPRs, which was shorthand for 'States/Provinces/Regions'.

10  Billy Cobbett, who was in charge of the Local and Regional Government and Housing department, and Professor Albie Sachs, who was a member of the Constitutional Committee, were responsible for the overall document. The author of this chapter drafted the finance and resources chapter of the document.

11  The author of this chapter was responsible for drafting the financial framework within the MIIF.

12  See Cameron's chapter on demarcation in this book.

13   This has traditionally been the International Monetary Fund approach and tends to be favoured by those responsible for managing national taxes, although current research within the Organisation for Economic Cooperation and Development and elsewhere has led to a significant shift in opinion.

14   The author led the Cape Town study and was involved in the DPLG work, which was led by the Palmer Development Group.

15   The final report, which ran to over 1 000 pages, had only one-and-a-half pages dedicated to implications for municipalities.

16   The intellectuals working with the civic associations and their networks, which I have described and of which I was a part in the 1980s and early 1990s, fell largely into this category.

## References

ANC (African National Congress, Constitutional Committee and Department of Local and Regional Government and Housing) (1992) *ANC regional policy*. Draft discussion document, October 1992. Cape Town: Centre for Development Studies, University of the Western Cape.

ANC (1994) *The Reconstruction and Development Programme: A policy framework*.

Bahl R & Solomon D (2000) The Regional Services Council levy: Evaluation and reform options. Unpublished paper, draft 25 October 2000.

Ministry of Provincial Affairs and Constitutional Development (1998) *White Paper on local government*. Pretoria: Government Printer.

RSA (Republic of South Africa) (1995) *Municipal infrastructure investment framework*. Pretoria: Ministry in the Office of the President and Department of Housing.

RSA (2004) *Trends in inter-governmental finances: 2000/01–2006/07*. National Treasury.

RSA (2005) *Budget review*. National Treasury.

Wheelan P (2002) Local government revenue. Occasional paper. Available at <http://www.idasa. org.za>.

Wheelan P (2004) A review of selected local government revenue reforms. Occasional paper. Available at <http://www.idasa.org.za>.

# Part 3: Developmental local government

# *Integrated development plans and Third Way politics*

Philip Harrison

## Introduction

The Integrated Development Plan (IDP) is the focus of South Africa's post-apartheid municipal planning system and is also now regarded as a key instrument in an evolving framework of intergovernmental planning and coordination. However, when it was first introduced – in a hasty addition to the Local Government Transition Act, Second Amendment Act, 1996 – the IDP was in direct competition with other instruments of planning, its purpose was vague, and its contents had yet to be specified.

This chapter traces the evolution of policy and legislation on IDPs, and also explores the outcome of IDPs (to the extent that it is possible to judge outcomes at this early stage of implementation). The IDP was a contextual response to challenges facing the post-apartheid government – in particular, the need to get a new system of local government working – but the nature and form of the IDP were strongly circumscribed by the international discourse and practice which prevailed at the time of its introduction and early development. Thus, after providing a brief introduction to the IDP, the chapter gives consideration to the international context within which the IDP emerged. In the chapter I argue that the IDP is linked to a second wave of New Public Management (NPM) approaches that took root internationally in the mid-1990s, and which is associated with the Third Way orientation of the 'centre-left' political parties of that decade (and currently). The bulk of the chapter, however, details the evolution of IDP-related policy in South Africa, and comments on some of the key influences on policy-making – in particular, the influences of Germany's *Gesellschaft für Technische Zusammenarbeit* (GTZ; in English, the Agency for Technical Co-operation) and South Africa's Council for Scientific and Industrial Research (CSIR). The chapter concludes with brief consideration of the outcomes of the new municipal planning system. It does so by considering the success or otherwise of the IDP as an instrument of joined-up government, participatory governance, modernised and efficient administration, and developmental governance.

## The IDP in outline

The IDP is prepared by local, district and metropolitan municipalities for a five-year period which coincides with the term of the elected council. It is primarily a plan concerned with directing and coordinating the activities of an elected municipal authority. The IDP does have a spatial component – the Spatial Development Framework – but it is very different from the spatial plans (eg. the town planning schemes, guide plans, and structure plans) which, traditionally, have been prepared for local authorities by town and regional planners.

The 1998 White Paper on Local Government identified the IDP as a key tool of 'developmental local government' (meaning local government that is concerned with promoting the economic and social development of communities) and linked the IDP to a broader package of instruments which include performance management tools, participatory processes, and service delivery partnerships. The White Paper emphasised the role of the IDP in providing a long-term vision for a municipality; setting out the priorities of an elected council; linking and coordinating sectoral plans and strategies; aligning financial and human resources with implementation needs; strengthening the focus on environmental sustainability; and providing the basis for annual and medium-term budgeting.

In 2000, the Municipal Systems Act specified the minimum contents of the IDP as:
*   A vision for the long-term development of a municipality;
*   An assessment of the current level of servicing, and of economic and social development, in a municipality;
*   The municipal council's development priorities and objectives for its elected term;
*   The local council's development strategies (which must be aligned with any national or provincial plans);
*   A Spatial Development Framework (which must include guidelines for a land-use management system);
*   Operational strategies;
*   Sectoral plans required by other legislation (eg. water plans, transport plans, waste management plans, disaster management plans and housing strategies);
*   A financial plan; and
*   A set of key performance indicators and performance targets.

Although the IDP was initially conceived of as an instrument of *local* planning and coordination, it is now linked, in an intergovernmental planning system, with instruments such as national government's Medium-Term Strategic Framework (MTSF) and the Provincial Growth and Development Strategy (PGDS) (Harrison 2003; DPLG 2004).

## The international context

The IDP is, arguably, one of the outcomes of a process of *policy convergence* that happened internationally in the 1990s. As soon as South Africa began its transition to democracy in the early years of that decade, a multitude of international influences came to bear on the policy debate in this country. A huge, interlinked global policy network influenced and significantly shaped the outcome of post-apartheid policy and practice. Key agents included major multilateral bodies such as the World Bank and the United Nations' agencies; the international development agencies of powerful nation states such as the USA, the UK and Germany; private sector consultants (both local and international); and academics. The accepted international discourse on governance and development forcefully constrained the horizon of possibilities for policy innovation after apartheid. The extent to which South African policy-makers could have taken more indigenous and original approaches is an interesting and important question but is not one that I deal with directly in this chapter.

The powerful influence of the NPM on the shaping of South Africa's systems of local government is now widely recognised (eg. Therkildsen 2001; Gasper 2002; Fraser-Moleketi 2003a; Bond 2004) and the connection between the NPM and IDPs has also been made (Watson 1998, 2003; Harrison 2001). However, insufficient attention may have been given to the complexity, diversity and evolving nature of the NPM, and the implications that this has had for public policy in post-apartheid South Africa. In this chapter I argue that the arrival of the IDP in South Africa can best be understood in the context of a second wave of NPM approaches associated with the Third Way (or centre-left) governance of the 1990s. As a progressive movement, the African National Congress (ANC) was cautious of approaches that were too obviously inspired by the conservative ideologies that were at their most extreme in the 1980s but, with the apparent demise of state socialism, the ANC leadership looked increasingly towards other models of 'progressive governance', including, initially, the developmental state model of East Asia but then, also, the Third Way approaches of Blair's New Labour and Clinton's New Democrats.

The NPM – which is no longer particularly new – is most commonly associated with the efficiency drive of the 'neo-liberal' approach to governance. A first wave of the NPM spread globally in the 1980s, beginning in Anglo-Saxon countries such as the UK, the USA, Australia and New Zealand, where radical neo-liberal administrations were in power, and then diffusing rapidly to other places, including countries in the 'third world' where the NPM was promoted by the powerful development agencies. NPM practices were, however, fairly diverse and, recently, attention has been given to cross-national differences and to different models of NPM practice (see Hood & Peters 2004). The common element, however, was the attempt to bring a corporate culture – concerned with businesslike efficiency and outcomes – into public agencies. Key elements of the approach often included professional and flexible management at the top of public sector bodies; the separation of policy-making from operations; the disaggregation of public sector departments into corporatised units; the introduction of competition into service delivery; outsourcing and competitive tendering; and an emphasis on output-based performance evaluation (Considine & Lewis 2003; Hood & Peters 2004).

This first wave of NPM reforms did not provide a planning-friendly environment. The 1980s focus was on individual, and mainly short-term, projects rather than on longer-term strategy and planning. However, this radical neo-liberalism created the conditions for a re-emergence of planning (although in a way that is very different to its traditional forms). One of the principal consequences of the NPM was the diffusion, fragmentation and growing complexity of governance. This was the result of decentralisation, privatisation, the separation of policy-making from operations, the creation of corporatised units, and the increasing involvement of non-state agencies in government (often through public–private partnerships). Increasingly, questions of coordination came to the fore (see Sullivan 2003).

In the 1990s, the traditionally left-leaning parties of Europe, and elsewhere in the north, challenged the hegemony of the conservative (or neo-liberal) politics that had dominated the 1980s. In making this challenge, they adopted a Third Way approach that accepted the fundamentals of 1980s neo-liberalism – conservative fiscal and monetary policies, the welfare-to-work approach, and a commitment to privatisation – but also emphasised progressive ideals such as building community, inclusion, participation, poverty alleviation, and integration. There was a shift away from the single-minded focus on economic rationality that had marked the 1980s but the Third Way approach was a complex, eclectic and uneasy mix (Béland, de Chantal & Waddon 2002).

Whilst Clinton and Blair are most commonly associated with Third Way politics, an international network of Third Way leaders emerged during this decade, including figures such as Jean Chrétien (Canada), Helen Clarke (New Zealand), Gerhard Schroeder (Germany), Vladimir Spindla (Czech Republic), Leszek Miller (Poland), Lula da Silva (Brazil) and Ricardo Lagos (Chile). There was, of course, also Thabo Mbeki of South Africa. These, and other leaders, met regularly and it is only recently, with the fall-out over the Iraqi war, that the unity of this coalition has been fractured. The reputation of the Third Way is now somewhat tarnished, as evidence suggests that it may have done more for the middle class than for the poor, but there is an attempt to revitalise the Third Way under the banner of 'progressive governance'.

Although there are commonalities with 1980s neo-liberalism (see the critique by Thomas 2001), one of the major departure points of the Third Way is its emphasis on integration (or on 'joined-up government', as Blair has put it). This, together with the Third Way focus on performance management and participatory governance, has shaped the new approaches to planning internationally, and in South Africa in the mid- to late-1990s. These three key elements of Third Way NPM are considered briefly next.

## Joined-up government

The 1990s saw a broad shift in the way the relationship between individuals and society was understood. Instead of seeing the world as consisting of isolated individuals concerned with maximising personal benefit, there was an increasing awareness of the ways in which agents are bound together in social, economic and governance networks. Metaphors of flows and networks (supported by advances in information technology) partially replaced the traditional metaphors of hierarchy and boundaries, and also the atomism – the individualism – of 1980s neo-liberalism (Simonsen 2004). Within governance, there was a growing concern with strategic partnerships, building trust, transcending organisational boundaries, and with coordination amongst the multiple agents involved in policy-making and implementation (Considine & Lewis 2003). Blair, for example, spoke famously of the need for 'joined-up solutions to deal with joined-up problems' (Knox 2002: 19) and, by the beginning of the 2000s, Perri (2004) was able to write of a widespread political commitment to coordination and integration.

Models of integration varied. In the USA, for example, the model remains one of loosely formed voluntaristic cooperation between agencies. In Ireland, national government plays a coordination and supervisory role within a broad social partnership (House & McGrath 2004), whilst in countries including the UK, Australia and New Zealand national government has set the policy framework, but expects local and regional government to perform most of the coordination and integration functions. As Hall (2003) explained, the joined-up government model in the UK involves continued devolution to subnational government and partnership structures, whilst consolidating powers for policy design and financial control at the centre. Long and Franklin termed this approach 'top-down direction for bottom-up implementation' (2004: 309). This may also be used to describe the system in South Africa where the IDP is an instrument of local coordination, but where the system is closely directed and monitored by national government.

In the UK under New Labour, as in South Africa, many national programmes and units have been set up to give support to decentralised initiatives, and instruments for local coordination have also been developed. In particular, area-based Local Strategic Partnerships have been introduced in the UK, tasked with preparing Community Strategies. It is striking how similar the Community Strategies (Community Plans in Scotland) are to the IDP. Community Strategies must link with national and regional priorities; show full evidence of engagement with the public, private and voluntary sectors; be preceded by capacity-building exercises; join up with national and local programmes that have area-based dimensions; and be based on well-researched strategies (Pearce & Mawson 2002; Allmendinger 2003). As is the case with South Africa's IDP, the preparation of a Community Strategy is often the prerequisite for accessing funding from national sources.

In recent years, *spatial policy* has re-emerged as an instrument of policy coordination (Healey 2004). The European Spatial Development Perspective, which provides a broad framework for public and private investment across the continent, has been particularly important in shaping the new spatial vocabulary and practice but there were other important national, regional and local initiatives (Jensen & Richardson 2003). This new-style spatial planning involves what the doyen of planning theory, Patsy Healey, calls 'self-conscious collective efforts to re-imagine a city, urban region or wider territory and to translate the results into priorities for area investment, conservation measures, strategic infrastructure investments and principles of land use regulation' (Healey 2004: 46). It is a form of spatial policy-making that has responded to a 'paradigmatic shift in geographical imagination' (2004: 48). It increasingly involves collaborative processes of dialogue and negotiation (Wolsink 2003). The idea of the Spatial Development Framework – a component of South Africa's IDP – is converging on this new international approach to spatial policy-making.

A further important dimension to integration is the idea of multi-level governance and coordination which is largely the result of developments within the European Union where complex mechanisms have been developed to link regional, national and supranational government. As shall be seen, a similar focus emerged in South Africa under Mbeki's leadership within the context of a complex constitutional arrangement of cooperative governance. On a continent-wide scale, the newly formed African Union and New Partnership for Africa's Development (Nepad) may offer the tentative beginnings of multi-level governance and integrated development planning. Significantly, Bill Clinton referred to Nepad as a form of Third Way planning in his speech to the British Labour Party Conference in 2002.[1]

## Performance management

Although outcomes-based performance management was a feature of 1980s-style NPM, it was really only in the 1990s that it became central to the functioning of public authorities and was explicitly linked to planning instruments. The Clinton–Gore administration in the early 1990s led the way with the introduction of mandatory outcomes-based performance evaluations for all federal departments linked to the preparation of Strategic Plans (see the 1993 Government Performance and Results Act). Very soon state and local authorities followed suit, and performance evaluation provided the core of the American 'Re-invention Movement' which was highly influential internationally. This new emphasis was largely the result of concerns flowing from the decentralisation processes of the 1980s which removed local officials from the direct control of higher levels of authority (Heinrich 2002). A related concern was with 'rational budgeting', that is, the linking of budgets to approved priorities and strategies. NPM reforms in Australia and New Zealand in the 1980s had emphasised rational budgeting but, by the mid-1990s, rational budgeting was widely used as an instrument of joined-up government (Grizzle & Pettijohn 2002; Long & Franklin 2004). As shall be seen, there are strong links between budgeting processes and South Africa's IDP.

*Participatory governance*

During the first phase of the NPM the emphasis was on citizens as clients or customers, and on the need for public agencies to provide their clients with an efficient service. However, as Vigoda pointed out, this increased responsiveness to the public was also 'accompanied by a *lower* willingness to share, participate, collaborate and partner with citizens' (2002: 528). However, in the 1990s, as the 'network perspective' on governance took hold, new attention was given to the need to collaborate with citizens as partners (often referred to as 'stakeholder engagement'), and a series of initiatives was introduced in countries including the UK and the USA, to promote a more participatory mode of citizenship. 'Collaborative governance' became a common refrain. However, there are contradictions between the idea of collaborative governance and a performance management culture which places officials under enormous pressure to attain targets within specified time frames. There is also a tension between participation and a model of joined-up government that seeks to maintain overall control for policy-making and finance at the centre, and between participation and the often technocratic approach to policy-making by Third Way administrations.

## The South African story

By 1996 when the IDP was first introduced – and especially by 1998, when the White Paper on Local Government clarified the objectives of the IDP – 'progressive' discourse on governance and planning internationally was centred on integration, performance management and participation. Internationally, a number of planning-type instruments had been – or were being – developed which supported these broad objectives.

*The origins*

However, although the South African story was to connect strongly with these international trends, there is a specifically local tale that links to the South African legacy of apartheid-induced fragmentation. From the late 1970s, the reformist wing of the (late) apartheid state was searching desperately for solutions to a growing political and economic crisis, and there was some hope that regional coordination (which cut across provincial and homeland boundaries) would resolve some of the more perverse consequences of apartheid. Within this context, there was experimentation with various forms of integrated development planning. There were, for example, integrated regional planning initiatives in the KwaZulu-Natal region, and integrated rural development programmes in the Gazankulu and Transkei homelands supported by the state's Development Bank of Southern Africa. However, without a fundamental reorganisation of political and administrative structures these initiatives had very limited impacts. There was also some shift towards a strategic planning approach at the local level, for example, Natal's Package of Plans, which linked the town planning scheme to forward-oriented structure plans and development plans, and Pietermaritzburg 2000, which was one of the earliest of South Africa's participatory and strategic urban planning processes.

However, a more important influence on post-apartheid policy was the struggles of the grassroots township-based civic movement of the mid- to late-1980s, which mobilised community activism around local issues such as housing and transportation. The famous slogan 'One city, one tax base' reflected a deep anger at the fragmenting effects of apartheid at a local level, and especially at the inequalities between the well-serviced white areas and the marginalised black townships and shack settlements. By the late 1980s a network of progressive academics and development professionals had connected with this grassroots struggle, and were providing a degree of intellectual support. Progressive planning and development non-governmental organisations (NGOs) established at the time – including, most importantly, the Johannesburg-based Planact – were important incubators for the ideas that came to shape official policy after 1994. With the transforming political context in the early 1990s, the focus shifted away from resistance, and progressive academics and NGO officials came together in networks – such as the Local Government Policy Project (Logopop) – which were important in furthering ideas around local government and planning. Connections were made to the policy think tanks that had been established by the ANC and the Congress of South African Trade Unions, such as the influential Macro Economic Research Group. By 1992/93 the emerging thinking within these networks was being fed into the policy negotiations taking place in the Local Government Negotiating Forum, which set the course of local government restructuring in South Africa, the National Housing Forum, and local structures such as the Central Witwatersrand Metropolitan Chamber. Within these arenas, ideas of integrated urban development and of post-apartheid planning were further developed, and consensus around new development and planning policies was gradually reached in a process that brought together an astonishing range of political and ideological positions.

All these negotiations and developments were happening within the context of rapidly changing positions on macropolicy. The ANC was always a 'broad church', and so came into the negotiating processes with a general commitment to the socialist ideals of the Freedom Charter but without strong coherence in its policy positions. The surprisingly rapid shift from a broadly socialist orientation to the economic orthodoxies expressed in the 1996 Growth, Employment and Redistribution strategy is now the subject of a number of critical commentaries (eg. Bond 2000; Marais 2001). It was clear that the ANC was under enormous pressure from western governments and international development agencies, as well as from private capital, to adopt economic and development policies that conformed to these orthodoxies and, with the collapse of state socialism, was hard-pressed to sustain a more radical approach to transformation.

With the apparent failure of state socialism, ANC intellectuals turned to the 'developmental state model' provided by Japan and the East Asian tigers in which the state plays a strategic and directing role in support of capitalist development. This model was hugely influential in the writing of the Reconstruction and Development Programme (RDP) manifesto. However, South Africa was a very different context to East Asia where state structures were very strong and, also, by the mid-1990s, with the economic crisis in East Asia, the developmental state model was in trouble. It was almost inevitable, perhaps, that key thinkers within the ANC alliance would be drawn to the Third Way approaches of New Labour in the UK and the New Democrats in the USA. These were approaches that offered both inclusion and economic modernisation. They were broadly acceptable to global capitalism and to global development agencies but could also be sold as approaches of the left, as Third Way discourse included reference to inclusion, community building and poverty alleviation.

The RDP, however, still offered a more traditionally left-oriented programme of state-led investment and service provision. The RDP was presented as 'an integrated, coherent socio-economic policy framework' (RSA 1994: Section 1.1.1) and the RDP Office within national government was set up to provide national coordination for the implementation of the RDP. For the RDP Office, 'integrated development planning' provided a potential instrument for delivering the RDP in a coordinated way. The RDP Office set up an interdepartmental Forum for Effective Planning and Development (FEPD) which was concerned with producing 'planning approaches which are integrated, multi-faceted, participatory, and long term' (FEPD 1995: Vol. 2), and participated in international tours to countries such as Malaysia, Indonesia, Botswana and Namibia where development planning was part of the national state apparatus. The FEPD defined integrated development planning as '…a participatory approach to integrate economic, sectoral, spatial, social, institutional, environmental and fiscal strategies in order to support the optimal allocation of scarce resources between sectors and geographical areas and across the population in a manner that provides sustainable growth, equity and the empowerment of the poor and the marginalised' (FEPD 1995: Vol. 1). It is a definition that is still widely used.

At the time integrated development planning still meant *national coordination*, and there were, in fact, proposals for the RDP Office to be reconstituted as a national planning agency, and also various attempts to put in place a National Development Plan. However, already by then, the ground was shifting. Attempts at national coordination were being deeply frustrated by departmental rivalry, whilst the ideological shift within government was undermining the idea of national planning (which, for many, still sounded suspiciously like a version of old-style socialism). Increasingly, also, the attention was shifting to the role of local government in the delivery of the RDP.

As local government came more prominently onto the agenda, so the influence of NPM-type thinking became increasingly apparent. The World Bank's Urban Reconnaissance Missions in the early 1990s had been hugely influential and, in 1994 and early 1995, World Bank staff in South Africa had been involved in infrastructure policy design for local government which informed early drafts of the Urban Infrastructure Investment Framework, later to become the Municipal Investment Infrastructure Framework, and which incorporated large doses of the NPM (Tomlinson 2002; Pieterse 2003). The government's strongly NPM-influenced Urban Development Strategy, released in October 1995, stressed the importance of local government in implementing the RDP and stated that 'local authorities will be responsible for development and physical planning as well as the preparation of 5-year infrastructure investment programmes' (RSA 1995a: 35). This was an early indication of the government's decision to make local government the key arena within which development planning and coordination would occur.

In April 1996, a few months after the elections for the new Transitional Local Councils, President Mandela announced the closure of the RDP Office, and with this office went the vision of national planning and coordination (in the traditional form, at least). The focus was now strongly directed at putting a new system of developmental local government in place. (For an insightful account of the origins of the system see Van Donk and Pieterse in this book.) The Constitution of the Republic of South Africa, adopted by the National Assembly on 8 May 1996, established local government as an autonomous sphere of government with its own constitutionally guaranteed functions (although still under the supervision of national and provincial government), and introduced the notion of 'cooperative governance' as the framework for the relationship between the three spheres. A simple model of national coordination and integration was no longer possible. Instead, coordination would have to be negotiated between the different spheres of government. Minds were, however, increasingly concentrated on what it would take to get the recently elected Transitional Local Councils working effectively (with the financial sustainability of local government being an especially large concern).

## The arrival of the IDP in 1996

By 1996 the need for a local planning instrument was obvious. The first post-apartheid planning instruments had been introduced in the Development Facilitation Act promulgated in October 1995, but these instruments – including the Land Development Objectives which local authorities were required to prepare, and Development Tribunals which were given power to override legal restrictions on land development – were intended primarily to be 'extraordinary measures to facilitate and speed up the implementation of reconstruction and development programmes and projects in relation to land' (RSA 1995b: 1). There was a need for a broader instrument to coordinate and direct the activities of local authorities.

The opportunity was provided in late 1996 by the preparation of a piece of legislation to amend the Act which provided the legal basis for the system of transitional local government. The Local Government Transition Act, Second

Amendment Act was drafted by the Department of Constitutional Development (DCD) and promulgated in November 1996. Fortuitously, key individuals who had a long history of engagement with ideas of integrated development planning – as political activists connected to the civic movement, policy researchers and negotiators in the early 1990s, and officials in the RDP Office after 1994 – had been recently transferred to DCD and were involved in preparing the legislation. These individuals included, most importantly, Dr (Chippy) Olver and Dr Laurine Platzky (Olver was appointed as Deputy Director-General of the department). They took the opportunity to incorporate within the legislation a requirement that all transitional metropolitan, district and local councils prepare an IDP.

This was done in haste, in response to a particular opportunity, and so there was no time to develop the concept of the IDP before introducing it in legislation. The Act does, however, provide strong indications of what the original intention of the IDP was. The IDP was primarily an attempt by national government to ensure that local authorities performed their functions diligently, in a way that was developmental and fiscally responsible. Section 10(G) of the Act makes it clear that IDPs were seen as a key instrument in promoting rational and developmentally oriented budgeting, and there was also a requirement that a local authority 'regularly monitor and assess its performance against its integrated development plan' (RSA 1996: Section 10), and use the IDP to promote economic development. There is a perception amongst some actors that DCD sidelined spatial planning in favour of a notion of planning that was directed at financial and performance management. Although the Act was very sketchy in its details, the newly emerging international discourse on planning was clearly reflected in the provisions it made for the IDP.

## The IDP policy process, 1996–2002

The drafters of the 1996 Act may have had a coherent view of the purpose of the IDP but there was a high degree of confusion amongst other actors. In particular, there was uncertainty around the relationship between the IDP and the Land Development Objectives, and between the IDP and the planning instruments that had recently been developed by provincial authorities (especially KwaZulu-Natal and the Western Cape). Newly established and still inexperienced municipal councils had little understanding of the planning process, and generally subcontracted the preparation of the IDP to professional planners, many of whom were still rooted in a strongly traditional and spatially oriented practice of planning.

There was an urgent need for further clarification of policy and for greater detail in terms of requirements, and also for support, training and capacity development for local authorities. An *ex post facto* process of policy elaboration unfolded after 1996 that connected with a series of international influences.

The most important initial development was the release of the White Paper on Local Government in 1998, which set out the principles and proposed arrangements for the new system of local government that would end the transitional period. The White Paper confirmed the IDP as a crucial instrument of developmental local government, and emphasised the links between the IDP and performance management. It also elaborated the objectives of the IDP. By 1998, there was no mistaking the connections between South Africa's approach to local government and planning, and the approach taken by the new wave of centre-left governments internationally. South Africa's White Paper was strikingly similar to New Labour's 1998 White Paper – entitled *Modern Local Government: In Touch with the People* – even though it was framed against the backdrop of apartheid legacies. The full range of connections between South African and British policy-making at this time has yet to be established but was clearly significant, and drew on the historic connections between the ANC and the Labour Party. Common themes included integrated planning, community participation, performance management, and service delivery partnerships. As indicated previously, there was also a remarkable similarity between South Africa's IDPs and the UK's Community Strategies. There were also clear similarities with planning approaches in countries such as Australia, New Zealand and Germany where Shroeder's centre-left administration had taken power in 1998.

The IDP, which began its life as a precarious and misunderstood instrument, in competition with other forms of planning, was now well entrenched within the post-apartheid system of local government. To a large extent the IDP, as an institutional plan, had eclipsed the previously dominant spatial planning approach although, by about 2000, a new form of integrative spatial planning was resurfacing within the framework provided by the IDP (see Harrison & Todes 2001; Watson 2002, 2003). For an excellent account of the broader context of spatial policy within which this new emphasis has emerged, see the contribution by Todes in this book.

In 1998, despite the clarity brought by the White Paper, there was still a great need to provide municipal authorities with substantive guidance and support in the preparation of IDPs, and to provide a more adequate legislative basis for IDPs. Responsibility for local government at the time fell under DCD (soon to be renamed the Department of Provincial and Local Government [DPLG]) but a government-to-government agreement between the Federal Republic of Germany and South Africa led to the formation of the Decentralised Development Planning (DDP) unit to oversee the introduction of IDPs. DDP was a semi-autonomous unit (which allowed it to operate with a reasonably high degree of flexibility) although it was housed within DCD and was responsible to a national IDP Steering Committee, which included the South African Local Government Association and various government ministries. The real direction for the DDP, however, came from the DDP Task Team which consisted of officials from DCD, an outside consultant (Marc Feldman), and officials from the German GTZ and South Africa's CSIR.

One of the first tasks of the DDP was to provide support to Transitional Local Councils which were struggling to prepare their first IDPs under extremely difficult circumstances. In 1998, the DDP, using the services of the CSIR, prepared an extensive manual on the IDP process. This was the first substantive guidance for municipalities but many users found it too detailed (437 pages) and technocratic. The first round of IDPs was completed, but rather inadequately. Nevertheless, a learning process had commenced, and the foundations were laid for the next and, arguably, more successful round of IDPs.

By 2000, most of the building blocks for the new (post-transitional) system of local government were in place. Local government boundaries had been redrawn and new local government legislation was in place. For the IDP, the key legislation was the Municipal Systems Act (2000) which specified the minimum contents of an IDP and set out the principles for the process to be followed in preparing an IDP (although it did not prescribe the process). In December 2000 the municipal elections were held and the new system of local government came into effect. Municipalities were then required to produce interim IDPs by March 2001 so that budgeting processes would be informed by some version of integrated development planning (with full IDPs being prepared by March 2002).

This time, however, there was a clear recognition by the DDP and DPLG that considerable support would have to be given to municipalities in the preparation of IDPs. The result was an impressive training and support programme that was to produce positive dividends. A training programme for municipal managers, other local officials, and councillors was rolled out across the country, and a new (more user-friendly) set of IDP guide packs was prepared by the CSIR and distributed nationwide. Very importantly, 31 Planning, Implementation, Management Support System centres were established at district level and were staffed and resourced by national government. The system provided many local and district municipalities with crucial technical support during the IDP process. Financial contributions to municipalities were made through a Municipal Systems Improvement Grant.[2]

Very few municipalities met the March 2002 deadline but all municipalities eventually completed an IDP with varying degrees of success. The DDP took seriously the idea of the IDP as a learning process and launched a comprehensive evaluation of the process using the services of academics, NGOs and other consultants (although the review was limited to an assessment of the process and institutions involved in preparing the IDP rather than an evaluation of the system as a whole).

*Key influences*

Key influences during this latter period of development were the GTZ and the CSIR, and it is interesting to speculate on the nature of these influences. The GTZ is a company under private law but it acts essentially as the international development wing of Germany's federal government. With a staff of over 9 500, and a presence in about 130 countries, it is a powerful global agency that forms part of a huge international network of influence and ideas transfer.[3] The focus of

GTZ support programmes internationally is good governance which it links with decentralisation, a market-orientation, and budgetary reform (GTZ 2003). GTZ is a zealous promoter of decentralised government. Whilst decentralisation is part of a global development discourse, promoted by other major development agencies, the force of emphasis given to decentralisation by GTZ has to do with Germany's own model of government which, for historical reasons, has an unusually high level of decentralisation, and is largely territorial in its organisation. Wollmann referred to it as 'decentralised territorialisation' (2001: 158).

In the German model, much of the coordination and actual delivery of state functions happens within municipalities and the Länder (the regional government), with federal departments being relatively unimportant (a smaller percentage of Germany's civil service is employed by federal government than is even the case in the highly decentralised USA). In South Africa, however, despite the enhanced role of municipal government, functionally organised state departments and agencies still play a critical role at the local level (in areas including education, welfare, land management, transport, electricity, telecommunications and water provision) and a German-based model of local coordination is not an entirely adequate instrument of integration in this context. Wollmann (2001) also points to the legal regulation culture in Germany, and to the greater emphasis on coordination by the local state than in countries where there is a stronger civic culture where partnership arrangements have been stressed.

Almost inevitably, home country experience will shape the perceptions and ideas brought to a new context. However, it is difficult to pass judgement on the influence of an agency such as GTZ. Inevitably, outside agencies will bring positions that are not entirely attuned to the local context but they also provide critical policy-related and technical capacity, and do transmit progressive ideas. GTZ, for example, has a strong international emphasis on gender-sensitive policies, and has worked to promote the gender angle in IDP processes. Other cross-cutting themes promoted by GTZ – including HIV/AIDS prevention, local economic development, poverty alleviation, and disaster management – are now widely accepted as key emphases within IDPs.[4]

The CSIR has also played a key role in the post-1998 evolution of IDP policy. The CSIR established an IDP team within its Building and Construction Technology Unit, Boutek, which has had direct representation on the DDP Task Team. This team has played a major role in producing manuals and guide packs on IDP process, in training local officials and councillors, and in monitoring the implementation of IDPs, and has also been responsible for important developments in the area of information technology.[5] Although the CSIR is primarily devoted to scientific and industrial research, its role has shifted significantly in recent years as it has worked to shed an image associated with the old order. Its current mission, which is to 'promote growth and quality of life via sustainable development' (CSIR 2003a: 4), has allowed this agency to become so deeply involved with municipal planning processes.

There can be little doubt that the CSIR, like the GTZ, has provided the state with much needed capacity at a critical time in the development of a municipal planning system. Inevitably, however, the CSIR has brought particular slants to the IDP. Despite its shift in orientation, the CSIR remains rooted in science- and technology-related research and it is not surprising that the CSIR has brought to the IDP a 'technical rationalism' with a strong focus on the details of procedures and institutional structures, and on the development of techniques. This has, however, been mitigated by the CSIR's strong emphasis on capacity building and training. The model seems to be to develop procedures and techniques and then to capacitate local authorities to use them. The CSIR has also brought a concern for sustainability. It has worked hard to link Local Agenda 21 processes, and notions of sustainability more broadly, to the IDP process, and it even showcased the IDP at the Johannesburg World Summit on Sustainable Development as an African path to sustainability (CSIR 2002).

### Recent shifts in policy and practice

The new planning system in South Africa is continuing to evolve through a learning process and in response to broader shifts in governance and macropolicy approaches. Until very recently, the IDP was seen almost entirely as an instrument of local planning and coordination (although there was a requirement that the IDP be aligned to national and provincial policies and programmes). However, from 1999, when Thabo Mbeki became president, a new emphasis was working its way through government. It was an emphasis on integrated (or joined-up) multi-level governance. As senior ANC official Fraser-Moleketi put it, 'issues of integration have been a cornerstone of the second term of democratic governance under President Thabo Mbeki' (2003b: 2).

One of Mbeki's first acts as president was to establish Cabinet Clusters to bring related portfolios together in a regular engagement. This was followed by the preparation of the MTSF, to prioritise, align and coordinate government programmes, and the Medium Term Expenditure Framework to ensure that departmental budgets are driven by the nationally agreed strategic priorities. Other integrating mechanisms included the development of a National Planning Cycle, a National Spatial Development Perspective – which takes its cue from the European Spatial Development Perspective – and an integrated information portal known as Gateway. Within the provincial sphere new attention has been given to the PGDS.

Since the IDP was an established mechanism of coordination within the local sphere, it became an obvious instrument to connect with the national MTSF and the PGDS. In December 2001 the Presidential Co-ordinating Council called for the 'implementation of a state-wide planning system wherein Integrated Development Planning serves as the basis for aligning policy, planning and budgeting processes across all spheres' (CSIR 2003b: 1) and, in May 2003, the Cabinet charged DPLG with preparing an Intergovernmental Planning Framework and putting together an Intergovernmental Relations Framework Bill that would strengthen the role of planning across the spheres of government. Recent reports from the Office of the President have mentioned the key role of the IDP within an unfolding system of intergovernmental planning. The IDP had now taken on a new meaning within a much broader context.

The first move towards an intergovernmental planning system was the establishment of the IDP nerve centre – an Internet-based information system that allows for the sharing of IDP-related knowledge and for direct communication within and between spheres of government.[6] In March 2004 the so-called Sun City Action Plan was prepared which reinforces the new emphasis on intergovernmental planning. In terms of the Plan, district and metropolitan council areas are designated as 'impact zones' in which national and provincial government departments must take unified action in a way that links with locally prepared IDPs.

Whilst national government was putting together a system of multi-level integrated planning and coordination, a more bottom-up and voluntary form of networking was coming together. This was the inter-locality networking that was formalised in 2002 as the South African Cities Network, which brings together South Africa's nine largest cities in a strategic partnership. This network is, in turn, linked to the international Cities Alliance Network which is closely connected to the major global development agencies. A 'new' approach to city planning – which both connects with and challenges the IDP – is being promoted through this extended network. This is the City Development Strategy (CDS) approach which has been implemented through the network in over 80 cities worldwide over the past few years, including in Johannesburg. The CDS approach allows for considerable innovation and variation in local methodology, and can be related fairly easily to the IDP. However, there are some potentially important differences in emphasis. The CDS, for example, has a longer-term perspective, is more strongly focused on economic development, and is directed mainly at managing the growth of large cities, whereas the IDP has largely been developed with medium-level local authorities in mind.[7]

The IDP-related system was developed almost entirely under the direction of national government (with strategic support from agencies such as GTZ). In the future, however, metropolitan authorities (with their large resources and planning capacity), supported and informed by wider networks such as Cities Alliance, are likely to be an important source of innovation in planning.

## Outcomes

It is still difficult to evaluate the effect of IDPs on developmental *outcomes*. Has the integrated development planning process produced more integrated and participatory ways of working – more joined-up government – and has this integration (if it has occurred) led to more effective delivery of services, and to more effective responses to problems such as poverty, HIV/AIDS, crime and spatial fragmentation? It will take a while before we are able to provide clear answers to these questions.

There have, however, been a number of evaluations of IDPs sponsored by DPLG, GTZ and provincial governments (for reports on these evaluations see Adam & Oranje 2002; Rauch 2002; Harrison 2003). These evaluations point to modest success for IDPs even if many problems and challenges remain. They suggest that, increasingly, local authorities are beginning to shape the way they operate around the IDP and this may be leading towards more effective developmental local government.

An important contribution by Todes (2004) evaluated the IDP in terms of its contribution to sustainability. Using the case of Ugu District Municipality IDP (in KwaZulu-Natal) Todes found mixed outcomes. She concluded that 'while the emphasis on integration and the multi-sectoral approach to development are strengths, greater attention needs to be given to environmental aspects, and the form of planning needs to be adapted to the context, and its social, economic and political dynamics' (2004: 843).

The IDP has many of the strengths and flaws of other Third Way planning instruments. As an *instrument of joined-up government* it has been limited by its inability to involve and bind the many other agents, apart from municipal government, that operate at the local level, although the emerging system of intergovernmental planning may address this issue. However, the IDP process has contributed to the development of networks and linkages, both formal and informal, within municipal structures and, to a lesser extent, between municipal structures and other agencies.

As an *instrument of participatory governance* the IDP has had mixed results. It has, undeniably, achieved a higher level of participation within municipal planning than ever before in South Africa's history (Adam & Oranje 2002) but there have been wide variations in the extent and success of this participation. Also, the participatory element of the IDP mixes uneasily with a performance management culture, driven by targets and time frames, that is not really amenable to the often 'messy', unpredictable and time-consuming processes of public participation. The IDP attempts to marry inclusiveness and participation with a largely technocratic managerialism, and top-down control with bottom-up processes. In the end it may not prove satisfactory in relation to any particular objective, although it may justifiably be regarded as offering a reasonable balance or trade-off between objectives.

As an *instrument of modernised, efficient administration* the IDP has also had ambiguous outcomes. Like NPM approaches elsewhere, South Africa's new system of local government is full of paradoxes and unexpected outcomes. One of the aims of the NPM is to increase the flexibility and independence of senior managers. However, performance management contracts have given politicians far greater control over senior officials, and the civil service in countries under the sway of the NPM has become increasingly politicised (Gregory & Christensen 2004; Hood & Peters 2004). In South Africa, there has been a strong motivation for local politicians to assert this control – first to take control of a civil service where the apartheid old guard was still strongly represented and then because of growing factionalism within local ANC structures. The local government officials I have spoken to have referred to the intense politicisation of administrative processes in South Africa. The problem for planning is not that the process is political – for planning is always political – but that the type of politics that surrounds planning in South Africa and elsewhere is often hidden from public scrutiny and falls outside accepted democratic procedures.

Performance management is also riddled with paradox. Hood and Peters, for example, use the term 'overcommitment' to refer to 'the extension of the specification and measurement of outputs to the point that unintendedly weakens the credibility and effects of such activity' (2004: 271). Simply put, this means that the system may become so focused on preparing and meeting targets that broader goals may be lost, and flexibility substantially reduced.

One of the other key objectives of NPM reforms is to introduce creativity and innovation into the public sector. However, the NPM, with its focus on benchmarking and best practice, often unintentionally leads to a 'one-size-fits-all' approach (Long & Franklin 2004). Adam and Oranje concluded that there was 'not much experimentation taking place as far as IDP methodology was concerned' (2002: 3), with the only real innovation coming from the metropolitan authorities. An unintended consequence of all the guidance and support given by national government to local authorities, and the detailed attention given to IDP methodology, is a standardisation which is likely to depress the long-term quality of planning. Fortunately, however, there is now an acceptance from national government of a 'differentiated and targeted approach' (DPLG 2004: 8), and also evidence of the incremental, often informal adaptations to the IDP, even within the smaller local authorities (Oranje 2003).

There are similar conclusions for the IDP as an *instrument of developmental local government*. There is wide agreement in assessment reports that IDPs have contributed to the significant shift in expenditure towards historically disadvantaged communities. However, it is not clear whether this more equitable expenditure pattern is having much impact on deeply entrenched social and spatial patterns of inequality. Mabin (2002) suggests that IDPs are not addressing the 'thorniest issues'; they are steering well clear of radical interventions that would be needed to alter deeply entrenched patterns. For Pieterse our conceptions of integration fail to 'address the legacy and systems of power that reproduce the apartheid city' (2003: 136). Pieterse would wish for a far more radical form of planned intervention than a Third Way approach would allow.

## Conclusion

The introduction of the IDP in 1996 was part of a programme to create and strengthen new forms of local government following apartheid, but was also strongly influenced by a global discourse on decentralisation, and by the approaches to planning taken by centre-left parties in influential countries such as the USA, the UK and Germany. Following Mbeki's succession to the presidency there was a subtle shift in the purpose and framing of IDPs. Increasingly, IDPs were linked to a system of *intergovernmental* planning and coordination, and were spoken of in technical and managerialist terms.

The landscape of planning, however, continues to shift. By 2005, instruments of planning such as the IDP were caught up in a growing crisis within local government. The doctrine of decentralisation was being challenged by the failure of many municipalities to deliver on their mandates, whilst systems of support and coordination across the three spheres of government were shown to be inadequate. For planning, the key question is whether the requirement to produce an IDP was one of the burdens on municipalities that detracted from their ability to deliver basic services, or whether the situation would be even worse without IDPs.

Preliminary evidence, in the form of DPLG-sponsored assessments, suggests the latter but the jury is still out. At best, however, the IDP is a modest and partial instrument that may support a municipality in providing a more strategic framework, and a more organised structure, for achieving developmental goals, and may, potentially, also assist with intergovernmental coordination.

Hood and Peters point to the long history in government of overconfidence in reform measures and of the common failure to anticipate unintended effects. They write of 'new gods, newly come to power [citing Aeschylus] who hubristically underestimate the difficulties they will face and the limits of their knowledge' (2004: 227). Local government in post-apartheid South Africa has proven to be more difficult to construct, and less effective, than was hoped for in 1996, whilst planning instruments like the IDP have also revealed their limitations. However, a long-term perspective which recognises the need for a sustained approach to building capability within government, and which acknowledges the advances that have been made, may offer a more hopeful view on the performance of South Africa's new planning systems.

### Notes

1   See <http://www.ndol.org>.

2   See <http://www.local.gov.za>.

3   See <http://www.gtz.de>.

4   See <http://www.gtz.de>.

5   See <http://www.csir.co.za>.

6   See <http:www.idp.org.za>.

7   See <http://www.citiesalliance.org> and <http://www.sacities.net>.

## References

Adam A & Oranje M (2002) A report on engagements with district and metropolitan municipalities on the first round of integrated development plans produced in terms of the Municipal Systems Act, 2000. Prepared for DPLG and the Municipal Demarcations Board.

Allmendinger P (2003) Integrated planning in a devolved Scotland, *Planning Practice & Research*, 18(1): 19–36.

Bèland D, de Chantal FV & Waddon A (2002) Third Way social policy: Clinton's legacy, *Policy and Politics*, 30(1): 19–30.

Bond P (2000) *Elite transition: From apartheid to neo-liberalism in South Africa*. Pietermaritzburg: University of Natal Press.

Bond P (2004) Contradictions confronting new public management in Johannesburg: The rise and fall of municipal water commercialisation. In P Dibben, I Wood & I Roper (eds), *Contesting public sector reforms: Critical perspectives, international debates*. Basingstoke, Hampshire: Palgrave.

Considine M & Lewis J (2003) Bureaucract, network or enterprise? Comparing models of governance in Australia, Britain, The Netherlands and New Zealand, *Public Administration Review*, 63(2): 131–140.

CSIR (Council for Scientific and Industrial Research) (2002) *Local pathway to sustainable development in South Africa*. Pretoria: CSIR.

CSIR (2003a) Annual report, technology impact and the state of science and technology in the CSIR, 2003. Pretoria: CSIR.

CSIR (2003b) Intergovernmental planning boosted by IDP Nerve Centre, *Akani*, November issue: 1–2.

DPLG (Department of Provincial and Local Government) (2004) Development Planning Indaba Report. A report on the deliberations of the Development Planning Indaba at Sun City, 29–30 March.

FEPD (Forum for Effective Planning and Development) (1995) *Minutes*, Volumes One and Two.

Fraser-Moleketi G (2003a) Quality governance for sustainable growth and development, *International Review of Administrative Sciences*, 69(4): 463–470.

Fraser-Moleketi G (2003b) On the integration of the public service. Paper delivered at the Second Annual Senior Management Service Conference held in Port Elizabeth, 15 September.

Gasper D (2002) Fashion, learning and values in public management: Reflections on South African and international experience, *Africa Development*, 27(3/4): 17–47.

Gregory R & Christensen J (2004) Similar ends, differing means: Contractualism and civil service reform in Denmark and New Zealand, *Governance*, 17(1): 59–82.

Grizzle G & Pettijohn C (2002) Implementing performance-based programme budgeting: A systems dynamics perspective, *Public Administration Review*, 62(1): 51–62.

GTZ (Gesellschaft für Technische Zusammenarbeit) (2003) *Annual report 2003: Good governance – state and society shaping development*. Eschborn, Germany: GTZ Corporate Communications.

Hall S (2003) The 'Third Way' revisited: 'New' labour, spatial policy and the national strategy for neighbourhood renewal, *Planning Practice and Research*, 18(4): 265–277.

Harrison P (2001) The genealogy of South Africa's integrated development plan, *Third World Planning Review*, 23(2): 175–193.

Harrison P (2003) Towards integrated inter-governmental planning in South Africa: The IDP as a building block. Report prepared for DPLG and the Municipal Demarcations Board.

Harrison P & Todes A (2001) The use of spatial frameworks in regional development in South Africa, *Regional Studies*, 35(1): 65–72.

Healey P (2004) The treatment of space and place in the new strategic spatial planning in Europe, *International Journal of Urban and Regional Research*, 28(1): 45–67.

Heinrich C (2002) Outcomes-based performance management in the public sector: Implications for government accountability and effectiveness, *Public Administration Review*, 62(6): 712–725.

Hood C & Peters G (2004) The middle aging of new public management: Into the age of paradox, *Journal of Public Administration and Theory*, 14(3): 267–282.

House JD & McGrath K (2004) Innovative governance and development in New Ireland: Social partnership and the integrated approach, *Governance*, 17(1): 29–57.

Jensen O & Richardson T (2003) Being on the map: The new iconographies of power over European space, *International Planning Studies*, 8(1): 9–34.

Knox C (2002) Joined-up government: An integrated response to communal violence in Northern Ireland, *Policy and Politics*, 31(1): 19–35.

Long E & Franklin A (2004) The paradox of implementing the government's Performance and Results Act: Top-down direction for bottom-up implementation, *Public Administration Review*, 64(3): 309–319.

Mabin A (2002) An assessment of the IDP in the Ehlanzeni District. Report prepared for DPLG.

Marais H (2001) *South Africa limits to change: The political economy of transition*. London: Zed Books/Cape Town: UCT Press.

Oranje M (2003) A time and space for African identities in planning. In P Harrison, M Huchzermeyer & M Mayekiso (eds), *Confronting fragmentation: Housing and urban development in a democratising society*. Cape Town: UCT Press.

Pearce G & Mawson J (2002) Delivering devolved approaches to local governance, *Policy and Politics*, 31(1): 51–67.

Perri 6 (2004) Joined-up government in the Western world in comparative perspective: A preliminary literature review and exploration, *Journal of Public Administration and Theory*, 14(1): 103–138.

Pieterse E (2003) Unravelling the different meanings of integration: The Urban Development Framework of the South African government. In P Harrison, M Huchzermeyer & M Mayekiso (eds), *Confronting fragmentation: Housing and urban development in a democratising society*. Cape Town: UCT Press.

Rauch T (2002) Evaluation of IDP processes in South Africa. Report for the Department of Provincial and Local Government.

RSA (Republic of South Africa) (1994) *White Paper on reconstruction and development*. Pretoria: Government Printers.

RSA (1995a) *Urban development strategy*. Pretoria: Government Printers.

RSA (1995b) *Development Facilitation Act, no. 67 of 1995.* Pretoria: Government Printers.

RSA (1996) *Local Government Transition Act, Second Amendment Act, no. 97 of 1996.* Pretoria: Government Printers.

Simonsen K (2004) Networks, flows and fluids – reimagining spatial analysis? Commentaries, *Environment and Planning A,* 36(8): 1333–1340.

Sullivan H (2003) New forms of local accountability: Coming to terms with many hands, *Policy and Politics,* 31(3): 353–369.

Therkildsen O (2001) *Efficiency, accountability and implementation: Public sector reform in East and Southern Africa.* Geneva: UNRISD.

Thomas H (2001) Joining up government – with principle, *International Planning Studies,* 6(1): 5–7.

Todes A (2004) Regional planning and sustainability: Limits and potentials of South Africa's integrated development plans, *Journal of Environmental Planning and Management,* 47(6): 843–861.

Tomlinson R (2002) International best practice, enabling frameworks and the policy process: A South African case study, *International Journal of Urban and Regional Research,* 26(2): 377–388.

Vigoda E (2002) From responsiveness to collaboration: Governance, citizens and the new generation of public administration, *Public Administration Review,* 65(5): 527–540.

Watson V (1998) Planning under political transition – lessons from Cape Town's Metropolitan Planning Forum, *International Planning Studies,* 3: 335–350.

Watson V (2002) *Change and continuity in spatial planning: Metropolitan planning in Cape Town under political transition.* London & New York: Routledge.

Watson V (2003) Planning for integration: The case of metropolitan Cape Town. In P Harrison, M Huchzermeyer & M Mayekiso (eds), *Confronting fragmentation: Housing and urban development in a democratising society.* Cape Town: UCT Press.

Wollmann H (2001) Germany's trajectory of public sector modernisation: Continuities and discontinuities, *Policy and Politics,* 30(1): 151–169.

Wolsink M (2003) Reshaping the Dutch planning system: A learning process? *Environment and Planning A,* 35(4): 705–723.

# 9 The evolution of local economic development in South Africa

Etienne Nel and Lynelle John

## Introduction

This chapter charts how Local Economic Development (LED) policy thinking and practice has developed and been interpreted and applied in South Africa since the 1990s. In terms of policy development, the thinking of the Department of Provincial and Local Government (DPLG), which has been primarily charged to oversee LED, clearly has played a key role in this process. This is, however, stated with a caveat, namely, that LED is also influenced by the Department of Trade and Industry, indirectly by National Treasury and by other departments and that various local municipalities have developed their own policy. The fact that, at the time of writing, there was still no nationally agreed-to policy framework for LED indicates the conceptual challenges posed by the concept and its focus. As policy development is still ongoing, the chapter explores how policy has been evolving, rather than presenting a *fait accompli* and analysing how it was arrived at.

At the same time that this evolution of policy has been under way, the legislative backdrop for LED was being put in place. Starting with the 1996 Constitution, the legislative basis for local authority action in the social and economic realms was laid. This was followed by the drafting of the White Paper on Local Government that introduced the concepts of 'developmental local government' and the Integrated Development Plan (IDP), which are integral to LED and which have laid the basis for subsequent laws that have strengthened the developmental responsibilities of local government.

Yet, by the very nature of what LED means, that is, local ownership and local-level action, while some local LED programmes will have been influenced by draft national LED policy and the various guidelines offered by government, others will have occurred with limited attention to, or even knowledge of, government LED thinking. The last section of the chapter is devoted to summarising and providing examples of LED programmes and projects. The evolution of national policy and local examples of LED illustrates how dynamic and diverse the field has become. This is particularly pertinent in the light of national government finalising LED strategy in 2005 and the emergence of many LED initiatives, especially among South Africa's nine largest cities, which are members of the South African Cities Network (SACN).[1]

Before proceeding, it is important to note that while there is no widely accepted single definition of LED, there usually is agreement on key aspects, including concepts such as local-level action, partnerships, in large part making use of local resources, and local solutions. The International Labour Organisation provides a useful working definition:

> LED is a participatory development process that encourages partnership arrangements between the main private and public stakeholders of a defined territory, enabling the joint design and implementation of a common development strategy, by making use of the local resources and competitive advantage in a global context, with the final objective of creating decent jobs and stimulating economic activity. (ILO n.d. a)

> ...[LED] must belong to the local stakeholders [including NGOs and communities]. (ILO n.d. b)

### Early LED discourse (1990–1998)

LED, as a defined strategic intervention, was thrust into the limelight as a development option in South Africa in the early- to mid-1990s. This was partially as a result of academics learning from oversees trends and identifying incipient LED-type processes in South Africa (Nel 1994; Tomlinson 1994), and partially as a result of policy-related investigations undertaken by a range of key local agencies, detailed later. Tomlinson's (1994) book was particularly significant in that it set the scene for subsequent discourse through drawing out the lessons of overseas experience, identifying the role of key stakeholders and distilling the lessons from emerging experience, particularly in Durban and the greater Johannesburg region. In addition, LED also came to feature on the agendas of three key organisations in the country, which all sought to envision a post-apartheid development context in which local action could contribute meaningfully to developmental processes. These were:
- The Urban Foundation
- The South African National Civic Organisation (Sanco)
- The Reconstruction and Development Programme (RDP) Ministry.

The private sector funded Urban Foundation, as part of its major investigation of a range of key urban management and policy options for the country, commissioned a study into LED (Urban Foundation 1995). The paper drew heavily on western experience regarding urban entrepreneurialism and how cities compete in the global economy. It argued that cities needed to abandon their traditional managerial focus and become more entrepreneurial in their actions. Notions of privatisation, partnerships, industrial districts and growth coalitions featured prominently in their recommendations.

A parallel process was that spearheaded by Sanco, with the direct assistance of the German social democratic agency, the Friedrich Ebert Stiftung, which drew on the community-oriented leanings of Sanco and sponsored consultants to help draft policy. Based on engagement with local-area actors actively pursuing LED and research undertaken both locally and internationally, Sanco released its own LED policy document in 1995 (Sanco 1995). The document stressed issues such as engagement, participation and partnerships. Issues such as public works, small business support and procurement featured prominently in their document. It was clearly influenced by both the civic character and the focus of Sanco and stood in quite distinctive contrast to the pro-market Urban Foundation paper.

Prior to the demise of the RDP Ministry in 1996, LED did start to feature in government development planning. In 1995, the RDP Ministry funded consultants led by Richard Tomlinson and Roland Hunter, now the Chief Financial Officer of the City of Johannesburg, to research and develop a draft policy document entitled *Local Economic Development: A Discussion Document* (Ministry in the Office of the President 1995). The work of the consultants was overseen by an official of the RDP Office, Pascal Moloi, who at the time of writing was City Manager of Johannesburg. The document provided an overview of what LED is, the role of various participants and a range of the more common approaches. It described the objectives of LED as being to 'encourage private investment, create jobs and enhance incomes and levels of affordability within a given locality, and to improve local government's ability to provide services' (Ministry in the Office of the President 1995: 1). It also stated that LED needs to promote investment in growth industries and services; mobilise public, private and community resources; and promote development in low-income neighbourhoods. The paper's strengths lay in the attention it devoted to the consideration of the role of government and other key partners in development. On the negative side policy prescriptions were weakly developed and funding and support for LED was not dealt with (Nel 1997). In parallel, a detailed research process was undertaken in the country that documented the incidence of LED in various institutional contexts.

Two other key government documents emerged in this time period that also reflected and helped shape current thinking and set a framework for LED debates in government. These were the draft Urban Development Strategy (RSA 1995a) and the draft Rural Development Strategy (RSA 1995b). The former argued that the country's 'economic performance will largely be determined in metropolitan areas, cities and towns' (RSA 1995a: 40) and improving economies was crucial to the eradication of poverty and the achievement of a more equitable society. Assertive LED-type strategies were called for, with a focus on small business development, public works and support for housing and infrastructural projects. In terms of the latter document, LED was seen as a mechanism to develop local solutions, through partnerships, for the development of rural towns (RSA 1995b). Though not taken further for several years, combined, these government documents laid the basis for LED thinking as it developed in government over much of the subsequent ten years, namely, with a focus on partnerships, small businesses and poverty-focused interventions. Government thinking on LED in the mid-1990s, though inconclusive, did show clear links with the principles contained in the RDP. The framing of documents which identified the need to encourage economic growth and address development backlogs, set the tone for local-level understanding of LED in the country. The demise of the RDP Ministry in 1996 dealt a blow to LED, through the loss of a host-ministry which could champion the process and this further served to delay policy debates until the role of local government more broadly had been defined in the country.

The three organisations, the Urban Foundation, Sanco and the RDP Ministry, differed considerably in their focus and orientation, ranging from the populist leanings of the Sanco document, to the Urban Foundation's market-focused approach, to the government's more middle of the road statements. Whilst none of the documents was taken further at this point, these early studies were useful for a number of reasons. First, they provided a useful summary of international approaches to LED, helping South African policy-makers to make more informed policy choices. Second, their overview of LED approaches helped define the parameters of the future LED policy debate, enabling subsequent policy-makers to start teasing out issues of implementation and intervention during policy deliberations. Third, they captured the practical issues that some local LED programmes had begun wrestling with (as reflected in the content of the Sanco/Friedrich Ebert Stiftung workshops which had tried to learn from applied experience and which were documented in subsequent publications [Nel 1995; Nel & Lindie 1996]).

Although it would be only in 1998 that explicit policy impacting on LED would emerge, several other noteworthy trends could be discerned in the mid- to late-1990s. As mentioned earlier, at a more 'hands-on' level, the Friedrich Ebert Stiftung helped Sanco with LED policy. In addition, for several years they sponsored a publication known as *LED News*, which was widely circulated to civic groups and municipal authorities. This publication helped to popularise the LED concept and celebrated applied successes. More recently, international agencies such as Germany's *Gesellschaft für Technische Zusammenarbeit* (the Agency for Technical Co-operation), the United Kingdom's Department for International Development, and the United States Agency for International Development have played an important role in terms of supporting LED research and promotional processes through training and the popularisation of the concept through the print and electronic media. In addition to the part played by international agencies, there was initial business support for LED research and programme development, primarily coordinated through the National Business Initiative. In the mid- to late-1990s the National Business Initiative actively supported research and tried to catalyse LED in various localities through direct support and the publication, in collaboration with government, of a LED manual. Together with the International Republican Institute, in 1998 they produced a handbook for councillors and officials entitled *The Local Authority's Role in Economic Development* (IRI 1998). The document provides an overview of laws impacting on LED, available strategies and resources.

## The White Paper on Local Government

The White Paper on Local Government, released in 1998, was the first definitive policy statement on post-apartheid local government and one that explored the economic development role of local government. The policy paper was issued by the Ministry of Provincial Affairs and Constitutional Development, which was later renamed the Department of Constitutional Development and subsequent to that the DPLG.[2] The final version of the White Paper was the culmination of months of intense debate amongst its key drafters – an ideological debate that occurred during highly formative years of policy-making in South Africa. For this and a host of other reasons, the White Paper's silences are as interesting as its policy assertions. This is certainly true of its pronouncements on LED. The White Paper developed at a time when the African National Congress (ANC) government had not yet taken a defined stance on its overall socio-economic strategy, which clearly impacted on the policy process. It is important to note that in the mid- to late-1990s, government policy thinking in general was increasingly reflecting the precepts of the country's macroeconomic strategy, the Growth, Employment and Redistribution (GEAR) strategy (RSA 1996a). According to Cheru (2002: 508), GEAR emphasised 'the need for improved growth to sustain the government's social and developmental programmes through fiscal discipline, monetary policy and the restructuring of state assets, in order to increase the competitiveness of the economy'. Debates regarding the White Paper, as a result, were dominated by issues of service delivery and finance and LED was not given much attention.

The White Paper policy process was driven by the White Paper Political Committee, which was supported in its efforts by the White Paper Working Committee. Research assistance was provided by the University of the Witwatersrand's Graduate School of Public and Development Management, the Centre for Policy Studies and the Foundation for Contemporary Research, amongst others.

The final document developed through a three-fold process, from *South Africa's Local Government – A discussion document* (1997), to the Green Paper on Local Government (1997) and finally the White Paper on Local Government (1998) (Ministry of Provincial Affairs and Constitutional Development 1997a, 1997b; RSA 1998). However, some key debates were never resolved during the 15-month drafting process. As a result, the final White Paper emerged as a document that makes very few explicit policy choices and fails to resolve a tension that every subsequent set of local government policy-makers and legislators ran up against. The discussion regarding LED was whether it should be a largely state-run initiative aimed at alleviating poverty or whether it should be a fairly private sector-driven affair, aimed at supporting business and maximising economic growth.

The formal LED section grew out of a set of research papers commissioned by the White Paper Working Committee that were undertaken by the Centre for Policy Studies. Research focused on a set of issues clustered under the theme 'A developmental role for local government'. Formative work was drafted by Ben Cashdan, a British consultant who adopted the view that LED in South Africa needed to be community focused and as such helped to shape the direction of future LED debates (Cashdan 1997).

The LED policy emanating out of the White Paper process may be read in two different 'places' or forms in the final document. First, it is seen most obviously in the formal LED portion in the section on Developmental Local Government (RSA 1998: section B). This subsection states that one of the characteristics of developmental local government is that of maximising social development and economic growth and it describes LED as one of the key developmental outcomes of local government. Second, much may be inferred from related sections on globalisation, public–private partnerships and so forth (RSA 1998: Sections A and F).

The document contains a series of key messages regarding LED. The primary message is that municipalities are able to substantively influence their local economies simply by using their traditional powers and functions. In other words, if municipalities do nothing but undertake their current responsibilities effectively, they will catalyse LED outcomes. The delivery of water and sanitation, waste removal and electricity, and regulatory functions are seen as especially important in this regard. The White Paper speaks of the value of 'investing in the basics – by providing good quality cost-effective services and by making the local area a pleasant place to live and work' (RSA 1998: 25).

Another significant and related message is that municipalities should review their existing policies and procedures in order to promote LED. This involves speeding up zoning applications, changing procurement policies to favour local or small businesses and so on. The White Paper makes specific mention of job creation. It argues that whilst municipalities are not directly responsible for job creation, they should actively create conducive conditions for it. The White Paper also advocates the provision of special economic services, which can range from sophisticated place marketing and support for growth sectors, to more low-key training and placement services.

The substance of the White Paper's LED messages is essentially about local government doing its 'normal job' well. Thus, despite some creative thinking on the use of traditional municipal functions to effect economic development, the formal LED messages emanating out of the White Paper process were relatively bland and cautious. This is particularly surprising in view of the document's parallel encouragement of the concept of *developmental local government* – of municipalities that proactively shape and influence their local spaces. However, if one remembers the focus of GEAR and concerns about the role of the state in the economy, perhaps this caution is not that surprising. What the White Paper did achieve was to actualise the vision of developmental local government that was inherent in the Constitution. Its urging of municipalities to become proactive, strategic and visionary conclusively changed perceptions about local government. The White Paper does not set out a bold vision for LED. Its failure to resolve an admittedly difficult policy debate also created problems for the next generation of local government policy-makers about whether the local state's role should be to intervene or merely to facilitate development.

## Parallel processes of government for LED

In parallel with the policy formation phase, a process of government support for LED started to develop from the late-1990s, in which the DPLG and the local government sector in general were particularly prominent. Within this context, a significant range of draft policy, research and applied LED interventions have taken place which have shaped the nature of LED thinking, policy and practice in the country. In the period since 1999 LED was formalised in the DPLG through a LED programme which was described as being responsible for policy and strategic management, coordinating LED studies, coordinating information and funding, and providing implementation management (DPLG 2003). Also put in place were funding mechanisms. In terms of policy, LED thinking and draft policy, for a period, came to assume a more definedly pro-poor slant as a result of the focus adopted by certain DPLG officials, which put LED interpretations in conflict with the views adopted by the Department of Trade and Industry and, at times, thinking in government more broadly (Tomlinson 2003).

In 1999 the Department of Constitutional Development commissioned the Isandla Institute to undertake a series of case studies of LED and poverty (DCD n.d. a) from across the country. This was accompanied by a discussion document that clearly linked LED to poverty alleviation and advocated explicit measures to address poverty alleviation through LED (DCD n.d. b). The study was funded by the United Kingdom's Department for International Development and drew on the skills of various non-governmental organisations (NGOs) and academics in the country. These studies and the pro-poor orientation clearly became the hallmark of a new generation of LED officials in DPLG, led by Karen Harrison who took charge of LED in 1999 (Harrison interview).

The poverty studies were followed in 2000 by a series of five LED manuals released by DPLG which provided comprehensive guidance on the DPLG's concept of LED to local governments, and which helped the latter to better conceptualise their role as development agents. In addition, it outlined available development, institutional and funding options (DPLG 2000). The manuals were developed by DPLG in consultation with a range of NGOs and academics and addressed the following themes:

- Institutional arrangements;
- Strategies and instruments;
- Management and measurement;
- Case-study experiences; and
- LED financing.

The underlying research process was driven by Karen Harrison who, as a supporter of the pro-poor standpoint, had commissioned the baseline studies which preceded the release of the documents. Research was undertaken by individuals who were deemed to hold fairly left-wing policy positions (Harrison interview), thereby signalling a key policy strand held by some members of the department at the time. While the manuals reflected the overall orientation of DPLG at the time, namely, the strong poverty-alleviation focus which was stated as a core aim in the documents, the strategies proposed were often more mainstream, referring to partnerships, and linking export-led strategies, industrial recruitment and place marketing to small business promotion and community economic development.

In October 2001, DPLG also released a LED resource book for municipal councillors and officials (DPLG 2001a). The resource book looked at a range of issues from practical matters like drafting project business plans to more policy-oriented issues like globalisation. Although released as a resource book, the document essentially set out the LED policy debate and clearly associated LED with pro-poor intervention. These documents helped to popularise the LED process, deepen local understanding and, for the newly established LED officers in municipalities across the country, provided an invaluable resource.

During this period one of DPLG's key activities has been the overseeing of the LED Fund. Even though policy debates were not fully settled, DPLG officials felt it was useful to 'get their hands dirty' (Africa interview). Launched in 1999 and linked directly to the then poverty relief programme focus of the government, funds were channelled though DPLG and then on to municipalities to fund a range of predominantly community-based development initiatives. The Fund, which ran from 1999 to 2003, provided municipalities with financial support of up to R1.5 million per annum per project to engage in interventions that would ensure job creation, poverty alleviation and redistribution (Urban-econ & Ukusa team 2003: 1).

Despite initial enthusiasm and a flurry of local-level activity in terms of drafting applications and, in many cases, direct local government involvement in project implementation, results were often a disappointment and a clear testimony to the disjuncture between economic forces and poorly planned efforts to create economically viable projects in the absence of adequate skills or understanding of market forces. Poor project selection, and the limited ability of municipalities to achieve targets and support for unsustainable ventures, led to a significant number of short-term interventions in projects which, though generating some short-term employment in the poorest areas, almost entirely failed to attain sustainability (MXA 2003). According to DPLG, the LED Fund yielded useful lessons (Africa interview). On the positive side, it enabled municipalities to begin grappling with LED issues. These practical experiences in themselves began to generate a very useful policy debate according to DPLG. However, DPLG acknowledged that a major concern was that the Fund was being used for poverty alleviation projects only (Africa and

Patel interviews). Evaluation reports also questioned the sustainability of many of the projects supported by the Fund (Urban-econ & Ukusa team 2003).

The effects of this funding process on the overall understanding of LED have been two-fold. Firstly, it has created the perception in the minds of many stakeholders – municipal and business – that LED is about poverty relief and not economic growth. This stemmed from the fact that funds came from central government for poverty relief and there was an absence of funds for more market-related projects. Secondly, the widespread failure of projects has tainted people's views about the efficacy of the concept. Getting beyond this scenario has been a major challenge for DPLG officials.

While there is a tendency to perceive LED as the mandate of DPLG and local municipalities and this chapter has focused on LED policy issues vested within the ambit of that department, one must also consider the local impact of a range of government programmes and funding mechanisms. Of particular significance in this regard are explicit Department of Trade and Industry spatial interventions, such as the Spatial Development Initiatives and Industrial Development Zones, which have impacted on local planning and development processes (Tomlinson 2003). Other interventions include support for the development of industrial clusters, small businesses, Manufacturing Advisory Centres and Tender Advice Centres, and the publishing of a range of supportive policy measures has had a clear impact on local development initiatives – often beyond the immediate scope of local government activities. Support for the establishment of Local Business Service Centres from the mid-1990s, through the actions of Department of Trade and Industry affiliated agencies such as Khula (which focuses on facilitating access to microcredit) and Ntsika (which supports small business advisory services), helped to identify economic development with local processes (Nel 2002). Department of Trade and Industry research into and support for issues such as knowledge-based development, export promotion and encouragement of clusters clearly matches the economic objectives of key SACN cities such as Johannesburg, Durban and Port Elizabeth. A key facet of LED in many cities is the adoption of Industrial Development Zone planning, one of the Department of Trade and Industry's core programmes since the mid-1990s, into local-level agendas. The Department of Trade and Industry's LED impact is clearly significant and in recent years the department has been collaborating directly with DPLG in policy formation.

Other government departments, such as Housing, Water Affairs, Public Works, and Environmental Affairs and Tourism, have similarly had a significant impact on LED through their funded job-creation projects which, though not defined as LED, have often led to not insignificant local development impacts. What this evidence suggests is the clear need to conceptualise LED as being a much broader entity than just what DPLG is focusing on and what local governments are capable of achieving. Policy, ideally, needs to be more encompassing in this respect.

## LED policy formulation

It is ironic that, by the early years of the 21st century, a LED Fund was in place, there were DPLG endorsed LED manuals offering guidance to local municipalities, and all municipalities were required to incorporate LED in their IDPs. However, there is no explicit legislative pronouncement on LED (beyond proactive support for development in general), nor is a formally approved LED policy in place. In order to rectify the situation, DPLG, primarily under the guidance of the then LED Director, Karen Harrison, commissioned a research process which drew in the skills of Richard Tomlinson and later Patrick Bond to help the department arrive at a more explicit statement of LED thinking and policy. The markedly different perspectives of the two consultants seemingly contributed to a delay in the preparation of a LED policy.

The effects of the absence of a national policy framework for LED became ever more evident as DPLG implemented its LED programme initiatives. DPLG officials were also aware that such a vacuum meant that old debates about pro-poor versus pro-growth approaches to LED remained unresolved. In 2001, certain departmental officials attempted to push that debate in a specific direction by releasing the first draft policy paper with an explicitly pro-poor stance. The document, *Refocusing development on the poor*, was released as a draft policy paper in June of that year (DPLG 2001b). However, it never materialised into a formal policy document as the process was halted. It is, nevertheless, a useful document to examine as it provides telling indicators of how LED policy thinking was evolving in the country at the time.

The document calls for 'an explicitly pro-poor method of achieving LED' (DPLG 2001b: 1), adding that 'the success of a pro-poor LED strategy must, in future, be judged on the basis not only of a simple increase in local Gross Domestic Product, but of how society's broader objectives are being realised' (DPLG 2001b: 2). However, later, in 2003, DPLG took a decision to stop because they felt the document did not necessarily capture all the current thinking on the subject (Africa interview). There was, however, another important issue that emerged at this time in terms of LED policy-making. With the release of documents like these, DPLG, as already observed, came to be seen as championing the interests of the poorer, rural municipalities exclusively. As a result, many large cities felt that national policies and programmes did not necessarily address their specific issues and concerns. The SACN, which was formed in 2002, has attempted to fill this void by encouraging debate amongst its members on what LED means to them (Boraine interview).

DPLG has since re-engaged in the policy formulation debate and at the time of writing was drafting a national LED strategy. This document started as a policy process in 2003 and was intended to produce a definitive national policy on LED. However, initial presentations to Cabinet and national government's Economic Cluster resulted in its status shifting to a national strategy rather than a policy framework (Africa and Patel interviews). The reasoning was that the South African government was now focusing on implementation and believed that there were sufficient policy frameworks in place to facilitate the application of LED. As noted by Tomlinson (2003), since 2001 the state has been shifting towards a more interventionist stance and as such it is inevitable that a range of policies will reflect a new genre of thinking and that LED will probably fall within the newer government ideas.

The national LED strategy was pending approval by Cabinet at the time of writing this chapter. This chapter is therefore only able to make a few tentative remarks on the initial drafts and the process to date. One of the most significant features of this process has been the unprecedented level of cooperation between the Department of Trade and Industry and DPLG. In fact, drafting has occurred through a task team made up of senior officials from both departments. Their respective policy perspectives have coalesced significantly during this process. Previous sections of this chapter mentioned the fact that DPLG officials had been wrestling with the dichotomy between pro-poor and pro-growth LED approaches for many years. This dichotomy appears to have been bridged through this process as the national LED strategy attempts to strike a balance between the two imperatives and is aligned with both RDP and GEAR principles (Patel interview).

For this and a host of other reasons, the national LED strategy reads far more confidently and assertively than preceding LED policy documents. The preparation of the document was driven by Yusuf Patel, the new LED Chief Director at DPLG, and Alistair Fray, one of DPLG's directors. The document aligns itself with the RDP, GEAR, the Microeconomic Reform Strategy and a range of current government policies. The Microeconomic Reform Strategy seeks to address the inequalities in the country and to build on the RDP, by focusing on issues of the geographical spread of activity, integration, black economic empowerment, knowledge-led growth, skills development and state responsiveness (DTI 2003). In contrast with the earlier LED policy document, investment promotion features more prominently, as does business retention and support for a range of enterprises, not just the smallest firms. In terms of alignment with current government thinking it argues the need to support both the first and second economies identified by President Thabo Mbeki as well as the need to work in collaboration with a range of government programmes.

## The emerging legislative context for LED

In parallel with the development of national policy and programmes, legislative processes were also taking place. While there is no definitive LED legislation, LED processes are implicit in two key laws, namely, the 1996 Constitution and the Local Government Municipal Systems Act (No. 32 of 2000).

The key driver in the development of the local government section of the Constitution was the Portfolio Committee on Constitutional Development and Provincial Affairs under the chairmanship of Pravin Gordhan and the ANC caucus within that Committee. The Committee drew on research undertaken by the Community Law Centre, NGOs such as Inlogov (Institute for Local Government), the University of the Witwatersrand's Graduate School of Public and Development Management, the Urban Sector Network and the National Land Committee to inform debate[3] (Mettler interview). This process brought to the fore broader development challenges, including LED, which needed to be dealt with.

Based on the earlier research, the Portfolio Committee members began to envision a new role for municipalities – one where they had to show initiative and proactively drive development in their local spaces. This meant that they had to have powers of general competency rather than a mere schedule of services listed in the Constitution (Boraine interview). Hence the inclusion of the clause stating that municipalities had to 'promote social and economic development' (RSA 1996b: s152 [1]). Once this idea became accepted, it was a natural progression for national policy-makers and municipalities themselves to begin to see LED as a key instrument of local governance. This was strengthened two years later when the Local Government White Paper (RSA 1998) overtly articulated the concept of *developmental local government.*

Even though the Constitution does not specifically refer to LED, it does, however, provide the framework that charges local governments to become more proactive as agents of social and economic development, which clearly has key LED implications (RSA 1996b). The Constitution established a strong local government system within a non-hierarchical cooperative government system. The Constitution also promoted the notion of subsidiarity: the idea that functions are best located at the lowest possible level within government. This ultimately paved the way for municipalities to take on multidimensional tasks, such as economic development. Whilst the Constitution does not contain an explicit policy stance on LED, it undoubtedly paved the way for this debate to evolve, albeit that GEAR would exercise a moderating force.

The Local Government Municipal Systems Act is the key piece of legislation which has had direct influence over the principle of popular participation in local governance and local-level development. The Act provides for 'the core principles, mechanisms and processes that are necessary to enable municipalities to move progressively towards the social and economic upliftment of communities, and ensure universal access to essential services that are affordable to all' (RSA 2000a: 2). The Act describes the 'core processes or elements that are essential to realising a truly developmental local government system. These include participatory governance, Integrated Development Plans (of which LED is an element), performance management and reporting, resource allocation and organisational change' (RSA 2000a: 48). This Act has key LED implications in terms of the operational procedures, powers and management systems discussed. DPLG officials chose not to devote a separate chapter to LED in the Act as they felt that further policy work was required on the subject before legislating (Africa interview). Instead, Chapter 2, which deals with the rights and duties of municipal councils, includes the duty to 'promote and undertake development in the municipality' (RSA 2000a: s4[2g]). A more explicit mention of the subject of LED is found in Chapter 5, which deals with IDPs. LED may also be promoted through the provision of special service tariffs for commercial and industrial users. A further LED provision is that municipalities may establish service utilities or contract out such services, for example, water provision. The parallel White Paper on Municipal Service Partnerships released in 2000 details how municipalities can enter into partnership arrangements with the private, public, community and NGO sectors to improve service delivery in a specific area (RSA 2000b). While there is no explicit section on LED, as stated earlier, LED has to be inferred from the Act and seen in relation to the significant support structure for LED which was emerging in the late 1990s, as detailed earlier.

## Local-level responses and policy impacts

Over and above the development of LED programmes and support at the national level, significant experience has been built up at the local level in terms of both local-level policy-making and applied experience. National programmes such as the LED Fund clearly exposed smaller centres to the concept of LED and influenced local understanding and application of the process. In addition, popularisation of LED through DPLG's publications and road-shows, parallel support for LED-type activities from the Department of Trade and Industry, and municipal recognition of constitutional requirements and the integrated development planning process have heightened awareness of LED. Besides this, the larger cities, partially in response to the support of the SACN, their economic diversity, pressing development needs and some measure of local capacity, are actively pursuing a wide range of locally determined interventions. Whilst national policy and support clearly has assisted the smaller centres to become more proactive, it would seem that the larger cities are not that dependent on central state support, such as from the LED Fund, and rather are pursuing a diverse range of development initiatives which are locally determined and driven, and often rely on locally unique partnership arrangements. City interventions range from the building of convention centres to inner-city renewal and efforts to alleviate poverty. In most of the cities the term 'economic development' is used in preference to LED to describe such activities. In the next section a brief overview of trends in the largest cities is provided, before proceeding to an outline of key themes in smaller centres.

### LED in the three largest cities

While all of the SACN cities are actively engaged in LED, an overview of what is happening in the three largest cities – Johannesburg, Cape Town and Durban (eThekwini) – serves to illustrate current policy, institutional and applied considerations.

In Johannesburg LED is overseen by the city's Economic Development Unit. Overall policy is influenced by an ambitious development plan called *Joburg 2030*, which sets the city's sights on rapid economic expansion and raising the standard of living of its citizens to that of a 'world-class city' (City of Johannesburg 2002). As the vision document states, 'In 2030, Johannesburg will be a world-class city with service deliverables and efficiencies which meet world best practice. Its economy and labour force will specialise in the service sector and will be strongly outward orientated such that the city economy operates on a global scale. The strong economic growth resultant from this competitive economic behaviour will drive up City tax revenues, private sector profits and individual disposable income levels such that the standard of living and quality of life of all the City's inhabitants will increase in a sustainable manner' (City of Johannesburg 2002: 13). The pro-market and economically aggressive tone of the document clearly charts a defined growth path for the city.

In Johannesburg key applied foci include economic and urban regeneration endeavours such as metropolitan marketing of the city as a key economic hub in Africa, privatisation of, for example, public transport and the fresh produce market, and inner-city renewal, which has seen significant public and private reinvestment in key central business district (CBD) precincts. In addition there is a focus on new industrial development and support for the small business sector. In the pursuit of such interventions, partnership formation, primarily with the private sector and provincial government, is clearly critical in actualising development (Rogerson 1997, 2000; Rwigema & Karungu 1999; iGoli 2002; City of Johannesburg 2002). Impressive results have been achieved in key projects such as the Newtown renewal area and the fashion district. However, questions could be raised about the ability of the pro-growth focus of the 2030 strategy to actually benefit all communities in the city (Nel & Rogerson 2005).

In Cape Town, LED is overseen by the Social and Economic Development Directorate and strategic guidance is provided by the key policy document *Going global, working local* (CMC 1999). According to that document, the vision of the city is that, 'Strong and sustainable economic development in the Cape Metropolitan area will depend on the ability of all stakeholders to work together to address the combined challenge of improving the Cape Metropolitan area's global competitiveness and reducing poverty' (CMC 1999: 4). In order to achieve this vision, a dual strategy has been identified. To achieve global competitiveness, issues such as the provision of world-class marketing and services are matched with support for business clusters, infrastructure and capacity development. Meanwhile, the parallel poverty reduction strategy seeks to provide affordable urban services and infrastructure, to integrate formerly separate areas within the conurbation, and to promote community development and job creation.

Cape Town has worked hard to image itself as one of the 'world's great cities'. Whilst projects are spread across the city, the CBD or 'city bowl' is clearly the locus of significant regeneration endeavours by both the public and private sectors, where the 'Central City Partnership' is active (Fouldien 2002). The value of development projects in and around the CBD since 2002 has exceeded R5 billion. The largest projects are the Waterfront redevelopment and associated housing construction, which will together cost R2 billion, the international convention centre costing R0.5 billion, while the station redevelopment will cost a further R1 billion (Cape Town Partnership in Robertson 2002). These developments are impressive, but it must be pointed out that while pro-poor and pro-growth goals receive equal emphasis in the vision, in practice expenditure patterns tell a different story. In a commentary on this experience in Cape Town, it has been noted that it appears as if 'there is a gulf between Cape Town's impoverished townships and its affluent areas, which appears to be widening in important respects. Development trends are tending to reinforce spatial divisions and fragmentation rather than assist urban integration' (Turok & Watson 2001: 136).

In Durban (eThekwini municipality), LED is overseen by the Economic Development Department. Overall policy guidance is provided by the Long Term Development Framework, which was developed in consultation with key local partners. This document identifies meeting basic needs, strengthening the economy and building skills and technology as the core objectives to be striven for (DTI 2002). It is significant that a local, informal growth coalition, predominantly representing municipal and private interests, is an important driver in the development process, facilitating public–private collaboration. In Durban, particularly significant initiatives include the redevelopment of the Convention Centre, the development of a major industrial estate and the promotion of the R1.4 billion Gateway Shopping Centre (*Business Day* 17.04.2002). The redevelopment of 55 hectares in the Point area at a cost of some R700 million for recreational purposes as uShaka Marine World, has clearly been a key project in the urban regeneration of the city (Chetty 2002). In terms of poorer areas, Durban is known for the establishment of the large Warwick Triangle informal market and the European Union-funded Cato Manor redevelopment initiative close to the central city, whereby significant resources have been allocated for the economic and social transformation of a low-income area. Hundreds of houses have been built, facilities upgraded and economic growth opportunities for low-income people investigated (Eising 2002). While many of Durban's achievements are impressive, Maharaj and Ramballi (1998) note that the poor have often been marginalised in the broader development processes taking place in the city.

In terms of pro-growth development, some dramatic achievements in terms of the provision of world-class facilities are taking place in South Africa's cities. In some respects what is being undertaken has close parallels with the achievements of large western cities (Clarke & Gaile 1998). Durban, for example, with its impressive business tourism facilities centred on the International Convention Centre, is now rated as one of the 'top-ten' business tourism cities in the world (Derwent 2002).

Meanwhile, Cape Town has become one of the world's leading tourism destinations, whilst Johannesburg gained much media publicity from hosting the 2002 World Summit for Sustainable Development. Most large cities were able to host a range of sporting mega-events in recent years, the rugby and cricket World Cups being the largest, and all will play a key role in the hosting of the 2010 soccer World Cup. The formation of key inner-city partnerships/growth coalitions in the major cities is indicative of the development direction which the cities are pursuing and the degree to which their economic development paths are being defined by local imperatives rather than directly by national policy. While this is noteworthy, questions have been raised about just how responsive these interventions are to the needs of the poor and whether they actually derive significant benefit from interventions which often focus on the local and foreign business and tourist elite.

## The experience of smaller centres

Smaller centres, by virtue of their limited economic diversity and what is often single-sector dependence, are often vulnerable to sector-specific economic shifts – either positive or negative, such as the closure of the key factory in the town or the establishment of a tourist resort. Various categories of small town can be identified, such as agricultural service centres, mining towns, factory towns, retirement/tourism towns, and in the South African context, 'homeland towns', that is, centres which were often artificially created, in the absence of an economic base, to meet the needs of apartheid planning (Nel & Rogerson 2005).

Local-level crises, such as the closure of mines or shifts in the agricultural economy, have a profound impact on the economies of many local towns, often forcing them to attempt crisis response interventions to try and reorientate their local economies. Centres such as Welkom (Nel & Binns 2002) have suffered heavily from mine closures and have tried to find new economic avenues to pursue. In Welkom, steps have been taken to try to strengthen the manufacturing industry, support urban farming and encourage tourism. In many other smaller centres, by virtue of inherent resources and/or local capacity, tourism promotion – tapping into the new demands of the affluent classes – is witnessing the growth of those small centres, for example the encouragement of second-home development in the case of Stilbaai, whale watching in Hermanus and trout fishing around Dullstroom (Nel & Rogerson 2005). This has been achieved through private sector investment and commitment to achieve change on the part of municipalities.

While the economically growing towns are often developing as a result of private sector investment, which may or may not be facilitated by local government action, for many declining smaller centres, lacking in funds and skilled staff in the face of private sector disinvestment, the municipality is often the only institution available to respond to economic change. For many of the latter towns, the first formal engagement with LED came as a result of the need to respond to the immediacy of local development crises. This situation, together with the availability of LED Fund support from the late 1990s and the 'developmental local government' mandate, has encouraged them to think strategically and identify community-based projects with economic growth potential. While success has been limited, as noted, what this experience and the integrated development planning process has meant is that all municipalities are aware of their new LED obligations and are actively engaged in attempts to improve local conditions. While it is true that most municipalities now have LED officers in place, or perhaps officials charged to take on LED duties in addition to other responsibilities, there clearly is room for more proactivity in this regard. Many of the smaller centres, however, regard LED as an 'unfunded mandate' and have yet to achieve meaningful results (Nel & Rogerson 2005). It is apparent that, in contrast to the large cities, smaller centres are far more dependent on state guidance and support to help them address development challenges and respond to economic opportunities.

## Reflections, critique and conclusions

This chapter has examined how LED policy and practice have developed and evolved in South Africa since the early 1990s. LED has become a key aspect of local government and development debates in South Africa and, at a policy level, has evolved through a series of quite distinctive phases. This development has been influenced by a variety of considerations, including international experience, broader government development thinking, and developments within the DPLG that have shaped the evolving form and focus of LED. This conclusion examines contextual considerations, the constraints impacting on LED, future research considerations which may influence later thinking on LED, and closing considerations.

LED in South Africa has not emerged in a vacuum. Instead, LED has been strongly influenced by international experience that has been modified to suit local circumstances. This international exposure has come about through various influences, including the study tours undertaken by national and local policy-makers, visits to the country by international experts, and an examination of international experience by researchers and policy-makers. From the start of the LED debate in the country in the early 1990s, consultants and academic researchers drew heavily on international experience, as reflected in position papers from, for example, Sanco (Sanco 1995) and the Urban Foundation (Urban Foundation 1995). In parallel, academics have published research papers on LED which have drawn on both international experience and emerging trends in the country. Such research has helped popularise the process and it has been circulated in government and municipal circles, helping to inform decision-makers of current thinking and international evidence (Nel 1994, 1997, 2001; Tomlinson 1994, 2003; Rogerson 1997, 2000; Nel & Rogerson 2005). Over and above this, local application has been framed in terms of key government policy pronouncements, especially the RDP, the Constitution, GEAR and the White Paper on Local Government, as well as a range of

Department of Trade and Industry and DPLG policy statements and strategies. These documents have served to set the parameters within which LED has emerged and the way it is understood and applied on the ground. The concept of 'developmental local government' is now firmly entrenched in the country and, within this context, LED is widely recognised by local municipalities as a core responsibility. As noted earlier, emerging government support mechanisms have clearly influenced the definition and application of LED in the smaller centres, while in the larger cities more locally specific action is discernible.

Despite the widespread recognition of LED as a key developmental strategy and the slowly accumulating body of applied evidence, LED suffers from a variety of constraints in the current South African context. Four stand out. The first is the delay in finalising a LED strategy that clearly spells out the objectives for LED and how these might be achieved. The second is the limited applied results achieved to date. This is partly as a result of the LED Fund process that has negatively impacted on broader government and business perceptions of what LED is and can achieve. The third, a challenge that one often encounters at the local level, is the commonly held view in localities that LED is only a local government prerogative. The latter has, in numerous cases, marginalised independent community and private sector initiatives. As a result, the principles of partnership need to be encouraged, particularly at the local level. Finally, local-level constraints, and lack of staff and resources, all inhibit local action to deal with tasks, and in many ways may be exacerbating rather than ameliorating poverty and the development gap in cases where no effective action to address unemployment and underdevelopment is being taken (Nel & Rogerson 2005).

Given that LED policy and practice are informed by both international and local experience, ongoing research will inform policy debate and strategy identification. As international and local experience reveals, LED is a dynamic field and one that is subject to change and adaptation, in response to shifts in the global economy, regional economic change and local realities. Close monitoring of the impact of globalisation on cities and evolving comparative experiences of cities as they respond to globalisation and local economic imperatives need to continually inform local debate and practice. Other more localised issues which merit close attention include the identification of appropriate LED funding and support mechanisms and ways in which to strengthen partnerships and involve multiple stakeholders more fully.

In conclusion, it is apparent that, despite certain inadequacies, LED is a distinctive component of development thinking and planning in South Africa and one which has emerged within the context of the evolution of broader economic and development policy debates, and questions regarding the role of the state in development. While the concept of 'developmental local government' has been entrenched, LED, as one of its key components, still needs more precise policy definition and applied support. Despite it being ten years since the release of the first draft government LED policy document, there is still no formally accepted national policy. In its absence, and partially in response to varying national and DPLG interpretations, LED has had a mixed track record. Until recently, clear differences existed between government departments regarding what it is, what the role of government should be and what interventions should be engaged in (Tomlinson 2003). Despite this, a significant LED literature has been generated in terms of draft policy, LED programmes and manuals and academic literature in the country. In addition, at the applied level, either through the independent actions of the cities or the application of LED Fund projects or various local endeavours, local knowledge has been expanded, which in turn further informs LED policy and practice. Government thinking on LED will, in all eventuality, be formalised in the near future. The relevance of LED will, however, be less determined by the outcome of the policy process than by applied experience. As a strategy designed to encourage local-level development, the test will be to see how effective LED actually can be in terms of the promotion of development and job creation within localities. Experience to date has been mixed and one can only hope that with more effective support and funding mechanisms, enhanced levels of success can be attained to help address the very real development challenges facing the country.

## Notes

1    The nine cities which constitute the South African Cities Network are Johannesburg, Cape Town, eThekwini (Durban), Mangaung (Bloemfontein), Msunduzi (Pietermaritzburg), Nelson Mandela (Port Elizabeth), Buffalo City (East London), Tshwane (Pretoria) and Ekurhuleni (East Rand).

2    The Ministry of Provincial Affairs and Constitutional Development, later known as the Department of Constitutional Development, which was later transformed into the current Department of Provincial and Local Government.

3    Observations on these parliamentary sessions are based on the author's personal involvement in them at the time.

## References

Cashdan B (1997) Local government and economic development. Unpublished paper.

Cheru F (2002) *African renaissance: Roadmaps the challenge of globalization.* London: Zed Books.

Chetty TC (2002) The Point Marine Park. Address at the International Geographic Union conference, Durban.

City of Johannesburg (2002) *Joburg 2030.* City of Johannesburg.

Clarke SE & Gaile GL (1998) *The work of cities.* Minneapolis: University of Minnesota Press.

CMC (Cape Metropolitan Council) (1999) *Going global, working local: An economic development framework for the Cape Metropolitan area.* Cape Town: CMC.

DCD (Department of Constitutional Development) (n.d. a) *Case studies on LED and poverty.* Pretoria.

DCD (n.d. b) *Linking LED to poverty alleviation.* Pretoria.

Derwent S (2002) Conference capital, *Sawubona,* September: 108–116.

DPLG (Department of Provincial and Local Government) (2000) LED manual series. Pretoria: DPLG.

DPLG (2001a) *Local economic development: A resource book for municipal councillors and officials.* Pretoria: DPLG.

DPLG (2001b) *Refocusing development on the poor – Draft LED policy paper.* Pretoria: DPLG.

DPLG (2003) *Local economic development programme.* Consolidated edition/2003. Pretoria: DPLG.

DTI (Department of Trade and Industry) (2002) *South African city economies.* Pretoria.

DTI (2003) *Medium-term strategy framework.* Pretoria.

Eising W (2002) The Cato Manor Development Association. Presentation at the LED Workshop, Welkom, 15 July 2002.

Fouldien G (2002) Local economic development in Cape Town. Presentation at the LED Workshop, Welkom, 15 July 2002.

iGoli (2002) Available at <http://168.89.27.5/iGoli2002>.

ILO (International Labour Organisation) (n.d. a) Available at <http://oracle02.ilo.org/dyn/empent/empent.Portal?p_prog=L&p_lang=EN>.

ILO (n.d. b) Available at <http://oracle02.ilo.org/dyn/empent/empent.portal?p_docid=PROCESS&pprog=C&p_subprog=LE>.

IRI (International Republican Institute) (1998) *The local authority's role in economic development.* Durban: IRI.

Maharaj B & Ramballi K (1998) Local economic development strategies in an emerging democracy: The case of Durban in South Africa, *Urban Studies*, 35(1): 131–148.

Ministry in the Office of the President (1995) Local economic development – Discussion document. Unpublished document.

Ministry of Provincial Affairs and Constitutional Development (1997a) *Green Paper on local government.* Pretoria: Ministry of Provincial Affairs and Constitutional Development.

Ministry of Provincial Affairs and Constitutional Development and the White Paper Political Committee (1997b) *South Africa's local government – A discussion document.* Pretoria: Ministry of Provincial Affairs and Constitutional Development.

MXA (2003) *Evaluation of the CMIP and the LEDF: Synthesis report.* Durban: MXA.

Nel EL (1994) Local development initiatives, a new development paradigm for urban areas: An assessment with reference to Stutterheim, *Development Southern Africa*, 11(3): 363–378.

Nel EL (1995) *Local economic development in South Africa: A review of current policy and applied case-studies.* Proceedings of a Workshop on Local Economic Development held at Midrand, 4 August. Johannesburg: Friedrich Ebert Stiftung.

Nel EL (1997) Evolving local economic development policy in South Africa, *Regional Studies*, 31(1): 67–72.

Nel EL (2001) Local economic development: A review and assessment of its current status in South Africa, *Urban Studies*, 38(7): 1003–1024.

Nel EL (2002) Manufacturing. In A Lemon & CM Rogerson (eds), *Geography and economy in South Africa and its neighbours.* Aldershot: Ashgate.

Nel EL & Binns JA (2002) Decline and response in South Africa's Free State goldfields, *International Development Planning Review*, 24(3): 249–269.

Nel EL & Lindie M (1996) *Local economic development in South Africa: Recent developments and strategies*. Proceedings of the Second Workshop on Local Economic Development held at Midrand in December 1995. Johannesburg: Friedrich Ebert Stiftung.

Nel EL & Rogerson CM (eds) (2005) *Local economic development in Southern Africa*. New Jersey: Transactions Press.

Robertson R (2002) Redeveloping the Cape Town CBD. Unpublished BA Honours project. Grahamstown: Rhodes University.

Rogerson CM (1997) LED and post-apartheid reconstruction in South Africa, *Singapore Journal of Tropical Geography*, 18(2): 175–195.

Rogerson CM (2000) Local economic development in an era of globalisation: The case of South African cities, *T.E.S.G.*, 91(4): 397–411.

RSA (Republic of South Africa) (1995a) *Urban development strategy of the Government of National Unity*. Government Gazette, Notice 1111. Pretoria.

RSA (1995b) *Rural development strategy of the Government of National Unity*. Government Gazette, Notice 1153. Pretoria.

RSA (1996a) *Growth employment and redistribution: A macroeconomic strategy*. Pretoria: Government Printers.

RSA (1996b) *The Constitution of the Republic of South Africa Act, no. 108 of 1996*. Pretoria.

RSA (1998) *The White Paper on local government*. Pretoria: Department of Constitutional Development.

RSA (2000a) *Local Government Municipal Systems Act, Act no. 32 of 2000*. Pretoria.

RSA (2000b) *White Paper on municipal service partnerships*. Notice 1689 of 2000. Pretoria.

Rwigema H & Karungu P (1999) SMME development in Johannesburg's Southern Metropolitan Local Council, *Development Southern Africa*, 16(1): 107–124.

Sanco (South African National Civic Organisation) (1995) *Strategies and policies for local economic development in the new South Africa*. Johannesburg: Sanco.

Tomlinson R (1994) *Urban development planning – Lessons for the economic reconstruction of South Africa's cities*. Johannesburg: WUP.

Tomlinson R (2003) The local economic development mirage in South Africa, *Geoforum*, 34: 113–122.

Turok I & Watson V (2001) Divergent development in South African cities: Strategic challenges facing Cape Town, *Urban Forum*, 12(2): 119–138.

Urban Foundation (1995) *Local economic development*. Johannesburg: Urban Foundation.

Urban-econ & Ukusa team (2003) National consolidation and assessment of the LED programme and fund for the Department of Provincial and Local Government. Unpublished paper. Johannesburg.

## Interviews

Africa E, Deputy Director-General: Department of Provincial and Local Government, Pretoria, 10 September 2004.

Boraine A, Chief Executive, Cape Town Partnership, 2 September 2004 (telephonic).

Harrison K, Boland district municipality, 6 September 2004 (telephonic).

Mettler J, senior consultant, Palmer development group, 3 September 2004 (telephonic).

Patel Y, Chief Director: Department of Provincial and Local Government, Pretoria, 22 September 2004.

# 10 Tourism policy, local economic development and South African cities

Christian M Rogerson

## Introduction

Under the Integrated Manufacturing Strategy issued during 2002 by South Africa's Department of Trade and Industry (DTI), tourism is identified as one of the country's 'priority economic sectors' for future support and promotion (DTI 2002: 30). During 2004, the tourism sector was recognised as a key contributor to national employment creation, gross domestic product (GDP) and foreign exchange earnings (Monitor 2004). Tourism is the only sector for the period 1998–2002 that records both positive growth in employment and contribution to GDP. Whereas for several other priority economic sectors the trend has been for employment to decrease whilst contribution to GDP continues to grow, tourism exhibits substantial improvements both in terms of employment and GDP contribution (Monitor 2004). Indeed, as the export earnings calculated from tourism surpassed that of gold exports, in the popular press tourism has assumed the mantle of 'the new gold' for the South African economy.

In this chapter the objective is to provide an examination of the making of national government's post-1994 tourism programmes and to focus specifically on tourism in South African cities. The material is organised in terms of three major sections of discussion. First, an analysis is undertaken of the changing policy environment concerning tourism development in South Africa since 1994. It is argued that in the early policy formulation process, local government was marginalised in terms of a developmental role. Essentially what occurred was a *dis-connect* between national policy processes and the rise of urban entrepreneurialism in South African cities, a movement that included a strong focus on creating cities as centres of consumption in order to build local tourism economies. In the second section of the chapter the focus turns squarely to examine tourism in South African cities and to an interrogation of local economic development (LED) activities concerning tourism. This discussion is contextualised against a backcloth of wider international debates and literature on so-termed 'urban tourism', a theme of research which one recent international volume stylised as 'still immature' (Wober 2002). Finally, Johannesburg, the country's largest city, is used as a case study for empirical analysis of the developmental role of tourism in cities.

Methodologically, the first part of this chapter draws primarily from a desktop survey of official documentation produced by the Department of Environmental

Affairs and Tourism (DEAT). The second and third parts draw upon a review of existing academic work on the role of tourism in South African cities, primary interview sources in Johannesburg and a critical analysis of international scholarship on urban tourism.

## The democratic government's tourism programme

In a landmark analysis of the local tourism industry, Cassim (1993) argued that the period of the early 1990s represents a crucial watershed for it is at this important juncture of South Africa's development history that tourism first enters the realm of policy debate. It is claimed that in the making of the new South African tourism policy, 'an elaborative and participative process was followed to allow especially previously excluded groups of society a voice and participation in decision making' (DEAT 2003a: 9).

### The tourism policy and process

The tourism policy process was launched under the logo 'Become Tourism Active' (DEAT 1995a). In terms of research inputs to the post-1994 tourism policy process the most important research sources significantly relate to nature-based tourism as well as to analyses of identifying potential market opportunities for South Africa's tourism products. At the heart of the policy process it was proclaimed that 'South Africa can become THE tourism destination in Africa if we, the people, want to make it happen' (DEAT 1995a). The country's major tourism resources were described as follows: 'South Africa has very special natural assets, a mild and enjoyable climate, a diversity of cultures and people that are friendly, hospitable and eager to share their arts, crafts, culture and surroundings with tourists' (DEAT 1995a).

During October 1994 the Minister of Environmental Affairs and Tourism convened a plenary meeting with a group of tourism stakeholders and role-players in order to discuss a new tourism policy (DEAT 1995a). At this meeting an Interim Tourism Task Team (ITTT) was established with the brief to compile a discussion document or Green Paper. The ITTT included representations from different constituencies, including labour, business, communities, and central and provincial government. The first draft of the Green Paper was discussed in April 1995 before redrafting, revision and another opportunity to comment from provincial tourism departments.

In September 1995 the 12-page Tourism Green Paper was released and distributed widely (DEAT 1995a). During October–November 1995 one-day workshops were held in 12 centres across all 9 provinces at which 'everyone interested and involved in tourism can participate and air their views' (DEAT 1995a). Before each regional workshop a pre-orientation workshop for community and labour participants was convened. In addition, community and labour representatives were trained 'in order to facilitate the discussion and empowerment process in the communities' (DEAT 1995a). The directions of the national tourism policy were influenced by the overarching context of the Reconstruction and Development Programme, which had the stated objectives of improvement of the quality of life of all people through the stimulation of economic growth and redistribution of wealth. It was argued in the Tourism Green Paper that tourism could contribute to these objectives, especially 'as an activity that can promote well-being and pride, as well as an industry that can promote economic growth, job creation and redistribution' (DEAT 1995b: 6).

The subsequent White Paper on the Development and Promotion of Tourism remains the essential core of South Africa's new tourism policy. Although some of the targets set in 1996 need recasting, government argues that 'the basic principles contained in the White Paper are still relevant' to inform contemporary tourism planning (DEAT 2003a: 9). In terms of policy and planning, 'the concept of "Responsible Tourism" emerged as the most appropriate concept for the development of tourism in South Africa' (RSA 1996: 19). Building upon the policy anchors provided by the White Paper, in 1998 DEAT produced *Tourism in Gear*, which sought to establish a framework for implementing these policies, particularly within the neo-liberal context of the Growth, Employment and Redistribution (GEAR) macroeconomic strategy (RSA 1998). This document is of particular interest as in initial macroeconomic planning, tourism was something of an afterthought and omitted entirely from the GEAR framework (Page 1999).

Taken together, the White Paper on Tourism and the *Tourism in Gear* document signal the need for a collaborative approach within which 'tourism should be led by government and driven by the private sector, and be community-based and labour-conscious' (RSA 1998: 1). As a policy and strategic leader for the tourism industry, among the most critical roles for national government is that of seeking 'to rectify historical industry imbalances, resulting from a discriminatory political system by promoting tourism entrepreneurship, human resources development, equity and ownership among disadvantaged individuals and communities' (RSA 1998: 1). Because the tourism industry, like most sectors of the South African economy, reflected the old policies of apartheid, particularly in terms of ownership and skills, the question of transformation is viewed by national government as critical, necessitating an expansion in the involvement of South Africa's historically disadvantaged black populations (DEAT 2003a).

### Newer policy initiatives and the tourism-LED nexus

The most recent addition to national government's policy arsenal has been the publication of guidelines for responsible tourism (DEAT 2002), which was subsequently released as the *Responsible Tourism Handbook: A Guide to Good Practice for Tourism Operators* (DEAT 2003b), which was funded by the Greening the World Summit on Sustainable Development initiative. The core input research was primarily a series of commissioned works that relate to nature-based tourism and pro-poor tourism. These important guidelines include a series of quantified targets for the tourism sector to aim for, as a means of addressing the objectives the 1996 White Paper set in relation to the triple bottom line of sustainable development (i.e. economic, environmental and social sustainability). Whilst providing practical guidance to what South Africa's 'new' or 'responsible' tourism system should constitute, these policy documents reiterate the importance of addressing key strategic challenges that had been earlier identified (DEAT 2003a).

An increasingly important role in the development of the South African tourism industry is played by South African Tourism (SAT), which is the restructured national tourism organisation and successor to SATOUR. The process of restructuring SATOUR resulted in a changed personnel and management composition and the introduction of new marketing strategies which are set to market South Africa as a whole 'rather than only the traditional features that have been mainly rich or white icons' (DEAT 2000: 5). An important role of SAT surrounds the development and implementation of national government's *Tourism Growth Strategy* (South African Tourism 2002), which was anchored upon extensive research into the various 'portfolio markets' for the country's tourism economy. The strategy essentially is founded upon five major objectives:

- To increase tourism volume at high and sustainable growth rates;
- To increase total spend by tourists in South Africa;
- To optimise length of stay to maximise revenue yield in South Africa;
- To improve volume and spend distribution around the country and throughout the year; and
- To improve activity and spend patterns to enable transformation and to promote black economic empowerment.

In terms of looking to the strategic challenges of growth, SAT is seeking to aggressively manage its portfolio across the key dimensions of volume, revenue and seasonality (South African Tourism 2002) and, more especially, to develop focused actions across a portfolio of markets where actions will be targeted to particular spaces in each market in order to achieve variously:

- Volume growth in markets where there is high potential to increase arrivals;
- Revenue growth in markets where there is high potential for growth in yields;
- Defending market share in those markets which are important to the portfolio but where growth potential is limited;
- Focused growth from markets and market segments where there is a potential to get increased volumes in off-peak periods to manage down seasonal fluctuations; and
- Facilitating the packaging of the product offering with industry to further transformation and redistribution.

South Africa's *Tourism Growth Strategy* document represents an important step to ensure the use of 'scarce resources to obtain the highest possible yield against the objectives of growth in volume, spend, length of stay, distribution and lower seasonality as the key tourism drivers of economic growth, job creation and transformation' (South African Tourism 2002: 30).

Finally, to complement the *Tourism Growth Strategy*'s focus on international visitors, in 2004 a new policy document was released concerning the promotion of domestic tourism. The stated objective 'is to create a holiday culture amongst all South Africans and to make travel "sexy" ' (DEAT 2004: 14). The DEAT's *Domestic Tourism Growth Strategy* is premised upon the significance of domestic tourism in the overall tourism economy (estimated at 70 per cent), the existence of further untapped potential for growth and a recognition that domestic tourism provides 'the base load' for the international market, reducing the exposure of the industry to the vagaries of international demand. Once again, the *Domestic Tourism Growth Strategy* was one outcome of research conducted by the Human Sciences Research Council into the organisation and flows of domestic tourism in South Africa (Rule, Viljoen, Zama, Struwig, Langa & Bouare 2004).

Over the past decade, therefore, it is evident that radical changes have occurred in the policy environment concerning tourism in post-apartheid South Africa. Of greatest significance are the changed roles of government, private sector and local people or communities in tourism development. The essential role assumed by national government has been to shape the policy environment to make investment attractive to the private sector and to provide incentives for local tourism development. One essential element of that role has been the commissioning of a series of research investigations which have informed ongoing policy development processes, the most recent being an ongoing investigation during 2004 into the global competitiveness and benchmarking of South Africa's tourism industry (Monitor 2004). To complement the activities of national government, investment and operation of tourism facilities is the defined role of the private sector. The role of the private sector enterprise goes beyond that of commercial profit-making to include even the development of arrangements with local communities for equity shares, benefit flows and/or contributions to local economic development (Ashley & Ntshona 2002). The fundamentally changed post-1994 policy environment provided the foundation for an emerging South African tourism system that is developmental in focus and viewed as offering opportunities for promoting economic growth and, very importantly, as a major sectoral contributor to poverty alleviation. What is critical, however, is the *lack of linkage* between the developing policy processes for national tourism development and parallel local processes surrounding a greater developmental role for municipalities. This policy dis-connect is particularly apparent with respect to the accompanying rise in the significance of LED planning (Nel & Rogerson 2005).

An incipient movement towards LED planning was already occurring as early as the late 1980s, especially in South Africa's largest cities (Rogerson 1997).

Certainly, by the mid-1990s when the national tourism policy was being formulated, LED initiatives were in place in Cape Town, Durban and Johannesburg (Tomlinson 1994). Moreover, in these cities a growing interest in the potential opportunities for tourism development and tourism promotion was taking place (Gretton 1995; MacMenamin 1995; Grant & Scott 1996; Rogerson 2002a; Lootvoet & Freund 2004). It is remarkable that in the context of the strengthening of the developmental roles and activities of these large cities, the proposals set forth in the tourism policy process saw only a minor developmental role for local governments. It is striking to review the list of functions that were allocated to local government in the proposals of the 1995 Green Paper:

- Ensure the application of integrated environmental management principles in land-use development proposals to facilitate sustainable utilisation of natural and cultural resources.
- Provide recreational facilities for residents and tourists (eg. theatres, parks, sports centres, museums, etc.).
- Ensure responsible urban planning, land use and land allocation.
- Develop control powers over land use and the maintenance of standards.
- Provide visitors' services.
- Provide and maintain camping and caravan sites.
- Disseminate information on attractions.
- Maintain historical buildings. (DEAT 1995b: 8)

Overall, it must be observed that only a limited policy connection seemingly exists between, on the one hand, the activities of DEAT and SAT concerning tourism marketing and new product development and, on the other hand, the activities of those municipalities – and especially of South Africa's largest urban centres – using tourism as a potential vehicle for pro-poor local growth. In the next section the focus turns to LED activities around tourism in South African cities and situates these as part of international trends for the making of cities as spaces of consumption.

## Tourism – an urban focus

It is significant to record that at national level post-1994 policy development in tourism has been relatively silent on the specific issues around tourism and economic development in cities. In terms of the importance of South Africa's cities within the national tourism space economy, this neglect is remarkable. At the city scale, however, the importance of the tourism sector has been widely acknowledged in terms of LED planning (Rogerson 2002a, 2002b) and reflected also in economic forecasting that seeks to predict tourism demands for certain localities (Burger, Dohnal, Katharda & Law 2001). In parallel with international trends concerning the rise of tourism in urban economic development planning, South African cities have embraced tourism enthusiastically as part of the LED policy agenda. More especially, with the growth in significance of tourism as a new economic driver for the post-apartheid economy, there has been considerable local activity and emphasis upon tourism-led LED planning across large cities and smaller localities (Rogerson 2002a; Nel & Binns 2003; Lootvoet & Freund 2004; Nel & Rogerson 2005). This section reviews the growth in importance of tourism in cities from the international and South African experience before narrowing the focus in the next section to an examination of Johannesburg as a case study.

## The rise of tourism promotion in urban economic development

Urban tourism, asserts Hoyle (2001), is set to become a major 21st century industry. Indeed, many large cities such as London, Paris, Amsterdam and New York have assumed the role of major focal points for tourism activities (Bull & Church 1998, 2001; Hoffman, Fainstein & Judd 2003). Beauregard (1998) and Law (1991, 1992, 1993, 1996) observe that during the 1980s, tourism became a major sector for economic promotion in US and European cities. Of the US experience, Beauregard records that many of the country's large cities now 'list tourism as one of their most important economic sectors' (1998: 220). Fainstein and Gladstone (1999) go so far as to argue that, other than tourism, US cities nowadays have few options for economic development. For cities confronted by the challenges of the service economy and information age, tourism provides an opportunity for them to reposition themselves and redefine their essential functions (King 2004).

Several analysts point to the benefits of using tourism as an element in urban economic development or revitalisation initiatives (Pearce 2001). For example, Law contends that 'tourism has been seen by policy makers at all levels as a major catalyst for urban regeneration' (1993: 216). Many potential benefits are viewed as associated with projects for tourism-based regeneration particularly in city centres (Law 2000). The most important is that of the direct or indirect effects for job creation and other wider economic benefits (Karski 1990). Indeed, it is hoped that profits from tourism 'will encourage further investment leading to a virtuous cycle of growth' (Law 1991: 50). Another critical benefit relates to the impact upon the image of cities of physical and environmental improvements that are associated with tourism-led regeneration initiatives (Karski 1990). Through the activities of marketing of the city for tourism, the image of localities will be enhanced leading to the gaining of civic pride (Shaw & Williams 2004). Re-imaging of places may have beneficial spin-offs for inward investment in relation to other economic sectors, either service-based or manufacturing (Coles 2003). Localities that are externally perceived as important and interesting visitor destinations 'tend to be significantly better placed to attract new businesses and industries as well as an appropriate workforce' (Karski 1990: 15). A further significant plus factor is that tourism development can bring improvements and better access for local residents to new leisure facilities. In association with this trend, as the tempo of visitor flows is increased, residents may gain civic pride which might have a further knock-on effect for environmental improvements. Karski maintains that urban tourism 'has much to offer as a component of economic and environmental regeneration' (1990: 15). Amidst such high expectations, not surprisingly, across much of Western Europe and North America, it has been observed that 'tourism-based urban regeneration has become a major phenomenon in the past two decades' (Swarbrooke 1999: 174).

The essential basis for tourism as a lead sector for economic development is the development and promotion of new or enhanced tourism products or attractions in cities (Hoffman 2000; Pearce 2001; Coles 2003). For example, the Singapore government has helped to create thriving arts, cultural and entertainment areas, as well as reviving and creating new historical attractions as part of an economic strategy to attract tourism (Teo & Yeoh 1997; Chang & Huang 2004). A focus on entertainment and sports has been marked in many US cities (McCarthy 2002). The promotion of creative or cultural products industries is a further facet of tourism promotion (Scott 2004). In the British experience there has been extensive use of heritage attractions to reclaim and regenerate redundant industrial spaces (Shaw & Williams 2004). A fundamental precondition for the attraction of any flow of new visitors to cities is thus investment in the local assets or tourism resources, which might involve new and improved facilities such as conference and exhibition centres, hotels, museums, heritage attractions, sports arenas, specialty retailing or enhanced physical environment improvements (Law 1996; Strom 2002). Another critical factor for successful tourism development in cities is public support for tourism. It is argued that tourism projects which are based especially in non-traditional tourism destinations are most likely to succeed with the support of local communities who, through their contacts, can 'sell' the city to potential visitors, particularly the friends and relatives market (Law 1991). Nevertheless, Shaw and Williams critique the use of tourism-led strategies in post-industrial cities as often being 'an exclusive process, producing new spaces of consumption for particular sectors of society' (2004: 267).

Based on existing international experience, several different tourism-led approaches in city development have been discerned (see Law 1991, 1992, 1993, 2000; Swarbrooke 2000). Building upon the work of Swarbrooke (1999) the following approaches have been used:
- A visitor-attraction-led strategy in which new physical attractions, such as waterfront developments, new museums or casinos are used to attract tourists;
- Expanding and using cultural attractions, such as the arts, theatre and music in order to attract visitors;
- Establishing a reputation as a city that is friendly to gay tourists;
- Selecting an events-led strategy which entails the creation of new festivals or the attraction of existing 'mega-events', such as major festivals and sports events like the Olympic or Commonwealth Games and the soccer World Cup;
- Exploiting the attractions for urban tourists of leisure shopping by developing new shopping-retailing complexes;
- Promoting the city as a host venue for important local and international fairs, conferences and exhibitions;

- Improving the nightlife of cities in order to attract particularly younger tourists for 'clubbing' as part of creating a so-termed '24-hour-a-day city';
- Attracting tourists to visit industrial sites or industrial heritage attractions and their related retail outlets;
- Using the attractions of local food and drink as a basis for encouraging new tourism flows.

The particular strategy or mix of strategies for any individual city will be clearly influenced by the character of its specific tourism resources that can be harnessed for tourism marketing and promotion.

## Tourism in urban areas of South Africa

Tourism is certainly not a new phenomenon in urban areas of South Africa. During the early 20th century leisure tourism formed the base for considerable employment growth in several coastal centres of South Africa. By 1930 the East London Publicity Association was already promoting the town as 'The Home of the Surfboard – where Sea and Sunshine Call' (ELPA 1930). The most important tourism focus was Durban, which established itself as a major tourist destination from as early as the 1920s (Grant & Butler-Adam 1992).

A new chapter in tourism planning in South Africa's cities began to open from the mid-1980s. In common with the international experience of urban economic restructuring, the promotion of tourism grew markedly in significance on the South African urban policy agenda. Recreation and tourism became a key influence on metropolitan planning, especially in Cape Town, Durban and Port Elizabeth (Grant & Kohler 1996; Van Huyssteen & Neethling 1996). In terms of the research agenda for LED, tourism has been an item since at least 1995 (Rogerson 1995).

Currently, tourism promotion is an element of economic development planning in all of South Africa's six metropolitan councils, including the unlikely case of Ekurhuleni (Ekurhuleni Municipality 2003). The most dramatic manifestations of tourism promotion are perhaps the waterfront redevelopments that have transformed areas of inner-city Cape Town and Durban (Grant & Scott 1996; Kilian, Goudie & Dodson 1996). Indeed, it is perhaps not surprising that the traditional leisure destinations of Cape Town and Durban were pioneers in the use of tourism in local development planning (Gretton 1995; MacMenamin 1995). New leisure markets are being sought, such as in Cape Town where the significance of gay tourism has recently been profiled (Visser 2002, 2003; Bennett 2004a). With the changes in gaming legislation since 1994, large casino investments in South Africa's cities have made them major national foci for casino tourism (Rogerson 2004a). A range of new tourism initiatives are occurring in all the coastal cities, not least in Port Elizabeth where a rebranding and repositioning of the city has been occurring (Heath 2004). Alongside new theme park developments, the most imaginative initiative is the planned construction of Africa's 'Statue of Liberty', a 65-metre-tall statue of former President Nelson Mandela, which is to be erected in Port Elizabeth harbour (Heath 2004; Van Zyl 2004). Overall, the growing significance of tourism as a vehicle for LED in urban South Africa was highlighted by the findings of a 2002 national survey of municipalities which disclosed that tourism was one of the most popular LED strategies (Nel & Binns 2003).

Despite its growth, the politics of integrating tourism in LED planning in South African cities have been little examined. In Durban's tourism development record, a range of flagship property development projects, including a new convention centre and tourism developments (Hall & Robbins 2002; Lootvoet & Freund 2004), have been interpreted as the beginnings of creating a new alliance between old and new business elites in the city (Moffett & Freund 2004). For Lootvoet and Freund (2004) the new commitment to projects such as the Shaka Island Development involves the creation of substantial business opportunities for the city's new elites through tendering opportunities for affirmative procurement. Nevertheless, it is argued that 'their impact on the mass of poor people is at best ambiguous' (Lootvoet & Freund 2004: 7).

The unfolding promotion of South African cities as centres for consumption has taken various forms and approaches which clearly reflect international patterns (Rogerson 2002a). First is the attraction of business tourism through the building of new international convention centres and linked hotel developments in Durban, Johannesburg and, most recently, Cape Town (Nel, Hill & Maharaj 2003; Gelling 2004; Ingram 2004). The critical and lucrative activity of MICE (meetings, incentives, conferences and exhibitions) tourism has been augmented by the attraction of mega-events such as the World AIDS Congress and the World Summit on Sustainable Development (Rogerson 2002b). Second, the traditional market of leisure tourism has been boosted through new waterfront redevelopment programmes (such as in Cape Town and Durban), and flagship projects such as the Shaka Island development in Durban (Lootvoet & Freund 2004). Cruise tourism is a further growing element of leisure tourism in coastal cities, in particular for Cape Town and Durban (Vos 2004). Third, the urbanisation of casino gambling, which has been such a distinctive feature of post-1994 South Africa, has further boosted the leisure tourism product offerings of cities (Rogerson 2004a; Rousseau 2004; Strydom 2004). Fourth, shopping tourism has been the target of developments such as Century City in Cape Town (Marks & Bezzoli 2001) and of Johannesburg's efforts to attract revenue from regional tourist flows from countries in sub-Saharan Africa.

Fifth, sports tourism has been an important element for growing the tourism economy in cities with the hosting of the rugby and cricket World Cups and the forthcoming 2010 FIFA soccer World Cup. Sixth, heritage and cultural tourism have been supported through the building of new museum complexes, such as Constitution Hill, the apartheid museum in Johannesburg and the Newtown cultural precinct (Rogerson 2002b, 2003; Sampaio 2004). The Constitution Hill and Newtown cultural precinct projects are joint initiatives between the Johannesburg council and Blue IQ, the Gauteng provincial economic development agency (Rogerson 2004b).

The significance of these projects is heightened for the regeneration and re-imaging of Johannesburg inner city and for the promotion of day visitors (McKenzie 2004). Seventh, the market attractions of political tourism or justice tourism linked to the struggle against apartheid are reflected in developments at Robben Island and the promotion of township tourism in localities such as Soweto, Alexandra and Inanda among others (Hughes & Vaughan 2000; Strange & Kempa 2003; Bennett 2004b; Kaplan 2004; Rogerson 2004c). Finally, South Africa's cities are the major focal points for domestic health tourism as well as key nodes in the lucrative international industry of medical tourism (George 2004; Bass 2005).

Overall, it must be stated that contemporary tourism flows – domestic, regional and international – are highly polarised in South Africa and in terms of the uneven tourism space economy, the nation's cities continue to function as major nodes. In the immediate years after the democratic transition the largest flow of investments in tourism projects was channelled into the cities, further strengthening their dominance of the national tourism economy (Rogerson 2002c). It is against this backdrop of the growing importance of tourism in cities internationally and in South Africa, in particular, that attention turns to review the experience and record of tourism development planning in Johannesburg.

## Johannesburg: a case study of tourism in urban South Africa

In Johannesburg, South Africa's major city, tourism has been identified as a potential 'sunrise' economic sector and designated for strategic intervention as part of wider restructuring of the urban economic base (Rogerson 2003). As a labour-intensive sector, tourism was identified as a sector with considerable potential for contributing towards alleviating the city's worsening problems of unemployment, especially in the context of the city's declining manufacturing base. Although Johannesburg is an unlikely destination for tourism expansion, in recent years the city has reinvented itself as a 'must-see for visitors seeking to experience the "real" South Africa a decade after the end of apartheid' (Harrison 2005). Under the banner heading 'Johannesburg: much more than you expect', the Johannesburg Tourism Company (2005) markets the city to international audiences as follows:

Take another day to enjoy Johannesburg. Travel beyond your assumptions. History is happening here.
Johannesburg is a sophisticated world-class African city, buzzing with enterprise, opportunity and attractions.
Escape grey skies and cold climates – here it's sunshine year-around with an average daily temperature of 22.4 °C.
An inspiring international destination, guilty of being untamed but never boring.

Overall, many observers view the future tourism potential of the city as promising, especially as visitors search for 'authentic' experience of South Africa's people and history. According to Harrison (2005), the latest *Rough Guide to South Africa* states, 'The tunes Johannesburg is playing are the new sounds of a new nation'. In similar vein, *Time-Out*'s 2004 Johannesburg guide informs visitors that, 'You can't understand South Africa without understanding Jo'burg' (cited by Harrison 2005).

Accurate statistics on visitor attractions, tourism flows into Johannesburg and the importance of tourism to the urban economy are difficult to obtain. The best current (2004) estimates are those provided by the CEO of the Johannesburg Tourism Company, which was founded in 2003 and charged with establishing tourism as a key economic sector in the city (Viljoen interview). The following profile emerges for Johannesburg tourism:

- Total annual visitor numbers to (Greater) Johannesburg are estimated as 6.2 million.
- The leading visitor (day and tourist) demand for cultural and leisure attractions in Johannesburg are Monte Casino, Gold Reef City, Bruma Flea Market, the Rosebank Rooftop Market and Johannesburg Zoo.
- In terms of geographical origins of Johannesburg tourists, it is estimated that 3 million are domestic tourists and 3.2 million are foreign visitors.
- The group of foreign visitors comprises an estimated 2 million regional tourists in terms of primarily cross-border shoppers from other parts of sub-Saharan Africa and 1.2 million long-haul international tourists.
- The estimated total contribution of tourism to the economy of Johannesburg is R7 billion per annum.
- The average tourism spend is calculated at R1 300 per trip to Johannesburg.
- The highest estimated spend is from international visitors, a value of R2 400 per trip.
- The average spend by domestic tourists visiting Johannesburg from other parts of South Africa is estimated as R500–700, and is lower because the majority of tourists stay with friends or relatives.

The above data underline the importance of tourism as a contributor to the economy of contemporary Johannesburg (Viljoen interview). Furthermore, it serves to reinforce the significance of strategic initiatives which are set to promote tourism in the city as part of wider LED programmes in the city.

The most significant city development framework for Johannesburg is that provided by the *Joburg 2030* document which was issued by the city's corporate planning unit (GJMC 2002). By 2030 the core goals are to elevate Johannesburg into the ranks of 'world cities' with a strongly outward-oriented economy, specialised in the service sector, and exhibiting strong economic growth which delivers increasing standards of living and quality of life to all the city's inhabitants (GJMC 2002). Of central significance in the strategic planning proposed for the city is the endorsement of targeted or selected sectoral interventions that would be made by the city authorities in order to enhance economies of localisation (GJMC 2002). The analysis identifies the high-skill and knowledge-based financial and business services sector as that sector which ranked most strongly on the basis of relative attractiveness and competitiveness for augmenting the future economic development of Johannesburg. Nevertheless, what is also significant is that tourism was among the small group of other targeted sectors that were identified. It was argued that the city's tourism industry and economy are currently significant, with the potential to make a meaningful contribution to the city's overall economy. Overall, tourism was viewed as a sector that can 'become a more important player in the City's economy' (GJMC 2002: 72) and was thus selected for targeting.

In 2001 the city prepared a Tourism Strategy, which was updated in 2004. The process of updating and revision did not change in any way the key conclusions from the 2001 analysis or affect the strategic directions identified in the 2001 strategy (Saunders interview). The Tourism Strategy recognises that Johannesburg does not possess a competitive advantage for the promotion of leisure tourism. Indeed, in terms of South Africa's nine provinces, Gauteng is ranked last in terms of leisure tourism but, significantly, first as a destination for business travellers. Of these business tourists, 66 per cent spent at least two nights in Johannesburg with 89 per cent coming to the city on general business and the remaining 11 per cent for the purpose of attending a conference or exhibition (GJMC 2001: 88).

The Tourism Strategy identifies two major growth areas as drivers for Johannesburg's future tourism economy based upon an analysis of the city's competitive advantage. The first is found in the general area of business tourism with a special focus on the so-termed MICE sector. The market for business tourism is the most critical and distinctive element in the tourism economy of Johannesburg (Rogerson 2002b). Business tourism is most significant as it offers a high spending form of tourism which also spreads its benefits more widely than leisure tourism because it makes use of a range of services that are not normally used by leisure tourists. For the tourism economy in Johannesburg, the activity of business tourism represents the highest-value customer segment. At the base of the city's competitive edge for business tourism is the fact that the Johannesburg metropolitan area contains overwhelmingly South Africa's largest cluster of headquarter offices of domestic enterprises, as well as a considerable group of the branch offices for international corporations which use Johannesburg as a base for wider African business operations. Further reinforcing the status of Johannesburg as business capital is the largest cluster of four and five star hotels in Africa. In light of the critical financial importance of business tourism, it is not surprising that the city tourism strategy highlights the retention of head offices as a fundamental strategy for building the urban tourism economy of Johannesburg.

In addition to individual business tourism, the business tourism economy also encompasses the MICE subsector, which involves bringing together senior managers and shareholders of companies (often with their partners) for conferences, exhibitions, team-building or training courses. The strength of this MICE subsector is recognised to be strongly dependent upon the quantity and quality of tourism infrastructure and available services. Johannesburg has strong tourism assets for the attraction of MICE tourism in terms of the city's asset base of conference and exhibition venues linked to the existence of high-quality graded hotel accommodation (Gelling 2004). The Sandton Convention Centre, Gallagher Estate, the Dome in Northgate and the Nasrec expo centre are viewed as convention and exhibition centres of world-class quality (Davie 2004). The existing data on MICE tourism in South Africa suggest that it is the fastest expanding segment of the tourism market as a whole and that Johannesburg is the leading South African focus for MICE tourism in terms of both the domestic MICE market and the international MICE market. Moreover, national data confirm Johannesburg's pre-eminence in the exhibition market – of 1 900 exhibitions annually held in South Africa, the city captures over half of the national share (Davie 2003). In the city tourism development strategy it was stressed that the MICE industry represents a significant element for the future of Johannesburg's tourism strategy. With the city's undoubted competitive advantage, business tourism is regarded as 'the potential jewel in the Johannesburg tourism market' (GJMC 2002).

The second sectoral driver for Johannesburg tourism was defined as building upon the city's existing advantage as the 'preferred destination of African tourists in South Africa' (GJMC 2001: 88). The importance of 'regional tourism', and more especially, of cross-border shopping relates to the growing number of tourist arrivals in Johannesburg from other parts of Africa for the major purpose of shopping (Rogerson 2003). Recent research discloses that for many regional tourists Johannesburg is seen as akin to 'the Las Vegas of Africa' in terms of its attractiveness (South African Tourism 2002: 10). The existing information points to the largest numbers of cross-border shoppers as emanating from the surrounding countries in the Southern African Development Community. But of growing importance is a trend for retail tourism to expand its geographical reach farther afield into countries such as Ghana, Nigeria, and Cameroon. Official recognition is accorded to the potential significance of this retail tourism in Johannesburg's tourism development strategy. Proposals are set forth for reinforcing Johannesburg's position as a shopping Mecca for cross-border retail tourism by establishing a dedicated cross-border hub linked particularly to tourists' shopping preferences, and by further marketing the retail attractions of Johannesburg (GJMC 2001, 2002). In addition, with Johannesburg positioning itself as the centre of New Partnership for Africa's Development, a continued growth of regional tourism is confidently expected (Palmary 2004).

In terms of overall support for tourism from the metropolitan level of government, the tourism development strategy for Johannesburg identifies a set of important development interventions, including the recognition that the primary contribution the council can make to tourism is to undertake activities which increase the flow of tourists in the city. The key institutional vehicle for support has been through the Johannesburg Tourism Company. Three potential areas for intervention and support are noted. The first is to increase aggregate demand through marketing and other city promotional initiatives in order to increase visitor arrivals, not least through re-imaging Johannesburg. Undoubtedly, the image of Johannesburg has been revamped and guidebooks which formerly counselled international visitors to stay away are now touting Johannesburg as the best place to experience the 'New South Africa' (Harrison 2005). In terms of retail tourism, the marketing of the city is to be intensified prior to planned promotional retail tourism weeks. Another critical element of this city marketing for tourism is to be focused on the strategy of 'landing the big one' as regards large international conferences. In this respect, it is estimated that a conference such as the World Summit generates in a single five-day period as much value as three months of average MICE and general business tourism in Johannesburg (GJMC 2001).

A second intervention is to indirectly increase tourism by addressing the issues raised most frequently by tourists and potential tourists as reasons for them either not visiting the city or minimising their demand for tourism products and services whilst in the city. The most important blockage is known to concern issues of crime and safety of tourists in Johannesburg (Ferreira & Harmse 2000). By addressing crime, the council would be indirectly assisting tourism development in the city. A third way in which it is acknowledged that local tourism planning can make a difference is related to infrastructure development, in particular for MICE and cross-border retail tourism (GJMC 2002). Few facility gaps are currently seen as urgent in terms of the city's strength for MICE tourism, other than issues of upgrading. In retail tourism, however, proposals have been made for designating a potential retail hub which would concentrate the goods and services most frequently sought out by African cross-border shoppers (GJMC 2002).

A remarkable omission in Johannesburg's *Tourism Growth Strategy* is the lack of promotion of 'alternative' forms of tourism and of geographically spreading the benefits of tourism into the city's poorest areas, although there has been an emerging link through Blue IQ projects such as the Newtown cultural precinct and Constitution Hill with issues of inner-city regeneration through tourism (McKenzie 2004; Rogerson 2004b). Nevertheless, the city has only recently begun to actively market tourism into township areas such as Soweto, which has experienced a considerable growth since 2002 of new tourism small enterprises in both the accommodation and the travel and tour operator sectors (Rogerson 2004c; Nemasetoni 2005). The expansion of tourism into Soweto and more recently Alexandra offers opportunities for tourism to become a stronger vehicle for contributing towards poverty alleviation, and for job creation in these spaces of high unemployment and limited job prospects (Kaplan 2004; Ramchander 2004). Lastly, new policy initiatives were formulated in 2004, in particular for catalysing township tourism in Soweto and building upon the critical role played by the locality in the struggle for democracy and freedom.

## Conclusion

As judged by the comparative findings of various 'ten year reviews' and assessments on various aspects of the economy and government's performance since 1994, tourism stands out as one of the 'bright spots' in the record of South Africa's new democracy (Rogerson & Visser 2004). In the first decade of democracy the tourism sector has maintained a strong performance and is now one of the priority sectors of government's microeconomic reform strategy and the DTI's Integrated Manufacturing Strategy (DEAT 2003a; Monitor 2004). This analysis discloses that the potential for tourism to be a strategic policy sector in urban economic development has not gone unnoticed in South Africa's major cities. In particular, the country's three leading cities – Johannesburg, Cape Town and Durban – have all grasped the opportunity to maximise tourism as a base for economic growth and increasingly also for contributing towards poverty alleviation. The detailed record of Johannesburg provides a case study of tourism policy assuming a new significance in urban economic development planning in a manner that exhibits many commonalities with the rise of tourism planning in British and American cities. Overall, however, there has been observed a policy dis-connect between national and local levels of government in the South African experience, with little direct linkage between the vibrant tourism-led economic development initiatives in the country's cities and processes of developing national tourism policy. Tourism-led LED in the cities is the missing link.

### Acknowledgements

The research reported here draws in part from ongoing work financially supported under award Gun No. 2050464 of the National Research Foundation, Pretoria, which is acknowledged with thanks.

### References

Ashley C & Ntshona Z (2002) *Transforming roles but not reality? Private sector and community involvement in tourism and forestry development on the Wild Coast.* Sustainable Livelihoods in Southern Africa, Wild Resources Theme Research Briefing. London: Overseas Development Institute.

Bass D (2005) Kidneys for cash and egg safaris – can we allow 'transplant tourism' to flourish in South Africa? *South African Medical Journal,* 95(1): 42–44.

Beauregard RA (1998) Tourism and economic development policy in US urban areas. In D Ioannides & KG Debbage (eds), *The economic geography of the tourist industry: A supply-side analysis.* London: Routledge.

Bennett A (2004a) The Cape of Storms. In A Bennett & R George (eds), *South African travel and tourism cases.* Pretoria: Van Schaik.

Bennett A (2004b) Robben Island: The conscience of a nation. In A Bennett & R George (eds), *South African travel and tourism cases.* Pretoria: Van Schaik.

Bull P & Church A (1998) Urban tourism in the 1990s: Understanding the figures for London, *Geography Review*, 12(2): 37–40.

Bull P & Church A (2001) Understanding urban tourism: London in the early 1990s, *International Journal of Tourism Research*, 3: 141–150.

Burger CJSC, Dohnal M, Katharda M & Law R (2001) A practitioner's guide to time-series methods for tourism demand forecasting – a case study of Durban, South Africa, *Tourism Management*, 22: 403–409.

Cassim R (1993) *Tourism and development in South Africa.* Economic Trends Working Paper No. 18. Cape Town: University of Cape Town.

Chang TC & Huang S (2004) Urban tourism: Between global and local. In AA Lew, CM Hall & AM Williams (eds), *A companion to tourism*. Oxford: Blackwell.

Coles T (2003) Urban tourism, place promotion and economic restructuring: The case of post-socialist Leipzig, *Tourism Geographies*, 5: 190–219.

Davie L (2003) Joburg – country's top exhibition venue. Available at <http://www.joburg.org.za>.

Davie L (2004) Joburg – an 'emerging giant' for business tourism. Available at <http://www.joburg.org.za>.

DEAT (Department of Environmental Affairs and Tourism) (1995a) *Become tourism active.* Pretoria: DEAT.

DEAT (1995b) *Tourism Green Paper: Towards a new tourism policy for South Africa.* Pretoria: DEAT.

DEAT (2000) Transforming the South African tourism industry. Unpublished report. Pretoria: DEAT.

DEAT (2002) *Responsible tourism manual.* Pretoria: DEAT.

DEAT (2003a) *Tourism 10 year review.* Pretoria: DEAT.

DEAT (2003b) *Responsible tourism handbook: A guide to good practice for tourism operators.* Pretoria: DEAT.

DEAT (2004) *Domestic tourism growth strategy 2004 to 2007.* Pretoria: DEAT and South African Tourism. Available at <http://www.southafrica.net>.

DTI (Department of Trade and Industry) (2002) *Accelerating growth and development: The contribution of an integrated manufacturing strategy.* Pretoria: DTI.

Ekurhuleni Municipality (2003) *LED policy and strategy implementation framework.* Department of Local Economic Development, Ekurhuleni Metropolitan Municipality.

ELPA (East London Publicity Association) (1930) *East London, where sea and sunshine call – The home of the surfboard.* Johannesburg: South African Railways and Harbours Department.

Fainstein SS & Gladstone D (1999) Evaluating urban tourism. In DR Judd & SS Fainstein (eds), *The tourist city.* New Haven: Yale University Press.

Ferreira SLA & Harmse AC (2000) Crime and tourism in South Africa: International tourists perception and risk, *South African Geographical Journal*, 82: 80–85.

Gelling J (2004) Business tourism in South Africa – structure, geography and transformation. Unpublished BA Honours dissertation. Johannesburg: University of the Witwatersrand.

George R (2004) Medical tourism: Surgeon & safari. In A Bennett & R George (eds), *South African travel and tourism cases.* Pretoria: Van Schaik.

GJMC (Greater Johannesburg Metropolitan Council) (2001) *Tourism strategy.* Available at <http://www.joburg.org.za>.

GJMC (2002) *Johannesburg 2030.* Corporate planning unit. Available at <http://www.joburg.org.za>.

Grant L & Butler-Adam J (1992) Tourism and development needs in the Durban region. In DM Smith (ed.), *The apartheid city and beyond.* London: Routledge.

Grant L & Kohler K (1996) Evaluating tourism as a policy tool for urban reconstruction in South Africa: Focus on the Point Waterfront Development, Durban, KwaZulu-Natal. In RJ Davies (ed.), *Contemporary city restructuring.* Cape Town: International Geographical Union Commission on Urban Development and Urban Life and Society for Geographers.

Grant L & Scott D (1996) Waterfront developments as tools for urban reconstruction and regeneration in South Africa: The planned Point Waterfront Development in Durban, *Urban Forum,* 7(2): 125–138.

Gretton D (1995) Local economic development in Cape Town. In E Nel (ed.), *Local economic development in South Africa: A review of current policy and applied case studies.* Johannesburg: Friedrich Ebert Stiftung and South African National Civic Organisation.

Hall P & Robbins G (2002) Economic development for a new era: An examination of the adoption of explicit economic development strategies by Durban local government since 1994. In B Freund & V Padayachee (eds), *(D)urban vortex: South African city in transition.* Pietermartitzburg: University of Natal Press.

Harrison R (2005) From seedy to sexy, Joburg seeks a revival. Independent Online, 14 January 2005. Available at<http://www.iol.co.za>.

Heath E (2004) Branding and positioning of the Nelson Mandela metro. In A Bennett & R George (eds), *South African travel and tourism cases.* Pretoria: Van Schaik.

Hoffman LM (2000) Tourism and the revitalization of Harlem, *Research in Urban Sociology,* 5: 207–223.

Hoffman LM, Fainstein SS & Judd DR (eds) (2003) *Cities and visitors: Regulating people, markets and city space.* Oxford: Blackwell.

Hoyle B (2001) Lamu: Waterfront revitalization in an East African port city, *Cities,* 18: 297–313.

Hughes H & Vaughan A (2000) The incorporation of historically disadvantaged communities into tourism initiatives in the new South Africa: Case studies from KwaZulu-Natal. In M Robinson, N Evans, N Long, R Sharpley & J Swarbrooke (eds), *Management, marketing and the political economy of travel and tourism.* Sunderland: Centre for Travel and Tourism and Business Education.

Ingram Z (2004) Cape Town International Convention Centre. In A Bennett & R George (eds), *South African travel and tourism cases.* Pretoria: Van Schaik.

Johannesburg Tourism Company (2005) Johannesburg: Much more than you expect. Available at <http://www.joburgtourism.com>.

Kaplan L (2004) Skills development for tourism: Alexandra township, Johannesburg, *Urban Forum,* 15(4): 380–398.

Karski A (1990) Urban tourism – a key to urban regeneration, *The Planner*, 76(13): 15–17.

Kilian D, Goudie S & Dodson B (1996) Postmodern f[r]ictions: history, text and identity at the Victoria and Alfred Waterfront, Cape Town. In RJ Davies (ed.), *Contemporary city restructuring*, 520–530. Cape Town: International Geographical Union Commission on Urban Development and Urban Life and Society for Geographers.

King B (2004) Book review on 'Managing urban tourism', *Tourism Management*, 25: 290–291.

Law CM (1991) Tourism and urban revitalization, *East Midlands Geographer*, 14: 49–60.

Law CM (1992) Urban tourism and its contribution to economic regeneration, *Urban Studies*, 29: 599–618.

Law CM (1993) *Urban tourism: Attracting visitors to large cities*. London: Mansell.

Law CM (1996) Introduction. In CM Law (ed.), *Tourism in major cities*. London: International Thomson Business Press.

Law CM (2000) Regenerating the city centre through leisure and tourism, *Built Environment*, 26(2): 117–129.

Lootvoet B & Freund B (2004) Local economic development: Utopia and reality in South Africa; the example of Durban, KwaZulu-Natal. Paper presented at the conference on the First Decade of Democracy and Development in South Africa, Durban, 20–22 October.

MacMenamin V (1995) Local economic development in the city of Durban. In E Nel (ed.), *Local economic development in South Africa: A review of current policy and applied case studies*. Johannesburg: Friedrich Ebert Stiftung and South African National Civic Organisation.

Marks R & Bezzoli M (2001) Palaces of desire: Century City, Cape Town and the ambiguities of development, *Urban Forum*, 12: 27–47.

McCarthy J (2002) Entertainment-led regeneration: The case of Detroit, *Cities*, 19: 105–111.

McKenzie K (2004) Two paths to renewal: Johannesburg vs Cape Town, *Delivery*, 28–30.

Moffett S & Freund B (2004) Elite formation and elite bonding: Social structure and development in Durban, *Urban Forum*, 15: 134–161.

Monitor (2004) Global competitiveness study – preliminary executive summary. Report on Work in Progress prepared for the Department of Environmental Affairs and Tourism and DTI, May.

Nel E & Binns T (2003) Putting 'developmental local government' into practice: The experience of South Africa's towns and cities, *Urban Forum*, 14: 165–184.

Nel E, Hill T & Maharaj B (2003) Durban's pursuit of economic development in the post-apartheid era, *Urban Forum*, 14: 223–243.

Nel E & Rogerson CM (eds) (2005) *Local economic development in the developing world: The experience of Southern Africa*. New Brunswick NJ/London: Transaction Press.

Nemasetoni I (2005) Contribution of tourism towards the development of black-owned small, medium and micro enterprises (SMMEs) in post apartheid South Africa: An evaluation of tour operators. Unpublished MA research report. Johannesburg: University of the Witwatersrand.

Page S (1999) Tourism and development: The evidence from Mauritius, South Africa and Zimbabwe. Unpublished report prepared for the Overseas Development Institute, London.

Palmary I (2004) City policing and forced migrants in Johannesburg. In LB Landau (ed.), *Forced migrants in the new Johannesburg: Towards a local government response*. Johannesburg: University of the Witwatersrand, Forced Migration Studies Programme.

Pearce DG (2001) An integrative framework for urban tourism research, *Annals of Tourism Research*, 28: 926–946.

Ramchander P (2004) Soweto set to lure tourists. In A Bennett & R George (eds), *South African travel and tourism cases*. Pretoria: Van Schaik.

Rogerson CM (1995) International issues, strategies and models. In E Nel (ed.), *Local economic development in South Africa: A review of current policy and applied case studies*. Johannesburg: Friedrich Ebert Stiftung and South African National Civic Organisation.

Rogerson CM (1997) Local economic development and post-apartheid South Africa, *Singapore Journal of Tropical Geography*, 18: 175–195.

Rogerson CM (2002a) Tourism-led local economic development: The South African experience, *Urban Forum*, 13: 95–119.

Rogerson CM (2002b) Urban tourism in the developing world: The case of Johannesburg, *Development Southern Africa*, 19: 169–190.

Rogerson CM (2002c) Driving developmental tourism in South Africa, *Africa Insight*, 32(3): 33–42.

Rogerson CM (2003) Tourism planning and the economic revitalisation of Johannesburg, *Africa Insight*, 33(1/2): 130–135.

Rogerson CM (2004a) New directions for casino tourism in post-apartheid South Africa. In CM Rogerson & G Visser (eds), *Tourism and development issues in contemporary South Africa*. Pretoria: Africa Institute of South Africa.

Rogerson CM (2004b) From spatial development initiative to blue IQ: Sub-national economic planning in Gauteng, *Urban Forum*, 15: 74–101.

Rogerson CM (2004c) Urban tourism and small tourism enterprise development in Johannesburg: The case of township tourism, *GeoJournal*, 60: 247–257.

Rogerson CM & Visser G (eds) (2004) *Tourism and development issues in contemporary South Africa*. Pretoria: Africa Institute of South Africa.

Rousseau GG (2004) The Boardwalk Casino and Entertainment World. In A Bennett & R George (eds), *South African travel and tourism cases*. Pretoria: Van Schaik.

RSA (Republic of South Africa) (1996) *White Paper on the development and promotion of tourism in South Africa*. Pretoria: DEAT.

RSA (1998) *Tourism in gear: Tourism development strategy 1998–2000*. Pretoria: DEAT.

Rule S, Viljoen J, Zama S, Struwig J, Langa Z & Bouare O (2004) Visiting friends and relatives: South Africa's most popular form of domestic tourism. In CM Rogerson & G Visser (eds), *Tourism and development issues in contemporary South Africa*. Pretoria: Africa Institute of South Africa.

Sampaio D (2004) Johannesburg – city or art: The use of art galleries in marketing. Unpublished BA Honours dissertation. Johannesburg: University of the Witwatersrand.

Scott AJ (2004) Cultural-products industries and urban economic development: Prospects for growth and market contestation in a global context, *Urban Affairs Review*, 39: 461–490.

Shaw G & Williams AM (2004) *Tourism and tourism spaces.* London: Sage.

South African Tourism (2002) *Tourism growth strategy.* Johannesburg: South African Tourism.

Strange C & Kempa M (2003) Shades of dark tourism: Alcatraz and Robben Island, *Annals of Tourism Research,* 30: 386–405.

Strom E (2002) Converting pork into porcelain: Cultural institutions and downtown development, *Urban Affairs Review,* 38: 3–21.

Strydom L (2004) Hail Caesars. In A Bennett & R George (eds), *South African travel and tourism cases,* 28–38. Pretoria: Van Schaik.

Swarbrooke J (1999) Urban areas. In J Swarbrooke, *Sustainable Tourism Management.* Wallingford: CABI Publishing.

Swarbrooke J (2000) Tourism, economic development and urban regeneration: A critical evaluation. In M Robinson, R Sharpley, N Evans, P Long & J Swarbrooke (eds), *Developments in urban and rural tourism.* Centre for Travel and Tourism, Sheffield Hallam University and University of Northumbria, Sunderland.

Teo P & Yeoh BSA (1997) Remaking local heritage for tourism, *Annals of Tourism Research,* 24: 192–213.

Tomlinson R (ed.) (1994) *Urban development planning: Lessons for the reconstruction of South Africa's cities.* Johannesburg: Witwatersrand University Press.

Van Huyssteen MKR & Neethling JPN (1996) Resort development in the False Bay recreational fringe of Metropolitan Cape Town. In RJ Davies (ed.), *Contemporary city restructuring.* Cape Town: International Geographical Union Commission on Urban Development and Urban Life and Society for Geographers.

Van Zyl I (2004) Municipality kick-starts major tourism developments, *Imiesa,* March: 24–25.

Visser G (2002) Gay tourism in South Africa: Issues from the Cape Town experience, *Urban Forum,* 13(1): 85–94.

Visser G (2003) Gay men, tourism and urban space: Reflections on Africa's gay capital, *Tourism Geographies,* 5: 168–189.

Vos K (2004) Starlight cruises. In A Bennett & R George (eds), *South African travel and tourism cases.* Pretoria: Van Schaik.

Wober KW (ed.) (2002) *City tourism 2002.* Vienna: Springer Verlag.

### Interviews

Saunders G, Director of Tourism Research, Grant Thornton Kessell Feinstein, Johannesburg, 6 April 2004.

Viljoen D, CEO of Johannesburg Tourism Company, Johannesburg, 24 March 2004.

# Part 4: Housing and services delivery programmes

# 11 Reaching the poor? An analysis of the influences on the evolution of South Africa's housing programme

Sarah Charlton and Caroline Kihato

## Introduction

This chapter contains an analysis of the housing policy process in South Africa, and the factors that shape policy. The housing policy, adopted in 1994, has evolved over the years into a complex, multifaceted entity with many components. We select key aspects of the housing programme to illustrate two points: firstly, that a variety of factors influence the evolution of policy. Whilst research is one of these, other pressures such as politics, power struggles, pragmatism and constraints in the external environment mean that the influence of research on policy is at times limited or not always clear. Secondly, we argue that understanding this range of influences on the policy-making process contributes to explaining the gaps between policy intentions, policy articulation and practice. In particular, it helps us understand why policies intended to improve the lives of the poor sometimes fail to do so.

To illustrate these points, we draw on the current discourse around government social programmes, including housing. This discourse emphasises the extent to which policy improves the lives of the poor and contributes to poverty alleviation, key questions in the recent period of reflection on the decade of democracy (see RSA 2003a). The Ten Year Review comments that 'programmes to alleviate poverty have brought improvement in the lives of millions' (RSA 2003d: 3), and cites the housing programme as one of these programmes. Housing is listed under the category of 'boosting ownership of assets and access to opportunities' (2003d: 4), and is considered to be one of the 'lead programmes relating to the elimination of asset capital poverty' (RSA 2003e: 25).

These extracts from state documents emphasise, *inter alia*, the notion of *assets*, revealing a sophisticated understanding of the multifaceted nature of poverty. However, indicators used to assess the impact of housing, whilst located within this conception of poverty, remain quantitatively focused around elements such as numbers of subsidies approved and numbers of title deeds transferred (see RSA 2003d) – measures which, it is argued, *in themselves* do not necessarily demonstrate a contribution to poverty alleviation.

This tension highlights a key argument of this chapter: that current discourse used by government in relation to housing, and used by us in this chapter as a lens with which to reflect on the housing programme, is applied to a policy which was formulated with reference to other imperatives. As we indicate, the original policy was developed in response to the notion of meeting basic needs, which was the basis for the Reconstruction and Development Programme (RDP) (ANC 1994), and was significantly shaped by a concern with delivery. Nevertheless, we note that during the 1990s some linkages were made between the idea of satisfying basic needs and impacting on poverty. These assumptions appear to have become increasingly entrenched over the years, with the discourse of the housing programme now reflecting a belief in the underlying linkages between the delivery of housing and poverty alleviation.

Our argument is that there remains a gap between the current focus in government discourse around the contribution of housing to poverty alleviation and the ability of the policy to do so. Part of the reason for this can be found in the nature and character of the policy-making process. While the original policy has been adjusted over the years, its evolution has not been shaped by a clear agenda of understanding of the housing programme's impact on poverty alleviation. The lack of engagement with this issue is partly explained by the other pressures driving policy formulation.

## Structure

We begin with a brief description of key elements of the housing policy in South Africa. The analysis of the housing policy process is then structured into three sections: firstly, an exploration of the main policy amendment of 2004 and the process that led to this; secondly, we consider selected policy adjustments in the late 1990s; and thirdly, we explore the process that led to the adoption of the original post-apartheid policy in 1994.

We recognise that hindsight often has a strong influence on our understanding and interpretations of history, providing new ways of seeing past events that may not have been apparent at the time that they took place. This is particularly true of South Africa's housing policy, as a remark by the previous Minister of Housing illustrates: '…there are many new challenges in the housing sector which were not as obvious in 1994 as they are now' (Mabandla 2003: 10). Given that policy processes do not always follow readily intelligible processes, and that it is often difficult to identify with certainty the causality of a policy decision, personal evaluations and reflections increasingly become data that we rely on – the end product not only reflecting the interpretations of key informants, but our own as well.

## Research method and approach

The substantial experience of housing programme implementation since 1994 has been matched by a considerable body of work which researches, comments on and evaluates policy and practice to date. This chapter draws on this work, as well as documentation and research of the Department of Housing, to consider key examples of policy adjustment and the influences on these.

In addition, the chapter draws on primary research. We conducted interviews with key informants between August and December 2004. Individuals included those involved in the early policy negotiations that culminated in South Africa's first democratic housing policy, as well as actors in the housing sector involved in implementing and influencing current policy directions.

## Key components of the housing policy in South Africa

The post-1994 housing programme has been highly significant in a number of ways. Housing delivery has been important in demonstrating the distribution of a tangible asset to the poor, and in this sense it can be argued to have played a key role in establishing a degree of state legitimacy among low-income households.[1] In addition, it is contended that 'the government housing programme is one of the few state interventions which places a physical asset directly in the hands of households living in conditions of poverty' (Mabandla 2003: 6). In general, the programme has provided beneficiaries with access to basic services, security of tenure, shelter, and fulfilled an important 'psychological need' in fostering a sense of pride and dignity in having a place to call home (Zack & Charlton 2003).

The dominant element of South Africa's housing policy is an income-related capital subsidy, aimed at purchasing land, securing tenure, delivering infrastructure services and a basic house for qualifying households. The subsidy is a once-off 'contribution' by the state aimed at meeting the African National Congress' (ANC) objective of 'housing for all'. The subsidy amount has been intermittently increased since its introduction in 1994, but has not kept up with inflation.

While the subsidy takes several forms, its most visible manifestation has resulted in the production of the 'RDP house'.[2] The nature of the 'basic house' has been contested since the formulation of the policy. On adoption of the policy in 1994, the intention was to deliver a starter house,[3] which beneficiaries would add to and consolidate over time. This incremental way of achieving the right to housing was related to a key assumption in the policy that beneficiaries would be able to access loan finance which would be spent on improving the house (Khan & Ambert 2003a). By the late 1990s, the nature of the house to be delivered using the state's capital subsidy had shifted from the open-ended concept of a starter house, which was subject to wide variations in interpretation, to a minimum 30 m² unit of defined specification.

Applicants qualify for the capital subsidy by meeting a range of criteria, most notably by demonstrating South African citizenship, household income[4] below R3 500 per month and, if the applicant is single, that he or she is supporting dependants.

A relatively new introduction has been a mandatory beneficiary contribution, either in the form of a cash payment of R2 479, or through participation in the delivery process, for example through providing labour.[5] This condition has been introduced in part in response to the need to fund an insurance against quality defects in starter houses. In addition, it responds to a desire to 'cultivate a sense of ownership' in beneficiaries (Minister of Housing, cited in Khan & Ambert 2003a: xi). Similarly, the restriction for five years on the sale of their RDP house by beneficiaries, originally introduced by government in 2001, is based on the belief that some recipients do not appreciate this 'free gift' from the state. The regulation is therefore intended to inculcate in beneficiaries an appreciation of the value of the house.

The original housing policy aimed at creating an 'enabling environment' in which the state supports and facilitates the delivery of housing by the private sector, or by community-based organisations, rather than engaging directly in shelter provision itself. This is referred to by some as both a 'state-assisted, market driven delivery approach' (Khan & Ambert 2003a: v) and 'state-assisted self-help' (Wilkinson 1998: 226) – therefore involving both market and people-driven production (Goodlad 1996). In recent years, the state has taken a more direct role in low-cost housing production, influenced by a range of factors which are discussed later, including reduced delivery by the private sector.

Policy as encapsulated in the 1994 Housing White Paper envisaged that the subsidy scheme would do more than just build houses, but would also result in the creation of 'viable, integrated settlements where households would have convenient access to opportunities, infrastructure and services' (Khan & Ambert 2003b: xxv). As implementation has rolled out over the years, however, this dimension of well-functioning neighbourhoods has largely failed to materialise. Gilbert (2004) suggests that although housing performance has in fact been far superior to that in other sectors such as education, health and employment, the housing 'experiment' has been widely critiqued inside the country, largely because of the lack of settlement integration and the poor connectivity between housing delivery and opportunities in urban areas.

Analysts in the sector contend that for various reasons such as poor location, cost of home ownership in the form of rates and service charges, and unemployment, increased access to low-income housing by the poor has had a limited impact on poverty alleviation (see for example Charlton, Silverman & Berrisford 2003; Khan & Ambert 2003b; Rust 2003; Zack & Charlton 2003). This is despite intentions and claims to the contrary expressed in some official documentation and statements (see for example DoH 2000; Mpofu n.d.). The programme has been much criticised for contributing to urban sprawl, perpetuating the marginalisation of the poor, and for failing to play a key role in the compaction, integration and restructuring of the apartheid city (Narsoo 2000; Huchzermeyer 2001; Todes 2003; Zack & Charlton 2003). Indeed, some commentators argue that social programmes such as housing have, in some cases, economically and spatially marginalised the poor further (Bond 2003). Thus, while the housing programme has had some positive impact on beneficiaries, end-user satisfaction with the subsidy scheme has varied widely (Tomlinson 1999b) and, in addition, it remains unclear whether South Africa's most vulnerable households are unreservedly better off as a result of the programme (see for example Baumann 2003).

## Policy adjustment in 2004

### Breaking New Ground – *a housing revolution?*

In this section we consider a potentially important policy development in 2004, and the factors that shaped key elements of it. A newspaper story in September 2004 suggesting 'Low-cost housing for elite suburbs', raised an uproar in the public domain in describing what some considered a 'housing revolution' (*Sunday Times* 05.09.2004). While some welcomed the Department of Housing's proposal 'to build a non-racial society' as long as it was 'well managed', others decried the impact of such an intervention on their property values, fuelled partly by not-in-my-back-yard emotions and fears around race and class integration. The Minister of Housing, however, was quick to allay fears: 'There is no intention by the Department of Housing to build a "low cost house on the doorstep of a R3 million house" as claimed by the *Sunday Times* report on Sunday September 5, 2004; there is no reason for the Department of Housing to negatively affect the high income market' (Sisulu 2004e).

But this publicity, focused on the location of state-provided low-income housing, in some ways obscured a meaningful discussion around the content of the Department of Housing's new programme of action – encapsulated in the document *Breaking New Ground*,[6] which was approved by Cabinet in September 2004. While not clearly introducing any new policy direction, the document outlines a comprehensive plan 'for the development of sustainable human settlements in the next five years' (DoH 2004: 2). This plan should be understood within the context of President Thabo Mbeki's State of the Nation address in May 2004. In this speech he promised that the Housing department would present to Cabinet within three months a policy document that addressed human settlements and social infrastructure (Mbeki 2004).

The Housing minister's reply to this statement makes it clear that *Breaking New Ground* was framed to respond to the president's speech and the specific concerns that it raised with respect to poverty alleviation: 'When the President spoke on 21st May giving deadlines and injunctions on what should be done in pursuit of the eradication of poverty, we were immediately able to contextualise our own plans' (Sisulu 2004d). Soon after this the minister noted that, 'We will be pushing back the frontiers of poverty by reducing the housing backlog' (Sisulu 2004b: 3). It is clear that there was political pressure for the Housing department to generate a new document that engaged with socio-economic issues around human settlements.

This pressure may in fact have compromised the plan's ability to address some of the underlying problems of the housing programme, such as the marginalisation of vulnerable households.

## Content of Breaking New Ground

*Breaking New Ground* is unequivocal about the housing programme's responsibility in the creation of viable human settlements. This notion of housing as a *leverage* for influencing and controlling the way human settlements develop, is significant. While encapsulating the aim of creating integrated settlements, the nature of the housing programme to date has in effect been biased towards meeting delivery targets. The new plan makes clear in its objectives that housing provision should address poverty alleviation, economic growth, improving the quality of life of the poor, creating an asset[7] for the poor and ultimately developing sustainable human settlements (DoH 2004). In other words, housing delivery is more explicitly framed as a catalyst for achieving a set of broader socio-economic goals. The Minister of Housing's Budget vote speech to Parliament in June 2004 echoed this shift when she said that the programme aims at 'promoting good governance and attaining sustainable, integrated human settlements' (Sisulu 2004b: 5).

*Breaking New Ground* also reflects the entrenchment of 'new' terminology into official housing parlance. Here, the concept of 'sustainable human settlements' in the document is noteworthy. Whilst the original housing policy document of 1994 mentions sustainability often, the notion of 'sustainable human settlements' does not feature. Its entry into official parlance can be traced back to the late 1990s, and linked to the department's relationship with United Nations (UN) Habitat and its commitment to the Habitat Agenda.[8] This is one clear indication of the influence of international organisations in South Africa's housing policy (see Huchzermeyer 2001; Tomlinson R 2002; Khan 2003b). Yet the concept of sustainable human settlements may not have gained much currency in the country if the internal conditions had not been conducive to change.

By the late 1990s, housing specialists had begun raising concerns that the delivery of RDP houses was inadvertently creating unviable, dysfunctional settlements. From about 1999 onwards, therefore, there is increasing focus by the Department of Housing on the intention to produce 'quality' rather than mere quantity (Housing in Southern Africa 1998; Huchzermeyer 2001; Khan & Ambert 2003a; Rust 2003). Underlying this focus, however, is the assumption that there is a direct link between the delivery of infrastructure and services such as shelter, water, sanitation, waste removal and energy, and poverty alleviation. A report on the Minister of Housing's media briefing in June 1999 notes that, 'Government would continue to reduce the housing backlog while introducing programmes to alleviate poverty and improve quality of life through creating access to basic services within the new settlements' (Housing in Southern Africa 1999: 2).

Speeches referring to *Breaking New Ground* also reveal an energetic focus on the eradication of existing informal settlements and, presumably, those that are formed in future (Sisulu 2004a, 2004b, 2004c).

> The Premier of Gauteng has fired the first salvo in our war against shacks. His bold assertion that informal settlements in his province will have been eradicated in ten years, is the best news I have heard in my tenure as Minister. (Sisulu 2004a: 3)

The determination to eliminate informal settlements corresponds with the Cities Alliance[9] 'Cities without Slums' 1999 initiative, featuring also in the former minister's Budget vote for 2000/01 (Khan 2003b). However, the discourse permeating this emboldened stance around informal settlements is somewhat confusing. In the new plan, 'eradication' is said to refer to the integration of these settlements 'into the broader urban fabric to overcome spatial, social and economic exclusion' (DoH 2004: 12) – part of the drive for sustainable human settlements. While this suggests the upgrading of settlements through providing services and tenure, it is also acknowledged, however, that in many instances 'where development is not possible or desirable' (2004: 12), this may mean relocation of residents to other areas.

To date political discourse has often equated informality with inferiority (Marx 2003), with the visible manifestations of informality interpreted as a failure of government to deliver to its citizens. This has extended to concerns about the type of dwelling delivered within an otherwise formal development. This has been a highly contentious political issue since the National Housing Forum (NHF) negotiations in 1992–1994 where organisations loosely aligned as the left rejected site and service schemes in which end-users would build their own houses. The current ambiguous discourse on informal settlements appears to be influenced by some of these concerns, reacting to the visible dimensions of these settlements without a clear understanding of the complexities of these highly visible manifestations of poverty, mobility, and survival strategies.

Some of the suggested strategies in *Breaking New Ground*, such as funding well-located land for low-income housing, paying for certain community facilities in new housing projects and supporting *in situ* upgrading of informal settlements in desired locations, illustrate the concern over the impact of the housing programme on the poor (DoH 2004; Napier interview).[10] The document also pledges to support legal non-South Africans in informal settlements, a population group that is often considered one of the most vulnerable (Napier interview). In addition to these, the department aims to widen the income band of those benefiting from its programmes to include those earning up to R7 500 per month.

Nevertheless, in its fundamental elements the plan does not seem to have essentially departed from the original housing policy (DoH 2004; Nell interview), although some hail it as a 'radical departure' from previous policy (see Isandla Institute 2004). In addition, the plan appears not to fully address key weaknesses with the existing policy identified in research and in reports commissioned by the department in recent years. It certainly does not offer the clear direction with respect to the difficult political issues of land ownership, the land market and rights around property values that the initial media publicity around it suggested. Although the programme strives for broader outcomes, key indicators of performance appear to remain largely quantitative, focused around numbers of houses produced and budgets spent. In addition, some of the weaknesses of policy identified to date remain outside the power of the Department of Housing to remedy on its own (see for example RSA 2003c). Seemingly, therefore, there is no clear alignment between the current focus in government on the contribution of housing to poverty alleviation, and the ability of the policy to deliver on these objectives.

Yet this lack of clarity on the policy's strategic direction is surprising given the extensive research driven by the Department of Housing during 2002 and 2003, and the opportunity this seemed to provide for developing a coherent strategy that responded to the challenges faced by the sector. For at least 18 months prior to the release of *Breaking New Ground* many people in the housing sector were aware of a process of research and consultation that was intended to inform policy direction. If viewed as a culmination of this process, however, *Breaking New Ground* appears confusing and disappointing.

This is perhaps unsurprising, given that the document originates out of an amalgamation of 19 different business plans from various sectoral programmes within the national department. This range of plans was then given to a consultant with links to the World Bank to consolidate into a more rational document. Despite this refinement, the document does not clearly demonstrate a unifying conceptual foundation which offers policy direction into the future. What is also surprising about the process of formulating the plan is the lack of involvement of the Deputy Director-General: Policy and Programme Management, and the Acting Chief Director of Research. Both of these officials were instrumental in driving an extensive research process in 2002/03 intended to lead to what was dubbed a 'second generation' policy (Khan 2003b; Sigodi Marah Martin 2003).

## The research initiative preceding Breaking New Ground

In 2002/03, the national Department of Housing managed a research process aimed at providing new policy direction and establishing a research agenda to inform and support policy decision-making within the housing programme (Napier interview). This was an attempt to counter the 'dispersal of knowledge and intellectual capability' that had occurred over the last ten years in which ideas had been lost in the complex layers of bureaucracy and the technicalities of reconstruction (Vawda[11] interview). Within government, complex questions of space and the economy were being raised but were not centred anywhere; and there was an opportunity for – and an obligation on – the Housing department to try to focus debate on these issues (ibid.). This initiative was headed by Vawda and supported by externally commissioned researchers.

Occurring concurrently was the realisation that the department would benefit from developing in-house research capacity to support and inform policy. Thus, in April 2003, it established a research chief directorate, aimed at, *inter alia*, establishing a research culture within the department, enhancing its position as a significant player in international and national debates around human settlements, and influencing practice (Napier 2004). This intervention was significant given that limited in-house research had been done to direct policy shifts to date.[12] Official statements of the need to redirect policy from a quantitative to a qualitative intervention, for example, were often not backed by a supportive policy framework, nor was there coherent research done to inform and direct any programmatic shifts (Rust 2003). There was, however, by this time a considerable body of research and commentary on the housing programme, produced by academics, researchers and consultants, including those attached to institutions such as the Centre for Policy Studies, the Council for Scientific and Industrial Research, and the Housing Finance Research Programme.

The research commissioned in 2002/03 included an intensive process of consultation with housing stakeholders at national, provincial and local levels and a beneficiary survey on perceptions of the impact of the scheme on their lives. In addition, six research papers were commissioned, which were intended to provide recommendations on future directions of the programme, and result in the articulation of a research agenda (Napier 2004). Two of the research papers reviewed the appropriateness of current policy, the first with reference to outcomes and impacts of the programme, and the second using a human rights perspective. Three other papers considered the contemporary context in relation to the changing nature of housing demand, the role of the private sector in housing delivery, and international shifts in shelter and settlement policy. A final paper synthesised the various findings and identified issues for the policy and research agenda (Development Works 2004).

The research provided empirical evidence that showed that the housing programme needed to concern itself with creating socially and economically integrated habitats. Further, background documents commissioned by the department – such as *Chopping Block* – began to articulate and debate what this would mean in terms of designing a supportive policy framework (see Khan 2003a). Concepts such as housing as an asset, integrated development, and sustainable human settlements received high focus in the research, and the empirical evidence reinforced the view that these were major gaps in current policy (Charlton et al. 2003; Khan 2003a; Sigodi Marah Martin 2003). As the research documents during this period show, this process was clearly intended to lay the foundation for a new housing policy and research agenda, and to contribute towards the design of a 'second generation' housing policy for the next ten years (Khan 2003b; Sigodi Marah Martin 2003; Development Works 2004). Indeed, the then Minister of Housing stated that the process was to lead to a new policy framework and the establishment of a research agenda (Mabandla 2003).

Ironically, this never happened – at least not as was intended by the drivers of the research process. The aim was that the new strategy would be 'unveiled' by the minister at the Housing Summit held in November 2003 (Napier interview). But as Napier notes, rather than the research leading up to new housing strategy, the summit was 'downgraded' to a 'listening process' (Napier interview). One may speculate as to why it may have been considered an inappropriate time to introduce new policy: national elections were around the corner and it was rumoured that Mabandla was a caretaker minister until after the elections.

However, it remains unclear why the research process failed to result in a more substantive change in policy beyond the Summit. The 2003 financial year was marked by significant underspending of housing budgets. Concern around this from the Treasury and the Presidency resulted in discussions between senior officials in these departments and those of the Department of Housing in early 2004. Some hard thinking produced a 'turnaround strategy' that contained seeds of a new policy direction, based on elements of the preceding research. However, this strategy was not implemented, nor did it enter the public domain. To date the research undertaken has no status within the department, and is used merely as reference material (Napier interview). Meanwhile, the position of research within the department remains precarious as the caretaker Acting Chief Director, Mark Napier, has returned to his long-term post outside the department and a permanent member of staff for this post has yet to be found.

Despite this, Vawda is optimistic that the research process did have value. While it may not have resulted in a turnaround policy, it began embedding 'pro-poor language' into government parlance (Vawda interview). But as we argue in this chapter, the discourse is far ahead of practice. The challenge of translating underlying intentions into practical outcomes remains.

It is not clear whether the 18-month research process would have ultimately resulted in strategies that addressed the problems in the low-cost housing sector, including the impact of the programme on the poor. But there was a clear process which was intended to shape the development of policy. That this process has not progressed to its conclusion suggests that the potential for aligning policy with the needs of the poor remains limited. This is notwithstanding the minister's assurance at the Summit that 'the Department of Housing reaffirms its commitment to addressing the needs of individuals, households and communities who experience poverty, social exclusion and vulnerability' (Mabandla 2003: 16).

## Selected policy adjustments in the late 1990s

This section of the chapter takes three facets of the housing programme that demonstrate policy shifts in the 1990s – namely the reconfiguration of stakeholder roles, social housing, and the introduction of norms and standards – and considers what the influences on these were. It also considers why more substantial policy evolution did not occur during this time. It comments on whether these policy adjustments have been influenced by a consideration of a poverty alleviation agenda.

If the 21st century housing policy in South Africa is concerned with the broader socio-economic impact of housing delivery, and notions of housing as an asset, discourse in the 1990s was framed around assumptions that infrastructure delivery contributes to poverty alleviation.

> Poverty is the single greatest burden of South Africa's people...it is not merely lack of income which determines poverty. An enormous proportion of very basic needs are presently unmet. In attacking poverty and deprivation, the Reconstruction and Development Programme... aims to set South Africa firmly on the road to eliminating hunger, providing land and housing to all our people, providing access to safe water and sanitation for all... (ANC 1994: 14)

The Housing White Paper, while cautioning against unrealistic expectations being attached to the housing programme, also makes the link between housing delivery and the impact on poverty:

> To impact on poverty a coordinated, multifaceted approach towards initiating and maintaining sustainable socio-economic development is necessary. Housing interventions by Government can at the most be seen as part of (an) integrated approach by Government to resolve the problem of poverty...The resolution of this problem (of grinding poverty) is something that a sustainable housing programme can significantly contribute to, but cannot remotely seek to solve on its own. (RSA 1994: Section 4.6 and Section 3.3.10)

Similarly, the Housing Code reflects the link between housing provision and poverty intervention, with statements such as 'the housing programme has a positive influence on the alleviation of poverty as well as contributing to the redistribution of wealth' (DoH 2000: 89).

These assumptions of the link between housing delivery and the alleviation of poverty are located in the belief that large-scale public expenditure on infrastructure such as housing, health and education is a significant contributor to resolving problems of poverty. This belief has its roots in the basic needs approach, first presented at the International Labour Organisation conference in 1976 (Esteva 1993). Increasing disillusionment with the failure of those development interventions that focused on economic growth models to reduce poverty in the sixties and seventies resulted in a mounting call for improving basic needs such as shelter, health, and education. The basic needs approach which aimed at 'the achievement of a certain specific minimum standard of living before the end of the century' (see Esteva 1993: 15) laid the foundation for large investments in social infrastructure in the belief that this would eventually help to eradicate poverty.

To some extent the South African government's recent Ten Year Review has this as an underlying belief – it assesses sectors through quantifiable delivery targets and uses these numbers to illustrate the extent of poverty alleviation (see RSA 2003a). But this conception obscures a meaningful understanding of the multidimensional nature of poverty. Statistics that show that access to water, electricity, housing and education for households has increased over a given time period, do not necessarily tell us that poverty has decreased. Similarly, increased government social spending on the poor does not guarantee the improvement of the quality of their lives (see Gelb 2003). In the housing sector in South Africa, the link between housing and poverty reduction is also contested (see for example Tomlinson 1998; Baumann 2003; Smit 2003). Nevertheless, Khan (2003b) citing Mokate, Schwabe, Makinta and O'Donovan (1999) makes the argument that both government and academics hold the view that the provision of houses is a key development intervention in reducing poverty.

This perspective is important in understanding the motivations for, and effects of, policy changes in low-income housing over the last ten years. We argue that the adjustment of policy that has occurred has not matched the rhetoric around addressing the negative impact of the programme on marginalised beneficiaries, nor has it been rooted in a specific understanding of how housing can contribute to poverty alleviation. Some commentators observe that policy adjustments in the 1990s were in fact not the result of research or conceptual deliberations (Smit interview) and that few modifications resulted in substantial policy changes (Khan & Ambert 2003a; Smit and Nell interviews).

### Stakeholder roles in housing delivery in the 1990s

A fairly significant shift was the move towards a more state-centred housing delivery programme, from a position in which the state played a facilitatory role and delivery was achieved by a range of players. The introduction of the Housing Act of 1997 paved the way for greater local government involvement in housing development (Tomlinson 1998). An announcement in 1998 signalled the intention to change what was termed the procurement regime, to allow only local authorities, as long as they had the capacity, to be developers of low-income housing projects with effect from April 2002. The Director-General in the Housing department labelled this 'a fundamental departure' (cited in Housing in Southern Africa 1998: 9), signifying as it did a shift away from the public–private partnerships approach of the NHF and towards a more state-centred, state-driven approach (Smit interview).

A range of possible influences on this policy shift can be identified; what is more difficult, however, is to make direct causal linkages. Some of our respondents saw this increase in the role of local government in housing delivery as reflecting a broader move towards the creation of a strong local state (Smit interview). It was important politically for local government councillors to gain greater control over one of the most visible aspects of state delivery (ibid.), particularly with respect to the sequence of implementation of housing projects and the allocations of houses to beneficiaries.

In addition, investigations by government suggested that a more active role for the state was needed to overcome obstacles which had become evident in the development process and to speed up delivery (Tomlinson 1998). Also, problems caused by a project-by-project approach to housing delivery had begun highlighting the need for spatial and programmatic alignment with integrated development planning (a local government planning tool under discussion in the late 1990s), particularly with respect to the delivery of bulk services. This suggested greater involvement of municipalities in the process than had been the case to date (Walker interview).

Apart from this, the focus on state-centred delivery can also be related to a reaction against the negative perceptions of the white construction sector, and a concern for getting the best deal for beneficiaries through maximising value gained from the subsidy (Tomlinson 1998). There were increasing indications of shoddy construction and perceptions of developers 'fleecing' the system (Smit interview). Some say that these problems had arisen from a misplaced faith in the integrity of the private sector and a failure to adequately manage their involvement in housing (Nell and Rust interviews).

It was also becoming apparent that there was increasing discomfort amongst private developers with the difficulties associated with low-income housing delivery. New procedural requirements were being introduced – such as environmental requirements in terms of the National Environmental Management Act (No. 107 of 1998) – construction costs were increasing, demands for bigger and better quality houses were surfacing (Tomlinson 1998) and the subsidy was not being adjusted for inflation. In addition, some of the subsidy milestones that secured payment to developers – such as township establishment, and transfer of title deeds – were fraught with complication and delays, increasing the financial risk to developers, who were unable to make a profit within the constraints of the policy (Tomlinson 1998). Eventually, these problems led to the withdrawal of private sector actors, and consequently a downturn in low-income housing delivery (see for example CMDA, BESG, First Metro & Metro Housing 2001).

Nevertheless, caution must be exercised in attributing the announcement of the new procurement regime to this downturn in delivery. Whilst housing delivery rates have since declined, they were at a peak in 1997/98 (DoH 2003). It is not clear that the withdrawal of developers and the downturn in delivery prompted thinking on the procurement regime which, while taking effect only in April 2002, was mooted in 1998 and approved by Housing MinMEC (the meeting of national and provincial housing ministers)[13] in May 2000. The Department of Housing's website suggests other factors, explaining the shift towards more state-centred delivery as follows: 'In response to the requirements of the Constitution, 1996, and the Public Finance Management Act,

1999, as well as the trend of uncoordinated and non-integrated housing development practices, the Government revised the process and rules for housing development through project approval under the Housing Subsidy Scheme' (DoH n.d.).

But the new procurement regime, it is argued, did not take into account the underlying rationale of the original partnership approach to delivery between the state and private sector, which was related to real limitations in the state's capacity to deliver or manage delivery (Nell interview; Tomlinson 1998). The procurement regime, placing yet another set of demands on an overburdened local government, has since been identified as one of the factors leading to a downturn in delivery volumes since the peak of delivery in 1998 (Charlton et al. 2003).[14] Importantly for our analysis of policy influences, this shift in policy was only partly related to enhancing the impact of the housing programme on the lives of the poor, and as Tomlinson (1998) notes, key questions in this regard remained unanswered at this time.

The reconfiguration of roles in the housing sector had another facet to it. As the state strengthened its role in low-cost housing delivery, another parallel process was occurring which emphasised increased *beneficiary* involvement in housing. In 1998, the department formally introduced the Peoples' Housing Process (PHP), a programme aimed at involving greater beneficiary input in housing delivery – at least, the 'top-structure' component of it (Huchzermeyer 2001). Notions of community participation had been part of the original housing policy, manifesting in the early years in the requirement for a 'social compact' between developers and communities. However, the meaning of community participation had not been clearly defined and its interpretation had varied widely across projects.

The introduction of the PHP resulted from a range of internal and external influences, including local grassroots organisations – such as the Homeless People's Federation – which were lobbying for greater beneficiary participation in the production of housing (Nell interview), and the UN, whose international experiences showed that beneficiary participation resulted in more responsive and effective low-cost housing delivery. The efficacy of the PHP is widely contested, and its realisation has encountered many problems. For example, it has tended to institutionalise a community-based process that is often organised around community networks. The random nature of plot allocations by government has tended to disrupt these networks and may unfavourably impact on the social and economic structures of the beneficiary communities. Comments acclaiming the benefit of the PHP for the poor, and the 'meaningful and lasting improvement in their quality of life' (see Napier 2003: 351), are therefore countered by perceptions that the state is abrogating its responsibility and shifting the burden of delivery to the poor (Khan & Ambert 2003a). But this debate aside, the introduction of the PHP into housing policy highlighted the conception of beneficiaries as active participants in the production of their own housing structures – a conception that some contend is important for responding to the housing needs of the poor. Notable for this chapter, however, is the point that participation is largely limited to house construction, with little influence by beneficiaries over key issues that may have a bearing on poverty such as the location of housing projects.

## Social housing

A second policy development during the 1990s saw the introduction of social housing – an institutional form of housing management which is often, and confusingly, conflated with rental housing in South African policy discourse. Although a mass state rental programme was clearly not envisaged in the policy adopted in 1994, the notion of rental housing provided by institutions was included in the White Paper on Housing as one of the subsidy programmes. However, this form of housing took some time to get off the ground.

Delivery of social housing during the 1990s was driven by a strong external influence. Through agreements with governments and organisations in the UK, Norway, Netherlands, European Union, and Canada, these social housing lobbyists have had a strong influence in South Africa, providing a significant amount of multilateral aid, technical support, international travel and exchange (Nell interview). Internally, the trade unions have been vocal in demanding a form of social housing delivery (Tomlinson 1999a), promoting the creation of a public housing agency to develop and own formal rental stock (Huchzermeyer 2001).

Increasingly, social housing is seen to be the solution to critiques that the RDP housing programme reinforces urban sprawl and the spatial form of the apartheid city. However, the complexities of the financial model, *inter alia*, have meant that social housing has had limited impact in terms of numbers of units delivered, accounting for only about 1.5 per cent of housing production by 2003. This is despite a high-profile Presidential Jobs Summit Pilot Project on Housing launched in 1998, which aimed to deliver 50 000 rental units by the end of 2000 (Huchzermeyer 2001: 316). In addition, social housing has generally only been able to reach a very narrow target group at the upper end of the main subsidy income qualification limit of R3 500 per household, relying as it does on a capital subsidy from government and no operating subsidy. Thus, it has had a fairly limited reach on the poor and until recently it was not considered an effective housing solution for very low-income beneficiaries.[15]

## Shifting norms and standards

A third policy shift can be seen in the introduction of the 'norms and standards' in 1999, which placed increasing focus on improving the quality of the top-structure or house. Ironically, this resulted in a compromise on the service levels. Delivery to date had produced starter houses which varied widely in size and quality, and service specifications were consuming large portions of the subsidy at the expense of the top-structure. Government was starting to have to deal with taunts such as 'Mandela's houses are half the size of Verwoerd's' (Nell interview; Tomlinson 1998). Consequently, regulations were introduced specifying the minimum size and specification of the top-structure.

A corollary of this was that limited money was spent on services, and as such pit latrines, communal stand pipes, and gravel roads – standards which were informed by models of health and safety accepted by other government departments – were viewed as acceptable by the Department of Housing, anxious to be able to deliver on the number and size of houses. In practice, some municipalities – such as the Durban Metropolitan Council – were able to provide higher levels of service through providing additional infrastructure grants. Nevertheless, in other areas the minimum levels of service prescribed by the department reinforced the trend for housing projects to be located on peripheral land where lower service levels were more acceptable.[16] This policy adjustment, driven by a political need to deliver acceptable houses, was not rooted in a deeper understanding of the consequences of the service levels/location/top-structure trade-off on beneficiaries. Rather, it was a reactive move related to the historic rejection of the notion of incrementalism – the gradual consolidation of a starter house over time by the end-user[17] – and may again, in fact, have further contributed to the spatial marginalisation of the poor.

## Lack of substantial policy evolution

The policy shifts described, and others not dealt with here,[18] are by and large reactions to weaknesses with the experience of policy implementation or, as illustrated, are driven by other agendas such as political pressures or internal departmental politics. They are not, however, explicitly rooted in a rigorous interrogation of the needs of the poor, such as the impact of the housing programme on livelihoods and economic activity of the poor beneficiaries.

In fact, this lack of a clear process of policy evolution, underpinned by a rigorous conceptual framework, has been highlighted by some of our respondents. They argued that at its inception, the 1994 housing policy was understood to be the beginning of a policy process of evolution rather than the final product (Cobbett and Nell interviews). From this perspective, instead of the shifts in policy described earlier, it was envisaged that a more fundamental conceptual progression of policy would occur. The subsequent lack of follow-through is seen to be directly related to the personalities of those involved: 'If Cobbett[19] had stayed there would have been a second-phase reconceptualisation of policy. He was strong conceptually – and he was fully aware of the compromises that had been made and why. Subsequent personalities, while strong politically, were not strong conceptually' (Nell interview). Other commentators (see for example Huchzermeyer 2001; Khan & Ambert 2003a) argue that the Housing White Paper of 1994 makes it clear that further debate was not the intention, at least at that time: 'The time for policy debate is now past – the time for delivery has arrived' (RSA 1994: 4).

In any event, in the early days of implementation of the policy, various pressures restricted the potential for policy refinement (Cobbett interview). One of these pressures was the imperative to deliver in the face of high expectations (Smit interview): to mobilise the bureaucrats and 'go and do it' (Narsoo interview). Delivery had to live up to the commitments made by the new government to deliver 'one million low-cost houses' in five years (ANC 1994: Clause 2.5.2).[20] Other processes contributed to the 'rooting' of policy in its initial form. Firstly, key players in the NHF negotiating process moved into government housing administration[21] or became advisers to officials. Secondly, the NHF didn't just produce a *policy*, but also the machinery of housing – 'the operational stuff' was negotiated and put in place[22] (Nell interview). In addition, Narsoo notes that housing was designated as a concurrent national and provincial function. Consequently MinMEC – which, as noted earlier, is a meeting of *political* leaders in the provincial and national spheres – became a significant forum for policy adjustment (Narsoo interview).

Constraints in the broader policy and institutional environment also contributed to the entrenchment of the initial policy. Housing was 'ahead of its time' – the formation of related urban policies lagged behind.[23] There was no legitimate local government in place until several years later. A new housing policy was being introduced and implemented at the same time as government was redesigning itself. 'It was like driving a bus with one hand tied behind your back'[24] (Cobbett interview). The notion of integrated development planning and the operationalisation of this were still some years away. In many parts of the country, therefore, the planning framework proved to be too weak to moderate or address the negative impacts of the housing programme (Smit interview), which developed its own momentum through the vigour of implementation. 'It may be that (the) failure to explicitly and systematically integrate housing policy into a coherent strategy of "urban restructuring" is the current framework's most important deficiency' (Wilkinson 1998: 226).

Other factors influenced the lack of engagement with key policy weaknesses in the early years, such as the highly charged issue of accessing well-located land for housing. In the mid-1990s 'no one wanted the boat rocked too badly' (Cobbett interview). The subsequent failure of housing policy to engage with the complexities of the land market (see for example Huchzermeyer 2001; Khan 2003b) is referred to by Berrisford as the 'reluctance of the nation's urban elite' (1999: 1) to grapple with an issue in which they themselves may hold a significant stake. A consequence of this is that in the early years the rapid delivery of housing ended up happening where existing institutions – such as the Urban Foundation's New Housing Company, and the South African Housing Trust – had already acquired land, which was predominantly on the edge of former townships (Narsoo interview).

Some aspects of policy did receive ongoing attention, such as the issue of access to finance by the poor. The assumption in the policy was that 'in addition to their subsidies from the government, low-income families would be able to obtain mortgage bonds that they would then be able to use to help acquire something more in line with the vision of a four-room house' (Tomlinson 1999a: 288). Attempts by government and the financial sector to reach agreement on their participation in low-income housing have been ongoing, and there is substantial research and commentary on the complexities of access to finance by low-income households (see for example Tomlinson 1997). Observers have commented that this reflects a narrow focus on the supply of housing finance 'while the more complex demand-side issues (related to low-income and poverty) are still little understood and given less attention' (Khan & Ambert 2003a: xiii). Indeed, questions have been raised on the extent and nature of the focus on the financial sector when the vast majority of the target group have not been in a position to access formal financial products (Tomlinson 1999a; Jones & Datta 2000).

The focus on access to loan finance was rooted in the notion that the best producers of housing were in fact the urban poor themselves, supported by government. This concept of the 'progressive' realisation of the housing rights over time was deeply unpopular amongst some sectors of the ANC. It was supported, however, by the first Minister of Housing, Joe Slovo, who prevented an attempt on the day of the signing of the milestone Botshabelo Accord in 1994 (discussed later) to remove the keyword 'incremental' from the document[25] (Cobbett interview). Nevertheless, it is clear that this issue of incrementalism remained highly contentious, as is illustrated by very negative statements by the first premier of Gauteng in 1994 (cited in Goodlad 1996) and subsequent attention accorded this issue.

## The formulation of the post-apartheid housing policy

The apparent lack of policy development during the 1990s needs to be viewed in light of the policy that was adopted in 1994, and the processes that had led to this. Housing was a key component of the RDP, the ANC government's manifesto for a post-apartheid South Africa (Nell interview; RSA 1994). Housing was considered to be one of the basic services whose delivery was seen as a means of poverty alleviation. However, it has also been noted that while the housing policy formulation process was happening in parallel with the RDP drafting process, the two processes did not connect as well as they should have (Cobbett interview), with some commentators arguing that while organised labour and community were instrumental in producing the RDP, the private sector dominated housing policy formulation (Huchzermeyer 2001).

On 27 October 1994, the newly elected post-apartheid government hosted the National Housing Summit in Botshabelo, which enabled it to secure formal support from key stakeholders for the new housing policy and strategy (Wilkinson 1998). This strategy was by and large the result of an extensive period of multi-stakeholder negotiation which took place between 1992 and 1994 at the highly significant NHF where the nature and form of a post-apartheid housing policy were debated.

Ultimately 19 different interest groups were represented at the NHF.[26] Despite this range of participants, critics have noted the lack of participation by certain marginalised groupings, including intended beneficiaries of the programme (Lalloo 1999; Jones & Datta 2000). In particular Huchzermeyer (2001) highlights the lack of influence of the thinking of the non-governmental organisation People's Dialogue and the grassroots organisation Homeless People's Federation, both concerned with savings and credit for the poor, and neither of which participated at the NHF. This may be because the Homeless People's Federation was only formalised in 1994. Huchzermeyer (2001) argues that its thinking has subsequently influenced policy.

*Positions at the National Housing Forum*

Huchzermeyer (2001) identifies two main 'camps' with different strands of thinking amongst those represented at the NHF: one was the Mass Democratic Movement (the ANC, the Congress of South African Trade Unions and the civic movement), and the other was the 'profit-making sector' (business, mining and industry). Two key issues under debate at the NHF were the nature of the product to be delivered in the housing programme, and the role of the state in the delivery process.

The business-aligned grouping promoted 'site and service' – individual plots of land with basic services, on which beneficiaries would build their own houses. The Mass Democratic Movement, on the other hand, was in favour of formal state-provided rental accommodation, and looked to examples from Europe and the UK. Tomlinson notes, for different reasons, both 'the constituencies on the Left and the private construction sector argued that the government should provide mass rental housing' (1999a: 286), one from the point of view of a high-quality end product for the users, and the other from the point of view of maximising profit through their role as contractors of a formal product.

For the ANC, self-build and site and service were 'seen as falling far short of the demand for a decently located genuine mass-housing programme' (Tomlinson 1999a: 284). Similarly, the position of the small not-for-profit delivery sector was that of 'no more toilets in the veld' (Nell interview), a reference to the site and service programme of the Independent Development Trust (IDT), the apartheid government's development agency.

In the early 1990s, the IDT had been servicing sites through the use of a capital subsidy to the value of R7 500 per site (Lalloo 1999; Tomlinson 1999a: 284). The notion of capital subsidies, shaped by Urban Foundation thinking (Huchzermeyer 2001), was brought onto the agenda of the NHF through a high-level think tank at the Foundation (Smit interview; Adler & Oelofse 1996), a private sector-funded development organisation.

In the face of the capital subsidy option, 'the left' was challenged to 'put on the table clear proposals' with respect to a mass rental programme – how it could be financed and managed. It was unable to convincingly do so (Smit interview). Therefore '…lessons drawn from providing rental housing, both in South Africa and around the world, were used in the debates to demonstrate the financial and administrative burden such an approach would create for a fledgling government' (Tomlinson 1999a: 286).

However, while international experience could point to the financial and administrative dangers of state rental housing, reservations had also been expressed in the literature on site and service (Walker interview). Discussion at the NHF highlighted the tension between targeting as many as possible with some form of basic housing provision versus targeting a lucky few with a complete housing package – the 'breadth versus depth' debate.

Attention focused on what was economically feasible. Some of our respondents suggested that there was a pragmatic recognition in certain circles in the left that a massive state rental housing programme was not possible, given the scale of the backlog (Smit and Walker interviews). This was influenced by an understanding of the need to grow the economy, and that housing should not become a financial drain (Smit interview).

Goodlad notes also that a case was put forward for incremental development – site and service supported by a capital subsidy – 'as the only form (of housing) which took account of the need to avoid large rental, maintenance or loan payment for the poorest people' (1996: 1643). There was also recognition that the ownership of assets had a high political priority: 'people wanted land and housing' (Nell interview). As Wilkinson notes, it had 'become conventional wisdom that most, if not all, households should become homeowners with full freehold tenure' (1998: 224), and that this should take the form of detached dwelling units.

Supported by international trends which were moving away from interest-based subsidies towards capital subsidies (and the control over the budget that this represented), it was also recognised that capital subsidies are simpler to implement where government capacity is limited (Smit interview). This recognition of the need to deliver – or, as some see it, the 'preoccupation with delivery' (Pottie 2003: 136) – was another major influence on policy formulation. Politically related violence in the hostels in the late 1980s and early 1990s had been a catalyst for the formation of the NHF (Rust 1996). Visible intervention into poor living conditions was considered crucial, therefore. Fuelled by the palpable feeling of political tension in the build-up to the first democratic elections, the NHF was focused on structuring a major delivery initiative. Debates were shaped by the need for simplicity in process, focusing around what worked in delivery terms (Smit interview).

This highlighted a second major area of debate at the NHF: the role of the state versus the market. 'Early on, the NHF had to decide whether the government should provide the housing or set up the framework within which the private sector would provide it' (DoH White Paper, 1994, cited in Tomlinson 1999a: 286).

While the Urban Foundation and its partners advocated a market-driven approach (Nell interview), the ANC and the not-for-profit sector envisaged the leading role in housing delivery being state driven. However, the ANC position had not been formalised and negotiators did not have a clear, approved position or mandate (Cobbett interview). Arguments swayed in favour of the partnership approach – a facilitative state which drew in the resources and implementation capacity of the private sector (Smit interview).

When the IDT announced the end of its capital subsidy programme in 1992, it was recognised at the NHF that there was an urgent need to continue with delivery whilst policy deliberations were unfolding (Rust 1996). The NHF proposed that a R1.2 billion special off-budget allocation be made to a Joint Housing Board, which would provide subsidies for low-income earners. It is acknowledged that there were 'more sophisticated gains for housing policy' which arose from this proposal: it forced consensus on a set of common policy principles, and necessitated the creation of interim capacity for delivery (Nell, Mkhabela, Rust & Du Plessis 1996: 53). Some analysts also argue that this focus on delivery sidetracked deliberations at the NHF away from critical debates on the spatial impact of capital subsidies and urban restructuring, which were never resolved (Adler & Oelofse 1996 and Lalloo 1999, both cited in Huchzermeyer 2001). Others note that the NHF had working groups[27] dealing with different aspects of policy formulation, including land and services, and restructuring the built environment, and that ultimately responsibility for building integrated cities was passed on to municipalities for consideration in the future.[28]

A grouping on the left accepted an approach which mixed housing associations (for rental) with a capital subsidy approach (Smit interview). Crucially, some say, at a point Billy Cobbett, chief negotiator for the ANC at the NHF, bought into the capital subsidy approach (ibid.). Huchzermeyer suggests that acceptance of the capital subsidy model was because key elements of the approach coincided with 'the ANC's interpretation of democracy' (2000: 11). Classifying the capital subsidy model as that of the Urban Foundation, she suggests that 'the political gain to be made out of the Urban Foundation proposal overshadowed key contradictions' (2000: 12).

The subsidy scheme is by far the most enduring and dominant contribution to the policy legacy of the many negotiations of NHF. Indeed, it has been noted that 'the work done by the NHF on housing subsidies was perhaps its key contribution to the new national housing policy' (Adler & Oelofse 1996: 109). In selecting a capital subsidy approach, what was chosen, in effect, was a system that could be defended fiscally – a clear, once-off amount with apparently no hidden costs to the state (Narsoo interview[29]).

However, the product that was agreed to was a variation of key positions at the NHF. The inclusion of a basic starter house was a compromise of the Urban Foundation's site and service approach (Nell interview), and distinguished the new policy from that of the previous government (Huchzermeyer 2001).

Some therefore hold the view that agreements reached at the NHF were, to a greater or lesser degree, a compromise for all of the negotiating positions taken at the NHF: 'The NHF came up with something which everyone (at the Forum) could live with but which suited no one in the end' (Walker interview). Others, however, refer to the 'tyranny of expertise' that dominated processes at the NHF through the reliance on technical inputs (Marais cited in Pottie 2003: 131), which were based on both current research, and also earlier research undertaken at the Urban Foundation.[30]

## A dominant business agenda?

Some analyses of the negotiating process at the NHF have focused on the manipulation and domination of the process by the outgoing government and big business (see for example the synopsis in Khan 2003b), whilst Narsoo, without elaborating, refers to the ANC as the 'dominant organisation within the NHF' (2000: 2). Nevertheless, it is generally acknowledged that not all parties had the same capacity to engage effectively at the NHF, with the establishment (profit-making sector) – articulated by the Urban Foundation – having disproportionate strength and resources (Smit and Cobbett interviews; Khan 2003b). This, it is argued, related in part to the resource limitations of the proponents of the left (see for example Pottie 2003), as well as the generally disadvantaged position of the Mass Democratic Movement in that unstable, pre-democracy period, for a variety of reasons (Lalloo 1999).

However, some of our respondents argued that it is misleading to characterise the debates at the NHF as a simple bipolar debate between the profit-making sector and the left (the Mass Democratic Movement) (Smit interview). They argue that processes were much more messy, with overlapping positions and similarities in thinking that cut across political divides. In part, it is suggested, this related to the actual process of debate, in which parties with different interests worked together and got to understand each other's thinking (ibid.). As a result, some observers comment, the NHF *collectively* looked at different models from around the world (Cobbett interview).[31]

Forging consensus was in keeping with the mood of the time, which was marked by a shift in thinking from oppositional politics to 'how do you run this place' (Smit interview). This was the time of negotiation, in the spirit of 'let's do a deal' (Nell interview). The ANC was concerned with finding a solution, recognising the need for operational pragmatism to achieve impact. 'What worked counted' (Smit interview).

Khan (2003b) warns of the danger of this consensual or lowest common denominator model of policy formulation. Conflicting views are not engaged with, and contradictory goals are accommodated within a policy framework. Hendler contends that, 'The NHF emphasised consensus building, which resulted in a relatively undefined housing process that was all things to all people…the result was not the formulation of a new housing policy but rather the continuation and development of the existing one' (1999: 14).

This consensual approach is seen by Huchzermeyer to relate to 'the "pacted" nature of the South African transition, in which the private sector had a powerful leverage over both the outgoing National Party government (which was rapidly losing power) and the incoming ANC, which was increasingly dependent on support from the established business sector' (2001: 308). It is also argued that compromise and mutual co-option of ideas – 'transplacement' – happens in times of negotiation in ways that do not threaten dominant established interests (Khan 2003b: 13).

This critique of the housing negotiation process is located within a particular perspective that contends that the extent of 'transformation' of South Africa has been limited and that transition has involved the co-option of an 'acceptable' socio-economic order and a reconfiguration of the elite, thus limiting the range of pro-poor development options under consideration (Khan 2003b). The shift to the Growth, Employment and Redistribution strategy in 1996 is seen to have further entrenched the belief in a market-friendly economic order, limiting 'policy manoeuvrability' and resulting in the 'consequent neo-conservative straightjacketing of development policy deliberations' (Khan 2003b: 5). Increasingly, the ANC is seen to be defending its housing and infrastructure development policies by extolling the virtues of fiscal discipline and sustainability (Pottie 2003), rather than direct benefit to the poor. Pottie further argues that housing policy 'failed to redress the prevailing balance of power that determined the development process and compromised the prospects of socio-economic policy that favoured the working class and the unemployed' (2003: 122).

*External influences on policy decisions*

A variety of other factors influenced the content of the housing policy negotiated between 1992 and 1994. Influences included the World Bank through its missions to South Africa (Jones & Datta 2000). Gilbert (2002) notes, however, that despite a considerable number of visits and advice from the World Bank, *overt* adoption of World Bank thinking was limited, *inter alia*, he argues, because of the ANC's wary attitude to the Bank as well as the pressure to reach a compromise on policy quickly. Knowledge on housing options was acquired from a wide range of sources, including international study visits to various countries by development professionals (Gilbert 2002). Nevertheless, whilst his general impression is that 'South Africans invented their own capital subsidy policy' (2002: 1919), the policy bears many similarities to policies elsewhere in the world and 'some kind of learning process was involved, even if there was not much sign of copying' (2002: 1928). Goodlad, on the other hand, notes that 'although some international influences are apparent (the housing strategy) has no close similarity to any other nation state's strategy' (1996: 1644).

The international context was also critical in shaping outcomes at the NHF. In the late 1980s communism collapsed in eastern Europe. Other influences included the existence and imminent closure of the IDT's capital subsidy model, which was in line with the Urban Foundation's negotiating position, supported by their research of international experience. Furthermore, macroeconomic concerns about the cost of a future housing programme, central in other debating forums at the time, were significant. Pragmatism around operational implementation of a housing programme was also a crucial influence, fuelled by a heightened sense of urgency of the need to demonstrate delivery.

Oelofse (2003) argues that the policy was founded on the RDP's basic human needs approach, which emphasised the provision of public services to the poor. Crucially for the analysis in this chapter, however, a range of untested assumptions were made about the needs of the poor (Wilkinson 1998) and, it is argued, negative aspects of past experience of capital subsidies were not interrogated (Jones & Datta 2000). Tomlinson questions whether the formulators of the policy 'overestimated the positive impact on poor people's budgets of a subsidised dwelling' (1998: 21). As one respondent put it, 'What we didn't look at were livelihoods. Is that a failure? Maybe, but things were driven by RDP targets' (Narsoo interview).

## Conclusion

In considering the influences on the post-apartheid housing policy in South Africa we have used the lens – prevalent in government discourse in 2004 – of the contribution of the housing benefit to the lives of the poor. We note that the emphasis in policy adopted in 1994 is on meeting basic needs. Nevertheless, an underlying assumption, alluded to in some official documents, is of the relationship between housing delivery and poverty alleviation. However, policy *drivers* at this time are not clearly related to an analysis of what intervention would make the most impact on the lives of the poor, but are largely those of pragmatism, workability, and feasibility.

Over the next ten years, policy was adjusted to greater or lesser degrees, but has remained largely within the original framework adopted in 1994. These adjustments have been largely reactive to negative aspects of the policy which become evident through implementation, and have been influenced more by political agendas and international influences than a rigorous examination of what works for the poor. Furthermore, it is suggested that a critical phase of policy evolution did not ever materialise in the 1990s. Nevertheless, as we have illustrated, the link between housing delivery and poverty alleviation persists in various official documentation and statements.

By 2004, a far more explicit focus on poverty reduction in relation to housing was evident in government discourse. A new housing plan was announced and introduced within this discourse. Again, however, the policy adjustments contained in this plan are not clearly related to an analysis of the impact on beneficiaries' lives (see also Huchzermeyer 2001). In addition, the policy direction announced is only in part the result of a fairly extensive research process initiated by the Department of Housing and intended to influence policy direction.

The lack of clear process evident in policy formulation over the last 13 years is indicative of the range of factors influencing policy. These include the difficulties of tackling major areas of political sensitivity (Huchzermeyer 2001), other contextual issues such as personalities, political pressure and underlying policy contradictions. Research is also an influence on policy, but its direct impact is not always clear – its focus is often not clearly aligned with recently articulated policy intentions, as is indicated by the limited range of research which explicitly focuses on the relationship between housing policy and poverty. This, it appears, is part of the explanation for the gap between policy and its impact on the lives of the poor.

*Notes*

1   By the end of the 2002/03 financial year almost 1.5 million houses had been delivered (RSA 2003b).

2   Named after the ANC government's Reconstruction and Development Programme.

3   During the mid-1990s this 'starter house' sometimes consisted of building materials in projects where land and servicing costs consumed most of the subsidy amount.

4   Household income is defined as the combined income of household head and spouse.

5   Certain categories of 'vulnerable groupings' – such as the disabled – are exempt from this requirement.

6   Although *Breaking New Ground* has been approved by Cabinet, we are unclear about its status as a public document as it seems to be unavailable in publicly accessible forums such as the Internet or the Government Communications Department.

7   The term 'asset' is used in different ways in the discourse, but is generally meant to include both a use value and an exchange value. Recent research by the Finmark Trust into the townships residential property market has highlighted the latent but trapped financial value of existing housing stock.

8   To show its commitment to the Habitat Agenda, signed at the UN conference on Human Settlements in Istanbul in 1996, the Department of Housing established a Directorate of Human Settlement Policy and Integration, responsible for the formulation of the Urban Development Framework (Huchzermeyer 2001), although the Framework has had no real influence on policy (Napier interview).

9   A World Bank and UN-Habitat initiative which takes the form of a global coalition of cities and development partners focused on improving the living conditions of the urban poor.

10  It remains unclear whether the Treasury will provide the fiscal support to implement all of these plans (Napier interview).

11  At the time of writing Deputy Director-General: Policy and Programme Management, Department of Housing.

12  Some comment that most housing research post-1994 was happening through organisations such as the United States Agency for International Development-funded Housing Finance Resource Programme (Rust interview). While some of this research was linked directly to

concerns of the Department of Housing, Vawda emphasises the lack of research capacity within the department at this time.

13  In 2000 Narsoo contended that the Housing Minmecs 'remain the most influential forums for policy making in relation to housing' (2000: 3).

14  Interestingly, *Breaking New Ground* re-emphasises the role of the private sector in housing delivery, perhaps in reaction to the downturn delivery figures.

15  A new social housing policy has now been drafted which explicitly tries to include at least some lower-income beneficiaries.

16  When projects were located in close proximity to existing townships, a key area of negotiation was that projects should have the same or higher levels of service.

17  Interestingly, while it was anticipated that the first group of beneficiaries would indicate dissatisfaction with the policy because of the basic nature of the starter house they received, research indicated that this was not the case and press reports in this regard appeared to reflect rather the view of the MECs of Housing and the provincial premiers who, on taking office, began to challenge aspects of the policy (Tomlinson 1999a).

18  Such as the responses to the Grootboom judgement.

19  The first Director-General in the post-apartheid Housing department, who resigned in 1996.

20  Lalloo contends that 'the ANC felt compelled to do this in response to (pre-election) rhetoric from the apartheid state about its own commitment to "build houses for everyone"' (Lalloo 1999: 40).

21  For example, Billy Cobbett (head of the ANC negotiations at the NHF) became the first Director-General of housing in the post-1994 administration. Monty Narsoo (NHF negotiator for the South African National Civic Organisation) moved from the NHF to the Gauteng provincial government's housing department (Nell interview).

22  In the early 1990s the institutional environment in the housing sector was severely fragmented.

23  It has been noted that its particular genesis, during the transition period but prior to the achievement of democracy, means that housing policy is 'rooted in the pre-1994 era' (Khan & Ambert 2003a: iv), unlike other policy and legislation of the post-apartheid government.

24  Nevertheless, the institutions of the Mortgage Indemnity Fund, Servcon, the National Housing Finance Corporation and the National Home Builders Registration Council were all established in record time (in global terms) (Cobbett interview). In this regard Khan comments on the influence of conventional development wisdom of the time in the drive to establish corporatist institutional arrangements as a means to defuse conflict and 'stabilise a new regime of state-society relations' (Khan 2003b: 13).

25  Others contend that the incremental policy was endorsed by Minister Slovo during a period of unrealistic expectations about the economy and the nature of the transition (Bond & Tait 1997).

26  These were: African National Congress, Association for Community Housing and Reconstruction, Association of Mortgage Lenders, Azanian People's Organisation, Building Material Suppliers Consortium, Business South Africa, Congress of South African Trade Unions, Construction Consortium, Democratic Party of South Africa, Development Bank of Southern Africa, Independent Development Trust, Inkatha Freedom Party, Kagiso Trust, Life Officers

Association, Non Profit Housing Delivery Sector, Pan Africanist Congress, South African National Civic Organisation, South African Housing Trust, Urban Foundation (Rust 1996).

27    Richard Tomlinson, commenting on an earlier draft of this chapter, notes that substantial research informed the deliberations of the Forum's Working Group 6 (dealing with hostels).

28    Richard Tomlinson, in commenting on an earlier draft of this chapter.

29    Narsoo in fact refers to the fiscal discipline of the housing programme as a 'fore-runner to GEAR' (interview), the government's Growth, Employment and Redistribution programme.

30    Research related to housing delivery undertaken at the Urban Foundation in the 1980s and early 1990s mainly focused on two areas, land and finance. Land issues included land assembly, land-legal obstacles, various tenure options and the identification of land for housing. Financial issues concerned capital versus interest-based subsidies, the extension of credit to the poor, end-user finance and new loan products of various kinds. Investigations took the form of both local and international research as well as the testing of ideas through physical projects. Examples of projects included housing delivery through site and service on vacant land, and informal settlement upgrading (Strelitz interview).

31    In commenting on this chapter, Monty Narsoo emphasised the persistence of different perspectives and interpretations of what transpired at the NHF deliberations.

*References*

Adler T & Oelofse M (1996) The housing subsidy scheme. In K Rust & S Rubenstein (eds), *A mandate to build:  Developing consensus around a national housing policy in South Africa.* Johannesburg: Ravan Press.

ANC (African National Congress) (1994) *The Reconstruction and Development Programme.* Johannesburg: Umanyano Publications.

Baumann T (2003) Housing policy and poverty in South Africa. In F Khan & P Thring (eds), *Housing policy and practice in post-apartheid South Africa.* Sandown: Heinemann.

Berrisford S (1999) Redistribution of land rights in South Africa: Simply a rural question? Paper presented at the IRGLUS/CALS workshop Redefining Property Rights in an Era of Liberalisation and Privatisation. University of the Witwatersrand, Johannesburg, 29–30 July.

Bond (2003) The degeneration of urban policy after apartheid.  In P Harrison, M Huchzermeyer & M Mayekiso (eds), *Confronting fragmentation: Housing and urban development in a democratising society.* Cape Town: UCT Press.

Bond P & Tait A (1997) The failure of housing policy in post-apartheid South Africa, *Urban Forum,* 8(1): 19–41.

Charlton S, Silverman M & Berrisford S (2003) Taking stock: A review of the Department of Housing's programme, policies and practice (1994–2003). Report prepared for the Department of Housing.

CMDA (Cato Manor Development Association), BESG (Built Environment Support Group), First Metro, Metro Housing (2001) Housing projects trends analysis (Draft 2). Unpublished document submitted to the Institute for Housing of Southern Africa. Durban: CMDA Resource Centre.

Development Works (2004) Synthesis Report. Research in support of the Policy and Research Agenda. Unpublished document prepared for the Department of Housing.

DoH (Department of Housing) (2000) *National Housing Code.* Available at <http://www. housing.gov.za/content/housing_code/part1/chapter4.htm>. Accessed on 7 March 2005.

DoH (2003) *National Housing Programme overview of achievements and challenges 1994–2003.* Pretoria: DoH.

DoH (2004) *Breaking New Ground: A comprehensive plan for the development of sustainable human settlements.* Pretoria: DoH.

DoH (n.d.) *Project Linked Greenfield Housing Subsidy Projects.* Available at <http://www.housing. gov.za/content/Greenfields/index.htm>. Accessed on 5 February 2005.

Esteva G (1993) Development. In W Sachs (ed.), *The development dictionary: A guide to knowledge as power.* Johannesburg: Zed Books.

Gelb S (2003) *Inequality in South Africa: Nature, causes and responses.* Johannesburg: Department for International Development.

Gilbert A (2002) 'Scan globally; reinvent locally': Reflecting on the origins of South Africa's Capital Housing Subsidy Policy, *Urban Studies*, 39(10): 1911–1933.

Gilbert A (2004) Helping the poor through housing subsidies: Lessons from Chile, Colombia and South Africa, *Habitat International*, 28: 13–40.

Goodlad R (1996) The housing challenge in South Africa, *Urban Studies*, 33(9): 1629–1645.

Hendler P (1999) Living in apartheid's shadow: 25 years of housing and urban policies in South Africa, *Housing in Southern Africa*, February: 14–16.

Housing in Southern Africa (1998) *A new voice: The new Director General of Housing speaks out.* Johannesburg: Institute for Housing of Southern Africa.

Housing in Southern Africa (1999) *Housing Minister outlines 5-year strategy.* Johannesburg: Institute for Housing of Southern Africa.

Huchzermeyer M (2000) A legacy of control? The Capital Subsidy and Informal Settlement Intervention in South Africa. Paper presented at the Urban Futures 2000 Conference. University of the Witwatersrand, Johannesburg, 10–14 July.

Huchzermeyer M (2001) Housing for the poor? Negotiated housing policy in South Africa, *Habitat International*, 25: 303–331.

Isandla Institute (2004) *Isandla Development Communique* 1(7). Available at <http://www. isandla.org.za>. Accessed on 15 October 2004.

Jones G & Datta K (2000) Enabling markets to work? Housing policy in the 'new' South Africa, *International Planning Studies*, 5(3): 393–416.

Khan F (2003a) Chopping block. Unpublished document produced for the Department of Housing.

Khan F (2003b) Continuities, ambiguities and contradictions. In F Khan & P Thring (eds), *Housing policy and practice in post-apartheid South Africa.* Sandown: Heinemann.

Khan F & Ambert C (2003a) Preface. In F Khan & P Thring (eds), *Housing policy and practice in post-apartheid South Africa.* Sandown: Heinemann.

Khan F & Ambert C (2003b) Introduction. In F Khan & P Thring (eds), *Housing policy and practice in post-apartheid South Africa*. Sandown: Heinemann.

Lalloo K (1999) Arenas of contested citizenship: Housing policy in South Africa, *Habitat International*, 23(1): 35–47.

Mabandla B (2003) Minister's Opening Address to the National Housing Summit. Gallagher Estate, 19 November.

Marx C (2003) Supporting informal settlements. In F Khan & P Thring (eds), *Housing policy and practice in post-apartheid South Africa*. Sandown: Heinemann.

Mbeki T (2004) *State of the Nation Address*. Available at <http://www.info.gov.za/speeches/2004/04052111151001.htm>. Accessed on 5 February 2005.

Mokate R, Schwabe C, Makinta V & O'Donovan M (1999) Spatial allocation of infrastructure and development spending in South Africa. Paper presented to workshop on Spatial Guidelines for Infrastructure Investment and Development, Pretoria. Cited in Khan (2003b).

Mpofu N (n.d.) Strategic Statement by the Director General Ms N Mpofu. Available at <http://www.housing.gov.za>. Accessed on 10 March 2005.

Napier M (2003) Supporting the people's housing process. In F Khan & P Thring (eds), *Housing policy and practice in post-apartheid South Africa*. Sandown: Heinemann.

Napier M (2004) Purpose and objectives of the National Housing Research Seminar. Paper presented to the National Housing Research Seminar on 23–24 March.

Narsoo M (2000) Critical policy issues in the emerging housing debate. Paper presented at the Urban Futures 2000 Conference. University of the Witwatersrand, Johannesburg, 10–14 July.

Nell M, Mkhabela I, Rust K & Du Plessis P (1996) Strategy and tactics: Planning and management in the NHF. In K Rust & S Rubenstein (eds), *A mandate to build: Developing consensus around a national housing policy in South Africa*. Johannesburg: Ravan Press.

Oelofse M (2003) An analysis of John Rawls' principles of social justice to planning: Issues arising form the implementation of the national housing subsidy programme in the inner city of Johannesburg. Doctoral thesis submitted to the Faculty of Engineering and the Built Environment, University of the Witwatersrand.

Pottie D (2003) Housing the nation: The politics of low-cost housing policy in South Africa since 1994, *Politeia*, 22(1): 119–143.

RSA (Republic of South Africa) (1994) *A New Housing Policy and Strategy for South Africa*. White Paper. Pretoria: Government Printer.

RSA (2003a) *Towards ten years of freedom – progress in the first decade, challenges of the second decade*. Available at <http://www.gov.za>. Accessed on 3 November 2004.

RSA (2003b) *Ten-year review: Social cluster overview report. Social development: Housing input 01 September 2003*. Also available as: Overview – 10 years of freedom. Chapter 3 in *South Africa Yearbook 2003/04*. Houghton: STE Publishers.

RSA (2003c) *Public Service Commission: Report on the Evaluation of the Housing Subsidy Scheme*. Available at <http://www.psc.gov.za/>.

RSA (2003d) *Towards ten years of freedom – progress in the first decade, challenges of the second decade.* Summary report. Available at <http://www.10years.gov.za/review/documents.htm>. Accessed on 10 March 2005.

RSA (2003e) *Towards a ten year review.* Available at <http://www.info.gov.za/otherdocs/2003/10yrbook.pdf>. Accessed on 10 March 2005.

Rust K (1996) The National Housing Forum: 1991–1995. In K Rust & S Rubenstein (eds), *A mandate to build: Developing consensus around a national housing policy in South Africa.* Johannesburg: Ravan Press.

Rust K (2003) *No short-cuts: South Africa's progress in implementing its housing policy 1994–2002.* Johannesburg: Institute for Housing of Southern Africa.

Sigodi Marah Martin for the Department of Housing (2003) *Towards a national housing policy and strategy agenda for the medium to long term stakeholder sector issues.*

Sisulu L (2004a) Speech given at the occasion of the tabling of the Budget Vote for the Department of Housing for the 2004/05 Financial Year. National Assembly, Cape Town, 10 June.

Sisulu L (2004b) Speech given at the occasion of the tabling of the Budget Vote for the Department of Housing for the Financial Year 2004/05. National Council of Provinces, Cape Town, 11 June.

Sisulu L (2004c) Speech given at the Public Policy Forum Meeting of Cities Alliance, Elangeni Hotel, Durban, 11 November.

Sisulu L (2004d) Statement by the Minister of Housing at the occasion of the parliamentary media briefing convened by the Government Communication and Information Systems, Cape Town, 25 May.

Sisulu L (2004e) Media statement issued by the Housing Ministry, 6 September 2004.

Smit W (2003) Housing Finance Policy in South Africa. In F Khan & P Thring (eds), *Housing policy and practice in post-apartheid South Africa.* Sandown: Heinemann.

Todes A (2003) Housing, integrated urban development and the compact city debate. In P Harrison, M Huchzermeyer & M Mayekiso (eds), *Confronting fragmentation: Housing and urban fevelopment in a democratising society.* Cape Town: UCT Press.

Tomlinson M (1997) Mortgage bondage? Financial institutions and low-cost housing delivery, *Social Policy Series,* Research report no. 56. Johannesburg: Centre for Policy Studies.

Tomlinson M (1998) Looking to the local: Local governments and low-cost housing delivery, *Social Policy Series,* Research report no. 63. Johannesburg: Centre for Policy Studies.

Tomlinson M (1999a) South Africa's Housing Policy: Lessons from four years of the new Housing Subsidy Scheme, *Third World Planning Review,* 21(3): 283–295.

Tomlinson M (1999b) From rejection to resignation: Beneficiaries' views on the South African Government's New Housing Subsidy system, *Urban Studies,* 36(8): 1349–1359.

Tomlinson R (2002) International best practice, enabling frameworks and the policy process: A South African case study, *International Journal of Urban and Regional Research,* 26(2): 377–388.

Wilkinson P (1998) Housing Policy in South Africa, *Habitat International,* 22(1): 215–229.

Zack T & Charlton S (2003) Better but ... Beneficiaries' perceptions of the government's housing subsidy scheme. Housing Finance Resource Programme Occasional Paper No. 12. Johannesburg: Housing Finance Resource Programme.

## Interviews

Cobbett B, representative at the National Housing Forum and former Director-General in the Department of Housing, 15 November 2004.

Napier M, former Acting Chief Director of Research in the Department of Housing, 27 October 2004.

Narsoo M, Sanco representative at the National Housing Forum and former Deputy Director-General of Policy and Programme Management in the Department of Housing, 30 September 2004.

Nell M, chairperson of the Coordinating Committee of the National Housing Forum and housing practitioner, 6 August 2004.

Rust K, coordinator at the National Housing Forum, 22 September 2004.

Smit D, consultant at the National Housing Forum and housing practitioner, 6 August 2004.

Strelitz J, representative at the National Housing Forum, 11 March 2005 (telephonic).

Vawda A, former Deputy Director-General of Policy and Programme Management in the Department of Housing, 18 November 2004.

Walker N, non-profit housing delivery sector representative at the National Housing Forum and housing practitioner, 5 October 2004.

# 12 Free basic services: The evolution and impact of free basic water policy in South Africa

Tim Mosdell

## Introduction and context

President Thabo Mbeki first announced the intention of government to provide free basic services at the Congress of South African Trade Unions (Cosatu) congress in September 2000 (Mbeki 2000a). On 8 October 2004, whilst launching the African National Congress' (ANC) election manifesto in the Karoo, he reiterated this intention and pledged free basic services for the poor in those municipalities led by the ANC. He stated that:

> Many of our people are poor and cannot pay for a little bit of water or for a half day of electricity...So this manifesto of the ANC says when we get elected to municipal government we will ensure the poor get some water and electricity free of charge. (Mbeki 2000b)

The free basic services (FBS) policy represents a dramatic shift in government policy in that previously, the approach had been that government would pay for the capital cost of schemes, provided that beneficiaries would undertake to pay the recurrent costs. This philosophy underpinned all feasibility studies, business plans, Water Services Authority/Provider agreements and tariff structures (Still 2001).

In this chapter I explore the motivation and rationale behind this policy shift, identifying and analysing relevant research, policy formulation processes and policy pronouncements. The process has been by no means linear or sequential and represents a complex interplay between emerging policy direction, research activity, and political statements and announcements.

I employ free basic water (FBW) policy as an illustration of the origins and subsequent dynamics underpinning the FBS policy. FBW is the most prominent of the three free services, measured in terms of need, cost, and its being the first to be implemented. The other services are sanitation and electricity and these are mentioned briefly at the end of this chapter.

I trace the development of FBW policy from its earliest roots in the Reconstruction and Development Programme (RDP) where, it can be argued, the principles underpinning the notion of FBS provision were established. Research and policy work associated with the development of the Municipal Infrastructure Investment Framework (MIIF) is also analysed and represents an important foundation to the explicit public statements made by the president and other key officials.

## Research and policy work leading up to the announcement of the free basic water policy

At first glance, it would appear that because President Mbeki's announcement of the FBS was made at the Cosatu congress, the roots of the policy are political. While this announcement does represent the first direct official reference to a policy aimed at providing FBS, a significant amount of policy development and research had been undertaken in the years leading up to that point. The initial policy development is to be found in the RDP and the initial research in the MIIF.

At one level the FBW policy can be seen to have its early roots in the RDP. The right to water is emphasised in the RPD in the following way:

> The fundamental principle of our water resources policy is the right to access clean water – 'water security for all'…The RDP's short-term aim is to provide every person with adequate facilities for health. The RDP will achieve this by establishing a national water and sanitation programme which aims to provide all households with a clean, safe water supply of 20–30 litres per capita per day. (ANC 1994: 28)

The RDP, however, stops short of explicitly advocating FBW. On the issue of tariffs, the programme aims to ensure that every person has an adequate water supply, and that the national tariff structure must include a lifeline tariff to ensure that all citizens are able to afford water services sufficient for health and hygiene requirements (ANC 1994).

From the preceding excerpt it is clear that the RDP set the scene for many of the principles which underpin the current FBW approach. Firstly, the programme enshrines the right of a minimum level of water for all. It introduces the notion of a rising block tariff structure – a key mechanism in cross-subsidisation. The programme also firmly vests responsibility for providing water services in the hands of local authorities.

The RDP, however, represents a strong visioning document rather than a practical implementation plan. While the programme effectively mobilised support for the vision and provided the initial impetus for change, it was left to other initiatives and processes to give practical substance to the vision.

Perhaps one of the key research processes that had a bearing on policy for service delivery was the MIIF. The MIIF formed the basis for government's approach to planning and financing municipal service delivery, and resonates through legislation such as the Municipal Systems Act (RSA 2000) and the Municipal Structures Act (RSA 1998), which in turn are important pillars on which service provision in this country rests.

Responsibility for preparing the MIIF was at various stages located in the Ministry in the Office of the President, the Department of Housing and the Department of Constitutional Development, which later was renamed the Department of Provincial and Local Government (DPLG). The actual preparation of the MIIF was undertaken by consultant teams, for the most part managed by Professor Tomlinson (Tomlinson 2002).

The MIIF was prepared to reduce uncertainty regarding how many households, and where, have access to different services levels, what the capital and recurrent costs are of providing the infrastructure and operating and maintaining services at different services levels, how these costs could be financed and how services could be delivered in practice. Generally speaking, the role of the MIIF was to:
- Estimate services backlogs;
- Assess the capital costs that are involved in removing the backlogs;
- Calculate the recurrent costs of operating and maintaining the services;
- Propose a framework for financing the capital and recurrent costs on municipal infrastructure programmes;
- Propose methods for enhancing the institutional ability of municipalities to ensure that services are delivered; and
- Suggest how investment in, and the management of, municipal services can be used to promote the development objectives specified in the RDP.

The first version of the MIIF was released in 1995 and later came to use an economic modelling approach researched and designed by consultants for the Development Bank of Southern Africa.

Importantly, the model also allowed for financial analysis that was aimed at investigating affordability issues related to the elimination of these backlogs. Indeed, the issue of affordability was central to the financial analysis at a number of levels. It is important at the national government level where sustainable subsidy levels need to be set. It is important at the local authority level where an infrastructure programme needs to be within the means of the local authority to finance the capital and recurrent costs. It is important at the household level where households need to be able to afford to pay the charges applicable to the service packages they receive.

These institutional arrangements are particularly significant since later failures in delivery have typically been blamed on municipal incapacity. That is, as specified in the Constitution, municipalities are responsible for ensuring the delivery of water, sanitation and waste removal, and the financing of these services through appropriate tariff and local tax mechanisms.

On the issue of tariffs, the MIIF, while acknowledging that tariff setting is the responsibility of municipalities, suggested a number of principles that should be considered in the development of a tariff policy. One of these principles was around the issue of affordability, where it argued that the setting of tariffs should take household affordability into account, within the context of targeted subsidies for the poor (DCD 1997). On the face of it, this principle appears to be consistent with the notion of FBW, assuming that a certain number of households may be unable to pay for the service at all. However, another principle offered by earlier versions of the MIIF is clear and explicit in its statement that no services provided directly to an individual property or dwelling should be made available free of charge. In general, at that stage, the MIIF's view was that all households who get services delivered to their homes – typically water, water-borne sanitation, electricity and road access – should pay some charge. These are often set at the operating and maintenance costs of the services consumed. The MIIF argued that exceptions to this should only be made for indigent households (DCD 1997).

Clearly this principle is at odds with the development of an FBW policy, particularly one which advocates the universal application of the policy, that is, to all rather just low-income households. Subsequent iterations of the MIIF did begin to interpret the MIIF in the light of emerging FBS policy (Tomlinson 2002), effectively signalling a significant change of direction on this matter.

Clearly, despite the sometimes ambiguous contradictions between the MIIF and the emerging FBS policy, much of the methodological approach and research underpinning the MIIF informed the development of government's approach to the provision of municipal services and underpins core legislation and policy in this regard.

Another important initiative that impacts on the FBS project is the advent in 2004 of the Municipal Infrastructure Grant. The grant is a conditional grant to support municipalities in the funding of municipal infrastructure and to upgrade existing infrastructure with the primary objective of benefiting poor households. The grant is essentially a new consolidated infrastructure transfer mechanism geared towards improving transfers to municipalities and to facilitating development planning. It is designed to complement the capital budgets of municipalities and ought to lead to improved resourcing of service-related infrastructure to poor households, effectively supporting the creation of an enabling platform from which to extend basic services, free or otherwise. The grant is in effect a capital subsidy aimed at facilitating infrastructure development and maintenance.

A mechanism known as the equitable share subsidy is an equally important element in the FBS project, impacting on the operating budgets of municipalities. The equitable share is granted on the basis of the number of poor households in a municipality and is the sum of unconditional transfers (formula-based and current transfers) that flows from national to local government. The equitable share is an important source of operating income for municipalities and is frequently used to cover some of the operating costs associated with extending FBS to the poor.

It can be argued that the approach and sentiments inherent in the MIIF, supported by the equitable share and emerging mechanisms such as the Municipal Infrastructure Grant, indirectly formed the basis and rationale behind the president's statements outlining the government's intention of implementing an FBW strategy. Firstly, the MIIF represented the first comprehensive, systematic financial analysis and assessment of the implications of municipal infrastructure investment options in the country as a whole. Based on this analysis, government has deepened its knowledge of what kind of investment package might be affordable under a range of different assumptions. The modelling exercise identified a range of different packages suitable for varying contexts based largely on different service levels which may be appropriate to different circumstances. The model also took cognisance of the wide variety of different settlement types. The investment programme involved providing a combination of the selected packages in order to eliminate the services backlog within a specified number of households while also making provision for new households. The analysis was not intended to drive national targets, but rather to illustrate the financial implications of infrastructure decisions. It is interesting to note that this methodology and approach, as well as the information required on backlogs and resources that the associated research yielded, would have been, albeit in an indirect way, on the mind of the president when he made his landmark announcement on government's intention to embark on a programme of providing free basic services.

## The presidential policy statement and other announcements

President Mbeki's commitment to FBS caused the Department of Water Affairs and Forestry (DWAF) to initiate a study under the guidance of the Intervention and Operations Support Directorate aimed at investigating the viability of providing FBW to the poor. This study was coordinated at an intergovernmental level and involved the Treasury, South African Local Government Association (SALGA), the minister's special advisers and other water sector professionals.

Essentially the research approach involved a desk study to investigate the viability of providing FBW (DWAF 2004c). The study drew heavily on the Durban model as a possible approach that could be replicated nationally. In terms of this model, the first six kilolitres of water had been provided free to all consumers, regardless of whether the household was rich or poor. Durban had also applied a rising block tariff system that promoted cross-subsidisation to good effect. The desk study tested six areas nationally: Nelspruit/Nsikazi, Bloemfontein/Botshabelo/Thaba'Nchu, Harrismith/Qwa-Qwa, Wild Coast, DC 25 (Utrecht area), and Odi.

The study investigated the viability of providing six kilolitres of FBW to three distinct groups, including: all people, only those households with an income of less than R800 per month, and standpipe water consumers. The study also worked on the assumption that only the poor receive direct benefits from the equitable share and that the local authority received its full equitable share. The study also assumed a rising block approach with three bands: 0 to 6 kilolitres, 6 to 30 kilolitres, and greater than 30 kilolitres.

The results of the study concluded that the provision of free water to the poor was practically and financially feasible. In terms of providing free water to all, the study felt that there may well be areas where this may not be feasible, although it concluded that this option was attractive from an implementation point of view in that it meant not having to undertake an administratively onerous means test.

The study also concluded that it would depend entirely on local circumstances if free water could be made available or not, and that the successful implementation of such an approach would hinge on the management skills of each local authority. In addition to this, the study identified the availability of the equitable share for water as an important variable in the implementation of an FBW approach. For the implementation to be sustainable, municipalities would need to ensure that they receive their full equitable share allocation and that they use an appropriate portion of it to cover some of the costs of extending free water. The study noted that the implementation of the policy in larger cities would not necessarily be easier than in rural areas but added that, if Water Services Authorities in both rural and urban areas direct approximately 30 per cent of the equitable share to FBW, they should be able to meet the basic water consumption costs of the very poor provided that operation and maintenance (running) costs remained below R4.30 per kilolitre. The study was not prescriptive as to whether local authorities should allocate free water to just the poor, or to all on a universal basis.

The study concluded that cost recovery was an important principle, particularly in cases similar to Durban where no equitable share is directed towards water services provision, or where insufficient equitable share is allocated. In these cases, cost recovery from consumers who use higher levels of water is important if cross-subsidisation is to be implemented successfully. The investigation also concluded that FBW is only practical if the water is metered, technically limited through flow restrictors, or provided through standpipe sources.

The study arrived at the following recommendations:
- Area specific: FBW to the poor must be investigated by each local authority using financial models.
- Equitable share: The full equitable share must be allocated to the municipality and must be used appropriately. In circumstances where the service provider is not the municipality but some other agency, for example a public–private partner, then it is expected that the subsidy will be allocated to the service provider.
- Management capacity: Strong management systems need to be developed with regard to FBW to the poor and the administration of the subsidy.
- Strategy: A technical group comprised of SALGA, the Department of Finance, the DPLG, and DWAF will be formed to develop an implementation strategy.
- Piloting: The piloting of the policy is to be undertaken in at least four local authority areas.
- Communication: The policy needs to be effectively communicated to the public and the municipality, and it needs to be reiterated that the implementation of the policy is a long-term process.

- Flexibility/legal issues: Local authorities should be given the flexibility of providing FBW to either the poor or to all consumers. The study also noted that municipality is not obligated in terms of the Constitution to allocate the equitable share.
- Metering: The success of the FBW policy will depend on being able to meter and/or control the volume of water. (DWAF 2004c)

Following the conclusion of the study, the DWAF issued a statement on 14 February 2001 effectively formalising the president's policy statement made a few months earlier. The statement read:

> The Cabinet has approved an implementation plan for 6 000 litres of free water per household as part of the government's integrated rural development strategy and urban renewal programme. The date for implementation by municipal structures is 1 July this year. This date coincides with the start of the first financial year of our new local councils.[1]

It is at this point that the FBW policy can be deemed to have come into effect. As part of the statement, the minister indicated that FBW is to be funded using a combination of the equitable share of revenue and internal cross-subsidies from appropriately structured water tariffs in a manner which best reflects the specific situation in the local authority area. It also signified the intention of DWAF, along with DPLG and SALGA, to assist municipalities with implementation via a support programme. This support programme involved preparing detailed guidelines for municipalities, establishing dedicated support teams for municipalities, and developing mechanisms to finance and implement the required metering and billing of water supplies.

The following month the minister, at an FBW workshop on 27 March, introduced the notion of an implementation strategy to give effect to the policy. It was at this workshop that he tabled some of the findings of the early research which underpinned the Cabinet announcement in January 2001. He also referred to a study conducted in 2000 by DWAF which noted that of 97 local authorities sampled, 18 had already been implementing an FBW policy. He noted, however, that the bulk of these initiatives were located primarily in urban areas. He identified the lack of resources to be a problem in this regard but went on to point out that:

> National government has announced significant additional allocations to local authorities over the next three years. Local government's total share of nationally raised revenue will rise by 11% a year, at a faster rate than any other sphere of government. The increase in the equitable share allocation is the most direct contribution to the free basic services challenge.[2]

Having indicated that local authorities would, in the future, receive additional equitable share, the minister pointed out that the research being undertaken by the task team had revealed that financial resources were not always available for providing the necessary basic water supply to the poor. This was primarily due to the problem that subsidies were not always transferred to water services providers who were actually delivering services and incurring the costs of delivery. This problem was particularly evident in contexts where municipalities had extensive rural areas within their boundaries. In the workshop he urged municipalities to establish subsidy rules which would allow sufficient funds to be transferred to the water service providers appointed by the authorities.

The March 2001 FBW workshop essentially marks the beginning of the implementation of the FBW policy. While certain issues, including broad financing principles, were outlined at the workshop, a detailed implementation plan and approach was not clearly articulated at this point. The workshop represents the first steps in developing this approach and methodology and led to an intensive research phase aimed at developing a comprehensive implementation strategy. The process and the emerging content that arose from this research phase are outlined in the following section.

## Researching and developing the FBW implementation programme

Once the political imperative for the introduction of FBW provision had been established through the presidential and other political statements in this regard, the issue of implementing a free basic policy became an urgent priority, necessitating a significant amount of research in a number of distinct but often interrelated policy areas, including the financial, socio-political, institutional and technical realms.

Consultants played a significant role in this research phase underpinning policy development. The Palmer Development Group, for example, was appointed as lead consultant to assist DWAF in the development of an implementation strategy to give effect to the FBW policy. At the outset, the research team identified the following as the problem statement:

> Implementing a FBW policy successfully is a complex task which requires a wide range of issues to be addressed both nationally and locally. The process of implementation will also differ across municipalities. Given the very different income and service-level profiles of municipalities, some will find it relatively easy to implement the policy while others will face severe constraints. In general the constraints that an implementation strategy has to overcome are:
>
> **Financial:** how to finance and target the supply of free basic services in a sustainable and efficient manner.
>
> **Socio-political:** how to establish successful communication and cooperation between consumers, councillors, local authority officials and different spheres of government.

**Institutional:** how to develop the required organisational capacity and working relationships between different institutions.

**Technical:** how to choose the appropriate technical and service-level options to facilitate FBW.

Strategic approaches to overcome these constraints are provided, with reference to international experience; technical and service level issues; and the respective roles of different actors in the water supply system. (DWAF 2001a: 4)

Significantly, this process focused on the provision of a free basic level of water supply to those households already having at least a basic water supply and did not deal with the ongoing roll-out of water services in unserviced areas. At the outset, however, the research team made it clear that the implementation of the FBW policy should not slow or prevent the continued extension of services to other households and that close monitoring of the impact of the policy would be required to ensure that this did not happen. The research team focused on a fairly wide range of diverse but interrelated issues, including the following:

- Assessing the institutional and legal landscape;
- Identifying the intended beneficiaries of the policy, and eligibility criteria;
- Determining what constitutes a reasonable volume for FBW;
- Exploring different technical options;
- Estimating administrative costs;
- Investigating different revenue and subsidy options;
- Exploring different targeting approaches; and
- Researching international good practice.

The research indicated that a free basic level of water supply could be provided to consumers in three ways, each of which would be most applicable under certain local circumstances and could be implemented in a flexible manner at the discretion of individual local authorities. These three approaches include a rising block tariff with a free basic amount to all who consume within the first block, targeted credits or subsidies, and service-level targeting. The rationale behind the rising block mechanism is that the cost of water per kilolitre increases as consumption rises. Figure 12.1 illustrates this. In this case the first 6 kilolitres are zero-rated. Kilolitres 6–10 are charged at R3 per kilolitre, while kilolitres 10–15 are charged at R4 per kilolitre. In this case, consumption over 15 kilolitres attracts a tariff of R5 per kilolitre. Targeted credits, on the other hand, is a mechanism providing a credit or direct subsidy to consumers that qualify, usually on the basis of a means test. Service-level targeting is an approach which provides a minimum service level to all consumers within a targeted geographical area.

**Figure 12.1** *Illustration of a rising block tariff structure*

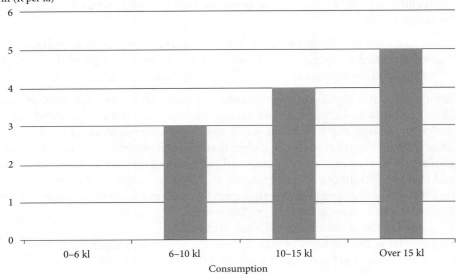

The research report outlined a methodology for allowing municipalities to choose between these options, setting out the advantages and disadvantages of each according to different circumstances. The implementation report, however, stressed that the choice of approach remains a local decision, determined by local circumstances, arguing that rising block tariffs are only viable where there is a sufficiently large number of middle- to high-income users to facilitate effective cross-subsidisation. The targeting approach is best suited for areas where there are many poor below or just above the poverty line used in allocating the equitable share. The research indicated that municipalities with low capacity and high levels of poor consumers may end up using a service-level targeting approach where limited service levels are used, which by their nature only supply a basic amount of water (DWAF 2001a).

In terms of financing FBW, the implementation strategy research team explored both internal and external funding options. The issue of internal cross-subsidies was examined in some detail, with a view to exploring how such subsidies could be incorporated into water tariff structures. The nature of, and extent to which, these subsidies could be used depend on a number of factors, including:

- Capital subsidies to, and capital requirements of, the local water system;
- Total equitable share subsidy made available to the Water Services Authority;
- Regional and local cost factors which influence the cost of supply;
- Total wealth of the supply area;

- Proportion of water consumed by the non-residential compared to the residential sector;
- Income distribution within the supply area;
- Consumption distribution within the supply area; and
- Local political feasibility of introducing cross-subsidies. (DWAF 2001a: 26)

On the issue of the equitable share, the research team concluded that the allocation is an important mechanism available to municipalities in financing FBW, particularly in contexts where the local revenue base is inadequate to meet these costs. However, because the equitable share is granted on the basis of the number of poor households in a municipality, it will not be sufficient to provide FBW to all households. Consequently, if the approach adopted by the local authority is one of universal provision, the equitable share will need to be mixed with locally-raised revenue.

In the final analysis, the research indicated that the process to implement a local FBW policy should rest on three elements. First, the approach should be phased, allowing low capacity and municipalities with little access to strong revenue time to phase in full implementation. Second, a set of national guidelines, choice options and benchmarks should be developed and made available to municipalities to allow them to select an approach suitable to their particular contexts. Third, management and institutional support should be made available to municipalities to allow them to find their way through the substantial planning and implementation support involved in the implementation of the FBW policy (DWAF 2001a).

In addition to commissioning an FBW strategy, DWAF also approached the Palmer Development Group to develop a set of guidelines for local authorities to assist municipalities to implement the strategy. Essentially, the guidelines provide a ten-step process towards implementing an FBW policy at the local level. These steps include:

- Understanding consumers and consumption;
- Establishing the institutional framework;
- Assessing technical options;
- Assessing links to sanitation;
- Understanding costs;
- Reviewing income sources;
- Selecting poverty relief options;
- Completing a pricing policy;
- Establishing financial arrangements with water services providers; and
- Setting up management arrangements. (DWAF 2001b: 2)

The guidelines set out each of these steps in detail, advising municipalities on how to negotiate their way through each phase, providing practical illustrative examples.

In addition to the guidelines and case studies which were developed and conducted as part of the initial implementation strategy, national government has undertaken a number of comprehensive communication campaigns in the years following the initial announcement of the policy. This communication strategy has gone hand in hand with the development of tools and resources to capacitate local authorities in the task of providing FBW. Provincial Support Units were also established by DWAF and have been tasked with assisting municipalities with practical, context-appropriate implementation of the FBW policy.

## Reflecting on the achievements and shortcomings of the policy in practice

This section explores the extent to which the policy has been rolled out and attempts to quantify the impact of the policy, particularly on the lives of the intended beneficiaries, namely the poor and marginalised. It also reflects on some of the difficulties and obstacles lying in the way of the successful implementation of the policy.

In a speech delivered by Minister Sydney Mufamadi of the DPLG in August 2004, he reflected on the progress made in the roll-out of the FBW policy. Across the board, 86 per cent of municipalities were at that stage providing FBW, although progress has been uneven, both within and between provinces. Significantly more progress has been made in the larger municipalities with poor rural municipalities struggling to give effect to the policy. As of November 2004, the proportion of Water Services Authorities providing FBW had increased to 95.3 per cent (DWAF 2004a). Tables 12.1 and 12.2 illustrate the distribution of Water Services Authorities providing FBW by municipality type and by province.

**Table 12.1** *Water Services Authorities providing FBW, by type*

| Type | Total | Providing FBW |
| --- | --- | --- |
| Category A (metro) | 6 | 6 |
| Category C (district) | 38 | 33 |
| Category B (local) | 126 | 123 |
| Total | 170 | 162 |

Source: DWAF (2004a)

**Table 12.2** *Water Services Authorities providing FBW, by province*

| Province | Total | No. providing FBW | % providing FBW |
| --- | --- | --- | --- |
| Western Cape | 30 | 28 | 93 |
| Eastern Cape | 17 | 17 | 100 |
| Northern Cape | 31 | 31 | 100 |
| Free State | 21 | 20 | 95 |
| KwaZulu-Natal | 14 | 14 | 100 |
| North West | 18 | 18 | 100 |
| Gauteng | 13 | 12 | 92 |

→

| Province | Total | No. providing FBW | % providing FBW |
|----------|-------|-------------------|-----------------|
| Mpumalanga | 23 | 16 | 70 |
| Limpopo | 12 | 12 | 100 |
| Total | 170 | 162 | 95.3 |

Source: DWAF (2004a)

From a Water Services Authority coverage point of view, these figures are impressive with almost all provinces, with the exception of Mpumalanga, approaching total coverage.

From a population coverage point of view, DWAF estimates that over two-thirds of South Africa's population of 46.5 million is currently served by the FBW policy. Figure 12.2 shows the population coverage broken down by province and illustrates a relatively wide range of coverage across provinces. The graph also illustrates FBW coverage of that population which is defined by DWAF as poor. The range of performance in this regard between provinces is even wider, ranging from 92 per cent in the Free State to just 26 per cent in Limpopo. The Northern Cape is an interesting case as it is the only province were the proportion of poor people served is greater than the proportion of total population served. This is significant as the entire rationale behind the FBW initiative has a strong pro-poor focus. Nevertheless, over 16 million poor people are now the beneficiaries of the policy. While there is still a great deal of work to do to ensure that the remaining 13 million poor people benefit, the achievements of the policy have been significant, particularly given the relatively short time that the project has been in effect.

**Figure 12.2** *Proportion of total and poor population served by FBW, by province*

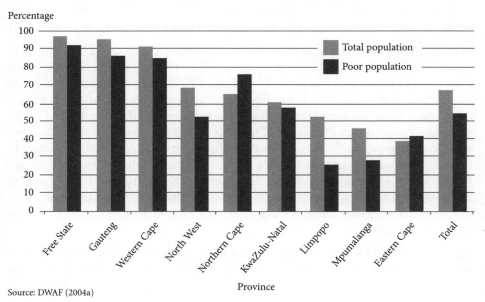

Source: DWAF (2004a)

The policy, however, has not been without its detractors and criticisms. A fundamental concern was the erosion of the principle of user pays. There is a view that where the long-term sustainability of government and society is concerned, the ethic of payment for services at some level is healthy and ought to be encouraged. A counter-argument to this is that the FBW policy will in fact encourage payment for services because it will allow government to take measures against those who use more than six kilolitres and who will not pay for it. The latter argument does not hold in rural areas where the six-kilolitre policy may lead to a situation where schemes become completely dependent on government handouts to keep running. This may well lead to the disempowerment of community-based water services providers, and to an escalation in municipal costs (Still 2001).

Another criticism of the FBW policy centres on the figure of six kilolitres, which has become a cornerstone of the way the policy is perceived. The South African Civil Society Water Caucus, in a submission to the parliamentary Portfolio Committee hearings on FBW, argues that the FBW policy is based on a flawed assumption that low-income households use less water due to their low-income status and that the six kilolitres referred to in the policy fail to account for the basic water requirements of households, which are influenced by a number of significant factors, including:

- Household size;
- Number of dependants;
- Illness status of household members as health-care demands (eg. of HIV/AIDS patients) increase water use;
- The use of flush toilets which need up to nine litres to flush;
- Different consumption patterns between weekdays and weekends, with an increased water use over weekends;
- Rural/urban location of households; and
- Water needs for productive use, for example to ensure food security. (PMG 2003)

Moving from the principle of user pays and whether six kilolitres are sufficient, a number of stakeholders have expressed concern regarding the inappropriate deployment of resources towards the funding of FBW implementation. The South African Association of Water, for example, makes the point that in municipal areas where there are not sufficient high-volume users to effect meaningful cross-subsidisation via the consumer tariff, the only source of revenue to cover the costs of FBW is the equitable share. However, this is an unconditional allocation to municipal authorities and the use of the funds is generally discretionary (although for 2003/04 a separate window was created under the equitable share for funding FBS, which is roughly 20 per cent of the allocation). This means that in some instances, insufficient funding is made available by municipalities to implement the policy (PMG 2003).

Similarly, the Water Research Commission points out that changes in the institutional and policy environment, including municipal demarcation and FBW, have meant that the challenge for municipal officials is not only to integrate and administer the disparate cost recovery arrangements they have inherited, but also to generate revenues to cover the costs of providing basic services free. They point out that prior cost recovery initiatives geared towards the lower end of the market are increasingly overshadowed by the implementation of the FBW policy (PMG 2003).

SALGA has taken the capacity issue further. In its submission to the Portfolio Committee hearings on the implementation of FBW, SALGA points to the lack of institutional capacity among certain municipalities as being an obstacle to the effective implementation of the policy. Similar sentiments were echoed in the South African Association of Water Utilities submission. SALGA does, however, point out that support for municipalities in implementing the FBW policy is available through the Masibambane programme and the Provincial Support Units which have been established in all provinces, and as such expects the situation to improve (PMG 2003).

Without attempting to downplay these problems, it would seem that most of the criticism levelled at the implementation of the policy has identified areas requiring intervention and improvement, rather than factors which are likely to result in the failure of the policy as a whole.

## Learning from the process: expanding the concept beyond water into sustainable FBS

While FBW represents the leading edge in terms of the extension and provision of free basic services, it is by no means the only sector where progress has been made. Indeed, significant progress has been made to expand the scope of providing free services in terms of both electricity and sanitation.

### Free basic sanitation

In the case of free basic sanitation, the emerging policy direction is clearly driven by the successes of the FBW initiative. The provision of free basic sanitation is also highlighted in the Strategic Framework for Water Services (DWAF 2003). In terms of the framework, the primary purpose of the free basic sanitation policy is to assist in promoting access by poor households to at least a basic level of sanitation service. DWAF, following on the methodology used by the department in the development of an FBW strategy, has developed a similar Free Basic Sanitation Strategy (DWAF 2004b).

The strategy identifies three main challenges related to providing free basic sanitation. The first concerns the fact that the key challenge with respect to the provision of free basic sanitation is the provision of the sanitation facility itself to poor households (together with the necessary supporting infrastructure). The second is that the promotion of health and hygiene must be provided in a coordinated manner, be properly managed and adequately funded if free basic sanitation is to become a reality. This requires close collaboration between district municipalities who are responsible for environmental health, the Water Services Authority and the water services provider. The last challenge concerns subsidising operating and maintenance costs. If the basic service is to be provided free to the poor then the Water Services Authority must ensure that the costs of providing the service are covered by the municipality equitable share and/or through cross-subsidies within the Water Services Authority area. These funds must be paid to the water services provider who operates the service or directly to the households (DWAF 2004b).

To date, the achievements of the free basic sanitation initiative have not been significant, in contrast to the FBW policy. As of November 2004, DWAF estimates that 13 out of a total of 170 Water Services Authorities were providing free basic sanitation, representing 7.6 per cent of these institutions. Approximately 7 million out of a total population of 46.5 million (15.1 per cent) citizens in the country were receiving free basic sanitation. DWAF estimates at this time that the free basic sanitation policy serves 11.1 per cent of the poor population.

### Free basic electricity

In terms of free basic electricity, the Department of Minerals and Energy implemented a free basic electricity policy effective from July 2003 (RSA 2003). The objective of the policy is to facilitate the implementation of free basic electricity services by municipalities as Service Authorities. As in the case of the FBW policy, the free basic electricity policy has its formal roots in government's statement of intent in respect of the provision of free basic services in 2000. Following from this, the Department of Minerals and Energy embarked on a research process aimed at developing an Electricity Basic Service Support Tariff. The research involved a number of pilot projects and culminated in a research report which assisted the department in arriving at policy recommendations.

The main issues influencing the implementation of free basic electricity to poor households are the same as those that faced the FBW, namely the level of free basic electricity allocation, the identification of recipients of the allocation, the cost implications of such an allocation, and there being sustainable sources of funding for such allocations (RSA 2003).

In terms of identifying the level of free basic electricity, the policy states that grid-connected households will be provided with 50kWh of free basic electricity, funded mainly through relevant intergovernmental transfers, subject to the contractual obligations between the service provider and the consumer being met. Any consumption in excess of the set limit (50kWh) will be payable by the consumer.

Recipients of the free basic electricity allocation are essentially self-selected and are identified as those households that either apply to their service providers for a current limited electricity supply, or who choose to be charged a special non-current limiting tariff that provides the free basic electricity allocation. The choice of mechanism to facilitate this self-selection is left to the Service Authorities and providers.

When it comes to funding the implementation of free basic electricity, the policy locates responsibility for the first phase of preparing the Electricity Basic Service Support Tariff with DPLG through a separate window of the equitable share or through an additional grant. The policy points out that municipalities with sufficient resources should be able to provide the free basic service without any national government support through cross-subsidies.

In terms of longer-term sustainability, the policy states that the Department of Minerals and Energy, in consultation with the DPLG and the National Treasury, will determine the extent of the provision of free basic electricity which can be funded through intergovernmental transfers on an annual basis, and that the cost of providing free basic electricity shall be included in the Medium Term Expenditure Framework budget allocation of the DPLG.

## Creating the conditions for free basic service provision

In an effort to ensure the ongoing viability of the FBW initiative, support for municipalities in implementing the policy has been available via the Masibambane programme and the Provincial Support Units, which were established in July 2001 as part of the Inter-Departmental National Free Basic Water Task Team. The objective of these units is to:
- Provide proactive technical and financial planning assistance in developing sustainable local FBW strategies;
- Monitor implementation of FBW by using technical and financial indicators;
- Act as a communication conduit for new FBW-related policies and strategies. (PMG 2003)

Provincial Support Units have been established and are currently functioning in all provinces. In addition to these units, DWAF has compiled and made available to local authorities a wide range of implementation documents and tools. These have been distributed to all municipalities and are available on the departmental website (DWAF 2004a).

From a financial sustainability point of view, an increase in the equitable share with effect from July 2003 is likely to assist municipalities to bridge the fiscal gap in instances where there are insufficient high-volume consumers to effect meaningful and sustainable cross-subsidisation. The Division of Revenue Act also now requires more stringent reporting on the part of municipalities regarding their free basic service-related activities, which should facilitate more effective implementation of the policy. Section 5(7) of the Act requires municipalities to submit information on their free basic service offering to National Treasury and Provincial Treasury and to the provincial local government department annually. It also requires municipalities to submit revenue and spending on infrastructure and free basic services on a quarterly basis (RSA 2004).

The most recent support initiative was announced by DPLG in October 2004 on the launch of the department's Project Consolidate. This project is essentially envisaged as a two-year engagement programme aimed at allowing national and provincial government to support and capacitate municipality. The initiative will be hands-on in nature and will involve the deployment of teams to work at municipal level to assist in addressing practical issues of service delivery and local governance (DPLG 2004).

## Conclusion

It is clear that considerable progress has been made in formulating policy for and delivering FBW. There has been considerably less progress in respect of free basic electricity and free basic sanitation. The extent of the political will to see the policy successfully implemented is evident by the interdepartmental nature of cooperation on this project and the resources that national government is committing to support the process. The chapter has shown that the emergence of the policy from an initial vision based on prior policy work and experience, through to the formulation of policy, supported by rigorous research and testing, through to a widely implemented and seemingly sustainable FBS programme, has been a non-linear journey that typifies the complex processes that characterise the development of public policy in South Africa in the current era.

### Notes

1    Ronnie Kasrils, media release, 14 February 2001.

2    Ronnie Kasrils, national workshop on FBW, 27 March 2001.

### References

ANC (African National Congress) (1994) *Reconstruction and Development Programme.* Johannesburg: Umanyano Publications.

DCD (Department of Constitutional Development) (1997) *Municipal Infrastructure Investment Framework.* Pretoria: DCD.

DPLG (Department of Provincial and Local Government) (2004) Press Statement on the Occasion of the Launch of Project Consolidate – A Hands on Programme of Support for Local Government, 29 October 2004.

DWAF (Department of Water Affairs and Forestry) (2001a) *Free basic water – Implementation strategy document.* Pretoria: DWAF Directorate: Interventions and Operations Support.

DWAF (2001b) *Free basic water – Guideline for Local Authorities.* Pretoria: DWAF Chief Directorate: Water Services.

DWAF (2003) *Strategic Framework for Water Services – Water is life, sanitation is dignity.* Pretoria: DWAF.

DWAF (2004a) Available at <http://www.dwaf.gov.za/FreeBasicWater>.

DWAF (2004b) *Free basic sanitation strategy.* Pretoria: DWAF Directorate: Water Services Regulation.

DWAF (2004c) Available at<http://www.dwaf.gov.za>.

Mbeki T (2000a) Address to the 7th National Congress of South African Trade Unions, Gallagher Estate, 18 September.

Mbeki T (2000b) ANC Election Manifesto Speech, October.

PMG (Parliamentary Monitoring Group) (2003) Water Affairs and Forestry Portfolio Committee, Free Basic Water Hearings, 4 June 2003, the Parliamentary Monitoring Group. Available at <http://www.pmg.org.za>.

RSA (Republic of South Africa) (1998) *Local Government: Municipal Structures Act, no. 117 of 1998.* Pretoria: Government Printers.

RSA (2000) *Local Government: Municipal Systems Act, no. 32 of 2000.* Pretoria: Government Printers.

RSA (2003) *Electricity basic services support tariff – free basic electricity.* Government Gazette, Notice 1693 of 2003, 4 July.

RSA (2004) *Division of Revenue Act no. 4 of 2004.* Pretoria: Government Printers.

Still D (2001) Free basic water in rural areas: Is it feasibile? Presented at the WISA CWSS seminar, March 8, Assagay.

Tomlinson R (2002) International best practice, enabling frameworks and the policy process: A South African case study, *International Journal of Urban and Regional Research*, 26(2).

# 13 Conclusion

Udesh Pillay and Richard Tomlinson

One might assume that the policy process involves negotiations during a certain period, agreements that find expression in a White Paper, with legislation and then regulations following that are intended to give effect to the policy. It transpires that the policy process is more complicated and differentiated.

The policy process generally occurs in a context of changing economic, political and social circumstances. For example, Mirjam van Donk and Edgar Pieterse in this book hold that the design of local government occurred over three phases between the late 1980s and the year 2000, with each phase occurring in differing political and economic contexts.

Yet the preparation of housing policy was characterised by negotiations during a three-year period that were characterised by collegiality among the major negotiators and an attitude of problem solving focusing on what worked in delivery terms. Agreements reached at the National Housing Forum (NHF) formed the basis of the 1994 Housing White Paper that was carried through without amendment into the Housing Act (107 of 1997).

An alternative is provided by free basic services, which was a sudden policy pronouncement at the time of the 2000 local government elections. It may have been informed by earlier research and policy frameworks such as the Municipal Infrastructure Investment Framework (MIIF), but the MIIF included principles like the user should pay for services, even if the service is heavily subsidised.

It is apparent that there are marked dissimilarities between the processes of preparing many of the policies. Yet rather than recount the policy process for each of the policies included in this book, it is more useful to trace the changing context for policies over time, and to locate the various policies and policy formulation processes within this changing context.

In addition to recounting the policy process, the editors take issue with some of the contributors and argue that they understate the relevance of academic research. We also inform the reader regarding urban policies that currently are taking effect or are emerging, and introduce the South African Cities Network (SACN) and its importance for policy purposes. The latter two undertakings, moving from *this is what the issues were* in 1994 and this is what government did about building a democratic urban future, to *this is where policy is headed,* are intrinsic to a service provided by this book of documenting the evolution of urban policy.

## Recounting the policy process

### Multi-stakeholder negotiations

Before 1990 civil society, in the form of the 'civics', played a key role in the struggle against the Black Local Authority system and then in negotiating an end to apartheid and the transition to democratic nationhood. The pre-eminent example is the Soweto rent boycott led by the Soweto Civic Association, the negotiations led by the Soweto People's Delegation, and the 1990 Soweto Accord. The role of the civics continued through 1993, in the case of Johannesburg in the Central Witwatersrand Metropolitan Chamber. The Chamber's ambitious agenda included, *inter alia*, an attempt to address the constitutional, institutional and financial structures of urban governance, and the demarcation of municipal boundaries. Indeed, all of these were successfully negotiated, but while the Chamber's consensus mode was useful for agreeing on matters of process and in preparing framework documents, it and other local negotiations were of limited use when it came to agreeing on products and seeing these through to implementation.

Thus it was that in 1993 the national Local Government Negotiating Forum (LGNF) was created comprising the national government, organised associations of local government, political parties and the African National Congress (ANC) alliance (that included trade unions, the South African Communist Party and the South African National Civic Organisation). The LGNF negotiated the Local Government Transition Act (No. 209 of 1993), which mandated local forums to negotiate solutions consistent with principles of non-racialism, democracy, accountability and one tax base. The task was to establish a new local government structure, the 'pre-interim phase'.

The consequence of the new process was to quash the contributions by civil society. For example, in the case of the newly created Greater Johannesburg Local Negotiating Forum:

> The power balance in the Forum differed from that of the Chamber.
> The Forum comprised a statutory side – essentially the pre-existing
> white local government structures (effectively led by the Johannesburg
> City Council); and the non-statutory side – where the community
> organisations and non-governmental organisations led by ANC-oriented
> white, coloured, Indian and African activists schooled in consensus
> politics gave way to 'a different breed' of mostly African ANC politicians
> more accustomed to a confrontational political style. They insisted
> on cancelling all agreements and threw out all the previous research.
> (Tomlinson 1999: 9, 10)

This curtailed civil society participation in negotiations of this sort and a concomitant centralisation of policy-making within the ANC.

In parallel with these local multi-stakeholder negotiations, there was the NHF that in effect, between 1992 and 1994, drafted the housing White Paper. This was a different circumstance to the Chamber. Whereas negotiations in the Metropolitan Chamber began before the unbanning of the ANC and thus were led by the civic associations, by the time the NHF started business the ANC had been unbanned and the ANC representative had a relatively 'free hand' to negotiate a housing policy. Although decision-making within the NHF required consensus among all representatives, the ANC was able to reach agreement with the private sector, represented as it was by the Urban Foundation.

## The Constitution

The process of formulating the 1996 Constitution arguably began when the National Party government met with the newly unbanned ANC for the first round of 'settlement' talks at Groote Schuur on 2 May 1990.[1] The three-day 'talks about talks' ended in the Groote Schuur Minute, a broad agreement between the two parties. The constitutional negotiation process formally began on 20 December 1991 when delegates from 17 political parties met at the World Trade Centre in Kempton Park. In July 1993, 26 constitutional principles (later expanded to 34) were adopted as building blocks for a new Constitution.

Chapter 7 of the 1996 Constitution is devoted to local government. Local government became a separate sphere of government and was granted powers of general competency rather than a schedule of services while operating as an arm of national government. Chapter 7 also refers to the 'developmental duties of municipalities', the first time that the phrase is invoked. This has to do with the delivery of services and the promotion of 'social and economic development' that, via the 1998 White Paper on Local Government and later the Municipal Systems Act (No. 32 of 2000), led to the notion of developmental local government, Integrated Development Plans (IDPs) and Local Economic Development (LED).

## The White Paper on Local Government

The Local Government White Paper was the key document when it came to the design of a post-apartheid system of local government. As described in the 1997 discussion document, *Towards a White Paper on Local Government in South Africa*, 'This process of drafting a White Paper on local government could almost be seen as drafting a "Constitution" for local government if one considers the importance of this sphere of government'.[2]

The central concerns of the White Paper were how best to deliver and to finance the delivery of water and sanitation, as well as other services. Service delivery was described as the 'essential' role of local government. The White Paper:
• Prescribed the types of local government;
• Determined processes and criteria for demarcating local government;

- Provided support for public–private partnerships for service delivery;
- Provided direction for financing local government; and
- Described the nature of developmental local government and specified the need for integrated development planning.

Looking at the policies that have followed on the 1998 White Paper, these have included research into, and the preparation of policy, legislation and regulations for municipal services partnerships; the same in respect of municipal finances; adjustments to the demarcation of municipal boundaries; and so on. In other words, the post-1998 policy process for local government has had more to do with implementation than the formulation of new policies.

The most important legislation that followed on the White Paper is as follows:
- Municipal Demarcation Act (No. 27 of 1998): The Act provides the criteria and procedures for the determination of municipal boundaries.
- Municipal Structures Act (No. 117 of 1998): The Act provides for the establishment of Category A (metropolitan council), Category B (local council) and Category C (district council) municipalities and for the allocation of powers and functions to and between these municipalities.
- The Municipal Structures Amendment Act (No. 34 of 2000): The Act shifted water, sanitation, electricity and health to district councils, and allowed that other functions can be decided by decree by provincial MECs. Then, in order to avoid interruption in service delivery, Proclamation Vol. 425 no. 2187 ruled that the status quo in respect of local councils providing water, sanitation, electricity and health would remain until the minister decides to the contrary.
- The Municipal Systems Act (No. 32 of 2000): The Act is important for municipal financial management as it confers on municipalities the powers, *inter alia*, to develop policy, plans, programmes and strategies providing for and regulating the provisioning of municipal services, and for imposing and recovering rates, taxes, levies, duties and fees. It is intended that these powers be given effect through IDPs.
- Local Government: Municipal Finance Management Act (No. 56 of 2003): The Act is intended to secure transparency, accountability and sound management of the revenue, expenditure, assets and liabilities of local government institutions.
- Local Government: Municipal Property Rates Act (No. 6 of 2004): The Act will shift all municipalities onto a system where the full market value of the property (including land and improvements) is taxed.

Finally, the local government elections marked the 'final phase' of the transition from apartheid to democratic local government structures. At the time of the elections the ANC, not government itself, promised the delivery of free basic services. Municipalities since then have rushed to provide free basic services, none more so than cities controlled by opposition parties that wanted to be first 'past the post'.

## Research matters

At the outset of preparing this book it was envisaged that the authors of the chapters would devote considerable attention to the role of research in the process of generating policy. However, many of the authors argued that, in fact, research had proven to be of little significance as the preparation of policies was guided more by the agendas of interest groups, and also that the urgency of the policies overwhelmed the pace at which researchers could proceed.

The editors believe that this perspective is overstated and here argue that research matters.

### Policy community

Academics in South Africa and academics elsewhere, from the United Kingdom in particular, have for decades undertaken research on urban issues in South Africa. The influence of this research has been extensive in creating perceptions of what the urban problems were, what urban policies might be appropriate and, more recently, informing perceptions of the success of urban policies and suggesting amendments and/or alternatives to extant policy.

As summarised by Carlsson (2000: 505), the notions of a 'policy community', 'policy networks', 'issue networks' and 'epistemic community' are not new. South Africa has an urban policy community, more in some areas (eg. housing and LED) than others (eg. local government finance), with some emerging (eg. urban poverty and HIV/AIDS), where academics, professionals, members of non-governmental organisations (NGOs), government officials and consultants share research projects, freely communicate research results and, often enough, move jobs from one institution to another. These persons share a profound commitment to improved urban livelihoods and an abiding interest in the post-apartheid transformation of South Africa's cities and urban areas.

The extraordinary range of housing research is a case in point. The lengthy housing bibliography included on the website of the Postgraduate Housing Programme of the University of the Witwatersrand is illustrative of the extent to which a 'policy community' has emerged in respect of housing policy.[3] A similar and overlapping policy group of researchers is emerging in the area of HIV/AIDS and urban poverty. They are promoting the need to mainstream HIV/AIDS in IDPs, and attempting to tailor housing and services policies to meet the needs arising from HIV/AIDS.[4]

Many in the urban community also share a passion in trying to influence urban policy. Thus, an interesting feature of this research is that it is often reported in the print media, with the *Mail & Guardian* being the preferred medium. Articles in the *Mail & Guardian* are interesting as well for pointing to the differentiated currency of the South African policy community. While there are the traditional academic articles and books, there are also research reports published by universities, development agencies like the United States Agency for International Development (USAID), and research institutions like the Human Sciences Research Council, academic and 'popular' articles on the Web, and also consultant reports. In a dynamic urban environment, the immediacy of the policy debate is quite striking, with this being especially so in the case of HIV/AIDS.

The editors argue that a mistake in 'writing down' the role of research arises from viewing the process of formulating policy and undertaking related research as involving a discrete set of steps with a clear beginning (eg. setting up a policy committee) and end (eg. publishing a White Paper). Whereas the contributors to this book readily recognise that political struggles during the 1980s influenced the policy agenda and also identified some of the participants in the policy process/policy committee, many have not allowed a similar role for urban research, including an individual's past research and perspectives leading to the selection of the individual to participate in the policy process.

*Best practice research*

The Urban Foundation provides an especially good example of best practice research that was intended to shape urban policy, although the expression 'best practice' was not in common use during the 1980s and early 1990s. The spur to the creation of the Urban Foundation was the 1976 Soweto uprising. The Urban Foundation was an NGO funded by the private sector that focused on policy changes around a range of developmental issues, including urbanisation, local government, housing and education.

An indication of the role adopted by the Urban Foundation is provided by the titles in its *Policies for a New Urban Future* series. Publications in this series include 'The International Experience', 'Regional Development Reconsidered', 'Rural Development', 'Managing the Cities', 'Governing Urban South Africa' and 'Housing for All'.

On the inside front cover of the publications, DL van Coller, the Urban Foundation's Chief Executive, described the purpose of the series as follows:

> This…series [deals] with the issue of urbanisation and how South Africa is going to manage this important dynamic. It is the product of a major five year study managed by the Urban Foundation's Urbanisation Unit under the aegis of the Private Sector Council on Urbanisation – a forum which brings together the major employer bodies, leaders from both urban and business communities and the Urban Foundation.

> This study has involved considerable research by a wide range of academics under the guidance of a number of working groups, the synthesis of that research, the development of policy proposals on the basis of the research recommendations and the testing of both the

research findings and the policy proposals with a large range of people…
it is hoped that the debate on this critical challenge facing South Africa
will be able to move forward on the basis of an understanding of the real
issues facing the country.

And on the inside back cover it is noted that the Private Sector Council 'set itself
the task of *formulating proposals for a new urbanisation strategy for South Africa*'
(emphasis added).

The research on urban policy significantly influenced the policies of the National
Party during the 1980s, and the Urban Foundation recommendations on housing
policy served a vital role at the NHF in creating perceptions of what the housing
problems are and what remedial solutions and appropriate policies might be (Rust
& Rubenstein 1996; Kahn & Thring 2003).

*Policy research*

The distinction being made between policy research and best practice research
in the first instance hinges on who commissions the policy research: in this case
government. Policy research might well include examining the relevance of best
practice or even simply how to apply best practice. For example, in the 1997
discussion document *Towards a White Paper on Local Government in South Africa*,
there is mention of 'how research on the South African and international experience
of local government best practice, will assist in drafting the Green Paper'.[5]

An early example of policy research can be found in the preparation of policy for
public sector hostels. The preparation of the policy was included in the NHF as
Working Group 6 and was completed in 1994, although research that led to the
preparation of an Operations Manual continued into 1995. The policy was based on
social surveys and studies by architects and engineers, as well as additional studies
concerning whether social housing might constitute a relevant model. This research
directly informed the views of the ANC, the Inkatha Freedom Party and the National
Party during the process of their negotiating a hostels policy. This is an interesting
case because the research informed policy negotiations among competing political
parties during the last few months of National Party rule, and occurred in the
context of the death of thousands in the struggle between the ANC and the Inkatha
Freedom Party, with the violence often centring on the hostels.

A post-1994 example is provided by the 1998 White Paper on Local Government.
Responsibility for the preparation of the White Paper fell under the Department of
Provincial and Local Government (at the time named the Ministry of Provincial
Affairs and Constitutional Development), and the drafting of the White Paper was
overseen by a White Paper Political Committee made up of politicians appointed by
Minister Mohammed Valli Moosa. The Political Committee was assisted by a White
Paper Working Committee comprising technical experts drawn from government

organisations, NGOs and political parties. The policy process described in the White Paper (DPLG 1998: vi; emphases in original) refers to six steps:

1. **Publication of a Discussion Document.** 'Towards a White Paper on Local government in South Africa'. March 1997.[6]
2. **Extensive Research.** Primary as well as secondary research on both local and international experiences.
3. October 1997. **Cabinet approval of a Green Paper.**
4. Provincial **Workshops/Conferences**, Parliamentary Portfolio Committee **Hearings**, Workshops on selected topics.
5. **National Conference** on Local Government White Paper 8–9 December 1997 to finalise policy options to be contained in the White Paper.
6. **White Paper submitted to Cabinet** for approval and then published. March 1998.

In his Foreword to the White Paper, Mohammed Valli Moosa refers to an 'intensive 18-month period of consultation and research' (1998: v), which are the two parallel thrusts for most policy formulation.

The later policy reviews that have been commissioned by government, or by donors on behalf of government, in order to inform revisions and amendments to policy are also a form of policy research. The extensive housing policy review research funded by USAID that preceded the Department of Housing's *Breaking New Ground* document is a case in point. Policy review research influences policy amendments in the light of experience with delivery, unforeseen difficulties and unexpected consequences.

## Policy implementation research

Although the distinction between best practice research, policy research and policy implementation research can be a bit tenuous, it does seem that one can differentiate between the preparation of policies leading up to the Local Government White Paper and policy research since then. Often enough the research will again be informed by best practice; this will especially be the case if the research is undertaken or supported by foreign consultants and funding agencies.

Municipal services partnerships were sanctioned in the White Paper on Local Government and provide an example of implementation research. In the White Paper it is specified that the 'central mandate' of developmental local government 'is to develop service delivery capacity to meet the basic needs of communities' (DPLG 1998: 92). The difficulty that arose was that the large majority of municipalities lacked the financial and institutional capacity to begin to overcome the service backlogs. It was for this reason that the White Paper proposed various forms of municipal services partnerships.

The Department of Provincial and Local Government, with the assistance of local and international consultants funded by USAID, set about developing a policy and rationale for these partnerships. A draft for the preparation of a Green Paper on municipal services partnerships was first prepared by a global consulting firm and circulated for comment in 1998. The revised draft and later comments on the Green Paper contributed to the preparation of the White Paper on Municipal Services Partnerships (2000). Minister for Provincial and Local Government Fholisani Sydney Mufamadi's Foreword to the document notes: 'I would like to thank the team of local and international advisors who assisted us to draw up this document. A special thanks is given for the financial support from the United States Agency for International Development.'

A striking role in research pertaining to the implementation of municipal services partnerships was played by the Municipal Infrastructure Investment Unit. The Unit was created and funded by USAID and the Department of Finance with a view to assisting municipalities to use partnerships to undertake the delivery of services and to raise finance for service delivery. The mission of the Unit involves enhancing 'deal flow' and helping to create a market for partnerships. The Unit was staffed by the American global consulting firm, PADCO. Owing to the length of time spent in South Africa and their increasingly well-informed role in promoting partnerships, PADCO's staff was involved in researching policy options and even, in a few instances, drafting legislation.

In sum, there is a policy community that is identified by past and ongoing urban research. The explicit policy content of this research dates back to university planning departments in the 1970s and the 1976 Soweto uprising and the formation of the Urban Foundation. The preparation of South Africa's urban policies was informed to varying degrees by policy perspectives beginning in the 1970s and continuing through the 1980s, with the implication being that to focus solely on research commissioned in the early 1990s to inform the preparation of a specific policy is to miss the influence of the earlier research. It is also a failure to observe that much of the research commissioned in the early 1990s consisted of summarising and reviewing past South African and international research and comparative experience and assessing the relevance to policy directions. Further, as already suggested, past research was imported into the policy process through including in the process academics selected on the basis of their past publications and their commitment to change, often manifested in their membership of NGOs. Of course, academics, consultants and members of NGOs are, on an ongoing basis, employed to evaluate the success of policy implementation and explore policy options. Research matters!

## 'New policies'

The first ten years of democracy have seen the creation of democratic, integrated and developmental local government; mass delivery of housing and services; a finely crafted array of capital and operating subsidies for delivery to low-income households; and a number of programmes intended to enhance the capacity of local government to undertake delivery.

The future agenda repeats the emphasis on delivery. For example, in *A People's Contract to create work and fight poverty*, the ANC electoral platform for 2004, the ANC again commits government to the delivery of housing and services, and then to reducing poverty and unemployment by half through speeding up the delivery of housing and services, 'economic development, comprehensive social security, land reform and improved household and community assets…new jobs, skills development, assistance to small businesses, opportunities for self-employment and sustainable community livelihoods'.

There are four potentially significant new 'urban policies'. These are the Presidency's 2003 National Spatial Development Perspective (NSDP), the Department of Housing's 2004 *Breaking New Ground* document, the Department of Provincial and Local Government's Local Economic Development Framework, and the pending, rewritten Urban Development Framework whose location within the Presidency, the Department of Provincial and Local Government or elsewhere had, at the time of writing, still to be determined. Each of these policies is briefly described and commented on later.

It does seem possible, though, that national policies of this sort may be of declining significance. The reason for this is due to the emergence of the SACN and the role of the major cities in setting their own and, in some respects, the country's urban agenda. As a result, following the review of the four 'policies', the significance of the SACN and the metros is explored.

## National Spatial Development Perspective

Within the NSDP it is noted that it is not, in fact, a policy. Yet a prominent academic and consultant to government in urban policy views the NSDP as an 'incipient urbanisation policy'.[7] Uncertainty is inevitable when the NSDP is presented as an:

> …indicative guideline that will encourage creative interaction and co-ordination between departments and spheres of government about the nation's spatial priorities. It will function as a basis for discussion and negotiation…the NSDP will function not as a policy that prescribes expenditure choices, but an instrument for discussing spatial development priorities for South Africa within government. (Office of the President 2003: 38)

Quoting from the Atkinson and Marais chapter in this book:

> The NSDP's main argument is that areas with 'potential' or comparative advantage should be pinpointed, and thereafter receive priority in the allocation of resources – in particular, in the allocation of

infrastructure funding ('hard investments'). Government spending on fixed investment, beyond the obligation to provide basic services to all citizens, should therefore be focused on localities of economic growth and/or economic potential in order to attract private sector investment, stimulate sustainable economic activities and/or create long-term employment opportunities. (Chapter 2)

There are similarities with the Department of Housing's 1997 Urban Development Framework in respect of not being presented as a policy, not being prescriptive, but rather a 'policy approach' and a guide that will 'foster linkages'.

A guide presented for discussion does not seem terribly promising unless there is a political obligation on relevant departments to take it forward. Encouragingly, President Thabo Mbeki mentioned the NSDP in his 2005 State of the Nation address. Reportedly, when national ministries are preparing their capital budgets and when provinces and municipalities are preparing their Growth and Development Strategies and their IDPs, questions are asked regarding whether these align with the NSDP.[8] Provinces are now more explicit about spatial development perspectives in their provincial growth and development strategies. In effect, the intended and possible outcome of the NSDP may be horizontal coordination among national departments, and vertical coordination between national, provincial and local spheres of government. Perhaps the NSDP is beginning to serve as an urbanisation policy of sorts and will continue to do so for as long as there is political weight behind the guide.

But does the NSDP actually have significance in the case of housing and services? In the case of housing, the judgment of the Constitutional Court in the case of Government of the Republic of South Africa vs Grootboom 2001 (1) SA 46 (CC) was that 'the state' must provide relief for people in 'desperate need' who are living in 'intolerable conditions or crises' situations. In recognition of the right to housing conferred in section 26 of the Constitution, the Department of Housing is required to provide for 'the fulfilment of immediate needs'. Similarly, the Constitution and the Grootboom judgment oblige all municipalities to provide services. It seems reasonable to assume that whereas the NSDP might influence the location of infrastructure investments for economic development purposes, it will have less bearing on the allocation and utilisation of resources in the scramble to provide serviced sites for housing and, in this respect, the realisation of *A People's Contract*.

## Breaking New Ground

The purpose of *Breaking New Ground* 'is to outline a plan for the development of sustainable human settlements over the next five years, embracing *A People's Contract* as the basis for delivery' (DoH 2004: 2).

*Breaking New Ground* is not presented as a new policy. Instead, it is noted that, 'Whilst Government believes that the fundamentals of the policy remain relevant and sound, a new plan is required...' (DoH 2004: 7). The document includes references to a 'new vision', 'enhancement', 'amendments', 'changes', 'redirection', 'new systems', 'new policy measures', a 'new subsidy mechanism' and a 'new plan that will be required to redirect and enhance existing mechanisms'. President Thabo Mbeki's view is that there should not be new policies or White Papers. Instead, the emphasis is on delivery, but *Breaking New Ground* arguably can be seen as a new housing policy.

The political underpinnings of *Breaking New Ground* separate this amended policy from the 1994 Housing White Paper, where private sector agendas and technical experts held greater sway. Whereas a defining concern in housing policy was with the sustainability of the financial institutions, in *Breaking New Ground* a defining concern is the sustainability of communities and settlements. The latter is in line with the Department of Housing being a signatory to the United Nations 1996 Habitat Agenda and the emphasis therein on sustainable settlements.

*Breaking New Ground* is a response to the sharp increase in the demand for housing arising from the decline in household size; increasing unemployment and numbers of households with incomes that qualify them for housing subsidies; the supply of housing on the urban periphery, with individual units not becoming '"valuable assets" in the hands of the poor' (DoH 2004: 4) and a slow down in housing delivery and under-expenditure of provincial housing budgets.

Synthesising from *Breaking New Ground*, government's new housing vision requires accelerating the delivery of housing as a key strategy for poverty alleviation and job creation; creating assets; promoting social cohesion and improving quality of life for the poor; supporting the functioning of the *entire single residential property market* to reduce duality within the sector by breaking the barriers between the first economy residential property boom and the second economy slump; and building sustainable *human settlements*, in support of spatial restructuring (emphasis in *Breaking New Ground*). This is a considerably more ambitious agenda than that in 1994, where the focus was simple: the delivery of a million units within five years to households having a monthly income below R3 500.

## Local Economic Development Framework

At the time of writing, the LED Framework was still unavailable. In the absence of the Framework document, the ensuing observations are based on the Department of Provincial and Local Government's (2005: 1–3) LED implementation guidelines, which are to be included in the Framework document.

> These guidelines were prepared following a consultative process involving provinces, [the South African Local Government Association], and key national sector departments through the Economic and Employment Cluster of Directors General.

A series of consultative workshops were held with independent experts and in the international donor community. Discussions were also held with tertiary academic institutions and practitioners.

A number of studies also within South Africa and abroad underpin these guidelines.

1. The aim of these guidelines is to influence the way government practitioners in all three spheres understand, approach and implement Local Economic Development (LED) in South Africa.

The policy context for LED guidelines noted in the document combines the Constitution and the White Paper on Local Government with the mandate of the Department of Provincial and Local Government. The specific context for implementing LED consists of:

2. The Ten Year Review of government
   • The 2004 electoral mandate
   • The Medium Term Strategic Framework
   • The January 2005 Cabinet Lekgotla
   • The Micro-Economic Reform Strategy

Further:

9. A government-wide approach to developing and supporting robust and inclusive municipal economies is required and should be facilitated through the active and dynamic alignment of the National Spatial Development Perspective (NSDP), Provincial Growth and Development Strategies (PGDSs), and District/Metro Integrated Development Plans (IDPs) [and their LED programmes].

If one considers this rather demanding context for local economic planning and the desire for horizontal coordination among national government departments, as well as vertical coordination within the three spheres of government, one can understand why there is so much attention in these various 'policy' documents to 'alignment', 'coordination', 'harmonisation', 'integration', and so on. This desire for coordination may become problematical when one notes that economic development in the cities relies on private investment, which may be little influenced by national policy for LED.

## Urban Development Framework

The 2005 draft Urban Development Framework appears to be an attempt to resurrect the 1997 Urban Development Framework. However, it is unclear whether the Framework will actually be finalised and agreed to by Cabinet. This brief assessment is based on an earlier draft of what was then called an Urban Policy/ Strategy. The first observation is, of course, that the significance of the document is diminished by its having been downgraded from a policy, which requires the approval of Cabinet, to a Framework that requires the approval of the minister of the department concerned.

The purpose of the draft Urban Policy/Strategy is to 'promote', 'initiate' and 'propose' (i) a *perspective*: 'initial set of practical interventions for investigation', 'deeper understanding', 'focus on certain policy issues', 'debate', 'developing a shared vision'; and (ii) *coordination*: 'integration and improved service delivery', 'alignment of government policies and programmes', 'appropriate funding framework'.

The intention, again, is to promote coordination, integration and alignment with national political commitments such as *A People's Contract*.

## The agenda of the cities

The counterpoint to the national perspective and frameworks is the agenda of the cities, especially those comprising the SACN. The SACN and its members have an increasingly robust role in setting the urban agenda and, in effect, leading urban policy. Many points contribute to this view.

First, the context for urban policy is ambivalence within government regarding the preparation of new urban policies. Reportedly, it was following debate within Cabinet that the NSDP was termed a perspective and not a policy. *Breaking New Ground* is presented as an 'amendment' or 'enhancement' to existing policy. The LED policy was downgraded to a framework. The Urban Development Framework is, of course, a framework. This national policy-shy approach to urban policy is in part a reaction to past accusations of government policy favouring urban areas (Development Bank of Southern Africa 2005).

In contrast, in its *State of the Cities Report*, the SACN, 'Through description and analysis of trends…hopes to set up a strategic agenda for further research, planning and action…' (SACN 2004a: 5). In addition, with the assistance of the World Bank-linked Cities Alliance, in its 2004 *People and Places: An Overview of Urban Renewal*, the SACN unabashedly specifies that, 'A national urban renewal policy framework must be developed as part of a broader South African urban policy framework' (SACN 2004b: 9); and, in the absence of a national policy framework, the document also indicates areas where cities can themselves take aspects of the policy agenda forward. It is further indicated that this should take the form of a City Development Strategy. City Development Strategies are explained as:

> A city development strategy supports cities in this critical decision-making process and is focused on implementation. It is an action-plan for equitable growth in cities and their surrounding regions, developed and sustained through participation, to improve the quality of life for all citizens.

The output of a city development strategy includes a *collective city vision and a strategic action plan aimed at policy and institutional reforms*, increased economic growth and employment, and implementation and accountability mechanisms to ensure systematic and sustained reductions in urban poverty.[9] (emphasis added)

As prescribed in City Development Strategies, the cities are taking their development forward in partnership with the private sector. The significance of the relationship with the private sector is that it further emphasises the independence of the cities from alignment with the national policy direction.

The presumptions and prerogatives of the SACN cities are further contributed to by the 'normalisation' of the urban agenda, with the legislative and institutional prerequisites for dealing with the aftermath of urban apartheid having been put in place. For example, the SACN now turns its attention to developing instruments of urban governance such as 'an effective regulatory system for land use planning that addresses the realities of informal settlements' (Boraine, Crankshaw, Engelbrecht, Gotz, Mbanga, Narsoo & Parnell 2005: 4).

To this should be added the role of municipalities in the delivery of housing and services. The Constitution, regardless of national urban policy, amendments and frameworks, requires that municipalities invest in services infrastructure for delivery to low-income households. This requirement is abetted by the Municipal Infrastructure Grant, which came into effect in 2004/05, which accords municipalities increasing independence in the allocation of resources for investment in services infrastructure. The same can be said for the Department of Housing's intention to accredit the cities to deliver houses.

Then, to add to the urban voice, there is increasing recognition of the facts that poverty is not solely a rural issue and there is an equivalent, if not greater, prevalence of poverty in urban areas; and that the cities play the central role of driving economic growth and employment creation (Development Bank of Southern Africa 2005: Chapter 5). Well-run cities are a precondition for both competitiveness in the global economy and for alleviating poverty in both urban and rural (owing to remittances and migration) areas.

The point is that in a context of ambivalence at the national level in relation to urban policy, the cities comprising the SACN are proceeding with an urban agenda that, to a significant degree, is self-defined, enabled by national housing and services policies and subsidy frameworks, and embodied in their commitment to city development strategies. The point is also that the SACN agenda influences that of non-member secondary cities.

Lastly, the SACN fills a key lacunae in national policy, namely that of mitigating the urban impacts of HIV/AIDS. The attention to this issue is evident in SACN newsletters and in ongoing research sponsored by the SACN.

# Conclusion

This book has described government's policies, and the preparation of the policies, which have created democratic local government institutions and enhanced their ability to promote socio-economic development in urban areas. The chapters dwell on three themes: *enabling*, *planning* and *delivering* in *consolidating democracy*, with the examples of delivery being housing and services. The book also first points to the need for more effective urban spatial policy and for urbanisation policy, and then deliberates whether current urban 'policy' initiatives will meet this need.

It is apparent that while there has been a coherent progression in introducing new policies in line with the Constitution, preparing the White Paper on Local Government and then preparing policies and legislation to give effect to developmental local government, and to meeting government's commitments in respect of the Reconstruction and Development Programme, the policy formulation processes have shown marked differences.

The role and contribution of research and the influence of international development agencies and 'best practice' was debated in most of the chapters and then at some length in this conclusion. Most authors allow that all three were (and remain) present during policy formulation, and then differ as to their contribution and significance. The editors have argued that there has been a consistent underestimation of the contribution of policy research.

Government has put in place the policy, legislative and financial framework to the extent that, as noted, Boraine et al. (2005: 4) write about the 'normalisation' of urban development issues. The institutions and policies are in place that enable local governments, other spheres of government and various other institutions to seek to reverse the impress of apartheid *and* to engage in a future no longer defined by 'post-apartheid'. Government has created the ability to set a policy agenda defined by the conditions and dynamics of modern South Africa in a global context.

It is the SACN cities that appear best prepared to look to the country's urban future and they are currently setting an urban agenda based on their mantra of 'inclusive', 'productive', 'sustainable' and 'well-governed' cities. It may be that the setting of the urban agenda and the impetus for urban policy have shifted to cities and their partners in the private sector and civil society.

## Notes

1    Much of the text for this section represents an edited but direct quote from Lynelle John's second draft of the LED paper.

2    See <http://www.polity.org.za/html/govdocs/discuss/localgov.html#l1>.

3    See <http://www.wits.ac.za/housingstudies/>.

4  Some of the publications include those by HEARD (2001), Thomas (2003), Rajaraman (2002), UNDP (2002), Van Donk (2002a, 2002b), Tomlinson (2001, 2003, 2004).

5  See <http://www.polity.org.za/html/govdocs/discuss/localgov.html#l1>.

6  See <http://www.polity.org.za/html/govdocs/discuss/localgov.html#l1>.

7  Discussion with Professor Susan Parnell.

8  Andrew Boraine, interview, 15 July 2005.

9  See <http://www.citiesalliance.org/citiesalliancehomepage.nsf/6FF87B591473087C0625687E 0058053D/3D8C401CF45EE33B86256BAC006D5C18?OpenDocument>.

## References

ANC (African National Congress) (2004) *A People's Contract to create work and fight poverty.* 2004 election manifesto.

Boraine A, Crankshaw O, Engelbrecht C, Gotz G, Mbanga S, Narsoo M & Parnell S (2005) The state of South African cities a decade after democracy. Draft paper.

Carlsson L (2000) Policy networks as collective action, *Policy Studies Journal,* 28(3): 502–520.

Development Bank of Southern Africa (2005) *Development report 2005 – Overcoming underdevelopment in South Africa's second economy,* Chapter 5. Midrand.

DoH (Department of Housing) (2004) *Breaking New Ground: A comprehensive plan for the development of sustainable human settlements.* Pretoria: DoH.

DPLG (Department of Provincial and Local Government) (1998) *White Paper on Local Government.* Pretoria: DPLG.

DPLG (2000) *White Paper on Municipal Services Partnerships.* Pretoria: DPLG.

DPLG (2005) Implementation Guideline version 1(3)(2). Pretoria: Governance, Policy and Research Branch.

HEARD (Health Economics HIV/AIDS Research Division) (2001) *Revised HIV/AIDS toolkit for local government.* Durban: University of Natal.

Kahn F & Thring P (eds) (2003) *Housing policy and practice in post-apartheid South Africa.* Sandown: Heinemann.

Office of the President (2003) National Spatial Development Perspective (NSDP). Policy Coordination and Advisory Services. Accessed at <http://www.idp.org.za/NSDP/NSDP.

Rajaraman A (2002) *An inventory of urban and local government actions to address the impacts of HIV/AIDS.* Pretoria: United States Agency for International Development, Regional Urban Development Office/Sub-Saharan Africa.

Rust K & Rubenstein S (eds) (1996) *A mandate to build: Developing consensus around a national housing policy in South Africa.* Johannesburg: Ravan.

SACN (South African Cities Network) (2004a) *State of the Cities Report.* Johannesburg: SACN.

SACN (2004b) *People and places: An overview of urban renewal.* Johannesburg: SACN.

Thomas E (2003) HIV/AIDS: Implications for local governance, housing and delivery of services. In R Tomlinson, R Beauregard, L Bremner & X Mangcu (eds), *Emerging Johannesburg: Perspectives on the post-apartheid city.* New York: Routledge.

Tomlinson R (1999) Ten years in the making: A history of the evolution of metropolitan government in Johannesburg, *Urban Forum*, 10(1): 1–40.

Tomlinson R (2001) Housing policy in a context of HIV/AIDS and globalisation, *International Journal of Urban and Regional Research*, 25(3): 649–657.

Tomlinson R (2003) An exploration of the shelter and services needs arising from HIV/Aids, Urban Management Programme e-Newsletter. Available at <http://www.unhabitat.org/ programmes/ump/newsletter.asp>.

Tomlinson R (2004) HIV/AIDS in the city of Johannesburg. Consultant report prepared for the City of Johannesburg.

UNDP (United Nations Development Programme) (2002) *Conceptual shifts for sound planning: Towards an integrated approach to HIV/AIDS and poverty*. UNDP Regional Project on HIV and Development. (Mirjam van Donk prepared the concept paper.)

Van Donk M (2002a) HIV/AIDS and urban poverty in South Africa. Prepared for the South African Cities Network.

Van Donk M (2002b) *The missing element: HIV/AIDS in urban development planning. Reviewing the South African response to the HIV/AIDS epidemic.* Working Paper No. 118. London: University College, Development Planning Unit.

# Contributors

**Doreen Atkinson** holds a BA Honours degree in Politics from Rhodes University (1982), an MA in Political Science from the University of California in Berkeley (1984), and a PhD in Political Studies from the University of Natal (1992). She is Director of the Rhodes University Karoo Institute, and is a visiting Professor at the Centre for Development Studies, University of the Free State.

**Robert Cameron** is a Professor in the Department of Political Studies at the University of Cape Town, and lectures in Public Administration. He has published almost 60 articles in journals and books in the fields of public administration and local government, including publications in international journals such as *Public Administration, Public Administration and Development, Local Government Studies* and *International Review of Administrative Sciences*. He is the author of a book on local government boundary reorganisation in South Africa. He is on the Board of the Comparative Local Government and Politics panel of the International Political Science Association. He was a member of the Municipal Demarcation Board in South Africa from 1999 to 2004.

**Sarah Charlton** is a senior lecturer in the School of Architecture and Planning at the University of the Witwatersrand. Prior to this she worked in a variety of positions in the non-governmental, local authority and private sectors in Gauteng and in KwaZulu-Natal, focusing on housing and urban development. Her work has been both in policy and strategy formulation, and in the implementation of housing projects through project and programme management.

**Jacques du Toit** is a lecturer in the Department of Town and Regional Planning at the University of Pretoria. He holds a Bachelor in Town and Regional Planning from the University of Pretoria and an MPhil in Research Methods from the University of Stellenbosch. He worked for an urban development consultancy during 2000 and joined the HSRC during 2001. In September 2003 he was appointed as coordinator of the Urban Renewal and Development Research Unit within the HSRC, where he served as project manager and co-editor of this book. His particular research interest focuses on issues of social sustainability in the built environment.

**Philip Harrison** is Professor of Urban and Regional Planning at the University of the Witwatersrand. He was previously Associate Professor at the University of KwaZulu-Natal and has also worked as a senior planner in the public and private sectors, and as a Research Fellow at the University of Sheffield in the UK. He has published in fields including planning theory, comparative planning systems, and planning education, and has served as consultant to the various spheres of government.

**Lynelle John** is a consultant in the fields of governance and urban development. She has worked on local government issues since 1994 and has been part of major transformation processes in that sector. Her early work included contributions to Chapter 7 of the Constitution. She was later appointed to a ministerial task team that drafted the Local Government White Paper. Since then, she has participated in key policy processes and helped develop national programmes and strategies for government and international donors. She also works with several municipalities across the country.

**Caroline Kihato** is a policy analyst at the Development Bank of Southern Africa, editor of the journal *Development Southern Africa,* and is associated with the Planning Programme in the School of Architecture and Planning at the University of the Witwatersrand. She has also worked as a senior researcher and project manager at the Centre for Policy Studies. Her experience includes research, evaluation and analysis of social policy on local government, civil society and governance in southern and east Africa.

**Alan Mabin** is Professor of Public and Development Management at the University of the Witwatersrand in Johannesburg. He holds a Doctorate from Simon Fraser University, Canada, and has worked in a variety of development fields for 25 years. He was involved in several aspects of the transformation of local government in South Africa, particularly in Johannesburg.

**Lochner Marais** is currently a researcher at the Centre for Development Support at the University of the Free State. Prior to this, he lectured at Vista University for seven years, and in the Department of Geography at the University of the Free State for two years. He obtained his BA, BA Hons, MA and PhD in Geography from the University of the Free State. He has authored, co-authored and compiled more than 70 publications, including some 30 refereed articles (including book chapters), and has co-edited a book. He has conducted research work for the Free State Provincial Government, the National Department of Housing, as well as GTZ, DFID and USAID.

**Tim Mosdell** has Masters degrees in Political Studies and Business Administration. He has 15 years research and consulting experience in the fields of development studies, public policy and public sector management. Since joining Palmer Development Group in 2000

he has worked extensively in the water sector, conducted a major evaluation of Treasury's *Special Poverty Relief Allocation,* consulted in the municipal restructuring field, developed knowledge management methodologies, and has contributed to strategic responses to urban poverty.

**Etienne Nel** is Professor of Geography at Rhodes University in Grahamstown. His teaching and research interests lie in the fields of urban and economic geography. He has published four books, two dealing with Local Economic Development, and some 90 articles and book chapters. He has interacted with government and various municipalities over the last ten years, primarily in terms of Local Economic Development policy and practice.

**Edgar Pieterse** is currently Special Advisor to the Premier of the Western Cape. He serves on the Board of Directors of Isandla Institute and is co-editor of *Voices of the Transition: The Politics, Poetics and Practices of Social Change in South Africa* (Heinemann Publishers 2004) and *Democratising Local Government: The South African Experiment* (UCT Press 2002).

**Udesh Pillay** is the Executive Director of the Urban, Rural and Economic Development Research Programme at the HSRC. He holds a PhD in Geography from the University of Minnesota, Minneapolis, and an MA in Geography from the University of Natal, Durban. Prior to joining the HSRC, he was the Head of the Delimitation and Planning Directorate of the Independent Electoral Commission. He has lectured at the University of Natal, and has consulted widely, including sustained involvement in the development of government's concept papers on urban development and the local government white paper. His publications in books and journals deal mainly with issues of urban development and social change in South

Africa, informal settlements, locality, global city competitiveness, demarcation, the impact of mega-sporting events on cities, and public attitudes. He is co-editor of *South African Social Attitudes: Changing Times, Diverse Voices* (HSRC Press 2006).

**Christian M Rogerson** is Professor of Human Geography in the School of Geography, Archaeology and Environmental Studies at the University of the Witwatersrand. His research interests include small enterprise development, local economic development and tourism studies. Among his recent publications are three co-edited books: (with D McCormick) *Clothing and Footwear in African Industrialization* (Pretoria: Africa Institute of South Africa 2004); (with G Visser) *Tourism and Development Issues in Contemporary South Africa* (Pretoria: Africa Institute of South Africa 2004); and (with E Nel) *Local Economic Development in the Developing World: The Experience of Southern Africa* (New Brunswick/London: Transaction Publishers 2005).

**Alison Todes** is Research Director in the Urban, Rural and Economic Development Programme at the HSRC, and Honorary Professor at the School of Architecture and Planning at the University of the Witwatersrand. She was previously Professor and Programme Director for Planning in the School of Architecture, Planning and Housing, University of KwaZulu-Natal, Durban. She has a PhD in Planning from the University of Natal and has published extensively in the field of urban and regional development.

**Richard Tomlinson** is a Visiting Professor at the School of Architecture and Planning of the University of the Witwatersrand. His research includes housing and infrastructure, urban development in a context of HIV/AIDS, urban policy processes and international best practice, and inner-city development. He has

published internationally in these areas and recently co-edited a book titled *Emerging Johannesburg* (Routledge 2003). He was a Visiting Scholar at the Massachusetts Institute of Technology and a Guest Scholar at the Brookings Institution, where he wrote books on urban development issues, and at the New School University. His research awards include Robert S McNamara Fellowship and Fulbright Scholarship. He currently serves on the board of Urban and Regional Research Committee 21 of the International Sociological Association. He also serves as a consultant in urban development and project management.

**Mirjam van Donk** works as an independent consultant on HIV/AIDS, gender and development, with a specific interest in urban development. She is particularly interested in the role of the state, from national to local level, in development processes. She holds an MSc in Development and Planning: Urban Development Planning from UCL, London.

**Philip van Ryneveld** has been involved in the development of South Africa's municipal finance system since 1985. He was a founder member of the Development Action Group in Cape Town and from 1990 to 1994 lectured in Economics at the University of the Western Cape. He was responsible for the municipal finance work within the Local Government Policy Research Project (early 1990s), drafted the Finances and Resources Chapter of the ANC's Regional Policy document (1992), was a technical adviser to the non-statutory side in the national LGNF, drafted the Financial Framework section to the MIIF, was a Commisioner to the FFC, was Chief Finance Officer in the City of Cape Town (1997–2001). Since 2001 he has worked as an independent consultant on municipal finance issues and is currently core consultant in a team working for National Treasury on a review of the local government fiscal framework.

# Index